PIMLICO

672

AFTER THE HOLOCAUST

Dr Eva Kolinsky is Emeritus Professor of Modern German Studies at Keele University, where she headed the Centre for the Study of German Culture and Society. Since 1999, she has been Professorial Research Fellow in German History at the University of Wolverhampton. Her books include *Between Hope and Fear: Everyday Life in Post-Unification East Germany, Political Culture in France and Germany, Women in Twentieth-Century Germany* and *United and Divided: Germany since 1990.*

D1580990

AFTER THE HOLOCAUST

Jewish Survivors in Germany after 1945

EVA KOLINSKY

PIMLICO

Published by Pimlico 2004

2 4 6 8 10 9 7 5 3 1

Copyright © Eva Kolinsky 2004

Eva Kolinsky has asserted her right under the Copyright,
Designs and Patents Act 1988 to be identified
as the author of this work

First published in Great Britain by
Pimlico 2004

Pimlico
Random House, 20 Vauxhall Bridge Road,
London SW1V 2SA

Random House Australia (Pty) Limited
20 Alfred Street, Milsons Point, Sydney,
New South Wales 2061, Australia

Random House New Zealand Limited
18 Poland Road, Glenfield,
Auckland 10, New Zealand

Random House (Pty) Limited
Endulini, 5A Jubilee Road, Parktown 2193, South Africa

The Random House Group Limited Reg. No. 954009
www.randomhouse.co.uk

A CIP catalogue record for this book
is available from the British Library

ISBN 1-8441-3317-6

Papers used by Random House are natural,
recyclable products made from wood grown in sustainable forests;
the manufacturing processes conform to the environmental
regulations of the country of origin

Typeset by Deltatype Ltd, Birkenhead, Merseyside

Printed and bound in Great Britain by
Mackays of Chatham PLC

For Zoë and Noah

Contents

List of Tables

List of Illustrations

14. Passover 1946 or 1947: distribution of matzot in Frankfurt (*Stadtarchiv Frankfurt am Main*).
15. Jewish Kindergarten in Frankfurt 1948 (*Jewish Museum, Frankfurt am Main*).

Preface

During Nazi control of Germany and Europe, Jews had been persecuted, deported, utilised as slave labour and murdered in their millions in the killing machine that has since become known as the Holocaust. For most survivors, liberation occurred inside Germany where many had to remain, as in an unloved waiting room because they had nowhere else to go. Some displaced Jews stayed on, fearful of moving to yet another unknown place. Some German Jews survived inside the Third Reich or returned from concentration camps. Together, survivors began to rebuild Jewish life and communities, hoping that a reinvented and democratic Germany might allow them a new beginning and a future there.

This book draws on oral testimony, personal memoirs, letters and contemporary reports, many of them written at the time and most of them unpublished, to ask how ordinary men, women and children managed to survive the Holocaust, how they saw their future after liberation, and how they were helped or hindered in rebuilding their lives. Some military personnel, aid workers and officials played a memorable role in assisting survivors, others fabricated red tape and denied special help. Many Jewish survivors remained impoverished after the Holocaust and dependent on welfare support from aid organizations, Jewish communities and public authorities.

I should like to dedicate this book to my grandchildren Zoë and Noah who are too young to know about the past, but young enough to shape the future.

Acknowledgements

Research grants from the Nuffield Foundation, the British Academy and the German Academic Exchange Service enabled me to collect materials from several archives over a number of years while the universities of Keele and Wolverhampton provided additional funding and sabbatical leave. Special thanks are due to the archivists and librarians who never tired of my work and offered excellent advice. Special thanks are due to Diana Spielman and Viola Voss at the archive of the Leo Baeck Institute in New York, Aron Kornblum, at the United States Holocaust Memorial Museum, Peter Honigmann, Alon Tauber and Eva Blattner at the Zentralarchiv zur Geschichte des Judentums in Deutschland, Werner Bergmann at the Zentrum für Antisemitismusforschung in Berlin, Ben Barkow at the Wiener Library and to George Promislow at the ADJC archive in Jerusalem.

I should like to thank Robert Dudley for his encouragement, Mike Dennis and Dieter Steinert for helpful comments on various aspects of the research, and my husband Martin whose careful reading of earlier drafts has been invaluable and who also assisted with the archival research. Finally, I am greatly indebted to Anita Lasker-Wallfisch, Kurt Thomas, Bella Tovey, Abe Malnik and Reuven Danziger for sharing their experiences with me, providing me with additional information and for taking such an active interest in my book. The publisher and I have made every effort to trace the survivors of those whose testimony I am quoting in this book, and obtain their consent. Any errors or omissions can be rectified in future editions.

Eva Kolinsky
Solihull, Summer 2004

INTRODUCTION

The Holocaust was brought to an end when military front-line units discovered concentration camps and slave labour compounds in the course of their advance and liberated their survivors. On January 27, 1945, the Red Army entered Auschwitz and freed about seven thousand hospital patients and children who had been left behind when the SS abandoned the camp. One hundred thousand of its prisoners and many times that number from other camps in the east were marched or transported into Germany before the Red Army arrived. Conditions on these forced returns were so bad and provisions of food and water so inadequate, that only one in ten reached Germany alive. Here, new arrivals were crammed into existing camps which became severely overcrowded and where starvation and complete neglect produced their own killing machine, even without gas chambers. In the closing weeks of the war, the death rate in many German concentration camps reached one thousand per day. Most of those who had survived until then were dangerously undernourished and often too weak and ill to walk. When the western Allies entered Germany in 1945, they became the main liberators of Holocaust survivors because the sites of the Holocaust had been relocated there from the east. They liberated two million concentration camp prisoners inside Germany. Official records at the time did not record who was Jewish and who was not. Some estimates put the number of Jewish survivors who were liberated in Germany at around 300,000.[1] Other estimates arrive at a much lower figure.[2]

Survival and Liberation

From the moment the Nazis seized power in Germany, they proceeded to impoverish and stigmatise Jews, then strip them of their citizenship and human rights before the state and its SS enforcers ordered their deportation and destruction. In the words of the poet Paul Celan, 'death is a master from Germany',[3] because the genocide of the Jews had been orchestrated there and the killer guards were German SS or their auxiliaries. Against this background and given the experiences of Jewish survivors with Germans as perpetrators, it was a cruel coincidence that Germany became the major site for their liberation and the unlikely location for a new beginning. Since all were starved, ravaged by disease, lice-infested and weak, they had to stay at least until they had regained some strength. Most tried, as soon as they could, to find out whether parents, siblings, relatives, neighbours were dead or living. Many began to walk home or scour other camps in Germany in search of family members and friends. Some were lucky and found someone they had known before the Holocaust; many did not.

While all had hoped to survive, there was no blueprint for a new beginning. Some craved revenge and imagined they would kill any German who happened to cross their path. Others thought that fortunes should be reversed, and Germans be made to hand over their homes and possessions to Jews in order to restore some kind of normality to their shattered existence. Most wished to go home but knew that they had no home to go to. While scenarios of a new beginning varied between individuals, all shared a fear of Germany. How could they live in a country where anyone and everyone might have been a perpetrator, a guard, a tormenter and killer, and where the vast majority of the population had looked on or away when Jews were deported and maltreated? In the eyes of Jewish Holocaust survivors, Germany was no place to live, let alone build a future in.

A Protracted Interim

In the closing months of the war, the western Allies had issued directives on how to deal with 'displaced persons', that is to say with civilian prisoners who would be found and liberated in Nazi Germany. These directives did not extend to identifying concentration camps or to speeding up their liberation. They also made no mention that many of the liberated persons might be in very poor physical condition but decreed that any help and care, including housing and food, would have to be secured from German resources without cost to the military. If need be, Germans had to occupy the emptied concentration camps while displaced persons lived in German houses until they could be repatriated. Repatriation was to take no more than a few months, with specially trained aid workers from the United Nations Relief and Rehabilitation Administration, UNRRA, supporting the military in caring for concentration camp survivors and in returning them to their countries of origin.

In devising these plans, the Allies had not foreseen several significant obstacles. The first pertained to the massive human destruction they discovered in the camps. It required a longer term and more extensive commitment to medical and personal care than had been anticipated. The second obstacle concerned the assumption that all additional resources could be procured from inside Germany. The care-needs arose while the war was still under way and arose, moreover, in a country that appeared too devastated by bomb damage and too hard-pressed by its own influx of German refugees from the east. Local officials argued successfully that they could not be expected to accept responsibility for former prisoners in the light of overwhelming German needs. Confronted with these realities, the western Allies abandoned their policy directives and organized their own support and care structures, including residential camps for survivors. Since UNRRA teams were slow to get off the ground, uncertain about their role and also depended on army resources for their operations, the military found itself taking the lead role. Finally repatriation, the linchpin of Allied post-liberation strategy, was based on false assumptions because the majority of survivors from eastern Europe refused to return. In preparation for rapid repatriation, all displaced persons including Jews had been classified as nationals of the country from which they had been deported. Immediately after liberation, therefore, Jews remained virtually invisible as a group. It took many months until they were recognised as a distinct group and no longer airbrushed out of the statistics. The Cold War also rewrote the original political agendas. Given the political divisions of Europe and Germany into hostile power blocs, the Americans quickly abandoned plans to return survivors into Soviet controlled eastern Europe against their will. 'Unrepatriables' had no 'nation' to which they belonged and no 'home' to which they could return. As attempts to repatriate them ground to a halt, Jews found themselves more irrevocably in Germany than they had wished or expected when they were liberated.

The special needs of Jewish survivors were recognised because repatriation could not be implemented. From the outset, however, there had been some exceptional individuals who found themselves, as regular soldiers, army officers or aid workers, in personal contact with Jewish survivors, tried to understand what they had lived through, and tried to help as best they could. The establishment of Jewish camps from the summer of 1945 onwards can be traced back to some inspired individuals who understood that anti-Semitism persisted among several national groups and that Jewish survivors deserved an everyday environment free from hostilities. Although DP camps tended to be located in decommissioned military installations, confiscated apartment buildings or on the site of former concentration camps, and offered none of the comforts of a private home, they provided their residents with a minimum of food and shelter. In addition, Jewish camps provided a space where survivors could rediscover their identity as Jews and explore meanings of their culture. During their unwanted sojourn in Germany, survivors were able to rebuild some kind of normality. Some got married and started a new family, others set up Jewish committees and contributed to running the camp in which they lived. A majority became ardent Zionists, a sizeable minority subscribed to ultra-orthodox religious beliefs. It took many months after the end of the war for Jewish aid organizations to begin work in Germany. Once they did, the additional provision of food, clothing, religious articles, books and other educational materials alleviated some of the poverty that had been imposed by the Holocaust and enabled Jewish survivors to set up religious, Zionist and vocational schools, start newspapers, run theatre groups and lead as full a life as possible in the interim to which they were confined.

This precarious normalisation was further consolidated from 1946 onwards when Jewish refugees began to arrive from Poland where they had encountered renewed and violent anti-Semitism. While other military governments in occupied Germany refused to accept these newcomers, the Americans turned their zone into a haven for all Jewish survivors, those who had been liberated in April and May 1945, and those who were later forced to flee from eastern regions. Over 150,000 sought refuge in the German interim, bringing the number of displaced Jews in the American zone close to 200,000. Overall, some 230,000 displaced Jews waited for resettlement in Germany. Their presence in the country and their Zionist leanings put pressure on international policy makers to 'open the gates' and allow Jewish immigration to Palestine to take its course. As the power holding the Mandate in Palestine, Britain was determined to limit the number of Palestine Certificates that were issued to Jews. This political constellation came to an end on May 15, 1948 when the State of Israel was officially founded. From this point onwards, resettlement became a realistic option for the Holocaust survivors and Jewish refugees who had been waiting in Germany for somewhere to go.

'Out of Camp' and in Poverty

Not all survivors or Jewish refugees wanted to live in camps, shielded and also segregated from German society. At least one in five chose to stay 'out of camp' and make their way among Germans as best they could. In addition, there were three groups of German Jews. The first consisted of nearly 14,000 individuals who had been classified as Jews by the Nazis but were not deported and survived inside the Third Reich. This group took the initiative in rebuilding Jewish communities after liberation. The second group consisted of about two thousand individuals who had survived in hiding, most of them in Berlin. The third group was similarly small and consisted of German Jews who had been liberated from a concentration camp. Like displaced Jews, German Jews of all groups were classified by nationality upon liberation. As Germans, they were, therefore, directed to live in the country that had driven them out.[4] In contrast to displaced Jews in camps who were cared for by the military and UNRRA, German Jews depended on local German officials and public authorities. Although they returned to their home towns, they remained impoverished and had to rely on benefit payments since none of their former possessions were restored to them when they returned from concentration camp.

The war had not yet ended when the first German-Jewish community after the Holocaust was founded. Within a year, there were about one hundred, most of them very small compared to those that had existed in Germany before 1933, and barely able to sustain prayer meetings or a religious culture. Yet, communities enabled German-Jewish survivors to find a public voice and put pressure on German and military government officials to acknowledge their special needs with regard to food, housing, clothing and other daily essentials. Some of these attempts succeeded, many did not. In 1945, Jewish communities, not the newly appointed German officials or the military governments that had assumed overall control, took the initiative to fetch survivors home. In Theresienstadt, survivors had been left stranded by the Russian liberators, and some returned only in August 1945. On coming home, many had to make do with hostel accommodation or a temporary shelter, since no provisions had been made for them. During the first years of their existence, the remade Jewish communities performed an essential care function of assisting impoverished and physically frail survivors on a daily basis. When Jewish aid organizations began to operate in Germany, Jewish community members were entitled to receive food and other parcels. These additional provisions constituted a lifeline in a country where food shortages had become chronic and where most Jews found it virtually impossible to purchase the foodstuffs or goods for which they held ration cards. The cigarettes or bags of coffee in the aid parcels allowed them to trade in the barter economy of the day and replace at least some of the items – shoes, a winter coat, a bed or blankets – that had been taken from them without redress.

Most of the German Jews who survived concentration camps were middle-aged or older and too broken by their experiences to attempt more than easing their daily hardship a little. Displaced Jews were younger and often more focussed on a future. Their survival had depended on slave labour where selection favoured young people – especially males – under the age of twenty-five. German traditions and values had no meaning for these survivors. On the contrary, their negative stance towards the society in which they found themselves made them particularly assertive and determined to get what they wanted. Thus, many displaced Jews utilised the economic dislocation in Germany, the collapse of monetary value and the rise of barter as a trajectory of a new start. Since they owned nothing when they were liberated, they needed everything in order to lead a life reminiscent of normality. Since they were not in a position to purchase anything in a regular way, even if it had been available, they had to trade coveted items such as cigarettes on the black market. Some became very adept at black market trading and at functioning in Germany's barter economy after the war. Displaced Jews were soon vilified collectively – by Germans, American service personnel who had arrived after the camps had been liberated, and by some Jewish observers – as black-marketeers and quasi-criminals. No reference was made by these critics to the loss of possessions and the injustice of Jewish poverty. Following violent clashes with displaced Jews, German police were banned from entering their camps. While this ban eased the fear of Jews that the German police might replicate Nazi practices, it encouraged rumours to grow unchecked that Jewish camps constituted black market strongholds and were housing cheats and criminals. German officials repeatedly accused Jews of undermining an already feeble economy and exacerbating the food crisis, especially by illegal slaughter and the disposal of large quantities of meat. None of these allegations was proven, yet they remained widely accepted and constituted the new face of anti-Semitism in the immediate aftermath of the war.

Despite popular misgivings about the presence and the treatment of Jews in Germany after the Holocaust, Jews had gained a public voice and, assisted by military governments, a protected space in the remade political culture. To some extent, German and displaced Jews had created parallel and competing organizations to articulate their interests in the local and regional setting, and to support their members in material and social terms. German Jews had created communities on the ruins of their predecessors while displaced Jews set up committees in their residential camps and in some German towns 'out of camp'. This bifurcated Jewish life began to disintegrate in 1948 when resettlement commenced and when the currency reform initiated economic reconstruction, improved living standards and the emergence of a stable parliamentary democracy in those parts of Germany that had been occupied by the western powers. The new constitution underpinning this democracy included an explicit commitment to human and civil rights for all. In such a political environment, Jews could, in principle at least, feel safe. Instead of making anti-Semitism, persecution and murder state policy, as Nazi Germany had done, the Federal Republic pledged equal status and treatment to everyone who resided within its borders. These safeguards made Germany a potential place of residency, although Jews remained marooned there and segregated from the bulk of the population by their Holocaust experiences and by remembering the inhumane treatment that had been meted out to anyone who was deemed to be Jewish.

Unable to Leave or Wanting to Stay?

In 1948, the creation of the State of Israel removed the restrictions that the British had imposed on immigration to 'Palestine'. Jewish camps in Germany had been Zionist strongholds and most of their inhabitants left within two years. Some, however, had contracted tuberculosis and other chronic illnesses during their captivity and had their applications to resettle turned down. Others could not face yet another upheaval and stayed on without actually deciding to stay for good. Revised immigration legislation in 1948 and 1950 also improved the chances of displaced Jews gaining entry to the United States whose quota system had earlier been an insurmountable barrier. The option of resettlement presented itself three and more years after liberation. By then, the camps had begun to close and many Jews, survivors as well as eastern refugees, had learned to live among Germans. In doing so, they translated their fears of a possible Nazi resurgence into distance, watchfulness, and a private determination to retain the sliver of normality they had secured for themselves: family life, some kind of business venture, Jewish community membership, a new beginning of sorts.

The 'stayers' included German Jews and displaced Jews, unevenly mixed across the regions, divided in their understanding and practice of Jewish religion and culture, yet thrown together in their unexpected diaspora because overall numbers were too small to support diversity and institutionalised difference. The new mix came to characterise Jewish life and communities only in western Germany and intensified the division that had turned the eastern part of the country into a separate state. When military governments determined the future of Germany after the Second World War, the Soviets refused to admit or accommodate displaced Jews in their zone. In contrast to developments in western Germany, therefore, Jewish communities in the east were exclusively German-Jewish in composition without the chance of rejuvenation arising from the influx of displaced Jews and, later, from Jewish migration. When the German Democratic Republic collapsed in 1989, Jewish communities in the region had virtually disappeared because there had been no renewal through migration and also because the socialist system equated religion with dissent and encouraged Jews to discard their identity in favour of the ideology prescribed by the East German state.

In West Germany, by contrast, Jews were at liberty to define how they wanted to live and redefine how they could relate to Germans and the German past in the land of the Holocaust. East Germany had simply exported the problem by blaming the Holocaust on the west and exculpating its entire population as working class freedom fighters. Jews, in this narrative, were portrayed as middle class and, in the great scheme of revolutionary justice, as agents of the capitalist system that had given rise to National Socialism which then, by way of rough justice, turned to destroy its makers. Although West Germany claimed to have risen – phoenix-like – from the rubble, helped by the hard work of its population, and had distanced itself from the Holocaust by locating it in an unsavoury and unrepeatable past, it did not deny, as the East had done, that the Nazi period and the Holocaust belonged to its own past. Moreover, the emergence of democracy granted rights of participation and voice to different groups and individuals, including erstwhile victims. From the outset, Jews regarded this commitment to democratic principles as a safeguard against persecution and a lifeline for their own future.

Displaced Jews postponed a decision to leave because they took this reinvented Germany to be a safe place, after all. German Jews justified their sojourn by a new sense of mission. Who would be better able to sense prejudice in German political culture and warn against a resurgence of anti-Semitism than Jews who had personal experiences of both? Who could be more committed to the success of the new democracy than Jews who had suffered most when German democracy was destroyed with impunity at the end of the Weimar Republic? Who other than Jews in Germany could fight for the return of synagogues, Jewish schools, old folks homes and cultural institutions, and also assist survivors in their rightful claims for restitution and justice?

From a Zionist perspective, and also from the perspective of most Jews in other countries, Jews who lived in Germany were vilified as aiding a whitewash of the Nazi past. These Jewish divides surfaced with liberation and have barely changed since. Any kind of Judaism inside Germany was deemed impossible after the Holocaust. How could anyone worthy of being considered a Jew choose to live there of all places? Similarly, German Jews who had survived inside the Third Reich were regarded as all too close to Germans. Had they been genuine Jews, could they have survived in the way they did?

The German and displaced Jews who remained in Germany after 1945 were divided from Jews as well as from Germans by the Holocaust. Jews accused them of minimizing the horrors of the past by their very presence in Germany. Germans, on the other hand, expected Jews who lived in Germany to disregard the past in favour of a redesigned future. For themselves, Jews in Germany constructed a complex identity of remembering the Holocaust inside the country that had perpetrated it, demanding restitution, keeping a watchful distance from their German environment and also subscribing to a firm belief in democracy as a safeguard. They also advocated emigration, especially to Israel, for the next generation who had no personal experiences of the Holocaust and who should, therefore, not be burdened with living in Germany and in the shadow of its past.

In the wake of the Cold War, and more intensely after the collapse of communist control in eastern Europe and the Soviet Union, Jews in Germany began to assist Jewish refugees from these regions with rebuilding a life. Since 1990, Jewish community membership more than trebled as newcomers from the former Soviet Union settled in Germany. The very size of this migration turned into a challenge of integration and accommodating diversity. In offering refuge, Jewish communities have affirmed their belief in Germany as a place where Jews might live safely. At the same time, they remain divided from Germans by their experiences and memory of the Holocaust, and by their fear that it could one day be repeated.

1

EXPERIENCES OF THE HOLOCAUST
AND STRATEGIES OF SURVIVAL

In 1933, when the National Socialists seized power in Germany, the persecution of Jews became state policy. It culminated in the system of deportations, incarceration, slave labour and genocide which the perpetrators and many historians have referred to as the 'Final Solution'. When historiography began to shift from chronicling Nazi policy and the process of 'extermination' to exploring how individuals were marked out and driven to their death, the terms ' Holocaust' or 'Shoah' replaced the Nazi phrase.[1] Central to recasting the terminology has been the determination to reverse the perception of Jews as nameless victims devoid of a personal history worth telling. Instead, researchers set out to unravel the dehumanisation inflicted on those who were caught in the Holocaust. This is the approach adopted here.

As the focus of research changed from the Nazi system to its victims, accounts of survivors about their experiences became a central component of writing about the Holocaust and communicating the enormity and inhumanity of what had happened. In his *The Holocaust: The Jewish Tragedy* Martin Gilbert combined painstaking reports on deportations and camps with personal testimony of individuals who survived them.[2] For Germany, Wolfgang Benz and Monika Richarz have shown that the collective experience of persecution after 1933 generated many different personal responses as individuals struggled to cope with the ever-narrowing scope of their daily lives.[3] While decrees set the same limits for all Jews, no two individuals experienced Nazi persecution in the same way. At the collective level, the 'social annihilation' through decrees and violent acts of exclusion was a prelude to the 'physical annihilation' in the death camps and slave labour compounds.[4] This collective experience pertained to all Jews who lived in any of the areas under Nazi control. It destroyed the normality of social environments and put life itself under threat. At the same time, the Holocaust constituted a personal experience, mediated for each individual by character traits, by favourable or unfavourable local circumstances, and by a complex mix of unpredictability, resilience and luck.[5]

The collective and the personal together constitute the Holocaust experience. Because Jews as a group – Nazi terminology referred to them as a 'race' – were denied personal rights including the right to exist, each individual who was regarded and treated as a Jew at the time, had to face up to these negations and develop personal strategies of adjustment or defiance. Survival itself, Yehuda Bauer argues, amounted to resistance since the whole gambit of Nazi measures and actions concerning Jews was aimed at their destruction and death.[6] The narrative of experience, therefore, constitutes an essential dimension of understanding the Holocaust. Through their testimony, Holocaust survivors show how their manner of coping with persecution and the Nazi killing machine was unique, and they also document challenges and risks, that were so common as to amount to shared experiences of survival, regardless of the specific setting.[7]

Parameters and Strategies of Survival

In Nazi Germany, the build-up and gradual intensification of anti-Jewish measures after 1933 reduced the choices for Jews over time. The order to wear a Yellow Star amounted to enforced self-stigmatisation. Six weeks later, in October 1941, deportations of Jews from Germany began. In the countries that fell into German hands and under Nazi control before or in the course of the Second World War, anti-Jewish measures were introduced immediately, without a build-up or time to adjust.[8] Both scenarios, however, left Jews devoid of choice, forcing them into situations over which they had no control and where personal preferences had been suspended.[9] In its most brutal form, the absence of choice equalled a threat of death. This threat constitutes a defining theme in the narratives of Holocaust survivors.[10] Without exception, they experienced physical violence and beatings at the hands of the SS and their auxiliary guards. They were surrounded by death on the deportation trains and forced marches, in their huts, on labour assignment, during roll calls. As the narratives collected in this book will show, survival entailed somehow and inexplicably getting away with life, although most others did not.

Strategies of survival were aimed first and foremost at reducing the risk of death. Thus, work indoors was more likely to offer a chance of life than work outdoors, especially if it had to be performed in subzero temperatures. Replacing concentration camp issue wooden clogs with shoes was necessary to avoid sore and infected feet. Obtaining warm clothing, socks, underwear, blankets, none of them standard concentration camp issue, were similar devices to preserve strength and avoid illness. In the chronicles of survival, illness is feared because in the camp and slave labour system, prisoners unable to work, march or stand through roll calls, some lasting several hours, risked being beaten or shot. Death sometimes happened in front of everybody and sometimes in hospital or other separate places. On the other hand, many narratives of survivors tell of falling ill and living through, and even of being taken to hospital in a camp and regaining strength there because they received some medical care or because they enjoyed a temporary reprieve from exhausting labour. In the camp hospitals, SS selections of the weakest were a constant threat, but prisoners working as orderlies or nurses often urged patients who had barely recovered to return to their hut, and in doing so saved their lives. Some hospitals dispensed aspirins. In Theresienstadt, life-saving operations were carried out. Most camp hospitals, however, offered no treatment other than rest. In Auschwitz, a special hospital existed where Josef Mengele carried out medical experiments on humans, in particular on twins.

The dominant theme of survival narratives is food. As Nazi decrees narrowed the scope of everyday life for Jews, food became scarce and hunger a pressing problem. In the camps and ghettos, access to food defined the dividing line between life and death. Survival was impossible without obtaining it, guarding it against thieves and making it last. This was especially true for bread. A piece given out in the evening had to last until lunch the following day. Gerty Spiess, who survived Theresienstadt, recalled in a short story how difficult it had been to keep food back for the next day when she was too hungry during the night to think of anything else:

My head aches. I really do not want to eat. I am determined to keep my bread and save it. But my hands are guilty. They automatically reach for the bread sack, touch it to feel whether there is anything left inside. And what happens now happens under some kind of magnetic spell. I have nothing to do with it. The bread tastes bitter and mouldy, horse chestnuts have been baked into it. . . . On my way to work, I fetch my coffee. Half a litre of some poisonous, black stuff, but it is hot and goes right through me. For a few minutes, I am completely happy. Then the toil begins. Breaktime. Everyone begins to eat. I have already eaten my slice of bread during the night. I close my eyes. I do not want to watch. The others do not say anything. They know what is up.[11]

After liberation, many survivors remained obsessed with food, feared it might run out and hoarded it compulsively, long after supplies had become secure and meals regular.[12] Liberation itself, as Lawrence Langer observed, did not mean 'closure' because the Holocaust experiences had written themselves into the biography and personality of survivors.[13] They could attempt to rebuild their lives, but not without looking back and revisiting their experiences.

Somewhere in their narrative, all Holocaust survivors hint at special motivations or hopes that had boosted their resilience at the time. There was no shared approach. David Bergman, for instance, drew strength from imagining that he would see his former house again. When he actually did so after he was liberated, the house had been taken by others and he could no longer live there. Yet, he perceived his return as a success:

> Because my survival was the ability that I saw myself opening the door of my home. I just wanted to have that. I opened the door. And this was the most touching moment for me, a vision that I had carried with me, and that finally came through.[14]

Ernest Weihs felt totally disorientated by what happened to him, and responded by living from one moment to the next without explicit hopes. He had been raised as a Christian but defined by the Nazis as a Jew, then used by the Gestapo to assist with deportations before being deported himself. In Theresienstadt, he noted that old people died because they did not get any food; he was young and got some. Later, he saw strong men dying around him from exhaustion and hard labour. His job was to bury them. He did not ask questions. After his liberation, he had no idea what to do and where to go:

> When you were supposed to go home, you could take a train. There was no need for money or anything. I do not know why, but I was hanging around there for a long time.[15]

Months later, he returned to his native Vienna, discovered that his wife had also survived, and that he could again work for the Swedish mission that had employed him before the Holocaust.

Many narratives of Holocaust survival mention that staying alive depended on stealing, lying and ruthless self-preservation. In the camp language, obtaining – by honest or dishonest means – additional food, clothing and other items of daily use, was called 'organizing'. While all survivors witnessed 'organizing' of some kind, the narratives draw a clear dividing line between actions that harmed fellow prisoners – which they condemn – and actions where the protagonist admits to trying to make a quick grab or use an opportunity.[16] Taking bread from a person who was dead or dying seemed permissible, while ripping it from someone's hand was not, nor was wolfing a piece of bread down after having agreed earlier in the day to swap it for something else.

Against this backcloth of brutalised behaviour, many survivors defined their own personal code of conduct in a desperate bid to retain a sense of self-worth. When the Nazis tried to confiscate her remaining money before deportation, Hedwig Geng did not hesitate to defy the order by refusing to complete the 15-page form that would have transferred everything to the German state.[17] Again defying orders, she hid 500 Marks in the seam of her coat when she was deported to Theresienstadt where the SS guards took the money and locked her up in solitary confinement for several months. Looking back, she was proud of her attempt at resistance although it did not succeed. In the camp, she appears to have alienated others by 'always behaving like a lady'.[18] By this she meant a refusal to steal or cheat at a time when everybody appeared to do it, and when normal rules of conduct seemed to have been suspended.

Hana Bruml was deported from Prague to Theresienstadt, Auschwitz and various slave labour compounds. She expressed her sense of personal integrity by trying her utmost to avoid an infestation with lice, although her surroundings and most of her fellow prisoners were infested. When she failed in her efforts, her confidence faltered:

> I remember sitting on the bed and looking, and finding my first louse. Finding my first louse was an absolute downer. This was the last drop of civilization gone.[19]

On arrival in Auschwitz, she and her group were herded into a hut where soup was dished out in bowls. Next to the entrance, she spotted a sack with a spoon sticking out. For Hana Bruml, getting hold of this spoon meant resisting some of the destruction of selfhood she feared would be her fate:

> So I pulled it out. So I was already more civilized. It was part of becoming less human when you have to slurp like a dog.[20]

The denial of identity is a recurrent theme of survivors' narratives. When their hair was shaved off, clothes replaced by ill-fitting striped dresses or pyjamas and their personal belongings taken from them, newly arrived concentration camp prisoners looked at one another in shock at the annihilation of individuality. The memory of being driven out of their homes, separated from their families and often forced to witness the murder of close relatives and friends, emerges in the narratives as a memory of personal destruction. Reuven Danziger, then aged thirteen, recalls that he felt totally cut off from his former friends, unable to talk to them and unable to laugh. The world and his place in it had collapsed when the Nazis entered his town in Poland and began shooting people he knew, including his mother. Abe Malnik and his parents had tried and failed to flee from Knovno in Lithuania, when the local population joined the Nazis in killing Jews. They had been out of town long enough to escape the murder of up to 10,000 Jews there, but many members of their family were killed in the 'Big Action'. In recalling what happened, Abe Malnik cannot but remember and resent that he and other Jews had been turned into non-persons:

> People have families. People have grandparents and uncles and aunts. They were all annihilated, taken away. We were, you became, nothing.[21]

In Their Own Words: Narratives of Holocaust Survival

The Holocaust did not include within its system a predictable way of survival. For the individual caught up in it as an intended victim, unpredictability was a central experience and risk. On paper, the Holocaust entailed a massive, bureaucratically managed operation of population movements and disposal. Some commentators even coined the metaphor of industrial-style killing, as if well-oiled machinery was set in motion and functioned to order, as if the floors were kept clean like in German factories, as if the processes of decision-making informing it all were rational and would be replicated time and again. Reality was nothing like it. Narratives of round-ups and deportations reveal wanton cruelty at every level. Deportees were kept waiting for hours, without food or water. They were beaten as they were herded along the road to the nearest railway station. Most of the trains consisted of cattle cars, filled to capacity and sealed. There is no record of how many collapsed and died during these operations. The only reliable, predictable components appear to have been the date on the deportation order and the timetables for the deportation trains. The deportees experienced chaos, fear and uncertainty. They were not informed of the destination of their journey and could not know whether they or the family members who travelled with them, would reach it alive.

Unpredictability took on a new urgency in the camps and ghettos where, as we have seen earlier, the lack of food, the threat of beatings, exhaustion and illness were constant risks. How survival was indeed possible can only be shown by looking at individual cases. Each narrative illuminates a unique set of experiences and reveals a personal mix of strategies and luck. It is, of course, impossible to capture the diversity of Holocaust experiences and do justice to all strategies of survival. Yet, the personal voices of survivors and knowledge of their distinctive biographies can show that Holocaust survival demanded extraordinary resources of resilience, courage and endurance and that each survivor, in his or her own way, commanded or won these resources against odds. These personal experiences also show, paradigmatically, what Jews had been through as individuals and collectively by the time the Holocaust came to an end, and to what extent all normality had been shattered and needed to be rebuilt in their lives.

The Story of Max Jacobson: 'These were hard times and we had to comfort one another'

When National Socialism turned the world of German Jews upside down, Max Jacobson was 59 years old; a widower with a married daughter, he lived in Leipzig and worked in the sales department of a German company.[22] In the summer of 1938, his employer honoured his achievements with a special certificate. By the autumn, he was dismissed because the employment of Jews was no longer permitted: his employer paid him only half the special bonuses owed. In November 1938, much worse was to come. In Leipzig, as in other towns and cities across Germany, synagogues were ransacked and set on fire. Max Jacobson was one of ten thousand Jewish men who were arrested and imprisoned without trial. He remembers intense hunger, horrid food consisting only 'of a black liquid and a piece of bread' and a sense of 'emotional oppression'. Like others, he was released on condition that he would leave the country, although, also like others, he had to pay 25 per cent of his assets to reimburse the German state for the 'Night of the Broken Glass' it had orchestrated. His daughter and her husband had already fled to Holland, and made their way from there to London where they were reunited with their twin sons whom they had earlier sent to a boarding school in Sweden. From England, they were hoping to obtain visas for the United States. Max Jacobson tried everything to get out of Germany. His best hopes rested on a cousin who already lived in the United States. But she refused to provide an affidavit until his daughter and her family had been accepted as immigrants. Efforts to join distant relatives in South Africa also came to nothing. After months of uncertainty, emigration seemed suddenly within reach:

In February 1941, the affidavit was finally dispatched. I had registered in good time with the consulate in Berlin and believed that I would soon be allowed to leave, but given the large number of emigrants it was impossible to receive a positive response from the consulate, or even any kind of response. After some time I enquired again and was told that I would soon be invited for my medical examination. I immediately moved to speed things up. I had all the necessary papers together, only the American visa was missing. I had even booked a passage on the steamer *Nyasse*, scheduled to sail from Lisbon on June 29 1941. Now, as I am writing this, I am still in Leipzig. There is no more hope of emigration. Nobody who has not experienced what had been done to us Jews can understand how I felt when I had to bury this hope.

He made one further, albeit abortive attempt to try and flee to Cuba. In November 1941, Max Jacobson knew that he was trapped. Around him, things got increasingly nasty. When a friend applied for a travel permit to visit his dying mother, he was told by the officer in charge that there was no need to do so since 'the pig will croak without you'. In nearby Dessau, his cousin Salomon, an orthodox Jew, was forced to wear a sign with an abusive inscription around his neck, beaten unconscious and taken to Buchenwald concentration camp where he died within days from his injuries. Street after street declared itself *judenrein*, cleansed of Jews, forcing Jewish occupants to move in search of shelter. Each time, German landlords insisted on advance payments and on tenants redecorating at their own expense, only to evict them just weeks later. Finally, Max Jacobson found a tiny room in a flat that also housed six Jewish families and three single people. Despite overcrowding, the residents gave each other support until deportations shattered all normality:

The shared suffering turned all of us into one large family. Here, Frau Gertrud Hahn in particular deserves to be remembered. When everybody had lost courage, and this happened often, she managed to give us new hope. Although she had to care for her sick husband, she was always ready to help when others needed her. How few of these 15 people are still alive! Most fell victim to the executioner. Conditions for us Jews worsened rapidly, we hardly dared to step out into the street. We had become powerless and outlawed and had to bear whatever happened. Then the dreaded transports to Poland and elsewhere in the east started. On January 17 1942, Frau Weinberger received the written order to prepare for departure and on January 18 she already had to leave for the unknown, together with eight hundred others from Leipzig. I tried everything humanly possible to free her, but because Frau Weinberger had been involved a few days earlier in an altercation with an SS man in the Dresdner Bank, all my endeavours were in vain. Nobody knows exactly where the transport was heading. . . . I myself and my friends were deeply troubled by the fate of our friends and there was hardly another topic of conversation. It was unbearable to have no news from anyone or anywhere to let us know where our loved ones were. We were tortured and made to suffer until our spirits were dull and blunted. Now, I am completely calm. Now, my rucksack is packed and sits beside me. On September 19 1942, I together with five hundred Jews from Leipzig have to go into exile. Rumour has it that we will be taken to Theresienstadt, but all this is uncertain, and I do not believe that we will stay there for any length of time. This transport includes all men and women above the age of sixty-five, the sick and war invalids. Fredy's mother was also taken to Theresienstadt a little while ago, as were Auntie Linchen from Göttingen and all the relatives from Hildesheim. Perhaps, I shall see them there again. In eighteen hours, I have to say farewell. I am going in the happy knowledge that my children are safe and I ask God to bless them and my grandsons Fritz and Peter. I am also leaving full of hope that the Almighty will protect me, that I survive the war and that I may live to see my children again. This is my one and only big and heartfelt wish.

Max Jacobson was deported to Theresienstadt where he found, as he had hoped, his aunt and other relatives. Most of them died from malnutrition within weeks of his arrival. At least 150 people died there every day. Dead bodies and transports to dispose of them were a daily sight. Two or three corpses at a time would be loaded onto open two-wheeled push carts and taken to the camp crematorium. These makeshift death carts went back and forth all day long while purpose-built Jewish hearses that had been taken in large numbers from Slovakia to Theresienstadt were used to transport all kinds of goods that needed to be moved inside the camp. In the past, these hearses had been pulled by horses, now they were pulled by prisoners. Max Jacobson was 'employed' pulling one of these hearses and shifting coal:

> These hearses gave the town a gruesome appearance which everyone who has been imprisoned there remembers all too well and which depressed us more and more. This, I presume, was the object of this order.

Hunger constituted a daily challenge to life. Rations consisted of a black liquid in the morning, watery soup at lunch time with three or four potatoes or a little tapioca, and in the evening again a thin soup and a disgusting brew called 'coffee'. Sometimes, a little marmalade was given out and a weekly allocation of 50g of sugar and margarine. Bread provided the main source of nourishment, but it was increasingly scarce. In December 1942, bread rations were halved and Max Jacobson exchanged some of the clothes he had brought from Leipzig for additional bread: a whole loaf for a good pair of shoes and a gabardine coat, half a loaf for a pair of trousers. He even rummaged in the garbage to find food:

> I struck up a firm friendship with the chap on the straw mattress next to mine, a comedian called Bendix from Berlin. We took turns in daily sifting through the dirt that had been swept out of the kitchen to look for potato peels. These were then washed, boiled, cut into tiny pieces and mixed in with the coffee suds. When we had some, we even added a little sugar to our daily extra nourishment. From time to time, we had to do without this addition for lack of ingredients, but also because our stomachs rebelled.

In the spring of 1944, Bendix died from malnutrition, although he had been taken off compulsory labour. While Bendix was still alive, the two of them and another man, Bernhard Löwenberg from Frankfurt, had developed a little entertainment routine which would earn them a slice of bread and help everyone to forget their plight for a moment:

> These were hard times and we had to comfort one another. . . . Bendix was brilliant in comical parts, I recited my own and other people's outpourings and Löwenberg delighted the comrades with song. Thus we tried to cheer each other up.

Death, however, was never far away. When Max Jacobson celebrated his seventieth birthday on October 18, 1944, only two of his many relatives who had been incarcerated in Theresienstadt were still alive. They congratulated him and even brought him a present: a tiny potato pancake with a paper 'Seventy' stuck on top. Inside Theresienstadt, hunger was a fearsome killer but even more of his family and friends perished after 'being selected for transports to the east and having to walk the bitter path of suffering to the very end'. On May 6, 1943, Max Jacobson himself came perilously close to being taken to Auschwitz. He had just been released from a five week spell in hospital where he had been treated for heart disease brought on by malnutrition and hard labour. Within hours of his release, he was ordered to be ready for transport:

> I found time to say goodbye to Willy and Margot Jacobson, but I could report back to them a little later, because – what luck – I was supernumerary and released together with five others. Nobody could have been more delighted, and the joy was justified because none of the people who were ordered onto this transport have ever been heard of again. Today and always, I am deeply grateful that destiny kept me

alive, yet the fate my friends had to endure continues to fill me with horror.

Luck was on his side again when he unexpectedly met an old friend, Anneliese Dickstein, whose husband worked in the kitchen. She began to provide Max Jacobson with some additional food. From late 1943 onwards, prisoners in Theresienstadt were allowed to receive parcels and although many did not arrive or had their contents raided, Max Jacobson was among the recipients and the additional food strengthened his hold on life. On October 20, 1944, he was again admitted to hospital, this time to undergo two serious urological operations – the first on January 30, 1945 and the second in late March. He was still recuperating when machine-gun fire shattered the hospital windows as the Russians occupied Theresienstadt and liberated its prisoners. Max Jacobson's surgeon, a Dr Braun from Prague, and the nursing staff had done their utmost to care for him and provide the best diet. On June 7, 1945, Max Jacobson was well enough to leave the hospital. His sleeping place in Theresienstadt had been taken by someone else, his luggage had been broken into and most of his belongings stolen. His last days in captivity were dominated by the fear of theft and an impatience to leave:

> In the days before the departure of the Czechs and Poles, thefts got out of hand, and it will forever remain a blotted page in history how they fought amongst themselves about things. I could not dare to leave my meagre belongings unguarded for fear that they would vanish. Nevertheless, someone managed to steal my only blanket but I consoled myself with the thought that the day of departure would soon also arrive for us Germans.

On June 23, 1945, three Red Cross buses collected seventy survivors from Leipzig and returned them to the town that had once been their home.

The Story of Hans Winterfeldt: 'I had been raised to do what the adults told me to'

When the Nazis seized power, Hans Winterfeldt was 7 years old and lived in Lippehne, a small town in northern Germany, where his father owned a shop and a house which Hans should have inherited, had life gone to plan. The family felt at home in the small Jewish community of thirty members with its shared rabbi and religion teacher. The father had served in the First World War, and like many Jewish war veterans, was proud to be German. Nazism seemed no more than a temporary aberration:

'Why should I emigrate,' my father would ask together with many thousands of other Jews. 'We are living in a state based on the rule of law. I have fought in the war. Nothing can happen to us.'[23]

Many Jews even believed that the violence on November 9, 1938 was carried out by isolated local party organizations. In December 1937, the family held a clearance sale to raise money – for the first time since 1933, there were customers in the shop – abandoned their house and left for Berlin where they hoped to live more anonymously and, therefore, in greater safety. Hans Winterfeldt's father built up a little business selling towels and linen to Jews who were preparing to emigrate. Since they were only allowed to take ten Reichsmarks with them, they would not be able to buy anything abroad and had to stock up beforehand. Like many Jews, the Winterfeldts tried to at least get their children out of Germany. Hans's older sister left for Palestine in 1939. He 'never liked the idea of emigrating to Palestine. I did not want to live only among Jews.' Efforts to secure a place for him on a *Kindertransport* to England came to nothing:

There was an office at the Jewish Community in the Oranienburger- strasse in Berlin where they dealt with emigration to various countries. My father tried his best, and I would have liked to go abroad. We spent innumerable hours waiting in the corridor in front of the office of the administrator and were fobbed off with promises again and again. . . . It seems that one needed to have the backing of an influential person, in order to be successful. Perhaps, the administrators wanted to be bribed.

Without relatives abroad to provide affidavits or to take them in, and without substantial funds to pay any sweeteners that may have been required, Hans Winterfeldt and his parents were trapped in Germany. In the run-up to the war, anti-Jewish decrees became ever more life- threatening and their mixture of humiliation and cruelty curtailed all 'personal freedom and lifestyle choices'. In March 1939, the identity cards of Jews were stamped with a 'J' as a mark of difference. When ration cards were introduced at the beginning of the war, those for Jews were also stamped with a 'J', although not immediately on every coupon. The family used this small loophole to disobey one of the many restrictions:

The letter 'J' was stamped into the centre of the ration card, in the space where the name had to be entered. While Jews had long been banned from going to restaurants, my parents often took me in early 1940 to a small restaurant in the Motzstrasse. It was run by an elderly couple. The husband was also the waiter. We were not supposed to cut the ration coupons off in payment for the meal we had chosen and the waiter was required to take the whole ration card before cutting the coupons off himself, but the old man was so busy that he was relieved when my parents handed him the correct number of coupons. My father would put the coupons on his lap under the table, so that nobody could see the 'J' printed on the card. We could not have cut the coupons in advance at home since we could not have known how many were required for each dish. Yet, the single 'J' did not last long. A little later, each ration card bore countless tiny imprints of the word 'Jew' (*Jude*) and each coupon would show the word *Jude* at least once.

Little acts of defiance such as this and kindly shopkeepers who kept goods under the counter until the afternoon when Jews were allowed to shop, enabled the Winterfeldts to take the edge off some of the restrictions although the list of forbidden items grew longer every day: eggs, meat and meat products, flour, coffee, tea, cocoa, fresh fruit and most vegetables, clothing, soap and razor blades, to name but a few. During Hans Winterfeldt's last year at school in 1939/40, Gestapo officers even made spot checks to search the lunch boxes of Jewish children for forbidden items. If anything was found, the parents were deemed to have a criminal record and, so it was said, would be the first to be sent 'to the east'.

Hans Winterfeldt left school at the age of fourteen in 1940. An apprenticeship as a locksmith at a Jewish vocational school and a short spell as a trainee cook in a Jewish old folks' home ended abruptly when the Gestapo closed both establishments. Like his father and other Jewish adults, Hans Winterfeldt had to sign up for *Zwangsarbeit* forced labour. While Jews had been removed from the labour market after the Nazis came to power, they were re-enlisted, albeit at the lowest and unskilled level, when Germans were mobilised in large numbers for war service and labour shortages intensified. By recruiting Jews, German employers could be sure of securing high-quality, cheap labour, not always only to work for the war effort. Hans Winterfeldt's first employer used his Jewish workers to build himself a luxury villa in a suburb of Berlin. His second employer, Otto Lebrecht who was a member of the Nazi Party, won a lucrative government contract to paint all air-raid shelters in Berlin in the regulation colours. The work was carried out by Jewish forced labourers. For Jews themselves, forced labour did not necessarily result in a deterioration of their situation. In many cases, it offered a welcome chance to obtain ration cards and improve access to food. Hans Winterfeldt believed that the direct contact with Jews as workers also challenged negative stereotypes about their character and abilities:

The Jewish unskilled workers were soon highly respected members of the workforce, not only with the Otto Lebrecht firm but in Germany overall where most were employed in factories, road construction or railway track maintenance. The German government had expected and hoped that Jews ... would make useless, lazy and unreliable workers. This would have confirmed the Nazi view of Jews. While the labour shortage during the war made it necessary to recruit everyone for work, it had been the intention all along to carry out the 'final solution of the Jewish question'. Yet, the Jewish men and women who were made to sign up for forced labour proved that at every level they performed their duties to the complete satisfaction of their employers. For this reason, the German government and the Gestapo were most embarrassed when large enterprises that made essential contributions to the war economy protested in 1942–43 against the fact that their Jewish unskilled workers were withdrawn in order to 'evacuate' them to the east.

By early 1943, even forced labour could no longer protect Jews from deportation. Towards the end of February, the Gestapo moved in Berlin and throughout Nazi Germany against Jewish forced labourers by rounding them up directly at their workplace. In most localities, transports were assembled; workers whom employers had regarded as essential were seized and sent to concentration camps. In Berlin, however, a week-long public protest in front of the Gestapo headquarters secured the release of two thousand Jews who were married to German women. These women had mounted the protests which became known as the Factory Action and forced the Gestapo to climb down. The Factory Action was only aimed at saving Jews who were married to Germans. As for the Winterfeldts, all three were Jewish and would not have been spared.

They had, however, already gone into hiding. The decision had been taken on February 15, 1943, one week before the Factory Action. The move had been carefully prepared. With the help of the caretaker of the house where they had rented a flat, they sold whatever they could, although Jews had long been forbidden to sell anything. By way of thank you they gave the caretaker their kitchen furniture. Then they took off their Yellow Stars and embarked on a life that Hans Winterfeldt recalled as 'engulfed by fear'. He found a friend where he could stay; his parents moved constantly from place to place. Parents and son barely met and never did so in public. While in hiding, Hans Winterfeldt made a new friend, a young Jew who boasted that he regularly flouted anti-Jewish rules, that he had been to the cinema and even that he had dated non-Jewish girls. Hans Winterfeldt never dared to behave in this way, but he admired the bravado of his friend, and always admired the daring of his father who seemed to find countless little ways of evading Nazi restrictions without being detected.

On June 12, 1943, disaster struck. His Jewish friend turned out to be an informer for the Gestapo and had him arrested while he attended a piano lesson. He was taken to a room, beaten and kicked repeatedly, and interrogated for four hours. His interrogators turned out to be Jews themselves who worked for the Gestapo. After his resilience had finally been broken and he had betrayed the address of his parents, they handcuffed him and led him, like a criminal, through the streets to a police station:

> The men intimidated me by their behaviour and by the way they spoke. I was in a state of shock, as if under anaesthetic. . . . Until this day, I have not lost an acute sense of guilt. In lonely moments, I revisit the events of June 12, 1943 and imagine how I might have or could have acted differently, and I stand powerlessly before unalterable facts.

From the police station, he was taken to a huge interrogation room where Jewish orderlies registered people who were to be deported. Most of these orderlies lived in mixed marriages, and their forced labour consisted of dealing with Jews prior to deportation, including collecting people from their homes and taking them to the assembly points. Despite his shocking experiences, Hans Winterfeldt believed these Jewish helpers to be 'decent people who tried to make things a little easier for the Jews who had been rounded up'. As he stood in line, his parents were brought into the hall, but they never once looked at him. He was completely crushed with guilt and self-doubt:

> I had not been strong enough to resist. I doubted my judgement, because I had not been brought up to have a will of my own, at any time. When was I praised for anything? Had anyone ever tried to boost my self-confidence? I was only used to being criticised. Did my decisions or aspirations ever find approval? No. I was being told off. I was called 'stubborn', 'strong-headed' and 'willful'. Did my parents ever like my friends? No. I therefore never took them home with me. I had always been the insecure child without a view of his own, and I had been raised to do what the adults told me to.

He met his father again on the deportation train to Auschwitz; the women, including his mother, had already been separated from the men. On arrival, father and son had consecutive numbers tattooed on their arms: A14317 and A14318. Although they were allocated to different huts and work commandos, his father managed to teach him a very important survival strategy: never to get noticed.

'You must not be noticed,' my father said to me. This he had obviously learned in the German army. When we had to line up and people were picked out for unpleasant tasks, my father and I always removed our glasses. In any case, it was not long before we had them knocked from our faces and broken. Somehow, we all looked the same. But when it came to selecting people, they would say: 'Hey you, with the glasses!'

On arrival, Hans Winterfeldt had made himself a little older to increase his chances of being selected for work. With four hundred others, he was kept in quarantine for four weeks, and suffered intensively from hunger, thirst and the disgusting conditions until his senses were blunted by the experience:

During the day, the heat was unbearable. In the morning we were served some dark liquid in large metal dishes, a sort of tea or *ersatz* coffee which was fetched in large wooden barrels from the kitchen. At lunchtime we received less than half a litre of indefinable soup, which we had to drink from the same metal dishes. There were no spoons. At the beginning, I felt revulsion that at least eight prisoners had to drink from the same bowl which was not washed. For 400 people there were only 50 bowls in the block. For weeks and months, the soup was the same in taste and smell. But it soon tasted much better than on the first day when I thought it was poison, because the taste of the soup in Auschwitz-Birkenau improved the hungrier I got. It is all relative!

After four weeks, he was transferred to a section of Auschwitz known as Camp D where male labour slaves were kept. Here, survival depended on managing to avoid 'commandos' with a high death rate from heavy work. On his first day, he was forced to unload massive tree trunks in front of one of the crematoria. At lunchtime, his hands were torn, and he was too weak to eat. He soon learned that new prisoners ended up in the most lethal commandos. Survival depended on working in a less destructive commando and on understanding the system. Commando leaders were required to supply a certain number of men. If they were short, they would grab anyone. Hans Winterfeldt was close to physical collapse when his hut was hit by an infectious disease. The SS, fearing disease among prisoners more than their death, ordered work to be suspended and the hut closed for four weeks. This unexpected rest allowed Hans Winterfeldt to recover some of his strength, defend himself better against having his food stolen and get more used to being constantly hungry. He also managed to find a less lethal commando, collecting and transporting human excrement in a wagon across the camp:

The wagon had an opening at the top into which we emptied the containers. When it was full, we covered the opening with a blanket while fifteen of us pushed and pulled the cart over the bumpy, boggy and stony paths all the way across Birkenau to where the manure wagon was emptied out. It was so far to go, and progress over the stony ground was so slow that we managed to make only four trips per day. Because the ride was so bumpy we were constantly splattered with faeces that was thrown up from the opening despite the blanket covering it, and dripped through chinks in the cart. After a few days, however, we no longer minded because we stank ourselves just like that.

This commando ended abruptly when the Hungarian women, whose excrement they had collected, were gassed. Hans Winterfeldt now used his knowledge of camp life to avoid another killer commando. He had observed that the Block Elders, two huge Russians, were supposed to keep the hut clean, fetch the food and ensure that all workers left for their commandos after a second bell had been sounded. Other than beating those who were slow to make it through the narrow doorway blocked by the crush of four hundred men, Hans Winterfeldt had never seen them do any actual work. He had already figured out that he could escape the blows if he left through a side entrance of the hut just before the commanding bell sounded. One day, he found himself a broom and as the second bell sounded, he began sweeping. He and three others who had done the same managed to stay inside the hut and take on the role of 'junior room service', scrubbing the cement floor with water, fetching soup from the kitchen. At lunchtime, thirty litres of soup were provided for the prisoners who were too sick to leave the block and people like himself who were working there. The Block Elders ate none of the soup since they had better things such as bread, margarine and sausage, allowing the 'junior room service' team to eat as much as they liked, and to keep some back to exchange for bread later on. This 'wonderful life' ended when the SS drove everybody out of the hut except the official Block Elders. Although ordered to serve in one of the harshest work commandos, Hans Winterfeldt knew by now that 'work avoidance equalled self-preservation'. After a few days, he managed to resume the 'room service'. His father, meanwhile, had adopted the same strategy. He performed 'room service' for German prisoners, *Reichsdeutsche*, who were held captive in Auschwitz. They received better rations and were feared by other prisoners. Every evening the father managed to exchange some soup for bread and share it with his son.

In November 1944, gassings stopped in Auschwitz and the crematoria were demolished. All prisoners were now forced to work outdoors, most of them shifting sand, stones and wood from one place to another and then back again the following day. Snow had fallen, it was extremely cold and the conditions were horrific. Hans Winterfeldt's strategy of survival now consisted of hiding under a bunk or behind a hut:

> Every day that could be spent without having to work in the cold and the snow, and without the maltreatment by the SS and the Kapos, was a day won.

On January 18, 1945, Hans Winterfeldt was one of nearly 100,000 prisoners who were marched from Auschwitz towards Germany. His father had become so weak that he had been sent to the camp hospital. From there he and seven thousand other survivors including more than a thousand children were liberated on January 27 when the Red Army entered Auschwitz. Hans, meanwhile, had been put on a train of open cattle trucks. In the first week, there was no food at all and many died of starvation and cold. In the second week, the train pulled into Prague station where Red Cross helpers had prepared some soup but did not provide enough bowls. Fighting broke out as people were forced to share, but especially because starvation and deprivation made them aggressive and unreasonable in their behaviour:

> Normally, one could talk to the other prisoners, but when food was distributed, they began to look and act like lunatics: their eyes stared rigidly at the ladle or at the arm that distributed the bread. When they had received their ration, they constantly watched the other prisoners to check that nobody had been given more. It was completely irrelevant what kind of person it was: uneducated and primitive, or educated and intellectually superior. I often wondered how cultivated human beings could behave like animals. Many prisoners were unable to judge the actual value of food. In Auschwitz, for instance, I found that they would exchange a large bowl of soup for a bread ration although the comparatively small piece of bread contained more nourishment. It even happened that prisoners bought extra soup at lunchtime in exchange for the bread they would receive in the evening. Later, when they had to hand over their bread, they would wail or wolf it down quickly themselves. This often led to fights.

From Prague, Hans Winterfeldt was taken to Mauthausen. The camp was situated on top of a mountain and the Austrian SS drove the prisoners, despite their weakened conditions, with rifle butts through the snow in a manner that Hans Winterfeldt remembers as a 'hunt' (*Treibjagd*). Some – especially those who appeared weak – had to stand for days by the camp wall, often until they collapsed or were shot. Those deemed fit for work were ordered to wash (they even managed to sip some water from the tap after a week without anything to drink). Then, still wet and clothed only in underpants, a shirt and shoes – socks were not issued in concentration camps – they had to wait in front of the accommodation block to which they had been assigned in temperatures of minus 15 degrees for at least half an hour. The Mauthausen roll call used the numbers that had been tattooed on their arms in Auschwitz. When a selection team asked him his name and age, he made himself three years younger than he actually was because he had picked up rumours that everyone over eighteen would be sent to work in the mines in nearby Gusen. Several of the men who arrived with him in the cattle car were sent there and never heard of again.

> For me, personally, Mauthausen was a lot worse than Auschwitz. In Mauthausen, there was a lot less food. I have no words to describe how I starved between January 18, 1945 and May 5, 1945. But it was not merely hunger that plagued us. We knew that the war could not last long and was lost for the Germans, and that this would mean the end of imprisonment for us. The most depressing thing was that none of this was apparent inside the camp. Everything went on as normal. The SS and the top-notch prisoners were as arrogant and cruel as on day one of my arrival in Auschwitz. It appeared as if the imminent end of the war could not change things for us. In addition, most of the prisoners were convinced that the Germans wanted to do away with us before the end of the war. I was full of unjustified optimism. I refused, categorically, to accept that I should die in the nineteenth year of my life, after I had, as long as I could remember, been oppressed, vilified, subjected to excruciating punishment, injustice and beatings and after having lived for eight months in hell before arriving in Mauthausen. Did I believe in a higher being, in a god? I can no longer answer this question today. I believed in or rather hoped for justice.

Within days, he was marched off to another camp where accommodation consisted of tents and everyone seemed destined to die of hunger and neglect:

> Many defecated wherever they lay, especially in the night, because they were either too lazy or too weak to get up. Rain turned the whole camp into a swamp and ensured that the shit was carried from one end of the camp to the other. It was unbearable. People died like flies. We hardly saw any SS inside our camp. We felt like lepers, who were supposed to finally eat one another.

Liberation came 'between the fifth and the seventh of May 1945' in yet another camp, Gunskirchen. Although it contained huts, they were 'full of sick people' and 'soggy with human excrement as people had lost the strength to go outside'. When somebody claimed to have seen 'Tommies', Hans Winterfeldt decided to get up, but felt too weak and kept falling asleep. It was only when the young man who slept next to him shook him by the shoulders and showed him the chewing gum in his mouth, that he managed to drag himself out of the hut. The liberators were American. One of them was sitting on the bonnet of his Jeep and threw chocolate, chewing gum and cigarettes into the crowd. The fitter ones could fill their pockets. Hans Winterfeldt was too exhausted to even try, let alone 'walk to freedom', as he had intended. Dropping onto the grass verge by the road, he noticed a small tin of salted nuts, prised it open and slowly consumed one quarter of its contents. After that, he shuffled to the nearby village where he joined several other liberated prisoners. They had obtained a sack of sugar and secured permission from a farmer to sleep in his barn. Hans Winterfeldt spent the night there, eating sugar. In the morning, he was strong enough to get up and make his way to an abandoned military barracks in the nearby town of Wels where, so he heard, survivors could find shelter. There were no beds, no care, no facilities. He felt completely alone and reduced 'to the mental level of an animal whose sense of self-preservation is totally focussed on finding something to eat'. It took Hans Winterfeldt many months to recover his health and to regain a sense of self that allowed him to look beyond his physical needs and think of his former life and his family. When he finally made his way to Berlin in October 1945, he found both his parents alive. The miracle of survival had not erased old misgivings and recriminations:

When someone asked my father why we were picked up by the Gestapo and deported, he told him that they only 'caught' me and that I gave away the address of my parents. Of course, this was the truth. But I did mind that he kept saying this when I was present.

Overall, Hans Winterfeldt felt that liberation did not meet the expectations and hopes that he and many others like him had harboured during their time in captivity:

We were free, but no more than that. I had fervently believed that the Allies had arrived in order to liberate us. Today, I know full well that they did not fight Nazi Germany to liberate a few million Jews. They pushed back the German army, defeated it and found us by accident along the way.

Bella Tovey's Survival: 'We were good looking Jewish women'

Bella Tovey was born in 1927 in Sosnowiecz, a Polish town near the German border where she lived with her parents and three younger siblings. The family were well off, owned a shop, lived in a spacious apartment and even employed a cook until September 1939, when the Nazis marched in, took away the shop, forced the family to move to an area set up as a ghetto, and stole most of their furniture.[24] In return for food rations, Bella Tovey's father had to work in his former shop while she, her mother and her sister Pnina were forced to perform forced labour in a nearby factory. Like in other ghettos, Jewish children were forbidden to attend school but the Toveys arranged some private tuition for their daughters. Since Sosnoviecz was an 'open ghetto', not surrounded by walls, inhabitants were able to barter and obtain some food from the local Polish population.

Conditions deteriorated in 1942 when transports out of the ghetto began. The family managed to avoid the first of these although their names appeared on the list and they were ordered to line up. Bella Tovey's father somehow persuaded the Germans to let them off, or perhaps the SS officer was moved when her little 6-year-old brother begged in German to be spared. In the autumn of 1942, the ghetto in Sosnowiecz was sealed off and conditions deteriorated sharply until all its inhabitants were deported and the ghetto itself closed. What the Nazis referred to as 'liquidation' took place in August 1943. Bella Tovey's parents and two youngest siblings did not survive.

Since they were deemed to be of working age, Bella Tovey and her sister Pnina had already been rounded up in 1942, sent to one of the sub-camps of Auschwitz in Gräben, and allocated as slave labourers to a garment factory in the town. Work for the women consisted of unloading huge bundles of flax and storing them in an open barn. There was not much food in the camp: one pound of bread for a week, some *ersatz* coffee and a bowl of soup per day. As time went on, the soup became more watery. Occasionally, there would be a teaspoon of jam or margarine. Looking back at this period of her Holocaust experience, Bella Tovey remembers that the woman in charge of her group was 'kind hearted and fair'. She had been a singer and also came from Sosnowiecz. One evening after work, she sang a Schubert song in the hut. This provoked an SS man to charge in and beat her severely, screaming that she had no right to sing this song, and no right as a Jew to sing that well.

Bella Tovey refused to accept the negative image of Jews. In the early days of her imprisonment she even believed that local people who saw her and others being marched from camp to factory, would notice that Nazi propaganda was false and distorting. She hoped that the bystanders would discard the stereotypes and see the individuals:

We had to walk through a little town to Gräben where the camp was, and we were, of course, walking on the street, never on the sidewalk. And the Germans were lining the streets watching us, and what I do remember is that they were surprised. We were still . . . we had come out of our homes. We were still wearing our clothing. We were good looking Jewish women.

Not only did the women not look like slaves, Bella Tovey also remembers that they did not behave like slaves. One day, when one of the women was seriously injured by a piece of machinery, the whole group demanded that she should receive medical attention, and refused to move on after roll call until their demand had been granted. The German owner of the factory appears to have valued his workforce and persuaded the SS to agree to treatment. Some months later, Bella Tovey had her first personal encounter with women who had been imprisoned in Auschwitz, deprived there of their personal appearance, clothing, hair and shoes, and who knew about the transports, selections and gas chambers. Some of these women came from her home town and told her that her family had been murdered.

In November 1944, the factory in Gräben was closed down and its Jewish concentration camp workforce death-marched towards Germany. From this point onwards, Bella Tovey was constantly surrounded and threatened by death:

It was very cold and we marched for days. Then they put us into cattle trains. I do not remember how long we were on the cattle train. We were finally brought to Bergen-Belsen. . . . They did not need gas chambers there. It was really a death camp. Almost immediately, people were dying all around us.

In Bergen-Belsen, she contracted typhus and only pulled through because her friend Frieda insisted that she could fight her physical weakness and sign up for work. Work meant being entitled to some soup. It consisted of 'doing inventory', sorting clothing and other belongings that 'they robbed, they took from Jewish victims'. Working in the camp storerooms provided her with a chance to steal things and swap them for better clothes. They kept her warm, but also boosted her sense of self:

I could put on a pair of panties. I was allowed under my uniform, I was allowed a pair of panties, a shirt or a blouse, maybe, and a sweater. And maybe some stockings.

A few days before liberation, she again contracted typhus and lay prostrate and feverish. Again, her friend helped by bringing her water and even 'organizing' some aspirins. When liberation came, she was too ill to take it all in:

> I was feverish. And my friend Frieda stayed with me that night, and in the morning the British came, and we were liberated.

A British soldier carried her to the camp hospital and later visited her to see how she was doing. When he asked her what she would like, she could only think of two things after all this time without choice: a pair of warm socks and sugar. In retrospect, she regarded her illness as another stroke of luck, since the special diet that was given to hospital patients protected her from the risk of eating too much too early or eating the wrong food after her experience of starvation:

> I survived – but many died in Belsen after the war. Many died, by the way, of dysentery because the British were so sympathetic, they felt such pity, that they gave the inmates their food rations, and that greasy food, you know, meat and things. People in the concentration camps, the inmates, could not take it.

After her liberation, Bella Tovey could not decide how to restart her life. Aimlessly, she stayed in Belsen until her sister found her there in the autumn of 1945. At the same time, a Red Cross message arrived from an uncle who had emigrated to New York. This offered some hope that she might rebuild a life, but it did not quell her fears that the Holocaust experience had deformed her for ever:

> I was filled up with a lot of anger and hatred and . . . I was afraid of myself.

The Story of Alice Cahane: 'I cannot tell you the humiliation I felt'

Alice Cahane was born in 1929 in Budapest and lived in a small town near the Austrian border until June 1944 when she was deported to Auschwitz with her mother, older sister and two younger brothers, one of them just 3 years old.[25] Her father had somehow managed to obtain Raoul Wallenberg papers for himself. These papers declared the holder to be a Swedish citizen and protected him from deportation. Alice Cahane's mother and little brothers perished in Auschwitz while she and her sister Edith had a chance of survival as slave labourers. They remained together until after liberation, when Edith died after eating tinned hash, given to her by well-meaning liberators.

Even before being deported, Alice Cahane and her sister were conscripted to forced labour in a brick factory. They worked there during the day, and slept in their own home at night. On the eve of their deportation, this little normality ended:

> So one day, that special permission of sleeping at home was not granted. We were ordered to go to the brick factory, and we went there and for one night we had to sleep on the floor. The next morning they took us to the railway station. And we were marching through our town. I cannot tell you the humiliation I felt, carrying our baggage, passing our house, looking into the windows, seeing the people who occupied our house looking at us, and nobody stopping. They marched us to the railroad.

On arrival in Auschwitz, she came face to face with Mengele, the notorious camp doctor and 'Angel of Death', and was sent with other women from Hungary to a section she remembers as 'Camp C'.[26]

> That was a place where nobody ever dared to go near, and we gave it a wide berth even when it was empty. Once the naked girls had been driven in, the doors were bolted and the windows barred, and they were kept there without food and water. All through the days and nights you could hear screams and sobbing, and an occasional snatch of prayers and singing. Hands stretched through the bars, begging for a sip of water. But it was out of bounds. Usually, lorries came to take the victims away. This time, they failed to arrive. At the end of the fourth day the SS men opened the doors. The smell made even them jump back. Most of the prisoners were dead, heaped on top of one another. Those still alive were sent back to their block, weeping with relief.

Soon afterwards, she was herded to the gas chamber but the gas did not work and she was sent back to the hut. Here, she was reunited with her sister Edith.

In the early days of her captivity, Alice Cahane was keenly aware of her own pitiful appearance, her hair shorn, her ill-fitting concentration camp issue clothes and she herself unrecognisable as feminine. By contrast, the SS seemed smart, clean, impressive in their uniforms. Female guards especially reminded her of her own shabbiness and depersonalisation:

> I remember Irma Grese.[27] She was SS and the most beautiful woman, with her blonde hair, beautifully coiffured, her beautiful skirt, blue shirt – starched, clean and crisp. Seeing her made us feel even more that we were less than animals. We are not human beings any more. We do not have individuality.

For Alice Cahane, as for other survivors, the chance of survival was linked to slave labour. In late 1944, a group of women from her hut, including her sister Edith, were rounded up to be transported elsewhere. Desperate to stay with her sister, she implored the SS guard to let her go also, claiming that it was her birthday. The guard consented. Travelling through the night, the women were taken by train to Guben, a sub-camp of Gross-Rosen, which was itself part of the slave labour system affiliated to Auschwitz. Work was in an ammunition factory. It was hard, but Guben seemed a safer place than Auschwitz where food was no longer distributed on a regular basis and the camp organization had begun to disintegrate as the Red Army drew nearer and the Germans prepared to destroy and abandon the killing machine they had constructed there.

The harsh normality of Guben even included a bit of fun. At Christmas 1944, the SS ordered the women to decorate their huts. Since they had nothing they could use for decorations, the women in Alice Cahane's group arranged themselves into a tableau depicting a candelabra and won the prize, 'a tin of snails'.

In February 1945, the factory in Guben was closed, its slave labour compound evacuated and the women who had been detained there death-marched in a westerly direction:

> In the middle of the winter, without socks, without underwear, without coat, just a blanket we had wrapped around us. We had to march from village to village.

Only once were they allowed to sit down at the edge of a field. At night, they slept in barns, during the day the guards forced them to march without a break. One night, Alice Cahane, her sister Edith and their friend Ibi managed to hide near the outer wall of a barn underneath some straw, and remain there undetected in the morning. Escape and freedom appeared within reach:

> They marched away. There is no way to explain what it is – freedom – at that moment, that you do not hear the voices any more, that you know they went away, and now you are somehow – your plot had worked – you are free!

For three days, they stayed hidden, sharing a small piece of bread between them. When the guards did not return, Alice Cahane and her two companions ventured from their hideout and sought shelter in nearby woods. There, they were found by Italian prisoners of war who had been assigned to work on a farm and were accommodated there in a cowshed. Although they were deployed as forced labourers, they enjoyed more scope of movement than concentration camp prisoners and were not under armed guard. Meeting these Italians gave Alice Cahane a first taste of what life might be like when things got back to normal. It also rekindled her sense of humiliation that she had been turned into an outcast:

> And the table was set. Three bowls, three spoons. Somebody took out a guitar and started to play music and we were stunned. . . . I watched their faces if they were not disgusted by the way we looked. Because we had sores on our legs. We had no coverage. But they were singing. They played the guitar. They told us to eat and they talked very rapid Italian.

The Italians tried to hide the young women in a shelter in the forest but an SS man discovered them. He did not march his captives to the village but told them to go there by themselves, report to the local police station and claim that they had lost contact with their group. Had they been identified as escapees, they would have been shot. Alice Cahane believes that the SS man saved her life. After spending the night in a police cell, the sisters and their friend were escorted to rejoin their original transport. Several days later, they arrived at Bergen-Belsen:

> Bergen-Belsen was hell on earth. Nothing ever in literature could compare to anything what Bergen-Belsen was. . . . When we arrived, the dead were not carried away anymore. They were crying, they were begging. It was . . . it was hell. It was hell. Day and night. You could not escape the crying.

When liberation finally came on April 15, 1945, Alice Cahane felt dazed and disorientated because nothing around her matched her expectation that the dehumanisation she had sensed so strongly should now be reversed. Should the liberators not provide survivors with some kind of normality, like the Italian prisoners of war had done, setting a table for them and serving a meal? Should the survivors not be able to wash, put on clean clothes, sleep on clean beds like real people? How could they be liberated if they remained in Belsen, in their huts, and nothing changed:

> I say to Edith: 'What is it, what does it mean: liberation? I do not understand that word. What is liberation? What does it mean?' She said: 'Free. Repeat it: We are free.' So I told her: 'But then I have to go and find us clean clothes. We are full of lice. We are full of this vermin all around our bodies. I will go and find us clothes. You stay here. I will bring you something.'

Alice Cahane was weak but still able to walk while her sister was too ill with typhus and dysentery to get up. As she wandered through liberated Belsen, Alice Cahane was struck by the 'incredible chaos' everywhere. At one end of the camp, she found a warehouse full of German uniforms and boots. She got hold of some uniform pieces and tried to put on a pair of boots but was too weak to walk in them. As she took off the boots to carry them to her sister, someone grabbed from her everything that she had taken. When she returned to the hut, empty-handed, her sister was no longer there. She had been moved to the camp hospital and all attempts by Alice Cahane to see her again were blocked by British soldiers who denied her access. She could never accept that her sister had died suddenly, after both had managed to survive together for so long. For many years after her liberation Alice Cahane hoped to find her sister alive and continued searching for her. Days after her liberation, she fell ill herself. In June 1945, she was among a group of young women who were taken from the hospital in Belsen to Sweden where they were helped, as far as possible, to recover their health:

> The Swedish people were incredible. They were so gentle and good to us. I felt like I woke up in heaven. Volunteers came into the hospital. They brought us magazines and we would show them from the magazines – because we could not speak Swedish – what food we wanted to eat. They would organize concerts for us. I could hear music. . . . But, you know, we were so sick, we were taken from one city to another. They could not figure out what was wrong with us. We had every illness that there was.

After several months, Alice Cahane insisted on returning to her native Hungary. A Swedish friend of her family had made contact with her and visited her regularly. He suggested that she could stay in Sweden and train as a nurse, but she was determined to see what was left of her previous life. As she prepared to leave, the friend pointed out to her that a young lady like herself should really wear a hat when travelling. For Alice Cahane, the seemingly mundane activity of choosing a hat for herself took on the special meaning of regaining her identity and shaking off, for a moment at least, the humiliations of the past:

> And so we went into a place, and there was a brown little 'chapeau'. I put it on and said bashfully, 'That's perfect. Thank you.' And that little hat was my dignity. It gave me back my dignity.

2

UNEXPECTED CHALLENGES: LIBERATING GERMAN CONCENTRATION CAMPS AND CARING FOR THEIR SURVIVORS

The concentration camps in Germany were liberated by American and British front-line units in the space of one month, between early April and early May 1945. As military ventures, these liberations were unremarkable. The Germans did not mount a defence of their concentration camps. The SS, who had organized them and supplied the guards, either fled before the Allies arrived or surrendered. In some camps, only bodies were found; in others, the liberators also discovered survivors. Overall, the Germans had created 1,634 concentration camps – six of them death camps equipped for mass killing – and nine hundred slave labour compounds affiliated to concentration camps.[1] Most of these camps and compounds were located in territories in the east that had been occupied by Nazi Germany. Many, however, were situated inside Germany. In the course of their military advance, American front-line units discovered about one hundred concentration camps and liberated survivors in seventy of them.[2]

Unplanned Liberations and the Shock Discovery of Conditions in German Concentration Camps

The military maps of the day do not appear to have listed concentration camps, since front-line units repeatedly stumbled upon them unexpectedly. Guidelines had been drawn up by the SHAEF, the Supreme Headquarters of the Allied Expeditionary Force that co-ordinated military activity in the closing phase of the war, about what should be done with civilians from other countries who had been imprisoned in Nazi Germany.

Field commanders were advised that these civilians should be regarded as 'United Nations displaced persons' and that their 'liberation, care and repatriation' constituted 'major Allied objectives'.[3] Brief reference was made to the fact that some of these civilians might originate from 'ex-enemy' countries and would have to prove to the liberating forces that they had been persecuted for 'activity in favour of United Nations' or on the ground of race or religion. The guidelines did not mention Jews, nor did they mention that most of these civilians would be ill, nearly-starved and generally in need of physical and personal rehabilitation after being freed. The guidelines were administrative in tone and without reference to a possible humanitarian challenge. This meant that military personnel had to decide for themselves how they could and should respond to survivors' needs:

> We had no actual instructions. What we did know was to take care of any survivors medically and also see to their welfare, that is proper food and a place to stay, and then have them interrogated by the CID. I do not recall any, at that point, any formal directives.[4]

The liberation of Ohrdruf on 4 April, 1945 confronted Allied soldiers for the first time with the reality of what had happened inside Nazi concentration camps. Ohrdruf itself was a small town in central Germany, made famous by Johann Sebastian Bach who had held a musical appointment there. During the Second World War, the Nazi leadership had chosen this remote spot to construct a massive telecommunications centre underground, using concentration camp labour. Eric Leiseroff, who was born in Germany in 1925, emigrated to the United States in 1941 and returned to Germany as an American soldier in 1945, recalled that his commander did have a map of the region that listed the town, Ohrdruf but made no mention of a concentration camp by that name.[5] Officially a sub-camp of nearby Buchenwald, Ohrdruf was no more than a fenced-in compound with very poor accommodation, no hospital or facilities of any kind, although it was controlled by its own SS guards and functioned as a self-contained camp. When the Americans arrived, it had been abandoned. The SS had marched 9,000 of its prisoners to nearby Buchenwald and killed 4,000 who were too weak to walk.[6] One of the liberators recalls having to climb out of his jeep because 'bodies were piled everywhere, making passage impossible':

> I was totally unprepared for what we found in Ohrdruf. I had heard of concentration camps, of course, but until the moment when we entered Ohrdruf and found the bodies strewn all about, I imagined them to be

giant work camps employing slave labour – three meals a day and a bed at night in exchange for unpaid labour.[7]

The liberation of Ohrdruf and the discovery of the unburied bodies there sent shockwaves through the advancing troops, many of whom visited the site as did General Eisenhower and other high ranking officers. Photos taken in the camp persuaded the British Prime Minister Winston Churchill to send a parliamentary commission to see for themselves.[8] The inhabitants of Ohrdruf town were more reluctant to see for themselves but forced to walk through the camp that had been on their doorstep. They remained stony-faced.

The tour over, the leading citizens of Ohrdruf went back to their town. The paint manufacturer returned to his castle.[9]

One day after Ohrdruf, the Third US Army reached Nordhausen, an industrial compound in the Harz Mountains where concentration camp labour manufactured V2 rockets and other military equipment in underground production sites:

We came across a town called Nordhausen. Of course, we knew nothing about it being a concentration camp, but about fifteen miles before Nordhausen, it hung in the air. I cannot describe it. It was just a penetrating odour. . . . We found out later that this was the odour from the camp itself.[10]

In the Nordhausen camp, the Americans again found a large number of unburied bodies, 2,700. This time, they also found three thousand survivors. Again, they ordered the locals to enter the camp that had existed in their neighbourhood and even forced them, despite strenuous objections, to shift some of the corpses:[11]

Maybe, we made some kind of impression. That is what we were trying to do. But we were a military unit. We were not actually supposed to be in that business but did what we could. Then we got orders to go south.[12]

While each liberation of a concentration camp in Germany occurred in a distinctive manner, there were common factors. The front-line troops turned liberators were not prepared for the evidence of Nazi brutality they uncovered nor for the humanitarian challenge arising from finding survivors. In each case, however, massive corporate efforts were made to provide food, hospital care and improve accommodation. In each case also, individuals tried to help over and above their normal duties and often in direct contravention of military rules. Liberation, like survival, depended on personal courage, not least because initially, the special suffering endured by Jews in the concentration camps and their special needs as survivors were not recognised because they were classified by national origin. But for the efforts of individuals among the liberators Jews would have remained invisible among the survivors of forty or more nationalities, each with their own experiences of persecution and in need of help.

Humanitarian Challenges After Liberation: Three Case Studies

Concentration camp liberations in Germany did not follow a standard pattern nor was there an agreed approach to meeting the needs of survivors. The three case studies below show what happened when the largest camps inside Germany – Buchenwald, Bergen-Belsen and Dachau – were liberated in April 1945. Not unlike survival, each liberation followed its own trajectory, driven by military objectives and guidelines, procurement processes and, of course, the number of survivors and the general conditions that were found in a given camp. Liberations were also driven by the ability of military men to understand the humanitarian challenges that confronted them and respond to the needs of survivors, be it by providing medical treatment and hospital care, be it by offering specialist diets for starvation victims, or be it by accepting that many survivors, including most Jews, resisted repatriation either because they had no country or home to return to or because they did not yet know what they wanted for their future.

The treatment of Holocaust survivors after their liberation required a degree of humanity, resourcefulness and empathy that no rule book could teach. The liberators, both collectively as occupying powers and individually as front-line soldiers, struggled to meet the vast humanitarian challenges that confronted them inside the camps. For many of the former prisoners, life after liberation remained buffeted by unpredictability and much depended, once again, on luck.

The Liberation of Buchenwald

On April 11, 1945, a reconnaissance battalion of the Third US Army came across an unusual fighting force on a forest road near Weimar in central Germany. Several thousand soldiers with a motley assortment of arms and outfits, marching as if they were a fighting force. Egon Flesch and Edward

Tenenbaum, whose jeep headed their column, described what they saw on that day:

> [We] saw thousands of ragged, hungry-looking men, marching in orderly formations, marching east. Those men were armed, and had leaders at their side. Some platoons carried German rifles. Some platoons carried hand grenades over their shoulders. Some carried 'potato masher' grenades. They laughed and waved wildly as they walked. Or their captains saluted for them. They were of many nationalities, a platoon of French followed by a platoon of Spaniards, a platoon of Russians, Poles, Jews, Dutch, mixed platoons. Some wore striped convicts' suits, some ragged uniforms of the United Nations, some shreds of civilian clothing. These were the inmates of Buchenwald, walking to war as tanks swept by at 25 miles per hour.[13]

When the Americans arrived, the SS had already withdrawn from Buchenwald. A camp committee, that had been created under Nazi control and functioned as an interlocutor between SS and prisoners, now took charge. As a concentration camp, Buchenwald contained committees at two levels: at the grass roots, national committees represented the prison population according to their countries of origin while a central committee operated as the collective voice vis-a-vis the Germans.[14] The Americans relied on this existing committee structure in administering Buchenwald after liberation although they did not share the political beliefs of the committee activists. Since Buchenwald had housed many members of the political opposition to National Socialism, the committees were dominated by communists. Moreover, the committee structure underlined nationality as the defining component of personal identity. Jews who originated in a variety of countries had no visible place in this nationalist framework and no committee. After liberation, the Buchenwald committees, their personnel and their patterns of representation, remained in place. This perpetuated existing injustices.

The Americans soon realised that committee members in Buchenwald may have been aligned all too closely with the SS. It had been up to the central camp committee to allocate individuals to labour commandos and compile transport lists. Both acts could send people to their deaths. While the SS gave the commands, the committees selected the individuals and thus shared the power over life and death with the perpetrators. Furthermore, prisoners in Buchenwald were permitted to receive food parcels but the central committee claimed the right to determine who should benefit from their contents, regardless of who the rightful recipients were. Needless to say, committee members took a share for themselves and, as 'trustees' of the SS, seemed to prosper compared with ordinary prisoners:

> Each German trustee obtained good clothing and numerous valuables. The communists of Buchenwald, after ten or twelve years in concentration camps, are dressed like prosperous business-men. Some affect leather jackets and little round caps reminiscent of the German navy, apparently the uniform of the revolution.[15]

Jews in Buchenwald

The Americans liberated 20,000 prisoners from Buchenwald concentration camp, four thousand of them Jews. Just days before, six thousand Jews were separated out, herded onto cattle trains and transported without food and water through Germany. These trains did not have a destination other than that the Germans expected they would be bombed, destroying their human cargo. Most of the four thousand Jews who escaped this final deportation had been in the camp for some time, and knew how to hide or were protected by other old-timers.[16]

The separation of Jews from other prisoners inside Buchenwald made Jews easy targets for the SS and particularly vulnerable. The camp consisted of two compounds with distinctly different conditions. In the Main Camp, prisoners were housed in brick-built barracks. This part of the camp held political prisoners and accommodated the camp committee. Separated from the Main Camp by a barbed wire fence, but located within the compound, lay the Little Camp. Here, accommodation was in tents or in wooden, poorly constructed huts. The huts contained some wooden bunks without mattresses although most of the prisoners had to sleep on the floor.[17] The majority of the captives in the Little Camp were Jews. The Main Camp had poor sanitary facilities and food was scarce. In the Little Camp, both were completely inadequate. As deportations back into Germany and concentration camps there gathered momentum, the Little Camp became vastly overcrowded and food was no longer distributed to its prisoners. The death rate in the Little Camp rose sharply in the closing months of the war.

From the first, the Americans had no doubt that prisoners who were found in the Little Camp had suffered worse than others in Buchenwald:

> In the Little Camp there are 27 low wooden barns. In these there are three-to-five-tier-wide shelves, running the length of the building. On them are sacks of rotten straw, covered with vermin. These are the sleeping quarters. In the centre of the camp are open sheds, covering

deep concrete-lined pits. These are the latrines, from which pour (sic) an incredible stench. The rated capacity of each of the blocks here is 450. Loaded down with 450, the barracks look like the interior of a slave ship. Yet, 1,000–1,200 newly arrived eastern Jews and Poles were often crowded in here. Daily mortality was high, 20–25 per block per day. Once, 160 out of 1,000 died in Block 57 within 24 hours. The block Chiefs in this small camp are Germans, and are considered the most brutal of the inmates.[18]

It seems that some of the military personnel understood that Jews had been treated worse than political and other prisoners. Reporting on April 16, 1945 about conditions and survivors in what he called 'Buckenwald', Brigadier General Wood stressed that Jews had fared particularly badly but does not mention any special measures that should be implemented to care for them. The same applies to another group with urgent needs: one thousand boys under the age of fourteen who were liberated in Buchenwald. The report mentioned that they were among the survivors but does not raise the issue how they might be helped.[19]

Since the liberators were front-line units, they set out to deal with Buchenwald and its survivors in accordance with military priorities although often emotional responses to the plight of survivors got in the way. One of the military priorities consisted of interrogating survivors in order to establish their credentials as 'displaced persons' or, in the case of German, Austrian and other 'ex-enemy' persons, determine the reasons for their imprisonment. Guy Stern served as an intelligence officer in the US Army and specialised in such interrogations when he arrived in Buchenwald on April 12, 1945. A native of Berlin, he had fled Germany in 1938 at the age of fifteen and joined the US Army in 1942.[20] His parents were unable to obtain visas to leave Germany, were deported to the Warsaw Ghetto in 1942 and murdered in Treblinka. For Guy Stern, therefore, coming to Germany and to Buchenwald constituted a chilling return. He tried to check his emotions by staying close to other members of his group, although they too were overcome:

> We did not arrive at the same time. I was looking around, I guess the emotions were so overwhelming that I was looking for some sign – maybe it was mental cowardice – but I was looking for some sign of something normal. So, I was looking for my buddies. . . . And I saw one who had sort of cradled his eyes with his arm. It was Sergeant Hadley from the Military Police, and he was bawling like a child.[21]

Liberation did not appear to have an immediate effect on how the survivors behaved. Guy Stern noted that they tended to huddle and line up as if they were still hounded by SS guards. 'This', he stressed in his recollections, 'was not Day One. It was Day Two, and still, some were so shaken.' Few could walk upright, and many continued to drink from puddles although containers with drinking water had been positioned at various points in the camp. Many also wanted to eat whatever they could get hold of and as much as possible while everyone from the ordinary soldier to the skilled medical doctor tried to persuade them to eat very little. More vividly than anything, Guy Stern recalled that Buchenwald was covered in mud and that survivors just had to live in it:

> The ground was so muddy, and many did not have shoes, and the mud and the grime all the way – this seems a silly thing to remember, because, you know, as a soldier you are trained to be always completely neat, even if you are going into battle. It struck me, this incredible filth and dirt. Each time they put their foot down, water from the mud would send sprinkles up to their pyjama uniforms and to their legs. This is the image that you saw as you were sort of stomping around the camp.

Harry Herder also entered Buchenwald as an American soldier and was assigned to guard duty. This consisted of keeping watch along the perimeter fence of the camp and making sure that none of the survivors would leave or enter the compound through the holes that had been ripped into the wire by American tanks. Although liberated, the camp was to remain closed and its inmates detained. As required, Harry Herder climbed into one of the watchtowers as armed SS guards had done before him. He had not been told why he should stand guard or what had happened to the people whose movements he was to curtail. He only knew his orders:

> We were to stand guard for four hours at a time, and then take eight hours off. There would be one of us in every tower most of the way around the camp. We could be covering all the holes we had ripped in the fence.[22]

Soon after starting his guard duties, he noticed a young boy climbing through the fence and back into the camp. Instead of acting in line with his orders and scaring the boy off, he let the young survivor pass unhindered and even encouraged him to climb the watchtower. Here, the two formed a friendship and Harry Herder heard the boy's story. As he listened, he no longer cared who went through the fence beneath him. He had lost the zeal to control the survivors and enforce a notion of military security that seemed ill-matched to their needs. One day, he noticed a group of survivors returning through the fence. They had caught a man whom they recognised as a former SS guard. After bringing him back into Buchenwald, they forced the man to hang himself. According to military rules, Harry Herder should have intervened and stopped the killing, yet he could not bring himself to do so. The little he had seen of Nazi concentration camps and the little he had understood about the experiences of survivors persuaded him that revenge might be justified and that he had to let it take its course.

The Limits of Care

Within two weeks of liberation, conditions in Buchenwald had improved significantly. An emergency hospital had been set up inside the camp with eighty doctors, among them several survivors. It looked after 5,490 patients, including 62 cases of typhus, 323 of tuberculosis and 208 of dysentery. Some 12,000 survivors had been dusted down with DDT in order to eliminate infestations with lice. The clean-up helped to reduce the death rate from an initial two hundred a day to single figures.[23] A group of French visitors even thought that the food in Buchenwald was excellent.[24] In a short space of time, much been achieved to improve care and living conditions. Only then could attention turn to the human cost and the prospects of individual normalisation. This is how things stood in Buchenwald on April 25, 1945:

> Most of the dead bodies that were piled around at the time the camp was uncovered have now been buried, but collections may still be seen as evidence of the conditions that existed. The condition of the inmates varies depending on how long they have been there and the kind of treatment they received. Some are fairly normal in appearance, others show the effects of abuse and starvation in all degrees. Numbers not yet determined are either on the point of death, or too weak and emaciated to move off the floor on which they are lying under cover of whatever scraps of cloths or clothing it has thus far been possible to collect. Large numbers of others who are veritable living skeletons are moving about inside the shacks although it is hardly conceivable that persons with such wastage of body tissue can have the strength to stand or walk. Many are clothed only in the thin cotton shirts which come half way to the knees and which are all the clothing they have had for an indefinite time.[25]

Despite the formidable efforts to reduce infection risks and provide health care, little seems to have been attempted to improve the daily living conditions of the survivors who remained there. Two months after liberation, most still wore the concentration camp uniforms in which they had been found.[26] The accommodation huts still contained the same tiered bunks, straw mattresses and filthy blankets, although these had been treated with DDT. Food was still doled out in the huts and had to be eaten there because Buchenwald lacked dining facilities for its survivor-residents. Survivors still ate from the same bowls as before their liberation. No organized activity of any kind was laid on. Any such activity was thought to be wasted on people whose minds seemed as 'anaemic and weak as their bodies', who appeared to have lost all individuality and whose lives were deemed to be 'beyond repair'.[27] One thing, however, had changed since liberation. The Little Camp was no longer inhabited. It had been abandoned albeit not cleaned up. 'The general impression (at Buchenwald) was one of filth.'[28]

From the point of view of survivors and their needs for clean clothes, clean beds with sheets, accommodation that enabled them to regain a sense of everyday normality, for instance, Buchenwald after liberation offered little more than cleansed concentration camp conditions. For the American liberators, however, these conditions served the purpose of preserving enough of the former reality inside a concentration camp to document to visitors of the site and to the world in general the horrors that had been perpetrated under Nazi control, and why the Second World War had to be won by the Allies. From the outset, the liberation of Buchenwald was a public event. As the American troops entered the camp, photographers and journalists entered with them, followed by military dignitaries, ordinary soldiers and a stream of political and other high level delegations. Germans, it seems, were forced to view the camp because the military leaders at the time assumed that they had not known what had been going on and needed to be shown. They also assumed – wrongly – that they wanted to know and were keen to condemn National Socialist control.[29] At the time, Germans only viewed Buchenwald when they were forced to do so. By contrast, Allied service personnel and in particular American soldiers were keenly interested to see for themselves what evidence remained of Nazi brutalities. Buchenwald and its survivors, therefore, became exhibits. Viewing these exhibits left no doubt that the war and its aims of destroying Nazi Germany were justified and that the Allied armies had arrived just in time to save those who survived. Gradually, however, reservations began to be voiced that turning survivors into exhibits 'in their rags, with their physical deformities' meant denying them the chance of a new beginning. The 'temptation to leave the camp as it is in order to have something left for the visitors to stare at' militated against cleaning up.[30] In early May, American field commanders were instructed to stop further visits by service personnel because Buchenwald could no longer evoke a sense of Nazi atrocities:

> Buchenwald has been cleaned up, the sick segregated and burials completed to such an extent that little evidence of atrocities remains. This negatives any educational value of having various groups visit the camp.[31]

Visits, however, continued until Buchenwald itself was handed over to the Russians on July 4, 1945 in whose zone of occupation the camp was located.[32] Since their Soviet allies chose not to accommodate and care for concentration camp survivors, the Americans emptied Buchenwald of its remaining residents. In June 1945, most of the six thousand so called 'unrepatriables', that is to say survivors who had become stateless or who could not return to their country of origin, were taken to hospitals or Displaced Persons Camps in the US zone of occupation. A special offer of help, however, had been proffered by Switzerland to accept some child survivors under the age of sixteen, provided they were free from disease. A Swiss nurse had arrived in Buchenwald to run a screening programme and to issue travel documents to those who passed it. Not everyone was happy with the arrangements. The child survivors, of course, feared that they might be rejected, while survivors above the age limit craved a chance of leaving Buchenwald and being taken to Switzerland. An American army chaplain, Rabbi Herschel, whose duties at the time included caring for Jewish survivors in the camp, suspected that the Swiss nurse was determined to keep the numbers as low as possible and compared her screening programme with SS selections in a concentration camp. He refused to accept what he regarded as arbitrary restrictions, obtained a copy of the relevant travel papers, had them reproduced by a printer in nearby Weimar, and set about completing dozens of them in order to increase the number of survivors who could leave Buchenwald for Switzerland:

> In the end, the Swiss nurse issued passes, and Reb Herschel issued two hundred more. A train was to take the children from Buchenwald to Basel, and Reb Herschel was appointed to oversee the operation on behalf of the US Army. As the boarding of the train got under way, the nurse was beside herself with fury at the sight of so many Jews boarding to whom she had not issued passes. Among those to whom Reb Herschel had issued documents were a 42-year-old mother and her two daughters. He told the mother to hide in a bathroom and not to come out during the entire long trip over the bombed-out tracks to Basel.[33]

How different the needs of survivors appeared at the time and how priorities varied between individuals can be shown with regard to the same programme of sending children to Switzerland. Rabbi Herschel's narrative suggests that he and others objected to the remit of the programme and interfered in order to make it more inclusive. From a military perspective, the programme seemed poorly administered and bogged down by incompetence. Since the US Army was to be in charge of procuring the required trains to take the children from Buchenwald to Switzerland, two officers were dispatched to finalise arrangements by collecting accurate lists of the number of persons intending to travel. They could not find any such lists and none of the travel documentation seemed to be ready.[34] In their frustration, they blamed the national committees in Buchenwald for failing to co-operate with registration and they branded UNRRA, the United Nations Relief and Rehabilitation Administration, as incompetent whose first ever aid team had only just arrived. From a vantage point of military efficiency, they all seemed incapable of keeping accurate records and of running things properly. The two military emissaries were not aware that the whole system of selecting children and of establishing transport lists was resented by the survivors as too restrictive. They also did not know that Rabbi Herschel, despite his position as army chaplain, regarded it as his humanitarian duty to torpedo the creation of restrictive lists. He wanted to maximise the chances for the survivors in his care of finding a future.

The Liberation of Belsen

The second major camp to be liberated inside Germany was Bergen-Belsen near Hanover in northern Germany. This time, the liberators were British and the liberation followed a handover initiated by the Germans in exchange for a ceasefire covering an area of 48 square kilometres. This extraordinary exchange marked the beginning of one of the most challenging and disturbing concentration camp liberations.[35] On April 12, 1945, an emissary from a German paratrooper regiment crossed the front line to propose to the British an agreement 'with regard to the concentration camp at Belsen'.[36] For the German side, a Col. Harries, who presented himself as the military commander of Belsen, and his deputy, a Col. Schmidt, led the negotiations. Later, Harries was to claim that he had no authority at Belsen which lay in the hands of the SS. He also convinced the British that the German soldiers who were stationed in army barracks at Belsen when the camp was liberated, were unfit for front-line duty and should be allowed to return home.

48

The version of events presented by Harries and Schmidt informed a memorandum sent on April 13, 1945 by a member of the British General Staff. In it, British military detachments in the region were advised that 'in the general area of Belsen 4867 there is a Concentration Camp containing approximately 60,000 prisoners'.[37] Identified by an accurate map reference, this camp was to be surrendered by the Germans because disease had become a problem including 'a serious outbreak' of typhus. This was blamed on a recently interrupted electricity supply (allegedly due to bomb damage inflicted by the Allies) and a lack of 'adequate water'.

Before setting foot into Belsen, its British liberators believed, as their German informants had suggested to them, that those held there were 'partly political and partly criminal', and detained for valid reasons. If there was a risk to life, it seemed to pertain only to the would-be liberators. Nobody considered that the conditions of imprisonment put the lives of the captives themselves at risk. In order to ensure a secure handover of the camp, the British insisted that seven hundred Hungarian SS auxiliaries, plus an unspecified number of *Wehrmacht* and SS guards who were deployed at Belsen, remained armed and in post for the time being. The liberators also thought of keeping German support staff such as cooks, orderlies and supply officers. High on the list of their priorities was to avoid direct contact with inmates as much as possible, and to take control of Belsen with a minimum number of British personnel:

> It is essential that this area [Belsen] should be kept as free of our troops as possible and that the persons at present in the concentration camp should be kept there until adequate arrangements can be made to sort them out – both from the point of view of preventing the spread of disease and preventing criminals from breaking out. . . . Troops will be instructed to uphold the authority of German and Hungarian guards and, if necessary, to render assistance. These guards retain their arms, and their orders and duties will be respected. It is thought that a serious risk of disturbance and attempts to break out will arise with the approach of British troops.[38]

The liberation matched the scenario outlined in this memorandum. To curtail the spread of disease and also to prevent anyone from getting out, the gates of Belsen remained locked and guarded even after the camp was liberated.[39] Initially, the British were convinced that the inmates were dangerous and had to be kept in check by armed SS. When Col. Taylor 'assumed control', he insisted on an SS escort and was accompanied by the German commander of Belsen, Josef Kramer. To broadcast his liberation message, he was driven through Belsen in the commander's car, addressing the prisoners by megaphone and from a safe distance. A British aid worker later observed that Taylor 'looked at the inmates as though they were an exhibition'.[40] Anyone who dared to approach the liberation party was shot. When a handful of prisoners tried to capitalise on the unusual turn of events by grabbing some turnips from one of the kitchens, the Germans presented the incident to the British as a riot. Several prisoners were shot in the course of liberation because they tried to forage for potatoes on a patch of land:

> The occasional shot was ringing out as we made our way further down the camp towards the potato patch. This consisted of a few rows of potatoes covered by earth, and on it were lying six or seven corpses which had obviously just been shot. There were other living skeletons that had been wounded and who were crying out in pain. No attempt was being made to relieve their distress, although SS troops were in the vicinity.[41]

The commander of Belsen, Josef Kramer, claimed that the camp had sufficient food on site for three days. This claim was more quickly shown up to be a lie than the claims about the nature of the camp and the state of its inmates. The liberation party did find ample supplies in the SS quarters. As soon as they entered the actual concentration camp and the areas known as Camp One and Camp Two, where most of the prisoners were held, they saw a very different Belsen than the image conjured up by the Germans. There was virtually no food in any of the kitchens, and the accommodation huts in both sections of the camp were so overcrowded that 'a large proportion were living in the open'.[42] Faced with such unexpected human misery, Col. Taylor extended his liberation message to reassure his listeners that food and water were on their way, that German rule was definitely over (although he was at that time still standing next to Josef Kramer) and that the British would be doing all they could to improve conditions for 'internees'.[43] In Camp Two, this message elicited cheers. Its fifteen thousand survivors, all of them men, suffered from starvation but were largely free from typhus. Most were mentally and physically alert enough to understand what was happening.[44] In Camp One, where forty thousand were imprisoned, the announcement was received in complete silence.[45] Starvation and disease had driven most of its survivors close to death. They had not received any food or water for at least six days. In Camp One, typhus and dysentery had spread unchecked. It was the 'real horror camp'.[46] Many of its survivors were too weak to leave the huts or take in what occurred around them. In Belsen's Camp One, 80 per cent of the captives were Jews.

The Belsen Challenge

Hard on the heels of the liberation party and its broadcast message of hope, the British army dispatched a reconnaissance team to see for themselves what Belsen was and what might be needed by way of food and provisions. Led by Captain W. R. Williams, the 'recce team' saw immediately that this was no ordinary camp. Finding no food in any of the five kitchens, Williams used his initiative and arranged for British army rations to be delivered the next day. Attempts at handing out tins of corned beef to survivors had to be abandoned when it became clear that most of those who had managed to get to the distribution point lacked the strength to twist the tins open. Again using his initiative, Williams had his team empty the contents of the corned beef tins into water in order to prepare a soup. This was dished out successfully. Of course, they could not know that eating regular army rations, even if dissolved in water, might prove fatal for people who had been severely starved. Nobody had advised them about such risks, just as nobody among the liberators appeared to have associated Nazi concentration camps with starvation.

During his course of duty in Belsen, Williams wrote letters to his son about conditions in the camp and his own efforts at making improvements:

> Everything you've read and more are absolutely true. I've seen everything and can swear to it. . . . The conditions, the dead bodies rotting in piles 6 and 7 high, no food or water – the rags which they wear. It's a miracle how many are still alive. 500 died the first night I was there. I could rattle off innumerable stories for you, but they must be seen to be really believed. You would never think human beings, including Germans, could stoop so low, or have such low morals. The first day I spent organizing cookhouses and trying to cope with the hungry mobs. Now I have a complete platoon working for me doing the detailed work in the cookhouses, which are inadequate, and cannot properly cope. There are no skilled cooks, and there was no lighting or water. Now we have both, and food for all who can walk to get it. Some are so weak, they try and get up and fall back dead. Nobody takes the slightest notice, and the bodies are everywhere.[47]

In the closing months of the war, Belsen had become a major destination to dump those who had survived death marches and transports from other camps, most of them in the east. The SS made no provisions for these new arrivals. The accommodation huts became extremely overcrowded, there was very little food, typhus and dysentery assumed epidemic proportions and a growing number of prisoners died of starvation. Medical care in Belsen was completely inadequate and most labour commandos, which might have offered some access to food and a slim chance of survival, had disintegrated. When the British liberated Belsen, they found ten thousand unburied bodies, many of them inside the huts where they had died, and they also found 60,000 survivors. All of them suffered from severe malnutrition, many were seriously ill and most were infested with lice. One third were so weak that they could not walk any more or swallow food. These 20,000 lay in their huts, unable to get to the places where food and water were distributed. Even if food was brought to them by a fellow survivor who was still able to walk, many were unable to swallow and could not eat it. Within six weeks, 13,045 who had still been alive on April 15, 1945 when the British entered Belsen died from the effects of the treatment they had endured during the Holocaust. Over ten thousand of these deaths occurred in Camp One. Between April 18 and May 26, 1945, 26,666 bodies were buried in Belsen. Leslie Hardman, the Jewish army chaplain who served in the camp, said prayers for the dead at 25,525 burials. Many of the bodies were never identified.[48]

The Belsen challenge consisted of caring for vast numbers of very sick people and keeping survivors alive who could not eat, were unable to walk, and whose bodies had nearly wasted away by the time help was within reach. When a British film team arrived in Belsen on April 17, 1945, they prepared a moving public record of the extent of human suffering and the shattered state of the survivors.[49] Yet, since the film makers did not enter the huts, they only saw and could only show those survivors who were comparatively strong, who could walk or sit outside and whose plight was therefore visible. In order to tackle the Belsen challenge, means had to be found over and above normal military procurement and practice to care for survivors and their huge medical and physical needs. The Belsen challenge consisted, first and foremost, of keeping as many as possible of those alive who had been alive when the camp was liberated. Nobody had a blueprint how this could be done because nobody had experienced such a vast human emergency.

Providing suitable nourishment in sufficiently large quantities and administering it to starvation victims seemed a sure way of rectifying things. On April 27, 1945, a senior officer from the Displaced Persons Branch at SHAEF visited Belsen to see things for himself and to make it known that arrangements were in hand to meet the Belsen challenge: 7,200 lbs of protein hydrolysate were on their way from London, enough to feed 1,500 advanced starvation cases intravenously.[50] The US Army had arranged to supply forty tons of dried skimmed milk, enough to feed all patients 'who cannot feed by mouth' for at least one month. Moreover, a specialist nutrition consultant, Dr Meiklejohn, a member of the Rockefeller Foundation Health Commission who had been seconded to work for the Nutrition Section at the European headquarters of UNRRA in

London, arrived on April 29, 1945 in Belsen to supervise the care of starvation cases. What could be arranged had been arranged. However, some patients refused intravenous treatment. They associated injections with killings undertaken by Nazi doctors in so-called hospitals. Even in the changed setting after liberation, they could not shake off these fears. As for the organizers of the special supplies, their confidence only extended to quantities. They were less certain about how many lives they could save:

> The situation as to nutrition and starvation is so critical that it has been necessary to attempt to select individuals as to chances for recovery. The result is that those individuals so obviously near to death will receive no care in order that the available means may be applied to those who have some prospect of recovery.[51]

At the beginning of May, one hundred British medical students were sent to Belsen to contribute to the enormous task of caring for so many seriously ill survivors. Their arrival, as we shall see below, marked a turning point. Yet, the young doctors were completely unprepared about what Belsen was and what they were expected to do there. Back in London, they had not been informed of their destination when they volunteered. Most expected to work in Holland to help resettle evacuees who had been displaced by the war. One of the pieces of information that was handed out prior to departure was a one page summary sheet of how to feed starvation victims. Nobody knew that this might be relevant to their work. On arrival, they were supervised by the nutrition expert Dr Meiklejohn, but had not received special briefing in advance. Dr Bradford kept a diary of the events that brought him to Belsen. His account tells their shared story. He reached Belsen three days later than expected because snow in England had upset travel arrangements, and assumed his duties on May 2, 1945. On the eve of their departure, Lady Falmouth met the volunteers and hinted at what lay ahead:

> She told us we were going to Germany. This was a big shock. . . . She also said that there were 40,000 in the camp, 22,000 of them women, and that they only hoped to be able to save 17,000.[52]

There were 97 students altogether. Each of them was put in charge of a hut where he had to ensure that 'inmates were properly fed'.[53] The Hungarian SS who had assisted the Germans in running their killing machine had been reallocated to assist with survival. Each young doctor had in his team two Hungarians. Some teams also included survivors who were strong enough to help. Two weeks after liberation, these teams were the first to enter the huts in Camp One and try to attend to those still confined there. One of the young doctors recorded in his notebook what he saw:

> Some huts contained bunks. In others, inmates were lying on the floor, mostly without any bedding. The conditions were indescribable because most of the internees were suffering from some form of gastro-enteritis and they were too weak to leave the hut. . . . The compounds were absolutely one mass of human excreta. In the huts themselves the floors were covered, and the people in the top bunks, who could not get out just poured it to the bunks below.[54]

Many of the students who found themselves so unexpectedly in Belsen recorded in letters and diaries their shock at conditions there, their practical efforts at improving things, their successes and disappointments. First priority was to get the huts cleaned, the bedding and clothing disinfected, the inmates deloused. This was carried out by the Hungarians under supervision. The young doctors concentrated on identifying the various illnesses; earmarked cases for quarantine, and administered food wherever possible. They also conducted a large number of autopsies to determine causes of death and gain information on the destructive impact of starvation on internal organs.[55]

After the initial clean up, priority was given to transferring patients from the huts to one of three hospitals that had been set up in former SS and *Wehrmacht* barracks. Here, British military doctors worked alongside forty German doctors and four hundred German nurses, all apparently devoted to their care functions.[56] From the first week of May onwards – three weeks into liberation – five hundred patients per day were moved to hospital. More patients could have been moved, but for a shortage of ambulances. The Jewish army chaplain immediately sent an urgent request to Jewish Relief in London for three additional ambulances. This worked its way through committees and officialdom and it was finally approved at the end of May 1945. By this time, the extra ambulances were no longer required. All patients who needed to be cared for in a hospital had been moved there. Camp One had been emptied. The last of the infested huts at Belsen was burnt to the ground on May 21, 1945.

Within one month of the young doctors' arrival, the death rate had fallen from its peak of 1,700 a day on April 23 and an average of over four hundred a day in early May to below one hundred on May 19, and to fifty per day at the end of the month.[57] The last death inside one of the huts occurred on May 18, 1945; after that, those who could not hang on to life died in one of the camp hospitals. Before the young doctors got to work, the small number of military personnel who were stationed inside Belsen prepared food and placed it in containers outside accommodation huts, assuming that the 'internees' would distribute it among themselves. This assumption did not take into account that the concentration camp experience had destroyed the normality for survivors and altered behaviour. Dr Meiklejohn who supervised the medical students during their course of duty at Belsen, described how things had been before their intervention:

> It is necessary to say, at this stage, that the morale of the internees had been completely broken by the ghastly events of the preceding weeks. The majority of the inmates had become quite indifferent to death, and could sometimes be seen taking their food whilst leaning against a stack of bodies awaiting removal for burial. It was a case of each man for himself. In consequence, when the food trucks arrived at the hut doors, those who were able to walk took all they could, with the result that very many became desperately ill from over-feeding, and numbers of these subsequently died. Within the huts, on the other hand, many sick patients were dying because there was nobody to feed them.[58]

By the end of May, Belsen had been cleaned up, its survivors moved to brick-built former German army barracks in nearby Höhne or specially created hospital areas for 12,000 of the most seriously ill patients. The Belsen challenge had been mastered. However, attempts to erase the name once all the infested huts had been burned, failed. The British military would have preferred to replace 'Belsen' with ' Höhne', the name of the complex of former military barracks where the survivors now stayed. The Jews among the survivors, at least, refused to let go of the name. As a DP camp Belsen (Höhne) became a temporary home for 13,000 Jewish survivors who waited in the British zone of Germany for somewhere to go. For most of them, this somewhere was called Palestine.

Jews in Liberated Belsen

A few days after liberation, Hermann Helfgott travelled to Belsen and persuaded the British guards to let him enter the camp. A native of Yugoslavia, he had fought against Nazi Germany before being made a prisoner of war and detained in a camp that had been near Belsen and was liberated at the same time. Instead of going home, Helfgott insisted on going to Belsen because he had heard rumours that tens of thousands of Jewish survivors had been found there and needed help. As a Jew who had also trained as a rabbi before enlisting, he felt compelled to make a contribution.[59]

When he arrived in Belsen, the two Jewish army chaplains who were stationed there seemed to be completely overwhelmed and shattered by the scale of the destruction around them. Leslie Hardman and his superior, Isaac Levy, whose responsibilities extended to the whole of the British zone, did not appear to know where to begin. Together with a Catholic priest they sat in one of the administration buildings when Hermann Helfgott stepped in, impassive with despair and quietly crying. Helfgott reports that he insisted on exploring the camp but none of the three clerics offered to accompany him. None had yet entered any of the accommodation huts. Helfgott, however, wanted to see with his own eyes. Inside the huts, he sensed a 'silence of death' and observed that some 'barely alive lie on top of corpses'.[60] Attaching himself to Belsen, he then embarked on a spell of desperate, unceasing activity. Until he came, no lists with the names of survivors had been compiled. No food had been brought into huts. Burials of the many dead bodies had not even begun. In his view, Leslie Hardman spent too much time writing letters to London and trying to persuade political and Jewish community leaders in Britain to support the cause of survivors instead of doing whatever needed doing on the spot. There were so many dead bodies in Belsen that individual burials were impossible. Not until the British camp administration ordered the former SS to dig pits for mass graves and deployed bulldozers to dump the corpses into these pits could the task of burial commence. Helfgott and Leslie Hardman, the Jewish chaplain, conducted grave-side services and said the prayers for Belsen's dead.[61]

When the immediate threat of death receded and survivors began to recover some of their strength, the question arose as to what should happen to the Jews in Belsen and where they could go to start their lives again. From a British perspective, the matter seemed self-evident: Jews were nationals of the country from which they had been deported during the Holocaust. Like other nationals, they were to be repatriated. A specifically Jewish problem of identity or destination was deemed not to exist. From a British point of view, the treatment of liberated persons could only be fair if Nazi criteria of race and difference were discarded and all survivors dealt with as nationals of their respective country, regardless of their status as Jews. The principle of returning Jews to their presumed nations and countries also applied to German Jews whose future was deemed to be located in Germany. In May 1945, Isaac Levy tried to draw attention to this problematic treatment of German Jews:

We are faced with the problem of the immediate future of German nationals in Belsen. Military government have already sent some of them out of the camp with a mere pittance in their pocket. They will now wander over the countryside in the vain attempt to look for families and a source of livelihood. I see no future whatever for Jews of German nationality who have spent so many years in the Concentration Camp. They . . . deserve special consideration. I fear the Military will not give it to them.[62]

Repatriation constituted a viable option for survivors from Western European and from other Allied countries, because they could normally return there without fear of new injustices or risk to their personal safety. For German Jews, such a return was more problematic, given that it meant living again among those who had supported and organized their exclusion. For most Jews from Eastern European countries, return also meant re-entering environments where local populations had frequently led the charge to destroy Jewish life, towns and culture and where most survivors had no homes or families left to return to. In addition, the advent of Communist control often generated new hostilities in Poland or the Baltic states as well as in Hungary and Czechoslovakia where survivors had initially been made welcome. Jewish survivors who tried to return to the east found themselves barred from the houses where they had lived and met with open hostility. The Holocaust experience did not shield Jews from anti-Semitism after liberation.

Inside Belsen, national divides as well as anti-Semitism remained strong. The shared fate of Jews and non-Jews who had been oppressed and persecuted by the Nazis had not extinguished prejudice. In a letter to the European headquarters of UNRRA, the United Nations Relief and Rehabilitation Administration, Isaac Levy, the senior Jewish chaplain, voiced his concern that Jews still encountered hostilities on a daily basis from other nationals in Belsen while the camp administration put them under pressure to return home at a time when they could not be sure of a welcome without hostility, and remained too shaken to know what they wanted and where they could go:

Anti-Semitism is still visible even in a camp of this type. The Poles and Hungarians are still playing havoc with the Jews in spite of the fact that they too are victims of the same beastly doctrine. Cases have been brought to my notice where Jews have been deprived of food, exposed to every form of insult and ignominy at the hands of their former compatriots. It is evident that the majority of these Jews cannot return to the countries of their origin. They fear a resurgence of the same ideology which has brought them to this present impasse. The youth in particular see no future in their former countries of adoption. They have oriented their much dreamed of future to settlement in Palestine which is the obvious solution for them. A large number, of course, still desire to return to their countries of origin in the hope that they may be able to find some trace of their relatives. But even this is a temporary measure. They realise that for them there is no other final destination but Palestine.[63]

Margaret Wyndham Ward, an aid worker for the British Red Cross who arrived in Belsen at the end of April 1945, also sensed the helplessness of survivors, although she seemed at ease with 'the gigantic task of repatriating 60,000'[64] and impressed by its speed and scale. When it came to individual cases, however, she understood that many survivors were afraid of repatriation. Writing to her mother, and in line with official Belsen categories, she mentioned Poles and did not mention Jews. Yet, the young women who sought her help could have been either:

> The trouble is that a great many people, especially the Poles, have no wish to return home as they are so terrified of the Russians, so I do not know what will happen to them. The whole thing must be a big problem. Every day I have girls crying round me saying they can't go home and will I arrange for them to go to England. I must say, I hope the British won't be so kind hearted as to invite them all! Although the individual cases are very pathetic.[65]

Until July 1945, repatriation from Belsen remained in force, and Jews from pre-war Poland who had been liberated there, were treated as if they were Poles. As survivors recovered and found a voice of their own, they were increasingly unwilling to comply. One of their number, Josef Rosensaft, emerged as spokesman for Belsen's Jews:

> Shortly after liberation, Rosensaft who was only 5 ft. tall, stood on a refuse can in the camp and proclaimed himself President of the Jewish Community in Belsen, and asserted that he expected everyone to recognize his authority and obey his orders.[66]

Much to the chagrin of the British administrators, Jews now spoke with a collective voice. Although Rosensaft and his committee were not elected, their self-styled role as agents of Jewish interests remained unopposed. The main function of the committee consisted at this early stage of challenging the assumption that all Jewish survivors could be repatriated and of insisting that repatriation should not be forced upon them.

In this climate of mutual unease between British liberators and liberated Jews from eastern Europe, 1,117 of them were moved at the beginning of June 1945 from Belsen to former army barracks near the German town of Lingen. Lingen had been established as a transit camp. When the Jewish contingent arrived from Belsen they were accommodated alongside four thousand Poles in order to be repatriated together.[67] On July 12, a further 950 Jews were brought from Belsen to Lingen. Nothing had been prepared for their arrival. There was no food, no accommodation had been set aside for them, sanitary facilities were inadequate for such large numbers and the general conditions so much worse than in Belsen that the newcomers refused to enter the camp. They were hastily taken to a camp in nearby Diepholz. After making sure that living conditions would not be worse than they had known in Belsen, they agreed to stay there. Since they were the only occupants at the time, they assumed that Diepholz would remain a Jewish camp. On the following day, however, a transport of two thousand Poles arrived. In order to make room, many of the Jews were forced to leave the accommodation huts they had chosen for themselves. All 950 Jews were squeezed into just 13 huts which were designed to house half that number. While this forced relocation was under way, many Poles taunted the Jews with anti-Semitic insults or even attacked them physically.[68] Faced with what they regarded as an injustice, the Jews demanded to be taken back from Diepholz to Belsen. From there, Josef Rosensaft and his committee sent transport to help with the return.[69]

The events at Diepholz marked a turning point for Belsen survivors. Not only were forced repatriations of Jews halted, Jews also gained recognition as a quasi-national group and were no longer thrown together with Poles and exposed to anti-Semitic hostilities arising from this. In the longer term, the events at Diepholz marked the beginning of Belsen as a Jewish camp for survivors in the British zone of occupation who had nowhere else to go.

From the outset, concerns ran high among those who were in daily contact with survivors about the future they might face. One of the young doctors who had been sent to Belsen argued that the deadlock could only be broken and countries of refuge found if Jews were to be declared stateless. He tried and failed to win the support of Belsen's Jewish army chaplain for his ideas. In a letter to his family, he explained how he thought help should be offered:

> The fact that a large number have been registered as Poles already, due to pressure being brought on them, is disturbing. I wanted chaplains to take action and they could have done so in time. This is a challenge for us and we must not fail. Should this [granting of statelessness] not be done and more Jews register as Poles etc., we shall have lost the struggle and all our fine efforts to save these people from the hell of Belsen will only lead to wasted time and energy. These people are stateless and have no country to go to. We are the instruments of their future and we dare not let them down.[70]

The Jewish chaplain whose backing had been sought, Leslie Hardman, had his own ideas about the future of survivors. His answer had clearer contours than a classification of Jews as stateless. Jews, Hardman believed together with many of his fellow Jews at the time, should be permitted to live among other Jews and settle in Palestine. In Britain, he lobbied political leaders and visited many Jewish communities in order to impress upon them that the displaced Jews of Europe who were stranded in Belsen and elsewhere in Germany, had an urgent need and a moral right to settle in Palestine. They did not require advice where to go but they did require help in getting there. As Hardman saw it, Britain, as the Mandate holder and the power in charge of the region, should issue as many Palestine Certificates as were required to respond to the vast and unexpected needs that had been unleashed by the Holocaust. More than anything, he tried to whip up a sense of unparalleled urgency:

> What of the Jewish future? Is the Jewish Agency to continue to compromise and vacillate in regard to the vital urgency of opening the doors to Palestine wide enough to receive some 250,000? . . . Enough of this back-scratching! Enough of dusting our bouquets! Let us get down to hard work and save these poor wretches![71]

The Liberation of Dachau

On April 27, 1945, American reconnaissance teams had spotted a large camp compound from the air near the Bavarian town of Dachau and estimated that it contained 30,000 prisoners.[72] Despite this advance information and the known risk of death in such camps, no troops had been diverted from their advance on Munich. It was only when two journalists asked for directions to the concentration camp on April 29 that the Forty-second Division was ordered to 'take a reading on the situation'.[73] Lt. William Cowling drove 'in a Jeep with a guard out ahead of the boys'[74] and became the first American to reach Dachau concentration camp. Just outside its perimeter fence, he stumbled on a train full of corpses. It had left Buchenwald two weeks earlier, on the eve of its liberation, packed with Jews. Upon approaching a railroad track, a large number of box cars were observed on the siding, and upon looking back at the cars, which were open on one side, the lieutenant discovered that they were stacked with dead bodies. The lieutenant stopped his vehicle and the two generals and the aide made a quick inspection of the cars. All the bodies were in an emaciated condition from starvation and many of the bodies showed signs of beating. Several were noted to have been shot through the head.[75] At first, Dachau seemed abandoned, without guards and without inmates. After a minute or so, the eery calm broke:

> People began pouring from the low, barrack type, black buildings. The people were thin, dirty, and half starved. They rushed to the American officer and the two newspaper reporters and attempted to shake their hands, kiss their hands or face, or just to touch their clothing. They even grabbed them and threw them up into the air, shouting in many different languages the whole time. Many of the men were crying and a good percentage of them were half-crazed with excitement and the brutal treatment which they had received in the camp. The lieutenant finally managed to break free, return to the gate and close it before more than one or two had gotten out. The people pushed against the gate and attempted to reach between the bars and shake the officer's hands or touch them.[76]

John Komski was one of the survivors liberated in Dachau. He had arrived there on a death march from Hersbruck, a camp built on a swamp with very poor accommodation facilities and a huge death rate from hunger and disease. Ten thousand were forced to march. Twenty days later, just two thousand were still alive. During the last five days, there had been no food and water. In Dachau, John Komski was not given any clothes, only a blanket to wrap around him. Because he had no clothes, he gained the 'survival advantage' of being excused from roll call and work. On liberation day, the camp routine was broken:

> There was no roll call any more, these famous drills taken in the camp. . . . And the day looks more quieter than usual. But after noon they order us into the blocks and they lock all the doors. . . . [Around five o'clock, they heard sounds of an attack.] And then came silence. And in those twenty minutes, we grabbed our things and we were ready to go. Nobody knows where, but we are ready to go.[77]

Looking through a window of his hut, John Komski could see hundreds running towards the fence and jumped out to join them. He heard some shooting but thought it came from prisoners firing rifles into the air 'and everybody enjoy. And I saw my first American soldier. Heaven.'[78]

For Lt. Cowling who headed the liberation party, entering Dachau was a more confusing experience. Armed SS guards remained in various sectors of the camp and stationed in the watchtowers. Surrender happened uncoordinated and in small groups. Thus, one German soldier and a civilian wearing a Red Cross armband stood by the entrance of the camp, waving a white flag. They also volunteered the information that Dachau contained '40,000 inmates of the prison'. Cowling himself accepted the surrender of two German officers and six soldiers. While the patchy liberation and surrender proceeded, SS guards remained armed, and the perimeter fence charged with electricity. At the same time, the survivors pressed for freedom. 'Thousands of yelling, screaming people' filled the square behind the closed gate. Several tried to scale the fence and were electrocuted, others were shot as the SS fired into the crowd. Lieutenant Colonel Walter Fellenz, who commanded the Forty-second Infantry Division when it entered Dachau, wrote his own account of the liberation. The gate, he found, resembled the entrance to a classy girls' school and was surrounded by extensive manicured lawns. The camp and its liberation had come as a 'complete surprise' to him and his men:

> Several hundred yards inside the main gate we encountered the enclosure itself. There, before us, behind an electrically charged, barbed wire fence, stood a mass of cheering, half-mad men, women and children, waving and shouting with happiness – their liberation had come! The noise was beyond comprehension! Every individual (over 32,000) who could utter a sound was cheering. Our hearts wept as we saw the tears of happiness fall from their cheeks. Amid the deafening roar of cheers, several inmates warned us of danger by pointing to one of the eight towers which surrounded the electrically charged fence. The tower was still manned by SS guards! Half-crazed at what we had just seen, we rushed the tower with rifles blazing. The SS tried to train their machine guns on us, but we quickly killed them each time a new man attempted to fire the guns. We killed all 17 SS, then in mad fury our soldiers dragged the dead bodies from the towers and emptied their rifles into the dead SS chests. In the excitement of the shooting, in full view of the inmates, the surging throng pushed one man against the barbed wire fence. It was heartbreaking to see the poor fellow electrocuted when freedom was within his grasp.[79]

In the meantime, 'the doughboys of the Forty-fifth Division' had arrived, and it was their commanding officer who gave the order 'to cut the switch which charged the fence'.[80] The Americans also fired live rounds of ammunition over the heads of the crowds who were pushing against the camp gates. Finally, an American, a British and a Canadian among the internees came forward. They could talk to the liberators in English and subsequently managed to calm the excitement and fears of their fellow inmates by explaining how their release would be organized. Accompanied by one of these ad-hoc interpreters who acted as a guide, the liberation

party then continued its tour and entered that part of the camp where the
dead and the living could barely be told apart:

> The guide took the group to numerous piles of bodies which were
> stacked between the various buildings throughout the camp. These
> bodies were in piles of anywhere between two and fifty. All of the bodies
> showed signs of starvation and were mere skeletons, and many showed
> signs of beating. The barracks were dirty, low, squat buildings with
> bunks stacked to the ceiling, four high, and so close together that a man
> could hardly squeeze between them, and in many cases probably had to
> crawl over them to get into them. In one building the people were all
> typhus cases and many of them lay on the bare floor, while a few had
> dirty straw pallets. The men tried to raise up and smile at the
> Americans or wave at them, but most of them were too weak to do more
> than look in their direction.[81]

Although few of the survivors were strong enough to walk, let alone cause
'considerable disorder', the American soldiers found it difficult to keep
them inside the compound or make them understand that release was
impossible without prior registration, medical checks, delousing as well as
the provision of food. No amount of training could have prepared the
military men for the challenge of dealing with the needs and expectations
of survivors. A telegram to headquarters conveys disbelief and anger at
what had been found:

> Treatment of prisoners by German SS operating camp brutal.
> Starvation diet. Now 2 rooms contain about 600 dead bodies awaiting
> cremation. Death due to starvation. Prisoners dying at rate of about 200
> per day. 21 box cars on railway siding contain dead bodies of prisoners
> dying in transit from starvation. Others dying in ditch by train. Camp
> closed. Typhus epidemic raging. There is gas chamber in camp and
> shooting gallery with evidence of executed prisoners.[82]

The crisp language of reports hides the emotional responses to
discovering Dachau. Private letters were more explicit by talking about
some of the survivors as individuals. Lt. Cowling, for instance, who led the
liberation of Dachau, wrote to his family that one day 'a wasted little man'
came up to him, touched him, and kissed his hand. Since the man spoke
good English, Cowling asked him if he was American and was told he was
Jewish, one of the very few Jews left while thousands had been killed. The
little man had spent six years in Dachau. He was twenty-eight years old,
but he looked as if he was sixty. 'It is unbelievable how any human can
treat others as they [the Dachau prisoners] were treated.'[83]

A Textbook Case

After some initial confusion between two army divisions on how to share responsibilities, Col. Worthing of the XV Corps assumed the role of Acting Camp Commander and put a camp executive into place to cover key aspects of administration such as public safety, relations with Military Government and the provision of food, health and sanitation. He also established contacts with the International Prisoners' Committee that existed in Dachau prior to liberation, included several English speakers, and had played a pivotal role in aiding communication between liberators and the liberated. Moreover, Col. Worthing nominated an officer to locate former SS guards and seize all camp records. By late morning of 30 April, he had created the framework for an internal organization as stipulated in the guidelines drawn up by the Allied High Command on how combat troops should handle any concentration camp they might (accidentally) liberate:

> You will assume immediate responsibility for the administration and control of all Concentration Camps in the areas of Germany occupied by you, using Combat Troops as required for this purpose. You will ensure that all camps, which are known to have been used, are covered whether there is evidence of their use at the time of your occupation or not. You will ensure the detention and segregation of all guards. . . . You will take all possible steps to ameliorate the living conditions of the internees . . . and to provide necessary medical services as a matter of urgency. No internee will be released before his or her case has been considered by a Committee appointed for the purpose.[84]

Turning Dachau round from a killing camp to a camp for survivors was something of a textbook case, although commanders were attached to front-line units and moved on after a short time. On the first day of army control, a medical survey revealed four thousand hospital cases and a further six thousand in need of urgent treatment, secured substantial medical supplies, enlisted the services of a specialist Typhus Control Team from Seventh Army, and directed two US Evacuation Hospitals to move into the camp.[85] One of them included among its staff Rabbi Abraham Klausner, who, as will be shown later, was to compile the first register of survivors and play a significant role in assisting Jews.

Food shortages were alleviated without delay, partly because a search of the compound revealed supplies for four days on the premises, partly because Seventh Army provided several truckloads of food which arrived between May 1 and 4. The discovery of warehouses full of food in Dachau and also in the Munich area initially persuaded the liberators that the

Germans had enough stocks to feed themselves as well as supply what was required in the liberated camps. The guide on the care of 'displaced persons' had laid down that provisions should be taken from the German population.[86] Within days, the assumption that the German population could or should provide what was needed by survivors was discarded, partly because the needs were so immediate and partly because no German resources seemed to be at hand. In contravention of the guidelines, the military used army transport to supply Dachau with army provisions, because this seemed to be the only way of meeting the challenge of feeding the hungry.[87] Fresh produce such as potatoes, meat and milk had to be requisitioned locally, although not without difficulties.

A total of 41,000 survivors needed to be fed, 32,000 of these had been liberated in Dachau itself and an additional 9,484 in nearby Allach, a slave-labour camp affiliated to Dachau and serving industrial enterprises in the region.[88] Paul A. Roy, Dachau's third commander in as many months, recalled some of the challenges and achievements after liberation that had to be met:

> Dachau was a horror of filth, almost impossible to describe. 32,000 victims were penned up in huts which, according to American standards, were adequate for 5,600 people, and according to German standards could accommodate 12,250 people, 8,000 people needed hospitalization. . . . I tackled this as a human job. We had more than 32,000 human beings on our hands who for years had been treated worse than animals. Our first job was their welfare. We had to nurse them back to health, and to rehabilitate them mentally. Many of them had been so completely starved that the fatty tissues surrounding their nerves had been used up, producing a kind of nervous short-circuit. They could not think consecutively, some of them had lost their memories, and their mental reactions were very slow and childish. They were human wrecks who had to be salvaged.[89]

Liberation brought an immediate end to starvation. Within days, regular diets of at least two thousand calories per person were provided for everybody. From the second week onwards, the Nutrition Officer managed to increase this to 2,445 calories and also offer an enhanced diet of 2,966 calories for severe cases of malnutrition need, while the very sick received a special diet of up to 4,200 calories per day. These intensive provisions included eggs, milk, cheese and fat in addition to bread, sausage, gravy, soup and coffee.[90] However, in spite of eating three meals a day, many survivors complained of feeling extreme hunger.[91] Some raided a local processing plant and devoured raw meat; others got hold of DDT powder and used it to thicken their soup. One person found rat poison and consumed it. When the camp personnel checked the garbage they noticed that even the egg shells had been eaten.

As in other camps, liberation could not halt further deaths. Between January and April 1945, 13,159 prisoners had died in Dachau. When the camp was liberated, the death toll stood at two hundred per day.[92] In May 1945, 1,127 died in Dachau. Within weeks of liberation, however, the number of deaths fell to single figures. Some died from eating unsuitable food, but most died from serious illnesses contracted during their incarceration. The effective installation of medical facilities played a major role in reducing the number of deaths. Within 36 hours after Lt. Cowling had driven his Jeep into the camp, medical services had been set up, and over one thousand typhus cases either isolated or treated. Within a week, three hospitals were functioning. On May 2, Col. Bradford of the 127th Evacuation Hospital and Col. Ball of the 116th Evacuation Hospital inspected the section of the former concentration camp that called itself 'hospital' to transform it. They found:

> Appalling conditions, sick people lying in three decker beds, sometimes two to a bed. In one 'Block' there were no beds at all. Here people were lying on the floor. . . . Among the sick, one would quite often notice a dead body, not yet removed. Buckets in the room served as toilets. All were suffering from acute enteritis, malnutrition and Tbc. The nursing care was completely inadequate. Typhus cases were discovered everywhere.[93]

They ordered German civilians and prisoners of war to clean up the premises before putting US military medical teams in charge of over one hundred former German army doctors and dentists as well as nursing staff. They also recruited the services of suitable personnel found among the liberated persons. The discovery of a warehouse full of mattresses helped to equip the hospitals. All blankets and clothing were disinfected to combat lice and disease. Additional large quantities of DDT powder had been procured on May 6, but appeared to have been used to treat prisoners of war, and it took until May 19 before enough supplies arrived to dust down the remaining 16,000 concentration camp survivors.[94] On May 8, a third hospital opened in a former SS hospital building. Together, the three hospitals in Dachau accommodated over eight thousand patients. They ran their own kitchens in order to offer special diets and ensure that all cooking utensils were sterilised. Laundry facilities were provided by the US army quartermaster. In mid-May, a screening programme of camp residents who were not hospitalised revealed a further 708 cases of typhus, most of them at various stages of recovery while the number of new infections was small. In early June, the transfer of six thousand patients, three hundred of them bedridden, to the tenth field hospital of the US Army, heralded the end of Dachau as a rescue centre for its former prisoners.

Exhibiting Dachau

The apparent textbook case with its impressive medical facilities and 'ample' food supply[95] had its darker sides. Since the American liberators were determined to expose Nazi crimes to the world and create a public record of the conditions they found in order to confront and punish the perpetrators, Dachau was opened to visitors as soon as the troops moved in. Not unlike Buchenwald, the camp became an exhibition. Even during liberation, journalists were present and a steady stream of political observers, journalists, military personnel and report writers filed through Dachau. Caught between the organizational imperative of cleaning up and improving conditions, and the educational mission of exposing the crimes that had been committed there, bodies were left where they had fallen. An inspection team noted on May 6 that 'none of the corpses has been disposed of and it is estimated that there were between 1,000 and 1,500 bodies (as no count had been made due to their condition this is only an estimate)'.[96]

The families of former SS guards continued to live in their homes on the edge of the camp while survivors were forced to remain in concentration camp huts. Some visitors were outraged that former prisoners rather than Germans were required to perform menial tasks such as removing bodies, digging graves or cleaning huts.[97] The only clothing to be distributed to survivors were concentration camp suits that had been found in Dachau and were dyed blue-black to alter their appearance. When liberated prisoners discovered an SS uniform store, they were prevented by US military guards from helping themselves. Only when survivors left Dachau to be repatriated were they given new clothes consisting of 'two shirts, two undergarments, two pairs of socks, a pair of shoes and a good suit'[98] to help them on their way.

Three months after liberation, Dachau ceased to be a camp for survivors and displaced persons and became an internment camp for German prisoners of war and suspected Nazi criminals. Paul Roy, 'our beloved Camp Commander', left on July 20, 1945.[99] By July 2, over 26,600 individuals (84 per cent) had been repatriated or moved to transit camps prior to repatriation. Of the remaining 4,935 residents, 2,310 (47 per cent) were confined to hospital and too ill to be moved.[100]

Survival and the Place of Jews

Registration in Dachau, as in other camps, classified individuals by nationality. The first list, compiled on May 6, recorded eighteen nationalities and 31,561 liberated prisoners. This count did not mention Jews as a distinct group.[101] Numbering 9,082, Poles constituted the largest group followed by Russians (4,428), French (3,700), Yugoslavs (3,089), Italians (2,184), Czechs (1,676) and Germans (1,178). The smallest national group consisted of six Americans. Most of the Russians, French, Yugoslavs and Italians would have been prisoners of war, while most of the Poles and many of the Czechs and Germans would have been Jews who were deported to Dachau in the course of the Holocaust.

A further report on the camp population was published on May 12, 1945, following a field trip to Dachau on May 6.[102] It presented a slightly different picture. While the numbers for Poles, Russians, Yugoslavs, Czechs and Germans and some of the smaller national groups tally with the earlier report, the later headcount mentions 2,800 Romanians where only fifty seemed present before, and also three thousand Jews where none had been mentioned previously. The report does not clarify how nationality was assessed but normal practice at the time was to ask respondents to define themselves. It took until November 1945 for US military government to recognise Jews officially as a distinct group and provide data in all demographic statistics. The unexpected appearance of 'Jews' in the second survey of Dachau's population suggests that some of the survivors refused to accept the nationality label given to them and insisted on being recorded as Jews. The figure of three thousand, however, underestimated the number of Jewish survivors who were in Dachau in early May 1945 since most were classified as nationals of the country where they had lived before the Holocaust and remained invisible as Jews.

The last statistical count completed at Dachau dates from July 2, 1945.[103] Written after repatriation from the camp had been completed, it refers to 4,935 'unrepatriables'. Included were 2,339 persons who gave their nationality as 'Jewish' and 2,310 hospital patients. In this category, Jews again do not appear, but it can be assumed that most of the 1,394 Poles and 276 Hungarians among the hospital patients were Jews.

The focus on nationalities was convenient for the purposes of repatriation but unhelpful to Jews who could not be repatriated. In Dachau, it was not imposed on Jews although nationality emerged as a salient symbol of belonging among survivors who celebrated their liberation in national groups and organized themselves in national committees. Colonel Roy, the last commander of Dachau as a Displaced Persons Camp, sensed some of the special difficulties facing Jewish survivors. When he addressed a meeting of national committees on June

22, 1945, he explained to those who were impatient to be repatriated that delays were caused by a shortage of transportation because many railway lines had been destroyed and millions of people were on the move. He assured his audience that these logistical problems would be resolved as speedily as possible.[104]

For the Jews among his audience, he could only offer words of comfort and advise them to be patient while they had nowhere to go and did not even know what happened to their families and friends:

> At present we will find out the way how many of the Jewish people and others can get in touch with their families, dispersed in different places all over Germany and other countries.[105]

Klausner's List

In Dachau, help for survivors to get in touch had already begun to take shape. On June 25, 1945, Abraham Klausner published a typed list of 25,000 names. The total list extended to five volumes. The names had been collected from survivors who had seen someone or heard about someone who had been seen elsewhere; or were sent to Dachau from other camps throughout Germany when rumours circulated that a list of survivors was being compiled. The list was typed by a group of survivors on paper they found in a Dachau warehouse. Overall, one thousand copies of the survivor's list were produced. Each volume included, in addition to names, a section outlining survivors' rights including their right to refuse repatriation.[106] In December 1945, a second edition of the list was published. It contained over 30,000 names, was produced at the expense of the US army and had made its mark as a vital tool in locating survivors and helping to reunite families.

The initiator of this remarkable project was a person who should not have been in Dachau at all, had military guidelines been followed to the letter: Abraham Klausner. He had arrived there as Jewish Chaplain with the 116th Evacuation Hospital immediately after liberation. Yet, the hospital should not have had its own Jewish chaplain, since the military rule book stipulated a ratio of 1,200 serving personnel to one army chaplain. In fact, Klausner's posting had been arranged by Judah Nadich, himself a Jewish chaplain at SHAEF headquarters in Paris who was later to serve as first Jewish Advisor to General Eisenhower.[107] Nadich had been warned by the senior Jewish chaplain of the Seventh US Army, Max Baude, that military withdrawal from the Dachau area was imminent and that the Jewish survivors in the camp would be left without support.[108]

Assigning Klausner to this challenging mission turned out to be an enlightened choice. As soon as he set foot into Dachau, he realised that he was needed in the camp rather than in the hospital. He worked tirelessly in burying the dead and comforting the living. When his unit, the 116th Evacuation Hospital, was ordered to leave its brief and effective assignment, Klausner pretended to leave with them but returned immediately by hiding in the back of an army truck to catch a lift back. In Dachau, he reported for duty in the 127th Evacuation Hospital that had not yet been relocated.[109] By way of explanation he declared that he had received a transfer order. Written confirmation would follow shortly. It never did. Klausner's superiors understood his intentions, waived traditional interpretations of military discipline, and turned a blind eye to the unconventional behaviour of this roving rabbi in uniform. Their unmilitary leniency allowed Klausner to focus on improving conditions for survivors before Jewish aid organizations arrived, helping when and where required.

After liberation, Dachau was no more than a staging post between survival and a new beginning. The camp itself had been designated to house German detainees while Jewish survivors were to be moved elsewhere. At this point, Feldafing, a DP camp near Munich on the site of a former slave labour compound, was on the verge of redefining itself as a camp for Jewish inhabitants because the majority of its residents were Jews. It was Klausner who actually turned Feldafing into the first Jewish camp in Germany by arranging for the remaining non-Jews to be relocated and for the Jewish Dachau survivors to move there. In helping create a Jewish camp, Klausner helped to provide Jews with a living environment that was free from anti-Semitism, somewhere to stay and start again for the time being in the interim until they found a country where they could settle or until they knew where and how they wanted to live after their survival.

3

BEYOND SURVIVAL:
IN SEARCH OF A NORMAL LIFE

The liberation of the concentration camps between April and May 1945 was a formidable challenge. Overall, two million survivors had been found and freed inside Germany, one in ten of them Jews. The majority were emaciated, ill and physically broken after their ordeal and had to be brought back to health; tens of thousands were close to death and needed intensive and protracted care. Many of these died after their liberation, despite all efforts to help them. The front-line units who, as we have seen, found themselves unexpectedly in charge of camps and their survivors, addressed their tasks with military rigour. In the absence of advance information, workable guidelines and a supply of special food and other essentials for victims of extreme starvation and deprivation, military men of all ranks and backgrounds used their personal initiative and compassion to respond to the humanitarian emergency that confronted them.

There had been no agenda for liberations and no advance warning about the state of survivors. Liberations differed between camps, army units and personnel on duty. Neither liberators nor survivors knew what life beyond survival might look like:

> When we were in Buchenwald, crouching on the floor and listening on our hidden radio to the speeches of Roosevelt and Churchill, we heard, coming through the air waves, promises of a golden future for the victims of fascism. We saw ourselves returning to our home towns, surrounded by crowds who cheered at our liberation and at their liberation from the yoke of Nazism. That was the dream.[1]

A different reality asserted itself in the liberated camps where survivors were forced to remain until diseases were under control, and where some were forced to remain because the camp had become their only home.

Beyond survival, uncertainties of how and where to live overshadowed any initial exhilaration about having survived:

> This is what freedom looks like! Behind us, a sea of tears, in front of us a tomorrow consisting of nothing but a huge question mark and the today full of obstacles, sad, dark and grey.[2]

Looking back at the time of liberation and the weeks that followed, Francesca Wilson, an aid worker for the United Nations Relief and Rehabilitation Administration, UNRRA, who arrived in Germany on May 7, 1945 and got to know former concentration camps and their survivors at first hand, had nothing but praise for the Americans and the British military and their 'magnificent' handling of the situation. She was particularly impressed by the success of front-line units in concentrating scattered survivors in camps and preventing them from roaming the countryside:

> We [the UNRRA workers] had visions of thousands struggling to get home on foot, blocking the highways and looting the countryside, massacring the population, fainting from want of food and epidemics. That this has never happened on any scale was thanks to the good planning and efficiency of the military in the early days.[3]

The confusion and population movements in Germany were unparalleled at that time. Holocaust survivors constituted only a small part in a much greater dislocation. Before taking up Francesca Wilson's point about picking up survivors and taking them to camps, let us review who else had been freed or dislocated at the end of the Second World War. Firstly, eight million former *Fremdarbeiter*, foreign conscript workers who been deployed in German industry and agriculture, were now at liberty to leave their compounds in search of food, clothes, goods and also revenge. Secondly, Germans had begun to be expelled or chosen to flee from territories in the east. By May 1945, at least four million were trekking along roads to find shelter with relatives or in transit camps. Thirdly, millions of Allied prisoners of war had been freed but had not yet been repatriated. Fourthly, several million Germans had been forcibly evacuated inside Nazi Germany and now tried to make their way back home to see if their houses had withstood the war and to find other members of their family. The smallest of these migrating and disorientated groups were the Jewish concentration camp survivors, some of whom defied military restrictions and left the camp where they had been liberated; others had been abandoned on death trains or marches and not been inside a camp when liberation came. A small number had managed to leave their transport and hide for the last days of the war.

For all Jewish survivors, making their own way was a first and significant step towards breaking free after years of incarceration and deprivation. Rudi Oppenheimer was one of them. He was 13 years old when he was liberated by Russian soldiers who found the death train that had taken him and two thousand others, without food or water, from Belsen two weeks earlier and come to a halt near Tröbitz in Saxony. Immediately, Rudi Oppenheimer and a group of other young men went into the town, entered German homes and took food and whatever else they could lay their hands on. When he returned to the train which still served as a shelter, he brought with him fruit conserves he had discovered in a cellar and even a motorbike. His sixteen-year-old brother Paul had been liberated with Rudi, but was too ill to make it into town. He could only crawl from the train to the nearest field where he sat, eating grass.[4]

Charles Bruml had been deported from Prague to Theresienstadt in December 1941 and from there to Auschwitz in January 1942 where he had been a slave labourer in the Buna works attached to the camp. On January 18, 1945, he was taken on a two day march to Gleiwitz, from there on a ten day train journey to Mauthausen, Nordhausen and finally, after other camps refused to admit new arrivals, to Belsen. He arrived there on the eve of liberation. As soon as the British moved in, he and others who could still walk escaped to nearby woods and obtained food from local farmers 'who knew that this was the end':

> After that, the British came and people were still running around trying to get to the farms, and they took some radios and some coats and so on, what they got. Some – they did not get anything. Then I got back again [from a farm where he had slept in a barn] to the camp because we were told by the British that we had to go back again.[5]

Benno Helmer was not yet sixteen when he and his friend Monyele were hiding in a hut after the guards of their camp had fled. Suddenly, an American soldier entered their hideout to ask for water. He became their liberator: 'Very short, with the rucksack, with the pack, with everything else. And a miracle, finally.'[6] Half a day later, French soldiers arrived with a soup kitchen. When they ordered everyone to sing the Marseillaise, Benno and his friend walked out, without tasting the soup. On the way, they grabbed a jacket from a German soldier, and watched American soldiers 'throwing a ball to each other with tremendous big gloves'. After walking for a while without destination, they decided to walk to France where a sister of Benno Helmer's friend had lived before the war. Near the beginning of their intended journey, an American soldier offered them a

73

lift 'in a jeep going to Paris. Except he – I do not know where he took us – he took us to a detention camp.'[7]

Abraham Levent was one of the Jews who had been taken by train from Buchenwald. After a brief stop at a camp without huts or clothing for the prisoners, he and his group were transported towards Dachau. When the train came to a halt, those who could still move forced the doors open, rolled out onto the embankment and tried to find food:

> The moment the train opened up, you see all [the dead] falling out. I told you, only young people could have survived. And after this, me and one more guy, we went over there. We took our little strength and we says: 'We're gonna walk to a town'. And we walked in that uniform. We felt more strength, and I remember like now, we came to a house with a German woman inside, and she saw us, and she started running. . . . She ran away. We walked in that house. What a beautiful house. All kinds of china, with closets, with clothes. First thing I did, I took off my things. I took out a shirt and I put on a shirt. This is the first time in three or four years that I had a shirt on my back.[8]

When the woman finally returned to the house, they asked her for food and she gave them some. She had hidden her child in a dog kennel, fearing that the strange-looking intruders would harm it, but revenge meant nothing to Abraham Levent and his friend. All they wanted was to eat and head for home. They left the house with the firm intention of walking back to Poland. Like Benno Helmer and his friend, they were stopped by American soldiers and transported to a compound of barracks that was still occupied by German prisoners of war. They refused to enter until the Germans had been moved out. The camp was to become known as Feldafing DP camp, housing many survivors who, like Abraham Levent, had been transported to Bavaria to be killed or to die from neglect, or who had worked there in one of the slave labour compounds.

Simon Schochet had been death-marched into the area. When the guards disappeared, they could already hear the guns of the Allied armies nearby. Together with about twenty others, he made his way to a house. Finding it abandoned, the group barricaded themselves in and climbed up to shelter in the attic. Some kept watch while the others tried to sleep, although their stomachs ached from hunger and everybody was in pain. In the morning, those who were able to, left the house to walk, excitedly in the middle of the street, towards their liberators.

> The little town of Feldafing on Starnberger See, and the barracks once used by the Germans as a Hitler Jugend [Hitler Youth] school have become our new home. Our original group liberated here is living

together in one of the buildings, but the number had dwindled to nine. Some were immediately taken away in Red Cross ambulances, a few just wandered off, and one died the day after we were set free. Roaming around Feldafing are new men of all nationalities. I recognized many as having been on the long march. A few have discarded their prisoner's uniform and wear civilian clothes of every shape and color, which hang stiffly from their skeletal bodies. None has yet dared to abandon the pot and spoon which are attached to his clothes with string or wire.[9]

Agnes Vogel was liberated on April 10, 1945 by front-line units of the Red Army. For days, there had been nothing to eat in the camp 'except whatever we could pick up, so to speak, almost like the garbage'.[10] When the Russians asked some of the women to work for them in the kitchen, many accepted eagerly in the hope of obtaining some food. However, those who volunteered were immediately raped, and fear of rape followed liberation for all the women in her group:

> It was pure hell. They [the Russians] look around and look for girls, and in the evening they would come back whoever, they would find, they would take. I was lucky enough to be hidden.[11]

After four days, Agnes Vogel, who had survived with her mother, decided to leave the place where her liberation had turned sour, and head for Hungary. She had taken a horse and cart from one of the local farms, because her mother was too weak to walk. With Agnes Vogel leading the horse, the two women headed for home. On the way, they were again harassed by Russian soldiers. This time, they stole a watch which her father had given to her. Even the homecoming was disappointing:

> We did arrive home which was not pleasant because we were walking down the street, and the people, instead of saying 'Well, how nice to have you here' said 'Oh, why did you come back? You were supposed to die.' So after that, I soon left.[12]

Abe Malnik and his father were liberated by the Russians from Gunskirchen concentration camp in Austria. The Russians, he recalled, just opened the gates and let survivors take care of themselves although his father managed to obtain some food from them in exchange for cutting hair. Together with other young survivors, Abe Malnik, who was eighteen at the time, scoured the surrounding countryside for food and clothes. The group also took what they needed from German refugees, 'who were walking in thousands and thousands'.[13] Once he and his father felt their energy return, they decided to return home. By this time, they had accumulated 'two suitcases and some clothes'. Travelling on the top of trains east towards Lithuania, they were robbed of their few belongings by Russian soldiers: 'Again, we had to start from ground zero.'[14]

Some survivors had positive encounters with the Russians who liberated them. Solomon Krug had been on a death march for three days when he and his fellow prisoners noticed that the SS guards started disappearing. During the night, a small group sneaked off to hide in a nearby forest. When they awoke, they had been liberated:

> And in the morning, we heard some horses running. And we looked up, and we saw some Russians. So we got up. And they seen us, you know. And they knew who we were. And they say: 'You are free. Go where you want. Do what you want'. And that was 30th April 1945. So, what do you do first? You go and look for something to eat. So we went in some houses. The Germans, you know, they seen us. They got scared. They gave us what we wanted. And sometimes, the Russians came with us, because they see how we looked. I weighed 80 pounds when I came out. We try to find us some food, you know, and some clothes. The only thing I found was a pair of pants. They went around me three times. I just wanted to get rid of this uniform. . . . The Russians were nice. They took us, you know, around, so we can get something good to eat, and we kept walking, just walking. We didn't know where we were going. Was five of us together. One was from my home town, one boy. And three from somewhere else. So we held together and kept walking.[15]

When Solomon Krug and his friends reached the Polish border, they met some young Jews heading west because the Polish Army had threatened to press-gang them into service. Other male survivors were picked up and made to join the Red Army. As for Solomon Krug, he had never liked the idea of being a soldier and decided to abandon his plan of returning to Poland. Instead, he went back to Germany.[16]

Liberation itself did not end confusion and uncertainties but it did provide a chance to regain the initiative on what individuals wanted to do and how they wanted to lead their lives. However, even survivors who had the physical and mental strength to focus on their future, could not just get on with life and forget about their Holocaust experiences. In the summer of 1946, an American psychologist, David Boder, interviewed Jewish Holocaust survivors in an attempt to determine how their experiences might impact on behaviour. The method he chose was to match the 'human experience' during the Holocaust to normal medical categories.[17] By the time he published his findings in 1949, the compassion of the first hour had faded and public thinking acquired a more negative hue. His book attempted to show how a psychologist would judge the burden that survivors had to carry:

> The displaced persons, in spite of their sorry state today, are not riff-raff, not the scum of the earth, not the poor devils who suffer because they don't know their rights, not idlers who declaim that the world owes them a living. They are uprooted people. They represent the members of all classes of society – farmers, industrial workers, teachers, lawyers, engineers, merchants, artists, housewives – and have been dislocated by a world catastrophe.[18]

Boder concluded that all Holocaust survivors were traumatised by their experiences. Although experiences of survival differed from one another, each survivor had been exposed to at least one experience which, by itself, would be enough to induce lasting trauma in the victim. Boder's 'traumatic index' extended to twelve points. The biographies of Holocaust survivors contain events and experiences that relate to many if not all these points:

The Traumatic Index
1. Brutal and abrupt removal from environmental stimuli.
2. Inadequate substitutes for the conditioning framework of normal life.
3. Introduction of new stimuli without relation to past experience and without reference to legal and moral traditions.
4. Insufficient food, clothing and shelter.
5. Lack of means and facilities for personal and community hygiene.
6. Enforced performance of meaningless tasks.
7. Chronic overtaxing of physical and mental endurance.
8. Seizure of personal property.
9. Blocking of habits of reading, writing, and worship.
10. Abolition of traditions of dignity and decency between sexes, in treatment of the sick, and in disposal of the dead.
11. Lack of medical and dental care, and wanton mutilation for purposes of alleged medical research.
12. Brutal punishment for trivial infringements of camp rules, and group punishment for alleged offenses perpetrated by unidentified persons.[19]

In assessing the traumatic impact of the Holocaust experiences on survivors, it is important to remember that for many the conditions of imprisonment had taken a sharp turn for the worse in the final months of the war. From late 1944 onwards, virtually all survivors endured extreme hunger, illness, exhaustion and were pushed near death because the minimal care of the concentration camp system had given way to total neglect as this system collapsed. At the same time, SS brutalities remained in place. Although many prisoners could hear Allied aircraft flying overhead or had witnessed air attacks on their compounds, the weeks leading up to liberation intensified uncertainties and their fear that, knowing that the war was lost for them, the SS guards would round everybody up and shoot them.

When liberation came, it came unexpected. Physically, survivors were more vulnerable than ever and mentally, they had no opportunity of anticipating that their imprisonment was nearing its end or looking ahead at what to do next. Beyond survival, therefore, individuals needed help to cope with what had happened to them. They needed a chance to tell their story in order to make themselves and others understand how their experiences had destroyed the life they used to lead and altered their behaviour, sense of self and prospects of a personal new beginning afterwards. Boder's 'traumatic index' underlines the size of the challenge that faced each survivor. It also underlines the scale of the assistance required to enable Jews to begin again and the tenacity shown by each survivor who carved out a new future.

The personal narratives presented below touch upon three different aspects of life beyond survival. The first tells the story from the point of view of an American soldier who found himself promoted to Displaced Persons Officer with a special responsibility for repatriation but who discovered within himself a special compassion for Jewish survivors and their needs. The second narrative tells the story from the point of view of an UNRRA care worker who ran a camp for orphaned children. Here, she tried to ease the after-effects of trauma by creating a secure and clean living environment. In talking to her young charges, she also learned to understand why some of them persisted with apparently anti-social or negative behaviour at a time when survival was no longer at issue. The third narrative tells the story of a young woman who survived Auschwitz and Belsen. In letters written while she waited in Belsen to leave Germany, she described her anguish about having nowhere to go and her impatience to lead a life of her own.

'The most immense piece of work': Displaced Persons Officer Albert A. Hutler

When the Seventh US Army advanced into Germany in April 1945, it established its headquarters in Mannheim, a leading city in the southwest of the country, and distributed various administrative tasks among its officers. First Lieutenant Albert A. Hutler was given the job of Displaced

Persons Officer. Writing to his wife, he had no doubt that this was a significant assignment:

> I began to do our displaced persons job. Lady, it is a job. It is the most immense piece of work I ever expect to do for the rest of my life.[20]

One month after assuming his duties, Lieutenant Hutler explained his sense of mission by describing the mood among people he was to care for and among his fellow US soldiers:

> The war is officially over but there isn't a great deal of excitement around here. It may sound horrible to say this but there isn't as much joy in my heart as I anticipated because I fear for the peace. The joy comes from the fact that I know it will bring me home sooner than if it had gone on another year. There isn't any joy in the fact that Germany is close to destroyed; there is a great deal of satisfaction that it is so. Germany and its people now know what war can mean, but I doubt if they will ever know what it means to have been a Pole, a Czech, a Russian, a Frenchman, a Greek under the domination of the barbaric, cruel people that the German has proved himself to be. Every day another camp has been liberated, another gas chamber, another hall of horrors. Every day body after body, one piled up on another in shallow graves, is unearthed. Every day American stomachs turn over and over from sights that they see, from smells that they smell, from things that they touch in camps thruout [*sic*] the country. Hour after hour we see striped suited, thin faced, sunken eyed, underfed, sickly, skin and bones political prisoners come shuffling into American DP camps. They are free but they are dazed. They are free but in their hearts they will never be able to cast off the last five years when they were under the protective custody, the benevolent guidance of their German teachers.[21]

Lieutenant Hutler was shocked at how brutalised survivors appeared to have become. Many hated Germans of any kind. Some wanted to kill as ruthlessly as the Germans had done, although talk was not matched by action. Most had, however, learned from their former masters how to loot and take whatever they could get their hands on. Germans now seemed to fear their former captives. Hutler acknowledged that survivors had been maltreated but refused to condone what he regarded as distorted behaviour. In his area of influence, he set about calming the hate, assuaging fears, restoring normal responses and rebuilding a sense of self-worth among the survivors.

When he assumed his new office, the southwestern region of Germany contained 20,000 displaced persons in six camps.[22] All camps were overcrowded. There was neither enough food nor an organizational structure to obtain and distribute it. A report from early May indicated that arrangements were in hand for Red Cross parcels to reach the camps – one parcel per person to last for two weeks – but they had not yet arrived.[23] Two months on, Hutler had set up two warehouses holding a fortnight's supply of food plus a further 525 tons of Army rations and ten thousand Red Cross parcels. These provisions ensured that displaced persons received a diet of two thousand calories per day, although the diet lacked variety and fresh produce was virtually unobtainable. Hutler's warehouses also held consignments of second-hand clothing that had been shipped to Germany by the American Red Cross. In addition, he had persuaded UNRRA to allocate two members of staff to run the warehouses and oversee the distribution of stock.[24]

Providing for displaced persons and achieving camps with stable populations – the technical term for this kind of stability was 'consolidation' – were complicated by frequent movements of residents between camps. Some of these were the unauthorised attempts of individuals to relocate, but most were initiated by the military in order to alleviate overcrowding and to create nationally homogenous camp populations. At the beginning of Hutler's period of duty as Displaced Persons Officer, all DP camps in his area were mixed with regard to nationalities. Two months on, all except two – Mannheim and the hospital camp at Heppenheim – were segregated by nationality. Moreover, Hutler set about curtailing overcrowding by increasing the number of camps from six to twenty-five. This approach enabled him to meet demand and accept newcomers. National camps constituted the backbone of 'consolidation'. On the one hand, adequate provisions could be arranged more easily. On the other hand, displaced persons of the same nationality could be repatriated en bloc when the time was ripe to do so.

As Displaced Persons Officer, Lieutenant Hutler pursued two aims of equal priority. The first consisted of providing accommodation and care of a suitable standard, the second of implementing repatriation as quickly as possible. Initially at least, he found these two aims compatible and underwrote both without misgivings. Some unease began to creep in when he discovered that transfers of specific national contingents from other US Army areas frequently included large numbers with different nationalities. In June 1945, for instance, the Ninth Army sent nine thousand Poles into Hutler's area of responsibility to be housed there and later repatriated. The group, however, contained 1,500 individuals who identified themselves upon arrival as Lithuanians and Estonians.[25]

Unexpected complications also pertained to the repatriation of Russians. The Soviet Union had insisted that all displaced persons whom it regarded as Russian citizens should be repatriated immediately. Personally, Hutler had no difficulty in complying with such orders but found that the Russians who were waiting to be repatriated 'caused great destruction at every center. Each center thru which the Russians have passed must be rebuilt, cleaned and fixed as if a new camp were being started.'[26] He also found that many resisted repatriation. In the face of such opposition, he chose to give in to the protesters:

> Yesterday in attempting to move some Ukrainians that the Russians classify as Russian, I found out what it can mean to be moved from one place to another, to fear, to be petrified. Our orders were to move these people to a Russian camp. The people refused to go; they barricaded themselves in their buildings; women knelt and prayed to the soldiers not to take them; soldiers fired in the air. People screamed and confusion was everywhere. When I saw the scene I sent the trucks away, ordered the troops out and called together the 3,000 Ukrainians. Speaking to them I told them what the story was and instructed them to stay in the camp while I went to higher headquarters. This is just part of a day's work. In the afternoon, a Russian Major came to make inquiries. It may cause an international rift but I told him to bring his own soldiers if he wanted people killed.[27]

Clearly, Displaced Persons Officer Hutler was not afraid to disregard regulations that he considered to be harmful or counterproductive. The Ukrainians, however, whom he defended so courageously, might not have deserved his ardour since many had moved to Germany of their own accord in search of work or even served in the SS as camp guards before using the post-war confusion to restyle themselves as victims and displaced persons. Yet, his courage in judging for himself which actions were required to help the people in his care made him one of the unsung heroes among military personnel whose responsibilities entailed direct contact with Jewish Holocaust survivors.

Before telling this part of his story, the story of Hutler as the champion of repatriation needs to be told. He proved himself exceptionally able to requisition trucks, locate trains and arrange transports. Not without pride, he wrote to his wife in early May:

> Our city [Mannheim] is used as a clearing house for French repatriation since I have been successful in securing transportation for these. We have the best record of any place in Germany for numbers and swiftness in moving people back to France. Our shipments have now hit 36,218 since April 9th. I have seen most of them pass thru. We set up the organisation to process them. It is the biggest job I expect to have to do in the rest of my life, and the greatest experience a man could ever have.

It is something a person interested in human beings prays for but never has the opportunity to do. They come to us shipped by freight cars, 40 cars to a train, 39 men to a car; we take them off the car, put them in a truck, take them to the camp, register them, delouse them, give them a medical examination, feed them, put them in a billet in a fine apartment house from which they continue their journey home.[28]

One week later, he and his repatriation success attained something like celebrity status which he clearly enjoyed:

My Dearest Family, I want this to include everyone. . . . Yesterday was sort of publicity day for me. It was the day we shipped our 50,000th Frenchman back to his country in a little bit over a month. General Immel came down to the station and shook the hand of the lucky Frenchman, made several speeches, while photographers had a heyday. I don't know if anything will ever be published but look out for the big news. These train shipments are really something to see. How we get them there with the staff we have I'll never know. But somehow they get out, deloused, medically examined, listed and happy. We turn them out as if they were on an assembly line.[29]

Despite his knack for repatriation, Hutler understood that it could not apply to Jews. Every Wednesday, he and the Jewish Chaplain held open house for Jewish displaced persons. Such personal contacts made Hutler aware of individual needs and of the collective impasse that many had no country or home they could return to:

Wednesday is Jewish day at my office. This is the day that Jews who are displaced persons gather to tell their stories to the chaplain. It is the day when they open their hearts, when they are able to talk, when they feel that they are free again. It is, however, the day when Chaplain Haselkorn and I suffer. We suffer not because of the people themselves but because we realize the almost complete hopelessness of the problem.[30]

One day, a Buchenwald survivor arrived in his office. His wife had been murdered, he did not know whether his two daughters were still alive but was full of hope that one day he might be able to go to England where he had a sister or to America where he had a cousin. In Hutler's office, however, the man only asked for a little underwear and a shirt: 'We can give him those. But can the Germans be made to give him back his wife, his girls or even his healthy, strong body?'[31]

Hutler soon found a cause and the means to help more meaningfully.

Having listened to experiences of Holocaust survivors, he was convinced that Jews who had been liberated from concentration camps – regardless of their original nationality and including German Jews – could only be helped towards a new beginning by finding a new country. In the interim, they needed Jewish camps as a shield against anti-Semitism and also to allow them to lead Jewish lives and rediscover their culture. The establishment of Jewish camps was to become official policy several months later after the Harrison Report castigated the treatment of Jewish survivors in Germany.

In June 1945, however, the administrators of displacement in Germany did not recognise Jews as a separate category but subsumed them under their former nationality. For this reason, a group of 150 Polish Jews who had been housed after their liberation by the French in a German village that had been requisitioned for the purpose but had to be vacated in the course of 'consolidation', were to be transferred to a Polish camp. The French were uneasy about what they perceived as an administrative injustice towards their charges and turned to Hutler for help. He visited the village and met the group who greeted him as if he were their saviour. Indeed, he was:

> We established a camp in the hills around Heidelberg for victims of concentration camps. It is an old, beautiful castle, hidden away in the hills. There, the people get plenty of fresh air, rest, relaxation and time to recover. They also draw a special diet.[32]

In addition to the 150 Jews moved from the French zone, Hutler agreed to transfer one hundred more to this enchanted place, Schloss Langenzell. Soon, he requisitioned another building to allow residents to be reunited with any family members they might have traced among the survivors. It needed special efforts to persuade his 'concentration camp boys' to keep the camp clean, since they felt that Germans should be brought in and forced to do the work while Hutler held that 'work is good for them'.[33] Such minor disagreements could not detract from the success of the venture. On June 24, the residents celebrated the formal opening of their DP camp with a service 'to let God know that their faith had been answered', followed by dancing, food and cakes, the recitation of poems thanking their liberators and tears of gratitude. For the first time since meeting survivors, Albert A. Hutler saw 'joy in their eyes'. The account to his wife tried to sum up his own sense of mission:

> Schloss Langenzell really is an unusual castle in that it houses great hate and great love. There is a spirit of revenge and yet a spirit of forgiveness. It is a castle filled with shadows who had been left to die

and melt away with typhus. These shadows know death and know it well. These shadows know nothing of their families, their children, their parents. We will nurse these shadows back to normal. We must help them forget a little of the past. The last six years cannot ever be erased from their minds and hearts. It is our hope that Schloss Langenzell will push a little of the horrible pictures from their minds.[34]

The retreat for 'broken minds and bodies' was short-lived. Further 'consolidation' led to its closure in mid-August 1945, and the transfer of its residents to Stuttgart. Lieutenant Hutler's involvement ended with ensuring that accommodation, food and other arrangements there were adequate.[35] During its short existence, Schloss Langenzell had gained fame as an exemplary DP camp, while the region administered by Lieutenant Hutler was hailed as offering some of the best provisions for survivors in the whole of Germany. Yet, he himself became increasingly disillusioned, not with his commitment to helping survivors but with the lack of recognition it elicited among his superiors. Promotion to captain had been promised and postponed repeatedly. The relevant paperwork never arrived from the United States and when it did, in September 1945, regulations had been changed and promotion made conditional on a further period of service in Germany. Lieutenant Hutler, having already opted to go home, found that his name would have headed the promotions list from first lieutenant to captain but had been crossed out because he had signed up to go home. He felt snubbed, even cheated and commented wryly to his wife: 'It is very humorous to me because they expect you to maintain a sense of loyalty to an organisation that treats you shabbily.'[36]

Other developments added to his disillusionment. The Military Police attached to the Seventh Army had, from the outset, shown a tendency to side with Germans and treat displaced persons as criminals. In the first weeks after liberation, Lieutenant Hutler had succeeded in alerting his commanding general who ordered restraint. By September, the negative stereotypes about DPs had resurfaced not just within the Military Police but also spread, he thought, to military government in the region:

The DP situation is about the same though many MG-Officers are beginning to take the attitude that these people are all criminals and are the cause of all the troubles communities are having.[37]

As his military career turned sour, Lieutenant Hutler received other job offers from the American Joint Distribution Appeal and from UNRRA. Both were major aid agencies concerned with displaced persons generally or, in the case of the 'Joint', specifically with Jews. His task would have been to liaise with the military in order to optimise co-operation. He declined both offers because he wanted to return to the United States, and wanted to do so in uniform, not as a civilian. Last highlights of his time in Germany were the creation of a Jewish community in Mannheim in September 1945, and a two hour consultation with Earl Harrison that, in Hutler's view, proved to be so successful that he regarded himself as an unacknowledged co-author of the Harrison Report. In September 1945, he also organized special seminars to instruct UNRRA personnel how to work with the army since UNRRA was supposed to take sole charge of administering DP camps from October 1, 1945. The seminars focussed on procurement and process, not on human or Jewish needs. These pragmatic priorities were also evident in the directives issued by the Seventh Army and through Lieutenant Hutler's office to UNRRA. They tried to spell out every detail of procedure. The lists specified precisely how DP camps should be equipped. They even stipulated the exact number of tables, chairs, cooking utensils, crockery and so on down to the required type of screwdriver.[38]

On the eve of his departure, displaced persons in many camps in the Seventh Army area as well as the members of the fledgling Jewish community in Mannheim celebrated the officer who had looked after them, and presented him with mementos and gifts, among them a handpainted book containing pictures and all the names of the Jews he had shielded in Schloss Langenzell. This book, Lieutenant Hutler wrote to his wife, 'will remain a prize possession'.[39] Like the tears of joy at the opening party at the castle, the farewell gifts signalled hope that lives might be rebuilt although he was convinced that the survivors deserved better than they got:

> The treatment of Jews is very patchy. Some places they are treated excellently, in others they are outcasts. . . . The whole thing is a problem close to my heart but I am certain that to me it is not a problem of Jews. It is a problem of people who need help and who are entitled to help.[40]

Child Survivors at Kloster Indersdorf

On June 20, 1945, team no. 182 arrived in Germany to play its part in meeting the humanitarian challenge of civilian displacement and survival. UNRRA, under whose auspices team 182 had been assembled and dispatched, had been created in 1944 by the wartime Allies as a specialist organization to provide welfare support in liberated Europe. As mentioned earlier, the Allies had expected to find a large number of displaced civilians who had to be cared for until they could be repatriated. UNRRA was designed to assist the military with providing this care in the interim between liberation and repatriation. Given the emphatic commitment to repatriating displaced civilians, UNRRA's special task seemed to be limited to a couple of months. As we have seen, repatriation did not constitute a viable option for all displaced survivors. Not only were many in need of medical care and slower to recover their health than the original timetable had envisaged, the whole project of repatriation did not go to plan.[41] The care needs of displaced survivors – Jews as well as non-Jews – were longer-term than had been anticipated, and UNRRA's role inside Germany less temporary.

There were other difficulties. UNRRA had been expected to field five hundred teams, each one international in composition and operating in conjunction with the military in a given region. The policy proved difficult to implement in full. Although team members began training for their tasks from January 1945 onwards in a specially created centre in Granville in Belgium, interest in working for UNRRA was lower than expected. When the concentration camps were liberated and welfare work needed, there were less than half the intended number of teams in training, and even this lower number was not staffed to requirements. UNRRA teams only began to arrive in Germany when the worst humanitarian challenges in the camps had been overcome. In August 1944, SHAEF had agreed to admit aid workers from the American and British Red Cross.[42] The latter sent personnel into the British zone shortly after liberation. In the American zone, it was left to the French Red Cross to dispatch care teams ahead of UNRRA.[43] The arrival of UNRRA teams was delayed further because the issue of how to co-operate with the military had not been resolved. In theory, UNRRA was to be in charge of running displaced persons camps, meeting the welfare needs within them and registering residents for repatriation. The reality was more complicated because the military controlled supplies as well as transport and was reluctant to hand too much power to another organization.

In the American zone of occupation, UNRRA teams began to arrive in June 1945. Team no. 182 was among these early arrivals. Its leader, Greta Fischer, had been instructed to report to the headquarters of the Third US Army where its Displaced Persons Division had requested welfare support. The special assignment of team 182 was the creation from scratch of a centre that would care exclusively for children who had been displaced in the course of the war or who had survived the Holocaust. This special assignment matched a strong commitment among UNRRA care workers to find children who had been hidden or who had been taken by the Nazis to be raised in German families. Data published by UNRRA in April 1946 underline the scale of the overall task that remained to be tackled. At that time, just over seven thousand unaccompanied children were cared for in

UNRRA facilities, most of them (5,145) in the American zone, the remainder (1,851) in the British zone of occupation.[44]

The children came from many different national backgrounds although for three thousand no nationality had been recorded. The ages of 'unaccompanied children' ranged from nought to eighteen. Two hundred and seventy were less than 1 year old, about 1,800 between fifteen and eighteen. Regarding the small number of children identified by UNRRA as Jews – just 446 in the American zone – most belonged to the older age group (fifteen to eighteen) who survived because they had been deployed as slave labour in ghettos and concentration camps. The special assignment given to Greta Fischer and UNRRA team 182 pertained to all children under the age of eighteen who were unaccompanied in June 1945 and needed help to cope with their wartime experiences. Her team was to help them find their families or prepare for a future life on their own. Having arrived in Bavaria on June 20, 1945 and received her instructions from her military superiors, it took Greta Fischer just three days to locate a suitable site for an UNRRA centre for lone children. On June 23, she came across a monastery that was operated by the Innere Mission, a Catholic order of nuns who specialise in medical and social care. During the Nazi era, the nuns had used the monastery, Kloster Indersdorf, to run an orphanage. After the war, the nuns remained but the orphans in their care had left. The site was an ideal find. In addition to buildings that were already adapted to accommodate children, Kloster Indersdorf included seventy hectares of farm land, and a good-sized garden where the German orphans had been put to work growing vegetables and flowers. The farm also included livestock consisting of eleven cows, thirty pigs, four horses and two hundred chickens. The only thing lacking were outdoor play facilities for smaller children. In October 1945, a report described this special place as follows:

> Kloster Indersdorf is a small Bavarian village five miles, but a world away, from dreaded Dachau. Here, an UNRRA team is looking after two hundred children in a twelfth-century monastery, and endeavouring to erase the horrors of the past and give them back their childhood. During the important formative years of their lives these children, and thousands of others like them, have known, instead of care, consideration and attention, a nightmare of beatings, torture and neglect.[45]

On July 9, 1945, Kloster Indersdorf officially opened its doors as an UNRRA centre, designed to house 361 unaccompanied or orphaned children. When full occupancy had been achieved, fifty of the children were under three years old, eight between four and twelve, and three hundred and three (80 per cent) between twelve and sixteen. Young people over the age of sixteen were not admitted to this special centre. Like unaccompanied children generally, the Kloster Indersdorf residents came from different nationalities and backgrounds. The majority were not Jewish. Many were the offspring of foreign workers whom the Nazis had placed in hostels or orphanages, possibly to raise them as future labour slaves.[46] Others had been abducted from Poland and other occupied countries to be raised in German families. A 'small group' was Jewish, among them fifty boys who were admitted to England in November 1945 in the context of a major programme of rescue and rehabilitation involving 732 young Jewish survivors.[47]

Greta Fischer asked the nuns to assist her team by looking after the younger children who needed, above all, 'good physical and emotional care'.[48] When they arrived, these children were pot-bellied, tended to toss their heads, scream and show a profound lack of interest in their environment. All were behind their physical age in skills such as sitting up, walking or talking. Here, the care provided by the nuns was to foster normality and catch up on missed development. In tandem with proper feeding and good, dependable care, the small children appear to have flourished and regained much of the childhood they had been denied.

For the older children care involved, first and foremost, rebuilding attitudes, redirecting behaviour and liberating minds from the distortions inflicted upon them by captivity and the challenges of survival. In her commitment to helping the young people in her charge, Greta Fischer felt let down by a constant shortage of UNRRA staff and by persistent difficulties recruiting displaced persons as assistants. When setting up the children's centre, Greta Fischer had envisaged that small groups would be assigned to a 'housemother' who was herself a displaced person and familiar with the children's experiences. However, it seemed impossible to find the required number of suitable candidates. On the one hand, she believed that 'quality DP workers' could not be found because 'the best were exterminated'. On the other hand, military regulations got in the way by stipulating that the number of displaced persons employed in any one camp must not exceed 5 per cent of its inhabitants.[49] This quota might have made sense for camps where the residents were adults. It completely ignored the fact that the care of children required more staff and had to be more labour intensive.

In order to run Kloster Indersdorf on a day-to-day basis, Greta Fischer recruited Germans to perform basic housekeeping duties such as cooking, cleaning and carrying out repairs. She was very surprised to discover that the displaced persons among her staff refused to work with these Germans and objected to their presence. Likewise, many of the older children were hostile. Some expressed their hostility by throwing stones at the German employees and also at Germans who happened to walk past the centre.

Many of the children not only refused to work alongside Germans, they refused to work altogether on the grounds that Germans had forced them into slave labour in the past and should now work for their former victims. Greta Fischer and her team tried to bring the two sides together but found the children, initially at least, unreceptive. All of them expressed and articulated hostility towards Germans. This hostility was at its strongest among the Jewish children:

> Nearly all the children have one attitude in common, that of intense hatred of the Germans. There are some German maintenance workers employed in the building and it has been difficult at times to explain to the youngsters why they should perform household tasks when, from their point of view, Germans should be working for them. One evening, a surprise party was held which had not been previously planned. There was no committee appointed to wash the dishes or do the general cleaning up after the affair. An UNRRA team member remonstrated that such special activities could be held only if full responsibility was assumed by the children. The youngsters were very upset by these instructions, feeling that the UNRRA team was not understanding of the treatment they had received at the hands of the Germans and not appreciative of the fact that the Germans owed them a great deal of service in return. However, after much discussion and explanation that the object was not to save the labor of the Germans but rather to prepare the children for life in a normal community in a free country, the children accepted the UNRRA position and planned a second party that was beautifully executed.[50]

Designed to restore children to mental and physical health, Kloster Indersdorf was based on tolerance as an 'inestimable value'. This, at least, was the intention of the UNRRA team. The children saw things differently. National identity continued to matter, and divides persisted. Notwithstanding the principles that governed daily life at Kloster Indersdorf, Polish Catholics and Jews did not like one another and objected to spending time together:

> Polish Jews had been oppressed by Polish non-Jews even before the growth of Nazism. Many of the Poles were admittedly anti-Semitic.[51]

UNRRA staff succeeded in persuading most of the older children that daytime activities should be integrated and include participants from all nationalities. The children insisted, however, that they should share their bedrooms only with members of their own group. When it came to sharing rooms, Poles wanted to be with Poles, Jews with Jews. The issue of nationality was complicated further by the contradiction that UNRRA staff tried to urge the older children to disregard nationality in personal intercourse with each other but insisted on classifying their charges by nationality in order to facilitate repatriation. In practical terms, the UNRRA team at Kloster Indersdorf tried to rekindle a sense of national belonging in the children by offering many activities in the language of their country of origin. This emphasis on national languages existed although the official language of the centre was German.

Within its walls, Kloster Indersdorf offered a microcosm of rehabilitation after survival. Organized activities included vocational classes in carpentry, painting and decorating, car maintenance, dressmaking and fine arts. Greta Fischer and her colleagues knew that learning a new trade and preparing for an independent life had to take place 'in a vacuum' because no-one knew what kind of future to expect. For the young people, on the other hand, the experience of learning itself constituted a new beginning and was celebrated by staff and students alike as an achievement. Religious services were on offer for Catholics and Jews, but attendance was strictly voluntary. The guiding principle at Kloster Indersdorf was to encourage its young residents to make choices and by doing so to develop their individuality. Neither choice nor individuality had been possible for any of the children during their displacement or incarceration. By way of example of how quickly her young charges learned that they had a right to choose and found the confidence to assert their preferences, Greta Fischer recorded what happened when a group of thirty youngsters travelled to Switzerland with a view of staying there. When they arrived, nobody greeted them by name. Instead, they were herded into a dining hall and ordered to sit down without being offered a choice where to sit. Worse still, their accommodation seemed to resemble a prison camp. Newly empowered with a sense of self-worth, they refused to accept the conditions imposed on them and demanded to be returned to their preferred place, Kloster Indersdorf:

> The children were shocked to be admitted, on arriving in that wonderful country, to a reception center that had the physical attributes of a concentration camp; barbed wire, uniformed guards, straw-filled ticking on raw wooden double-decker bunks. This was their first introduction after liberation to a 'free country' and they were deeply affected by it. This introduction may have been responsible, in part, for their uncooperativeness when they arrived at the very lovely hostel in which they were to live, a setting infinitely superior to that of Indersdorf although the children admitted none of this; they complained incessantly about the food, the covers, the people, and demanded to be taken back to Indersdorf.[52]

One of the special approaches adopted at Kloster Indersdorf consisted of encouraging the older children to tell their stories. All members of staff from UNRRA aid workers to housemothers took part, although the initiative appears to have come from the children themselves:

When the heavy doors of the monastery were thrown open to these little victims ... they wanted to talk. They did not ask for regular meals, a thing they knew little about after four or five years behind the wire of Nazi extermination camps. Their one desire was to release all their bottled-up self-expression, and by a flood of talk to wash away from their minds the years of fear and horror. For days the members of the UNRRA teams were followed about the monastery by hordes of children clamouring to talk and to be listened to.[53]

All children in Greta Fischer's care had survived in an environment where ordinary rules of social intercourse or moral values had been suspended because survival depended on the aptitude to function in an amoral and dehumanised system. One of these survival strategies concerned not telling the truth. In fact, most of the older children in Kloster Indersdorf had lied about their age without regarding such a lie as wrong. When their survival depended on being selected for work, they had pretended to be older than they really were. After liberation, the situation was reversed. Offers to move to countries such as Sweden, Switzerland, England or France tended to favour younger children. Without hesitation, child survivors made themselves one or two years younger in order to increase their chances of leaving Germany. Lying, Greta Fischer observed, had become a means of survival and lost all moral stigma.

A similar detachment from conventional norms and values pertained to nudity and relations between the sexes. When young survivors of concentration camps arrived in Kloster Indersdorf, they seemed to have lost all sense of shame and, ignoring completely adequate toilet facilities, performed bodily functions such as urinating and defecating in full view of others. Initially, male and female young survivors chose to share dormitories. They did not appear to know that gender relations were governed by certain social rules and moral codes. Many appeared to be oblivious of conventional behaviour and had to relearn it. UNRRA staff and housemothers were disapproving of transgressions but eager to understand their underlying causes. Rather than passing negative judgement, carers tended to interpret their problem behaviour as deformation that had been inflicted on the children and that could be remedied. Outside Kloster Indersdorf, such empathy was often lacking. Many aid workers were repelled by what they perceived as aggression, slovenliness or persistent immorality.[54] Some even thought that Jewish female survivors had lost all sense of decency, engaged in random sexual activity and were spreading venereal diseases.[55] When UNRRA published a review of its rescue work after the Second World War, Jewish survivors were depicted as infantile, deceitful, demanding, revengeful, jealous and constantly fighting among themselves.[56]

The absence of quick and negative judgement about survivors and an approach to their care that blended disapproval with practical steps to encourage behaviour change, may have been prompted by the fact that the residents were children who, it was assumed, could learn and relearn. Underlying all this was a general confidence that each of the young survivors could in fact develop, improve and build an independent future.

Re-Learning How to Live: The Story of Kurt Klappholz

By way of example, let us look at Kurt Klappholz, a Kloster Indersdorf resident whose story moved one of the UNRRA staff sufficiently to write it down.[57] Kurt Klappholz was one of the older children. He arrived there on foot and by himself in August 1945 because he had heard rumours that boys might have a chance to go from there to England. In November 1945, he was indeed one of 'the Boys'.[58] Lillian Roberts, a member of UNRRA team 182, met up with some of them three months later and could not but notice how quickly they had changed:

> I had tea with ten of these youngsters in London the following February. The conversation was animated – about their progress in English, school trips, preparing for the future. They were totally different persons than they had been in Germany.[59]

In 1947, Kurt Klappholz passed the entrance examination to study at the London School of Economics and Political Science (LSE). Of the five thousand who sat the examination in that year, only four hundred were successful, Kurt Klappholz among them. Three years on, he graduated with a first class honours degree, moved on to complete a doctorate at the LSE and remained there to embark on a distinguished academic career in Economics. Education played a central part in his efforts to move on beyond survival:

> After all, we did not have any education of any kind in the camps, and I never went to high school since I was too young and when the war broke out all education for Jews stopped as soon as the Germans marched in. I found my period of study at the LSE intellectually most stimulating. At

LSE, I associated with people who were interested in intellectual matters and this was extremely exciting for me.[60]

Born in 1927, Kurt Klappholz had been 12 years old when the Nazis occupied his home town of Bielsko (Bielitz) in Upper Silesia in 1939. He was an only child who had grown up in a comfortable and secular middle-class environment until persecution made life for Jews increasingly difficult. In June 1942, the Jewish inhabitants of Bielsko were rounded up for deportation. Before herding their captives onto a train, the SS selected all those who were deemed fit to work, while all others were sent to their death. Kurt Klappholz, then aged fifteen, found himself in the slave labour column. His parents were ordered the other way, and he never saw them again. From Bielsko, Kurt Klappholz was taken to a succession of concentration camps, all of them sub-camps of Gross-Rosen in Silesia, a sub-camp of Auschwitz. In late 1944, he was transported with other Jewish slave labourers to Germany where he worked for four weeks in an underground bunker near Bad Salzungen. From there, he was death-marched to Buchenwald, then taken by train to Flossenbürg, a concentration camp in Austria, and liberated by the Americans in May 1945.[61]

He was 18 years old, had survived three years of slave labour and concentration camps and had seen his childhood cut short from 1939 onwards when the Nazis arrived in his home town. When he saw his first American soldier drive into the camp, he climbed on his Jeep and kissed his feet with joy. At the same time, he was afraid that the Americans would seize him again and force him to work. Instead, they just said to him 'go eat'.[62] Like many other survivors, he fell ill with typhus a few days after liberation and was moved to an American field hospital to recover. From there, the US Field Artillery Battalion that was stationed in the area offered him work in their kitchen. They gave him food and shelter and adopted him as a sort of mascot. They also told him about Kloster Indersdorf and the chance of getting from there to England, and issued him with an official-looking certificate about the kitchen work he had performed. Kurt Klappholz was not alone among young survivors to receive direct help from American troops. Greta Fischer noted:

Entire groups of children liberated from the concentration camps by the American Army became army mascots. They worked in the kitchen, in the army billets. Many entered the UNRRA DP Centres, leaving the army units, only because the former offered the best or only chance for search of relatives, repatriation, or resettlement. In other instances, the liberating units were moved elsewhere; stricter directives were issued prohibiting mascots, etc. In general, reports of treatment by the army were excellent. In the first flush of excitement and joy of liberation, many of the army personnel made commitments they were not able to fulfill, particularly in regard to taking children home with them or sending for them later, offering adoption, etc. From a psychological point of view, however, the effect of having first association after liberation with people who were interested in and concerned about the welfare of the children was salubrious.[63]

At Kloster Indersdorf, Kurt Klappholz was one of the young survivors who told his story in order make others understand what happened to him, and in order to understand himself how he might start afresh. The camp system had made Kurt Klappholz behave in a manner that could not be transferred to normal living. He had stopped washing himself. He no longer bothered with using the latrine but performed his bodily functions in the open or in the hut, whenever he needed to. He would grab whatever he could get, and he would constantly think of food and how to obtain it. Looking back on his experiences and behaviour, he felt that he had been reduced to living like an animal.[64]

Other young survivors had lived through similar experiences and needed help to overcome their after effects. Food was a particularly sensitive area where anxieties continued to undermine conventional good manners and obstruct a return to normality. Looked at objectively, there was no shortage of food at Kloster Indersdorf. The children received three main meals and two supplementary meals a day. Although nobody went hungry, they continued to crave and hoard food as if there was a shortage:

> When some of the children still persisted with stuffing their pockets with bread, we discussed the matter with the representatives on the Center Council. The youngsters agreed that the practice was undesirable and agreed for monitors to stand in the dining room door and frisk the children as they left. One boy explained that they would try but that we could not expect complete compliance. He explained what bread meant while they were in the concentration camp. Bread was given out once, after work. 'One took the bread, put it inside one's shirt so that no one else could get it, and crept to bed. And then one remembered the terrible, gnawing hunger of the day at work and resolved, as had been done on other nights, not to eat the bread but to save it for the following morning for the hunger during the work period had been so terrible. But perhaps it would not be so bad to bite off one little corner. And so one little bit was broken off – and then another – and then it was impossible to stop, until all the bread had been consumed'. The youngster also explained further that he was not sure if the boys would ever get over their craving to have and to hold bread.[65]

An obsession with bread pertained to virtually all concentration camp survivors, not only to the children at Kloster Indersdorf. All survivors found it difficult to relate to food in a rational way, and many remained haunted by fears of starvation throughout their life. In order to assuage such fears and to interest the residents in their environment, staff at Kloster Indersdorf replicated, as far as possible, a family home for all activities, including meals. All important were:

neatness and an informal atmosphere of order. When two courses are served, different plates are used. Serving dishes and silver are used. The children are served in family style, eight to ten sitting at one table. The youngsters have been encouraged to decorate their own bedrooms. Bed linen is provided. This one factor has probably done as much to rehabilitate the children who came from concentration camps and who have previously lived in substantial middle-class surroundings than any other factor. Clothing is simple but fitted to size, and wherever possible, the children are encouraged to choose their own colours and patterns. One seems to see the entire personality of a child change when he discards his old, dirty, misshapen garments for clean, neat-fitting, non-institutional ones. The provision of clothing has been fully as important for the purpose of re-establishing a sense of personal dignity as for decency and warmth.[66]

Greta Fischer and her staff tried to re-educate their young charges by way of simple, pragmatic housekeeping rules such as appointing some residents to act as dining room monitors. They would stand at the exit at the end of a meal and collect the bread and other foodstuff that some of the children tried to smuggle to their bedrooms. Like other measures, the use of dining room monitors was designed to wean survivors off their obsessional behaviour, so that 'these victims of a world Holocaust may lead lives of independence, of security, of peace'.[67]

The goodwill of the UNRRA team at Kloster Indersdorf appears to have been obstructed somewhat by its dependence on the military for procurement. It was a complex chain of command. The teams in the camps were not permitted to use their initiative to obtain food, furnishing, transport or other supplies they required. They had to submit their requests to the army and wait to have them approved and delivered. The army, in turn, had to apply to the military government of the region before it could authorise anything. Food, for instance, had to be ordered centrally and was delivered to individual camps from centrally stocked warehouses. This elaborate process ensured that demand was monitored, but it also resulted in delays and confusion. The military system of procurement seemed particularly ill-adapted to meet the needs of babies and small children, yet forbade UNRRA workers to use their initiative and 'shop locally' for baby bottles and other essentials for infant care that did not normally figure in military procurement.[68]

As UNRRA staff saw it, their dependency on the military prevented them from being as effective as they might have been. However, after the military relinquished control, confusion continued and improvements failed to materialise. Staff at Kloster Indersdorf found that in the two key areas of transport and regular supplies, procurement deteriorated after UNRRA headquarters in Munich assumed control. The transport, for example, of young survivors from Kloster Indersdorf to England, had to be postponed five times because the required vehicles failed to materialise. Fifty boys were ready to leave, but depended on vehicles to come and collect them. These vehicles did not arrive. When they finally did, they came late and the boys nearly missed their plane to England. Greta Fischer would have liked to notify the airport, but her centre was not equipped with a telephone.[69] Despite practical and operational difficulties of this kind, UNRRA team no. 182 managed to assist their young charges in moving towards a life of their own. Greta Fischer believed that each of the children needed to know that they were accepted and valued as individuals before they could overcome the ravages inflicted on them by the concentration camps. For the children at Kloster Indersdorf and, more generally, for all survivors, a future came into view only after a sense of self-worth had been restored as the foundation for a different and essentially normal life.[70]

'I was 19 years old and felt like 90' : Anita Lasker-Wallfisch between Survival and a Future

Anita Lasker was 19 years old when she was liberated in Bergen–Belsen.[71] She had been deported in 1942 from Breslau, a German city in the border region of Silesia with a vibrant and non-orthodox Jewish community. The youngest of three daughters, Anita Lasker was born into a middle-class, cultured family and showed early promise as a cellist. Her sister Renate liked to sing. An older sister, Marianne, had left Germany for England in 1939. After deportation to Auschwitz, the parents were sent to their death while Anita Lasker and her sister had a chance of survival through work. Their survival depended on one of the most cynical institutions at Auschwitz: the camp orchestra which was ordered to play marches when the slave labour commandos moved in and out of the camp to disguise their deadly purposes and reinforce the pretence of normality enacted by the SS.

When liberation arrived for the two young women, the Russians had seized control of Breslau, their parents were dead, there was nowhere for them to return to. Like other survivors who had been death-marched there from camps further east, Anita Lasker and her sister found themselves inside Germany, the country that had stripped them of their citizenship and set out to destroy them in its killing machine. Until December 1945, Anita Lasker and her sister were trapped in Belsen, and it took several more months and a good deal of determination, ingenuity and luck before they could leave for a new home and country. Drawing on an autobiographical memoir and on letters written in Belsen, we can reconstruct how Anita Lasker and her sister fared after liberation and share the determination and desperation in their search for a new beginning:

> I would like to be able to describe what it feels like to be liberated. A daunting task. . . . For years, we have been dragged through the extremes of emotions and hardships. Despair – fears – hunger – misery – hatred – friendships. There is only so much one can take. We were completely numb. Our experiences had all been well outside the scope of what is normally heaped on people in the course of a lifetime. And suddenly it is all over. We were 'liberated'. Another monumental experience. After years of living for the moment and maybe if you were lucky, for the next day, there was suddenly this space in front of us. It was hard to believe. I was 19 years old and felt like 90.[72]

The liberation of Belsen was 'a mixture of confusion, helplessness and ignorance'.[73] Anita Lasker recalled how British tanks arrived and withdrew again, how the Hungarians – 'an extremely trigger-happy bunch'[74] – were left in charge, and how, when the British soldiers finally assumed control, they appeared like gods handing out food although this proved to be 'another terrible mistake'.[75] Both she and her sister somehow avoided eating the food, in particular the meat. Liberation meant, above all, that they no longer had to fear for their lives. The sense of shock felt by the liberators at the conditions of the camp did not affect survivors who knew no different:

> You must realize that the camp did not look to us the way it did to our liberators. We had lived surrounded by filth and death for so long that we hardly noticed it.[76]

Although weakened by their ordeal and recent bouts of typhus, the two sisters were able to move about when the liberation occurred. Within days, Renate, who had learned English at a boarding school in Florence, was recruited by the British camp administration as an interpreter and joined there shortly afterwards by her younger sister. Anita Lasker was employed to type English texts despite speaking no English and being unable to type. She learned both on the job.

Working for the camp administration was a lucky break for the sisters. It changed their status from ordinary survivors who lived in the camp to that of army personnel who were entitled to the benefits and privileges reserved for officers. Accommodation was no longer in huts or army barracks but in a small house inside the Belsen compound which they shared with two other interpreters. The place was nicely furnished, their beds had sheets and bed-linen, their living room a radio. They were free to enter and leave the camp, entitled to use the officers' bath – a special luxury after so much deprivation before – and obtain goods including cigarettes at the NAAFI store reserved for the military.

> Our life as Interpreters was really quite comfortable. Being attached to the British Army meant that we had all sorts of privileges. I have in my 'Scrapbook' umpteen little 'passes' to testify to these privileges.[77]

While employment secured a relatively high level of physical comfort, it also broke the deadlock of survival without a purpose, that had oppressed Anita Lasker after her liberation. She had felt stifled by boredom and frightened by the destructive force of revenge.[78] One day, she had joined a looting party. When she saw a German child staring in fear and without comprehension at the looters, she realised that this kind of revenge amounted to moral defeat: 'A thief is always a thief, whatever the circumstances.'[79]

In addition to employment with the British Army, Anita Lasker found two more lifelines to restore a sense of hope and purpose after liberation: establishing contact with her sister and other relatives in England, and being presented with a cello by one of the officers stationed at Belsen. Both were turning point events for her and both depended on coincidence and luck. One day, rumours circulated that a van from the BBC had arrived in the camp. There had been no announcement nor had it been made known that Belsen survivors could record a message and have it broadcast in England in the hope that it might be heard by relatives there or anyone who knew them. Along with many others, Anita Lasker went to see the van from the BBC and did in fact record a message that she and her sister Renate had survived and were still in Belsen. Completely by chance, her sister Marianne heard this message when she listened to the radio, as she usually did. She immediately wrote back to Belsen. The first letter from Marianne arrived in Belsen on May 20, 1945, followed by regular correspondence between the three sisters which soon also included a cousin and his wife who lived in England. Again, the Lasker sisters were privileged. Residents of displaced persons camps were only permitted to send a limited number of Red Cross open postcards, each containing a maximum of twenty-five words.[80] They were not entitled to send letters and no regular provisions existed in such camps for incoming mail. Their de facto status as employees of the army made it possible for Anita Lasker and her sister to bypass these restrictions by persuading one of the British officers to act as their postbox by sending and receiving letters on their behalf. Similarly, Hedwig Geng, whose story is told elsewhere in this volume, enlisted the services of a US soldier after she had returned to Munich although during her wait in Theresienstadt after liberation no such help was forthcoming. The regular exchange of letters allowed the Lasker sisters to talk about their daily lives and to get to know each other again after seven years apart and in totally different worlds.

For Anita, life after liberation took another positive leap in June 1945 when a British soldier presented her with a cello. It lacked proper strings, the bow needed rosin and she did not own any sheet music, but it was a defining moment. A letter to her sister Marianne celebrated the event:

> It is Sunday again: the third lucky Sunday. The first: Liberation on 15 April. The second: Your first letter on 20 May and the third one is today: 17 June. Have you guessed? I have a Cello. . . . Yes, I am a Sunday Luck Child. That is clear as mud.[81]

From then onwards, Anita Lasker's day was divided between working in the office and playing the cello. When Lady Montgomery, a 'high ranking officer in charge of entertainment at Belsen'[82] wanted to organize some concerts, she took Anita with her to visit an Italian POW camp and look for musicians among the prisoners. They found several, including the former principal cello of the Rome Radio Orchestra. On July 4, 1945, Anita Lasker 'played for the first time after such ages in front of a public audience'.[83] Together with the Italian musicians and Eva Steiner, a singer who had also been a member of the orchestra at Auschwitz-Birkenau, she began to tour POW camps in Germany, giving concerts.[84] When the violinist Yehudi Menuhin, accompanied on the piano by Benjamin Britten, performed in Belsen, Anita Lasker sat in the audience and found the occasion both auspicious and disappointing:

> At first it looked as if this concert was for Poles only and we were absolutely furious but then it transpired that this was not meant literally and we got tickets without trouble. I was a little disappointed. . . . I had the distinct impression that he [Menuhin] was saving himself. It could well be that it was hardly inspiring for him to play in this atmosphere. It was impossible to get complete silence in the hall.[85]

To Anita Lasker, playing the cello again, performing in public or hearing Menuhin's concert were, at one level, facets of a new normality. At another level, the abnormality of being confined in a displaced persons camp became all the more apparent. The comfortable living quarters, ample provisions, new clothes could not disguise the fact that living in Belsen was living in a trap without purpose or prospect:

> These days, spent rushing between office and cello, are lost days to me. Especially since my 20th birthday, I can actually hear myself getting older and older, without being where I should wish to be, and that is quite simply at Music School and not in the 'office' of the 'Chief Clerk of Belsen Camp'. I know, we are a thousand times better off than everyone else. It is only the waiting and waiting, and the fighting against a thousand idiotic difficulties.[86]

As soon as her sister Marianne had sent her first letter, Anita Lasker was consumed by hope and the expectation of leaving Belsen without delay and coming to England. On June 8, she wrote:

> Belsen camp is Belsen camp and however free of worries life may be at the moment it is just a passing phase and if you could hear how fast my heart is beating as I write this, you would feel how much I would like this 'phase' eventually to lead to England.[87]

Several obstacles lay in her path. The first concerned her sister Marianne. Although she had fled to England in 1939 and settled there with her husband Rolf, she had always been a Zionist and seen England only as a stopover point. As soon as the war ended, she applied to go to Palestine. No sooner had the sisters rediscovered each other, did it emerge that Marianne was set to start a new life elsewhere. Anita Lasker had come to regard England as the place of her future and hoped her sister would be part of this future. Neither of these assumptions matched the reality unfolding around her. For one thing, she was not a Zionist although she concurred that she might go to Palestine if that was the only option; for another, she sensed that years of different experiences had created distances between the sisters that had not existed in the past and might not be bridged easily in the future:

> These last few days I have been depressed because I am obsessed by a great fear, the fear that I could be a stranger to you. Your way is so different from mine, and I just ask one thing: don't take me any more for the little 13 year old Anita from the other day. If I say that your way is different, I mean that I know which is *my* way. I have three long,

heavy years behind me, with hard days and even harder nights. Enough time to keep testing, and the nearer one is to death the more one feels life. The result is that my life is music. When I say this now, it really has deep reasons. . . . It is this which frightens me so. That we should be strangers to each other before we even managed to get to know each other again. I am not a Zionist and shall probably never become one.[88]

One week earlier, she had begged: 'I hope you understand; I have not rejected Palestine !!!!! Only, please, please let the jumping off point of our new life be England. Please, Marianne, don't run away before we get there.'[89] Since her sister had made up her mind, however, she accepted that their preferences differed. Speaking for Renate and herself, she wrote on June 19, 1945: 'We are happy for you and Rolf that you shall now reach your goal.'[90] By that time, the Home Office in London had already turned down a first application to admit Anita Lasker and her sister Renate to Britain. They found themselves classified as 'German born refugees'.[91] Several 'British Army people' offered to help, and the Jewish chaplain who had arrived in June held out hope that the two sisters could join a transport of young Jewish survivors to Britain. As we have seen earlier, this transport of children had an upper age limit of sixteen and was intended to allow displaced Jewish boys who could not be repatriated to spend some time in Britain before proceeding to Palestine. The transport did not envisage that 'the boys' should stay in Britain (although most of them did), and did not include girls or Jews from Germany. Although Anita Lasker could not have known of these restrictions, she had heard that one thousand children were to be relocated and doubted that the organizers could find that many. She did not allow herself to hope too fervently: 'Yes, of course, we will continue to hope for the children's transport, but as the only hope it seems rather slender. When, oh when will all these problems finally end?'[92]

The administrative logic of treating her and her sister as Germans made no sense to Anita Lasker but infuriated her more than anything else. It seemed to her as if she, the survivor and victim of German brutality and destruction, was regarded as if she was no different from her persecutors and torturers. Just before her sister Marianne left for Palestine, Anita Lasker vented her frustration and disbelief:

The most difficult thing to stomach is that we are GERMAN Jews. What this does to me, I cannot express. If I had not taken a vow after liberation to conduct myself like a halfway civilised person, I would take the various ink pots which surround me and hurl them against the wall, or relieve myself in some other 'not ladylike' fashion. But one has acquired a large stomach and manages to swallow even the fact that one is a GERMAN Jew, although it sticks in the throat and I don't see how I shall ever come to terms with it.[93]

Nothing except collapsed hopes and false promises of leaving Belsen happened until November 1945 when the Houses of Parliament ruled that, as Anita Lasker put it in her memoir, 'displaced Persons would be allowed to join their relatives in England, provided they were UNDER THE AGE OF 21 and had no relatives ANYWHERE ELSE in the world'.[94] Had she been less determined to get to England at all costs, these restrictions might have shattered all hopes of leaving Belsen or Germany. Her sister Renate had already celebrated her twenty-first birthday and an uncle by the name of Edward was known to live somewhere in America. The uncle presented no real problem since nobody suspected his existence and the sisters were not yet in contact with him then. The age limit could be overcome by stealth. Here, the interpreter's privileged access to army supplies proved vital: 'It took fifty NAAFI cigarettes to have our dates of birth altered at the Registry Office in Belsen. . . . I sort of gave myself back two years.'[95] Since Holocaust survivors did, of course, not possess birth certificates or other official documents, identity papers were drawn up on the basis of personal statements and oral communication. In Anita Lasker's case, they were adapted to testify that she was 18 years old and her sister Renate twenty, and without a known uncle or other relatives elsewhere in the world, the two young women seemed eligible for England.

However, there was more red tape to deal with. In order to gain admission to England, the Lasker sisters had to present themselves and their documents at a British passport office. Belsen had no such office, nor did the British zone of Germany at the time. The nearest one was situated in Brussels. Friends from Jewish Relief who worked in Belsen tried to help by improvising some kind of uniform that would make the girls look 'official' and perhaps help them to cross zone and country boundaries in their path without difficulty. In December, they were promised that they could catch a ride to Brussels on a lorry scheduled to go there. It never arrived.[96] On Boxing Day in 1945, Anita Lasker, still stranded in Belsen, attended a dance where, suddenly, her luck changed. One of the officers, Captain Alexander, asked her for a dance and told her that he was planning to drive by car to Brussels on the next day. Would she and her sister want to come with him?

In her memoir she commented that her departure from Belsen had all the makings of a cheap movie but actually happened that way. In preparation for the journey and to make doubly sure of getting across the various borders, Anita Lasker used her office typewriter to produce a 'certificate' permitting herself to:

travell [*sic*] to complete a repatriation procedure. She is to report to the British Passport Office Control Officer at the British Embassy in Brussels.[97]

Having typed it, someone in the office put on an official looking stamp to make it look even more convincing, and completed a matching one for her sister. This time, the promise of transport came true. Although several hours late, Captain Alexander turned up and did so in style: 'We piled into the car, a Mercedes, chauffeur driven, and rolled out of Belsen.'[98] Their companion served as a War Crimes Officer and intended to make use of his right of crossing borders unhindered and with witnesses in case of encountering difficulties. His intervention proved to be essential. Although the small party reached the crucial checkpoint quite late in the evening and found it poorly manned, the home-made passes aroused enough suspicion for the two sisters to be ordered out of the car. Captain Alexander followed immediately, demanding to know what was wrong with the papers, screamed at the duty officer and demanded to telephone his headquarters to complain. This show of strength sufficiently intimidated the border guards to allow Anita Lasker and her sister to proceed.[99] They arrived in Brussels after midnight where Captain Alexander said goodbye to the Lasker sisters after finding them a room for the night.

They had no money, but had, as their most important landmark of orientation, the address of La Grande Hélène, a friend and fellow survivor from the camp orchestra in Auschwitz. They found the address and La Grande Hélène who lived with her parents in a tiny flat. Anita Lasker and her sister intended to stay there only for a day or two, until their papers were ready and departure imminent. On the very next day, they went to the British embassy to collect their passports and travel documents. At this point, their luck ran out. The British officials again refused them entry and they were, unexpectedly, stuck in Brussels. Clearly forced to stay on and unable to stay with their friend, they made contact with the local UNRRA office. Here, they received some spending money and UNRRA offered to pay for accommodation if they could find it themselves. It took another three months of waiting and resubmitting their applications in Brussels and in England until they could finally leave, eleven months after liberation. Anita Lasker's elation would have been boundless, had not the old insult of her national status surfaced again:

We had no difficulties with Emigration, but were subsequently issued with an 'Alien' Identity Book which had the charming word 'Enemy Alien' printed on it. Can you imagine – after all this – we were classified as ENEMIES.[100]

The new life held challenges of integration and disappointed expectations. It was the beginning of normality. Anita Lasker studied music and became a cellist of international renown. Her sister Renate seemed more broken by her Holocaust experiences and less resilient. The first letter she sent to her sister Marianne in England, dated June 9, 1945, tried to explain what kind of future she wished for and how the Holocaust had devastated what she had been:

> You ask me if I still like to sing. Yes, I do, but only for myself, because I practically lost all my voice after contracting typhus. You also want to know what I intend to study. Marianne, you forget that your sister is no intellectual genius. If you want me to be quite frank, I'll tell you that I wish nothing more than to get married, to help my husband (if I find one) and to lead a simple, peaceful life. Are you disappointed? Maybe you understand me better when I tell you that during these last three years I have used up all my energies. The reaction to this time makes itself felt only now. After all those years of misery and hatred and all the wickedness of life, you offer us so much love that we are quite dizzy with happiness. I hope you are not angry about this crazy letter.[101]

For each sister, survival depended on remaining together and giving each other support. Renate Lasker touched on this special bond in her first letter to Marianne in England:

> I am happy and grateful that I was fortunate enough to have her [Anita] next to me and that I could look up to her. It is only thanks to her that I have not totally given up in despair.[102]

The shared experience of Holocaust survival created a special closeness between the two sisters and among survivors generally. Their experiences of survival, however, also separated them from others who had not been caught up in the Nazi killing machine. In reflecting on the meaning of normality and the chance of social integration, Anita Lasker concluded that for Holocaust survivors, distance and difference from these others and their ordinary worlds would remain as irreversible as a deep scar:

> Survivors are a race apart. However complete the integration into 'normality', there will always be an untouchable compartment which will remain the sole property of those who have mysteriously been spared against the most overwhelming odds.[103]

4

UNTIL THE GATES OPEN:
WAITING IN GERMANY ON THE
ROAD TO SOMEWHERE

Liberation had ended the threat of death that characterised the Holocaust and removed the destructive dominance of the SS and their helpers. It had not generated a shared and collective experience of what should happen next. The liberators, as we have seen, did not subscribe to an agreed agenda, leaving front-line units to discover camps without preparing them for the poor state in which they might find survivors, and the special help that might be required. Individual survivors, on the other hand, had constructed their own scenario of what they might do when they were free, although they had no idea how to turn it from hope into reality. Common to all these personal strands of mapping an unknown future was the belief that the world outside Germany, by May 1945 at least, knew about the Holocaust and was waiting to compensate survivors for what they had endured, although nobody knew how this might be accomplished or what would be involved. Compared to such sweeping hopes, liberation lacked lustre. Tables had not been turned. With the exception of prisoners of war and apprehended Nazi criminals, Germans continued to live in their normal environments, albeit harassed by shortages of food, housing, and economic uncertainties. They had not been ordered from their homes into camps to make room for survivors. Beyond Germany, offers of refuge were limited to some very sick children and young adults. There were no offers of residency and permanent immigration from countries the world over. Once survivors had recovered their physical strength and might have attempted a new beginning somewhere, no such choices were on offer. Policy and practice of the liberators, and of UNRRA, were geared towards repatriation and based on the assumption that returning people to the places where they had been removed from would set them up to resume their interrupted lives. Some Jews, notably those from western European countries, could be repatriated, reinstated in their homes, reunited with their families and friends. For most Jews from eastern European countries, however, no such return was possible. These countries and their new governments did not extend a welcome, public hostilities often remained unbroken while homes and belongings remained in the possession of others. Moreover, whole families had been murdered and social environments destroyed. Jews from these places could not go home and could only go elsewhere if they found another country to take them, often because a relative sponsored them and would guarantee that they would not be a material burden to the state. The rules governing immigration worldwide had not changed since the 1930s and 1940s, when Jews had been desperate to obtain affidavits and visas to flee from the Nazis. In any case, most survivors had nobody to sponsor them in another country and were left to wait in Germany for somewhere to go. After repatriation had been completed, 40,000 Jewish Holocaust survivors remained in Germany.

Two months after the war had officially ended, those who were left in Germany began to convene conferences and public gatherings in order to generate a collective Jewish voice that might be heard outside the camps. A first such conference was held in Feldafing in Bavaria on July 1, 1945 followed on July 25 by a further conference, this time aimed at forging a cohesive body for liberated Jews throughout Germany and Austria. Although held in Munich in the infamous Beer Cellar linked to the Nazi movement, the first of these conferences has become known as the St. Ottilien conference after a Catholic monastery near Dachau where Zalman Grinberg, a medical doctor and Holocaust survivor from Kovno in Lithuania, the moving spirit behind the gathering and its chairman, had created a very special hospital. At the time, this hospital cared for eight hundred sick and wounded Jews, many of whom survived, like Grinberg himself, death trains and death marches before being abandoned in the Bavarian countryside. Taking the lead, he had collected as many together as he could, but found it impossible to locate shelter, food or medical supplies until he met an American soldier willing to cut red tape and commandeer for him a section of the St. Ottilien monastery. The main buildings housed a German military hospital. Since Zalman Grinberg's hospital had been created in self-help and without official authorisation, it was not recognised as a DP centre, and depended for supplies on the courage and individual initiative some of American soldiers who defied orders by taking food and medicine to the survivors they had discovered in the vicinity of their base.[1]

The St. Ottilien conference was to replicate Zalman Grinberg's reliance on self-help by forging a unified voice for Jewish survivors. In this aim, it did not succeed. Although delegates from all zones were invited, only those from the American and British zones received permission to attend. The

French and Soviet occupying powers deemed that survivors there had no need for such a special conference or voice. Moreover, the delegation from the British zone under its leader Josef Rosensaft, who headed the Jewish Committee in Belsen, refused to subscribe to a common approach whose organizational centre would need to be located in Munich, leaving Belsen 'subordinated'.[2]

Despite these divisions, the delegates agreed fourteen resolutions. They show what Jewish survivors hoped for at the time and where they demanded improvements. The list of resolutions was headed by the demand for a Jewish state and the right of survivors to live there:

I. Jewish State – Equal Member

The survivors of European Jews who have been annihilated as a people and led towards final extermination, whose sons and daughters fought the common enemy in the forests of Europe as partisans, in the streets and foxholes of the ghettos, in resistance groups of all European countries, in the Allied armies and in the Palestinian volunteer units in the Jewish Brigade claim:

1. Immediate restoration of Eretz-Israel (Palestine) as a Jewish State.
2. Its recognition as an equal member of the United Nations . . .

II. Emigration

Over the graves of seven [*sic*] million Jews who have been murdered in Europe we are claiming that the gates of Eretz Israel be immediately opened for the remainder of the Jewish population in Europe, the bulk of whose men and women have been killed in gas chambers and crematoria. The history of the last six years shows that there is no way back to our native countries because its soil is stained with our blood. It is in Eretz-Israel where our wounds will be healed, where in peace and freedom we shall build our new life.[3]

Survivors, so the St. Ottilien conference asserted, had been sustained during 'the dark days of disillusion and pessimism as eyewitnesses to the annihilation of our families' by the vision of 'a united population building its peaceful home in Eretz-Israel'. This vision could only be turned into reality, if Jews all over the world rallied to the Zionist cause in order to end 'the denial of our existence as a people'.[4] The Holocaust had demonstrated to the world that Jews could only lead a secure and peaceful life in their own state and among their own people. It had turned survivors into torchbearers of Zionism whose shared aim was to leave Germany for Palestine. While forced to wait inside Germany, they demanded 'the right to live as free and independent people, fairly fed and properly clothed'.[5]

In demanding a Jewish state where the survivors could venture a new beginning, the conference in St. Ottilien struck a defining note that would be repeated over and over by displaced Jews in Germany, their representatives in camps and committees, and their delegates at subsequent conferences until the State of Israel was founded on May 15, 1948 and resettlement became possible. After liberation, Zionism emerged as something like a credo, a shared belief about what the future should hold. Linked to the Zionist agenda were the realisation that survivors had to remain in Germany for an unspecified time and a feeling of frustration at the lack of material and humanitarian support extended to them. When the Liberated Jews in the American Zone held their conference in Munich in January 1946 – officially known as the first conference, although it was the second gathering of displaced Jews in the region – the twin themes of Palestine and the perceived abandonment of survivors dominated proceedings in a mixture of disappointment and hope. The *Frankfurter Rundschau* reported:

> The address by Dr. Grinberg turned into an accusation against Europe when he declared that the remnants of the Jewish people had been saved from being gassed and burnt, but had not been liberated. There is only one way out for the Jewish people. This is to open the gates of Palestine.[6]

In his closing speech, Grinberg stressed that Jewish survivors did not expect much help from the Germans who had been responsible for the Holocaust but had expected to be 'comforted' by the world. Instead, they found themselves kept in camps and excluded from anything resembling a normal life, and trapped in a country from which the Holocaust had divided them for ever:

> We cannot possibly be expected to contribute to the reconstruction of Germany. We want to get out of Germany, we want to get out of Europe, we want to go to Palestine.[7]

Breaking the Stalemate: The Harrison Report

Jewish survivors voiced their demands and expectations before audiences of fellow survivors with the aim of communicating them to a wider public,

and eliciting pledges of support from military government, aid organizations, German regional policy makers and other agencies. At the Munich
conference in January 1946, the list of special guests could not have been
more comprehensive.[8] Leading generals, aid workers, German regional
politicians, Jewish chaplains and even David Ben-Gurion attended, the
latter officially in his capacity of trade union leader in Jewish Palestine, and
unofficially as the embodiment of the Zionist dream.

Help for Jewish survivors had, however, already arrived from another
quarter. In Germany, Jewish chaplains in the US army had, from their
first encounter with the camps, sent letters and reports home on the
conditions endured by survivors. Between April and June 1945, Abraham
Klausner, the army chaplain who, as we have seen, attached himself to
Dachau, was instrumental in compiling a list of survivors and helped to
turn Feldafing into the first Jewish Displaced Persons Camp, dispatched
several such reports, each one intended to evoke pity and cajole Americans,
above all American Jews, into action. In June, Klausner wrote:

> Six weeks ago they were liberated. They were taken to a series of camps
> in the uniform of the Concentration Camp and remained garbed in this
> infamous outfit. They are housed in dwellings that are unfit for human
> occupation and are fed in many cases less than they received at the
> Concentration Camps. I do not use words recklessly. I have travelled the
> entire area [Bavaria]. I have visited each of the camps. I have spoken
> with the leaders, observed their mode of life and I turned aside in the
> best situation and silently cried – for all of Israel's sufferings, this!
> There seems to be no policy, no responsibility, no plan for these . . . for
> these stateless Jews. At some camps they are kicked around by some
> smart second Lt. At others an UNRRA man with less power than a
> glow worm sits at his YMCA desk and at best one or two conditions are
> a bit better because a Jewish officer is enraged. Twelve hours a day I tell
> my lies. 'They will come', I say. 'When will they come?' they ask me.
> UNRRA, JDC, Red Cross – can it be that they are not aware of the
> problem? It is impossible. The JDC representative did visit one of my
> camps. There he asked our people 'What can I do for you?'. What can
> you do for a broken, hungry, spiritless people! Red Cross has sent in a
> few packages here and there, but nothing more. Clothes? Only those we
> manage to steal. . . . Of what use is all my complaining. I cannnot stop
> their tears. America was their hope and all America has given them is a
> new camp with guards in Khaki. Freedom, hell no! They are behind
> walls without hope. Can not American Israel raise its voice? Can not the
> leaders of our people cry out demanding a new day for these who have
> hated the dawn of each day? There are so few left. Forgive my
> incoherence, calmness is not with me.[9]

Klausner and his fellow chaplains expected Jewish and other aid organizations in America to send immediate and practical help: clothing, shoes, food, toiletries, and care workers to support survivors. Jewish organizations and their leaders, on the other hand, were more concerned with persuading the US War Department, State Department, various government officials and ultimately the President himself to recognise the special needs of Jews and authorise special support.[10] From May 10 onwards, the American Jewish Conference, assisted by prominent political figures such as Congressman Emmanuel Celler, campaigned for the appointment of Jewish liaison officers within the US army who could identify and address the needs of liberated Jews.[11] Although the War Department and the US army rejected the proposal on the grounds that liaison officers always represented national groups and Jews did not constitute such a group,[12] continued lobbying finally persuaded the American President Harry S. Truman in June 1945 to send a special emissary on a fact-finding mission to Germany and Austria. He was to report to the American public how Jewish survivors were cared for and what was needed to secure their future.

Americans at that time knew that their victorious army had assumed the challenge of care. They also knew from reports published by delegations of journalists, congressmen and leading publishers who had been invited to tour the liberated camps, that the Nazis had committed unimaginable atrocities in these camps, and that conditions for the survivors remained bad.[13]

On June 22, 1945, President Truman instructed the Dean of Law at the University of Pennsylvania, Earl G. Harrison, to 'inquire into the US Army's treatment of the Jewish DPs'.[14] His report was to cover four aspects: 1. the conditions under which non-repatriables and stateless persons lived; 2. the needs of such persons; 3. how their needs were met by the military, relief agencies and other bodies and, 4. what the future destinations of such persons might be.[15] Truman's brief gave prominence to assessing the role of the army in caring for displaced Jews. No less significant was the issue of resettlement for Jews who could not be repatriated. There was an unspoken assumption that resettlement meant, above all, settling in Palestine, and Harrison's report was to lift this theme from the wish list of displaced Jews to the international political agenda.

Officially at least, Earl G. Harrison did not speak for any organization or political group, although he had been in close contact with American Jewish representatives and was aware of their concerns. He personally believed that the United States had a moral responsibility to improve the daily living conditions of displaced Jews as well as a political responsibility to facilitate Jewish settlement in Palestine or elsewhere.[16] By the time he left for Europe on June 28, 1945, he had chosen a small team of experts on refugee issues and Jewish welfare to accompany him.[17] The fact-finding mission commenced with gaining a broader perspective on policy by meeting key decision makers in London and Paris before inspecting actual camps and conditions. In Germany, the visit began with extensive discussions at the US military headquarters in Frankfurt am Main and at military government level. Following this, Harrison and his team visited twenty displaced persons camps and several communities where displaced as well as German Jews lived 'out of camp'. The touring part of the mission lasted from July 13 to 25. The return journey was again broken by consultations and meetings with key decision makers in Switzerland, Paris and London.[18]

The report submitted by Harrison after this *tour de force* found little to praise and much to criticise. What he described, often citing verbatim from conversations held with survivors' representatives, Red Cross care workers, displaced persons officers such as Albert A. Hutler (singled out for personal praise) or Jewish chaplains, seemed to reveal no more and no less than the virtual abandonment of the Jews. The report was published on September 30, 1945.[19] When it hit the headlines in early October, residents of Feldafing, the only DP camp where Harrison found anything to praise, protested that their situation was in fact much better than had been portrayed in the press.[20] Of course, more than two months had gone by since Harrison collected his information and many things had improved since then. In order to shield the army from embarrassment, Harrison had communicated his main findings unofficially in early August, even before his return to the USA. His conclusions so startled the Chief of Staff, General George C. Marshall, that he cabled them to General Eisenhower, the US commander in the 'European Theater', urging him to review army provisions and remedy what had been found amiss.

What Harrison Found

The report opened with a broadside of condemnation:

> Generally speaking, three months after VE Day and even longer after the liberation of individual groups, many Jewish displaced persons and other possible non-repatriables are living under armed guard behind barbed wire fences, in camps of several descriptions (built by the Germans for slave labourers and Jews) including some of the most notorious concentration camps, amidst crowded, frequently unsanitary and generally grim conditions, in complete idleness, with no opportunity, except surreptitiously, to communicate with the outside world, hoping for some word of encouragement and action on their behalf.[21]

Although survivors were no longer starving and received a diet of two thousand calories per day, most of these calories (1,500) were delivered in the shape of 'dark, wet and extremely unappetising bread' and potatoes. There were hospitals for the sick but not enough medical supplies. Some camp commanders had managed to obtain and distribute clothing, some survivors had found SS uniforms to replace their 'concentration camp garb' but many still wore, three months after liberation, the clothes in which they had survived. Essential items such as shoes were very scarce. To the chagrin of the survivors, the German population appeared well-dressed and, in particular in rural areas, better-supplied with food. Accommodation in DP camps was vastly overcrowded and lacked adequate sanitary facilities. Most DP camps were located in former Nazi camps or barracks, many of them damaged by bombs and without window panes or leak-proof roofs. Even in better locations such as Zeilsheim near Frankfurt am Main where former workers' housing had been turned into a DP camp, seven or more people shared one room. Elsewhere, vast halls or dormitories served as sleeping quarters where residents erected makeshift screens between mattresses on the floor to find some privacy. Sheets or other paraphernalia of normal living were unheard of. Many DP camps were surrounded by barbed wire and residents forbidden to move freely in and out. Harrison also criticised the army for failing to establish a tracing service and for restricting communication by post. Despite their liberation, he claimed, survivors remained outcasts:

> As matters now stand, we appear to be treating the Jews as the Nazis treated them, except that we do not exterminate them. They are in concentration camps in large numbers under our military guard instead of the SS troops. One is led to wonder whether the German people, seeing this, are not supposing that we are following or at least condoning Nazi policy.[22]

In the context of his fact-finding mission, Harrison was, of course, briefed that SHAEF directives had envisaged to provide for displaced persons by requisitioning from Germans. They even stipulated that Germans should be moved into camps if this was the only way of accommodating displaced persons in ordinary houses.[23] This aspect of the directives, however, had never been implemented. Their punitive aims did not seem to suit a military-style control of displaced populations and they were not shared by individual camp commanders. In any case, the belief in quick repatriation militated against even looking for longer term solutions to displaced living. Harrison argued that it was time to stop appeasing the Germans and do the right thing by the survivors. By way of example he cited:

... the very few places where fearless and uncompromising military officers have either requisitioned an entire village for the benefit of displaced persons, compelling the German population to find housing where they can, or have required the local population to billet a reasonable number of them. Thus the displaced persons, including the persecuted, live more like normal people and less like prisoners or criminals or herded sheep. They are in Germany, most of them and certainly the Jews, through no fault or wish of their own. This fact is in this fashion being brought home to the German people but it is being done on too small a scale.[24]

Rather than employing displaced persons for whom purposeful activity would constitute a step towards the normalisation of their lives, the armies of occupation preferred to hire Germans. Looking back on his visit, Harrison stressed the human cost:

Scarcely less terrible to me than my memory of the stench and squalor of the concentration camp is the memory of the corroding aimlessness of the life to which the refugees are condemned. Where camp residents were employed, they usually were Balts. For most of the inmates, one dull and hopeless day succeeded another, with the meagre meals the only break in the monotony. Nothing could be harder on morale, more degrading on the human spirit.[25]

The Palestine Issue

In the short term, Harrison's report was to put pressure on the army to improve the quality of caring for survivors, and on UNRRA to co-operate more effectively. The overarching aim of his detailed comments was to achieve for survivors 'a recognition of their actual status, and by this I mean their status as Jews'.[26] Since they had been 'more severely victimised than the non-Jewish members of the same or other nationalities', they now had special needs. Since they had been persecuted as Jews and not on the grounds of nationality, they had to be protected from anti-Semitism. Therefore, repatriation had to be abandoned in favour of what Harrison called 'evacuation': 'The evacuation from Germany should be the emphasized theme, policy and practice.'[27]

In the course of his whistle-stop tour, Harrison had met many different people and listened to their views. The sentiments prevailing in the camps were expressed forcefully by the chairman of the Jewish committee in Belsen, Josef Rosensaft, who informed Harrison: 'all Jews want to get out of this bloody country' and all wanted to go to Palestine.[28] In some camps,

UNRRA staff distributed questionnaires in order to obtain a more objective picture. Of 19,311 respondents, 18,702 opted for Palestine, the remainder for the United States.[29] A few weeks later, an exploration team of the American Jewish Conference conducted their own survey during an inspection tour with very similar results: 98 per cent of Jewish survivors who lived in DP camps wanted to leave for Palestine, the only place where they thought they could 'live as free Jews'.[30] The only discordant note during Harrison's fact-finding mission came from Chaim Weizmann, President of the World Zionist Organization. His vision of a Jewish state did not quite tally with the displaced individuals who were now pinning their hopes on living there. He confided to Harrison that, in his view, entry to Palestine should be restricted to children and young people under the age of twenty-five who were fit and could contribute to a Jewish future. It would not do to turn the Zionist homeland 'into an old people's home'.[31]

Drawing on estimates provided by Jewish organizations and their leaders, Harrison put the number of displaced Jews at 100,000, and demanded that the British government should issue that number of Palestine Certificates.[32] The demand for 100,000 Palestine Certificates went beyond the actual need he could have ascertained in the course of his field trip and included Jews who were known to have survived in eastern Europe, notably Soviet Russia. Many of them had begun to make their way to Palestine illegally. Given the enormity of destruction of lives, homes and environments in the Holocaust, Harrison regarded it as a moral imperative that the wishes of the survivors should be heeded:

> For some of the European Jews, there is no acceptable or even decent solution for their future other than Palestine. This is said on a purely humanitarian basis with no reference to ideological or political considerations, so far as Palestine is concerned. To anyone who has visited the concentration camps and who has talked with the despairing survivors, it is nothing short of calamitous to contemplate that the gates of Palestine should soon be closed.... No other single matter is, therefore, so important from the viewpoint of Jews in Germany and Austria and those elsewhere who have known the horrors of the concentration camps, as is the disposition of the Palestine question.[33]

The Palestine issue, however, was too complex to yield to Harrison's appeal on behalf of Jewish Holocaust survivors. Politically, Britain exercised control in the region and had committed itself to restricting Jewish immigration to no more than one third of the Arab population there. This ceiling remained in place even after, on July 16, 1945, the British Labour Party had won the general election and formed a new post-war government. At its party congress in November 1944, Labour had pledged to remove all limitations of Jewish immigration. In government, however, it continued the established practice of restricting the number of Palestine Certificates.[34] Despite the change of leadership, the British government rejected the demand for an additional 100,000 Palestine Certificates. Instead, it insisted on retaining the quota of no more than 1,500 certificates, most of them to be issued to illegal emigrants who had been intercepted and been detained in Cyprus. In order to diffuse the issue, the British government proposed to set up an International Commission of Inquiry whose task it was to ascertain actual demand for emigration to Palestine among displaced Jews. Harrison's head-on challenge to British policy on Jewish settlement in Palestine failed to the extent that no additional Palestine Certificates became available. It did, however, force the issue of Jewish settlement in Palestine onto the international political agenda and prepared the way for a process of international decision-making that, less than three years later, led to the proclamation of Israel as an independent state by the United Nations.

When the Palestine issue hit the headlines in the autumn of 1945, nobody could have predicted this outcome. The displaced Jews themselves were increasingly impatient to leave and could not understand why they had to wait. The Jewish Agency for Palestine (JAFP) who administered the distribution of Palestine Certificates reported after one year in Germany:

> The Jewish DPs gave the first group of JAFP personnel an enthusiastic welcome. They saw us as the embodiment of their hope for the future. They were ready to place in us a great deal of confidence, thus confidently facilitating our work. . . . So deeply convinced were they of their immediate admission to and resettlement in that country [Palestine] that they gave little heed to the fact that we had begun dealing in immigration certificates at the rate of no more than a few hundred per month. They could not conceive of the idea that the world might be deaf to their plight.[35]

Some thought that the Zionist fervour of displaced Jews reflected their lack of choice and would wane if other countries began to invite Jewish survivors to live there. David Ben-Gurion regarded the size of the displaced Jewish community as a powerful argument in promoting demands for a Jewish state. He even suggested that the camps should be emptied and displaced Jews moved to Italy, partly to keep them committed to Zionism and partly to ensure that the world would take notice. This idea came to nothing, but Zionist leaders did regard displaced Jews as a 'reservoir' who 'presented a one-time opportunity to give Jews a majority in Palestine, after which Jewish statehood would be inevitable'.[36]

'What we have done since July': General Eisenhower's Response to the Harrison Report

Harrison raised the Palestine issue as a humanitarian imperative that followed from the Holocaust experiences and the displacement of Jewish survivors in Europe. In doing so, he set in motion political processes that were too slow to offer a solution in 1945, when they commenced, but did eventually result in resettlement opportunities. The quality of life for displaced Jews in this interim was significantly altered by Harrison's critical comments and by the responses on the part of the US army. With more immediate effect than the Palestine issue and the problems of resettlement, displaced living inside Germany changed from detention and curtailment towards independence and normality.

On November 5, 1945, the Commander in Chief of the US forces in Europe, General Dwight D. Eisenhower, informed President Truman in a detailed letter 'what we have done since July'.[37] Although Eisenhower regarded the criteria applied by Harrison as unrealistic and claimed that he personally had found no evidence that food, medical care or clothing were of inferior standards during an inspection tour in August 1945, he assured the President that 'subordinated commanders' had already made improvements or were under orders to do so. Given the influx of German refugees, the need to detain a large number of German prisoners of war and to meet the requirements of the military and military government by requisitioning buildings, he did not accept that much more could be done to accommodate displaced Jews outside camps:

> Displaced persons have, and will continue to have, preference over Germans for housing, but the requirements of the distribution of supplies, the provision of medical care, and the need for welfare activities, makes it desirable that displaced persons be sufficiently concentrated so that these services may be performed efficiently by the limited supervisory personnel and transport at our disposal. Thus, considerable use has been made of large installations such as brick buildings in preference to scattered individual billets.[38]

When Harrison accused the army of stationing guards at residential camps for displaced persons and surrounding the compounds with barbed wire, he hit upon the truth that, as far as the military was concerned, the camp populations were troublesome and needed to be controlled:

> The assertion that our military guards are now substituting for SS troops is misleading, and demands a full explanation. One reason for limiting the numbers permitted to leave our assembly centers was

depredation and banditry by displaced persons themselves. Despite all precautions, more than 2,000 of them died from drinking methylated alcohol and other types of poisonous liquor. Many others died by violence or were injured while circulating outside our assembly centers.[39]

Despite Eisenhower's defiant tone, Harrison's report redefined the living conditions for displaced Jews in Germany. Barbed wire and armed military guards were removed, and all displaced persons camps treated as residential centres whose population could move in and out freely. Security at the gates and inside the camps was handed over to a newly created police force, staffed by and run on behalf of displaced persons themselves. The creation of Jewish camps proved more patchy. On August 22, 1945, General Eisenhower had ordered the establishment of separate camps for Jewish displaced persons.[40] One year on, 130 camps included Jews among their populations but only 30 were Jewish camps.[41]

Harrison had also highlighted the problems encountered by German Jews and displaced Jews who had opted to live 'out of camp'. They were treated like Germans, required to obtain German ration cards and rely on the German authorities to obtain food, clothing and other supplies. In his letter to President Truman, Eisenhower conceded that problems existed but appeared confident that orders were in place to put things right:

> In the past, a 2000-calorie minimum diet was prescribed for all displaced persons in approved centers. Our field inspections have shown that in many places this scale was consistently exceeded, but there have also been sporadic instances where it was not met. Three or four thousand persons of the persecuted categories, including German Jews, in the American Zone have returned to their home communities. Many are making a genuine effort to re-establish themselves. Until recently, there has been no clear-cut system of assuring adequate food for this group, although in most cases they have been given double rations. I have recently raised the daily caloric food value per person in approved centers to 2,300, and for racial, religious and political persecutees to a minimum of 2,500. . . . We are now issuing directives that those Jews and other persecuted persons who choose and are able to return to their communities will receive a minimum ration of 2,500 calories per day, as well as clothing and shoes, the same as those in centres.[42]

Unfortunately, these orders did not filter down to the rank and file who should have implemented them. On the contrary, local commanders understood the new directives as excluding everyone from any kind of assistance who did not live in a displaced persons camp.[43] Taking their lead from the army, UNRRA personnel adopted the same stance and limited their support to camp populations.[44] Following Harrison's report, two developments in particular improved the living conditions of Jews in Germany, above all those who were waiting in camps for somewhere to go. Firstly, from October 1945 onwards, a Jewish Advisor was assigned to the office of the military governor with the special remit to monitor all aspects of the life and treatment of Jews, and to ensure that policy and practice accommodated the special needs of Jews in the American zone of occupation. The second development concerned the admission of Jewish charities and aid organizations.

The involvement in Germany of Jewish charities had been delayed partly because the organizations themselves were not ready to dispatch personnel or aid, and partly because the US army and UNRRA could not agree who should authorise their presence. The insistence of UNRRA that Jewish aid workers should join their teams also became an obstacle. The Vaad Hatzalah, an American Jewish organization that focussed on supplying religious articles and kosher food to observant Jews, agreed to work under UNRRA and began to contribute in the summer of 1945. The much larger American Joint Distribution Committee had sent a first representative in June 1945 but took until the end of the year to position itself in Germany because it sought to set up a system of material support for Jews without subordination to UNRRA.[45] The third major Jewish charity, ORT, the Organisation for Rehabilitation and Training, entered Jewish displaced persons camps without difficulties in the early autumn of 1945. True to its mission, it established vocational and general education programmes inside these camps including, wherever possible, training farms for young people eager to settle in Palestine. The arrival of these charities in the wake of the Harrison Report ensured that Jews who were waiting in Germany until they could leave for somewhere else received help to learn, to develop their skills or acquire new ones, and to rediscover their religion and culture.

The Making of a Jewish Camp

Landsberg, a displaced persons camp on the site of a slave labour compound in the town of the same name in Bavaria, was one such camp where Jews were helped towards a new beginning. Instrumental in turning Landsberg from a detention centre to a residential place was Major Irving Heymont during his brief spell as camp commander between September and November 1945. He arrived in Landsberg on September 19 to take charge of the camp which at the time housed 58 Nazi officers in the local castle and six thousand displaced persons, among them five thousand Jews, in barracks and wooden huts. The assignment came as a complete surprise. In preparation, Major Heymont had been told that conditions in the camp were horrible and needed improving. He received little guidance how this might be achieved and what the overall aims were in running such camps:

> Regimental headquarters called to discuss the camp before I went to see it. I was told I had a free hand in getting the place into shape. As a weapon, I was authorised to cut the rations by one third to force them to clean up the camp.[46]

On arrival he was met by the camp committee, and by George Craddock, the head of the UNRRA team attached to Landsberg. As they set out on an inspection tour, General Rolfe, the Assistant Division Commander, joined the party, having driven close to one hundred miles to do so. Over the coming months, he was to become a regular visitor at Landsberg. And it was General Rolfe who hinted at the connection between Major Heymont's mission and the Harrison Report:

> The reason for his visit, he said, was that the camp was considered a scandal – and that General Eisenhower was personally interested in having it cleaned up. It seemed that some civilian VIP named Harrison had inspected DP camps for President Truman and had some harsh things to say about the Army. Landsberg, according to Rolfe, was one of the reasons Harrison had 'burned' the Army.[47]

Heymont's vision was simple. He wanted Landsberg to operate as a self-governing community with a camp committee that assumed responsibility for all aspects of daily life while the army took a back seat. The military should help, not manage or control. The US Army, he reasoned, had come to Europe to fight the Nazis, not to 'stand guard over their victims'.[48] Before a residents committee, however, could take on the responsibility of running the camp, it had to be elected in a democratic, essentially American fashion. Holding elections, in turn, depended on transforming living conditions in Landsberg and improving facilities. Elections, Heymont thought, had to be preceded by a change in residents' attitudes. They had to care for the appearance of their daily environment and take an interest in the quality of their lives. The Landsberg elections took place on October 21, 1945. One month later, Major Heymont's assignment as camp commander came to an end. In letters to his wife, he wrote in detail about his plans for Landsberg and his experiences with its residents. These letters constitute a unique record of conditions in Landsberg as it emerged as a Jewish camp and since Landsberg was soon recognised as a model, Heymont's letters also cast light on displaced living elsewhere in Germany.

Displaced Living, September 1945

On his second day as commander, Irving Heymont described in a letter to his wife what he found inside the camp. Apparently, it had already been improved since Harrison's inspection tour two months earlier.

> It is located in a former Wehrmacht artillery *kaserne*, or permanent military post. The dwellings, known as blocks, are three-storey brick barracks typical of any permanent Army dwellings. The rooms are very large and afford no privacy. Washrooms and latrines have long rows of the usual fixtures. From a military viewpoint, the barracks are modern and well designed. For housing families, they could not be worse. The DPs sleep in bunks of rough, unfinished lumber that are often double or even triple decked. Mattresses are straw-filled sacks. Bedding consists of shoddy gray Wehrmacht blankets or US Army blankets. Sheets seem to be unknown except in the camp hospital and among a few enterprising persons who must have black market resources. The people are provided with tall, narrow, wooden wall lockers. In these lockers (or occasionally in a wooden box, a battered suitcase, or a rucksack), they keep their worldly possessions, food supply, and utensils.[49]

Because the dormitory-style accommodation did not afford any privacy, its occupants had moved the wall lockers to form partitions and used blankets and bits of cardboard to shield neighbours from one another. In carving out a private space, the residents tried to live as individuals and not, as they had been forced to for so long, as a nameless and faceless part of an ordered mass. Heymont conceded that, for the survivors, these arrangements constituted a first step towards normal living, but their notion of normality did not meet his American and military standards:

> In the makeshift cubicles of the living quarters, groups are trying to revive family life. Eating together, it was explained to me, had come to be the high point of the day for the family group. Tables and chairs had been improvised from scraps of lumber and boxes. Almost every family group has an electric hot plate. . . . The wall lockers are littered with clothing, food, and eating utensils. The latter are generally quite filthy. I soon learned that there were no real facilities for washing them. While the bunk beds were fairly neatly made up, little or no sweeping had been done. Here and there, a very few family groups had spotless areas. The number of idle people is surprising. Many of the beds were occupied by people either dozing or just lying there listlessly. One could sense an air of resignation. The hallways are littered with trash and scraps of old food. Behind a number of staircases, I saw signs of human excrement

that obviously had been there for some time. In a few instances, I even saw human excrement in the corridors!

The toilets beg description. About half the bowls were inoperative but full of excrement. Toilet seats, while not entirely lacking, were smeared with excrement or wet with urine. No toilet paper was in sight. I was informed that toilet attendants had been designated – but not one could be seen on duty. In explanation of the deplorable state of affairs, I was told that the water pressure was low because of war damage to the water mains. However, the water pressure seemed more than adequate for at least the first two floors of each barracks building. What appeared to be low was the general sense of responsibility for communal sanitary facilities.[50]

In the washrooms, most sinks were out of order and drains blocked by food scraps since residents cooked in their bedrooms and used the washrooms to rinse their cooking utensils. Yet, Landsberg boasted two kitchens. Both of them failed to meet Heymont's standards. The first was designated non-kosher and 'encrusted with black grease and food debris'. By contrast, a small adjoining dining room – reserved for members of the camp committee – was neat, clean, furnished with tables and chairs and the walls decorated with pictures of Roosevelt, Truman and Ben-Gurion. The kosher kitchen seemed particularly dirty:

> The utter filth in this kitchen and its cooks and workers had to be seen to be believed. In a corner of the kitchen store room, I saw human excrement on the floor. I could not understand how it would be possible to eat food prepared in that kitchen and not suffer from diarrhea or dysentery. I instructed the man in charge that, unless the kitchen was cleaned up within 24 hours, I would close it as a menace to the health of the camp.[51]

As instructed, Heymont concentrated his efforts, first and foremost, on cleaning up the camp. This did not mean sending army personnel to do the job, nor hiring Germans. He insisted that the residents themselves had to comply, initially by obeying orders and eventually by developing their own sense of responsibility. In expecting a clean camp and involving residents in creating it, he did not pander to yet another inspection team but assumed that cleanliness constituted visible evidence of self-esteem for individuals and for the group as a whole.

Even before conditions in Landsberg had improved to Heymont's satisfaction, there were highlights. The camp hospital was run by the UNRRA team who employed German nurses. Despite persistent shortages of medical supplies and despite some thefts of equipment, the hospital offered exemplary care. Even more impressive were the schools that had been established in Landsberg. Under the leadership of a 'graduate of a concentration camp', Dr. J. Oleiski, 320 children and adolescents at Landsberg learned to read and write, or attended vocational training classes. Adults could study cultural subjects in the evening. In his native Lithuania, Dr. Oleiski had worked as a vocational teacher for ORT, the Jewish organization specialising in rehabilitation and training. This experience enabled him to create schools in Landsberg, although initially everything was in short supply from pencils to paper and books. Later, the American Joint and ORT played a major role in providing study materials and teaching staff for use in Landsberg and other Jewish camps. For Heymont, the discovery of these schools pointed the way to the future: 'I think the camp can best be helped by helping Dr. Oleiski – that is, after the camp has been cleaned up'.[52]

Cleanliness and Self-Esteem

Within two week, the new regime began to show results. While Heymont had insisted on cleanliness as a first and vital step to improving conditions, he had also shown that he understood the circumstances and personal experiences that had distorted behaviour and destroyed motivation. Whether addressing the camp committee or Landsberg's assembled residents, he mixed empathy with reprimand. He acknowledged that the treatment by the SS had destroyed people's sense of pride, but stressed that this had now ended. Misuse as slave labour had sapped the will to work, but work and its context had changed. He knew about the extreme starvation they had suffered and that it made them crave food at all times. For this reason, they tended to disregard the rules against hoarding food in their beds and his insistence on preparing and eating food under hygienic and orderly conditions. Heymont conceded that they had been dehumanised, but maintained that this could not be the end of it:

> All of that is true. But now is the time to relearn the habits of work and industry. Now is the time to relearn how to be self-respecting civilised persons. No man can ask you to forget what you and your families have been through. However, you cannot live in the shadow of the past forever.[53]

Not unlike a parent, Heymont promised rewards for behaviour he wanted to encourage. Thus, when firewood had to be chopped in preparation for the winter, he enlisted the help of young Landsberg residents who wanted to live as a group, calling themselves Kibbutz, and who needed a separate building to do so. When they delivered the firewood, they promptly received their building. In a similar vein, he tried to tackle what he perceived as lack of moral inhibitions. The family groups he had observed during his first inspection tour in September 1945 included men and women who were not married to one another and who would 'sleep in the same room in a manner that would be considered scandalous back home'.[54] By way of remedy, Heymont promised better accommodation to married couples and set in motion a 'rush of marriages'. Yet even before this incentive, Holocaust survivors were driven to create new families for themselves and find new partners as a mark of beginning a different life:

> Many couples live together without the sanctions of wedding rites. This practice is accepted in a very matter-of-fact fashion. If a couple has a child, I am told that a marriage ceremony will follow. Children are highly esteemed, even more so than in a normal community. Continually, people of the camp individually ask me for favors or small comfort items that are not available through the regular camp supply. Never once have I been asked for contraceptives by anyone from the camp, although our German employees frequently ask for them. I discussed this individually with several members of the camp committee. Each told me that the use of contraceptives is highly frowned upon by the camp people. They believe it is everybody's duty to have as many children as possible in order to increase the numbers of the Jewish community. It is their opinion that it will take several generations to replace the casualties of the Nazi period.[55]

By mid-October 1945, Heymont had arranged for non-Jewish residents to be moved elsewhere and for Landsberg to function as a designated Jewish camp. Yet another inspection tour by senior military personnel in early October had left Heymont in no doubt that the army felt under pressure 'to improve conditions for Jews'.[56] As far as he was concerned, improvements were under way. He had ordered the construction of a central dining room where families could eat in groups. Moreover, use of the dining hall was to ensure that cooking and storing food in the bedrooms and the hygiene problems arising from this practice would cease. Other innovations included opening a café inside the camp, partly to scupper the effort by some fast-acting business types to run a black-market operation, but mainly to offer leisure facilities and break the monotony of daily life. The café was officially opened with a celebration:

> The Café is a large recreation room used for dancing. Around the sides of the room are small tables at which coffee is served. Originally the

Café was a set of filthy, littered rooms. They cleaned out the filth, took out walls, and did a wonderful job of painting and decorating. The opening was a great success. It was good to see the people of the camp dancing to the music of their own orchestra. Dr. Oleiski made a little speech which is worth repeating. He said that it was incredible to stand in the beautiful hall and watch people, who only six months before were in concentration camps, dancing like normal individuals.[57]

Tensions and Divides

Even after being turned into a Jewish camp, Landsberg remained overcrowded. In the nearby town of Wolfratshausen, the army had requisitioned a former workers' estate in a village setting and turned it into a camp for one thousand Jewish residents. The camp was called Föhrenwald and equipped with everything, including an UNRRA team, but Heymont found it difficult to persuade Landsberg residents to move there.[58] Many were afraid of yet another transport and feared that a change of their circumstances might amount to a deterioration. It was only after a group was taken for an inspection visit to Föhrenwald and could see for themselves that this was as close as they could get to living in a normal environment without leaving the protective umbrella of a camp, that Landsbergers were persuaded to relocate. More than in any other camp, living conditions in Föhrenwald resembled those in civil society. It existed as a Jewish camp until 1957, and was the last of Germany's displaced persons camps to close.

To alleviate overcrowding, Heymont was also ordered to requisition several houses in the town of Landsberg itself. This time problems did not arise from persuading people to move there but from tensions that surfaced between Jews and Germans in the course of the handover. Some buildings had been used by the military and were simply reallocated. Others belonged to Germans who were evicted at short notice and ordered to leave all beds and furniture behind. They were, however, permitted to take some essential household items with them. As the eviction commenced, a large crowd of displaced Jews gathered to watch and soon began to object that the Germans were taking too much. The camp police – staffed by displaced persons – entered the houses that had been vacated to inspect what had been left behind and soon entered other houses that had not yet been vacated or not been requisitioned to take what they thought they required. Other DPs followed their example and joined in the looting and pillaging. Heymont was forced to dispatch soldiers and military police to restore order, yet he found it impossible to condemn outright what had occurred:

The people in the camp have an undying hatred of the Germans. Never, for most part, had they been able to slake their thirst for revenge with some physical act.[59]

Unexpectedly for Heymont, some of the Germans who had been evicted complained about the way in which they had been treated and even visited his office inside the camp – 'this is really bearding the ogre in his den' – to beg special favours and permission to take certain items they had been ordered to leave behind. Although he received them and listened to their requests, he remained unmoved:

The usual story goes that they have found other accommodation but could they please have their stoves or other items. I politely explained that those items cannot be removed because of orders of higher headquarters. I further pointed out that they were not being dragged off to a concentration camp with only the clothing on their backs and that they are not going to see their families starved or gassed or otherwise killed.[60]

When Heymont considered how the newly acquired houses should be allocated, he discovered unexpected divides within the camp population. He would have preferred to rehouse families who, in his view, needed privacy and a chance to lead normal lives. Although he made a recommendation, he left it to the camp committee to decide who should benefit. Since the members of the Landsberg Jewish committee had already managed to find private accommodation for themselves and no longer lived in the camp when the additional houses became available, their judgement would not be obstructed by self-interest. Unexpectedly, an American rabbi by the name of Rosenberg won the day by persuading the committee that the houses should be allocated to religious Jews. It was the first time that Heymont noticed that religious Jews constituted a distinct group within the Jewish residents. Rabbi Rosenberg was affiliated to the Joint Distribution Committee and eager to upstage the Vaad Hatzala with its known support for orthodox Jews among the survivors. The housing incident revealed that the inhabitants of Landsberg had begun to define different Jewish identities:

The Rabbi is not too popular with the general camp population. He is considered by many to be too partial to the religious minority. This antagonism between the religious and non-religious elements is one of the more obvious of the many inner tensions existing within the camp.[61]

Most Landsberg residents were, as we shall see below, secular and

Zionist in their orientation, although a minority were orthodox and determined to lead observant lives. Heymont had to learn how to adjust his own criteria of managing Landsberg to their religiously founded and inflexible expectations as to how they wanted to live. The different perceptions surfaced with regard to the construction of a *Mikvah*. During one of his visits, General Rolfe had discovered it. Neither he nor Heymont knew what it was, other than that it contravened the hygiene code of the camp. In a letter to his wife, Heymont described the incident:

> Going through the camp the other day, Gen. Rolfe found a small sunken pool in one of the condemned wooden barracks. The water in the pool was filthy. When he called my attention to it, I could only plead ignorance. The camp is so large and sprawling that any inspector can occasionally embarrass us by discovering a figurative skeleton in the closet. I never told Gen. Rolfe of all the skeletons that we uncovered.
>
> On investigation, we learned that the sunken pool was a 'Mikvah'. This is a ceremonial bathing pool in which all orthodox women are required to bathe after menstruating and before marriage. I was told that if an orthodox woman failed to use a 'Mikvah' at the prescribed time, she could not have sexual intercourse with her husband until after her next menstrual period. I also learned that the orthodox religious group had hired Germans to construct the 'Mikvah'.
>
> I sent for the leaders of the orthodox group and explained to them that the 'Mikvah' must be emptied at once. Scabies were rampant in the camp, and the use of a common stagnant pool, particularly when it was filled with filthy water, would only help it spread. The orthodox leaders – who are rabbis – absolutely refused to have the 'Mikvah' emptied. They told me that the 'Mikvah' must be filled with the purest water – rain water – and during the recent spell of good weather there had been no opportunity to accumulate fresh rain water. Words went back and forth, but they refused to budge from their position. I threatened to have the 'Mikvah' boarded up as a health hazard. They replied that they would call a strike, if I carried out such a drastic measure.[62]

A compromise was reached. Heymont promised to have showers installed where the women would clean themselves before and after using the ritual bath, while the *Mikvah* itself could remain in use. This incident underlines the determination of religious Jews to live by the rules and laws of their culture. Their regained identity as Jews and human beings manifested itself as insistence to adapt their present environment to their cultural needs, even if this environment was as temporary as a displaced persons camp or as unloved as Germany. Religious orthodoxy constituted a restored identity. Unlike Zionism, it did not depend on resettlement, but could be practised and implemented with immediate effect. Although a minority pursuit in Landsberg – Heymont noted that 'strict orthodoxy fails to attract most of them' – it was a cohesive voice. It was made all the more powerful by the official recognition and material support it received from the Joint, the Vaad Hatzala and other Jewish aid organizations who tended to equate a Jewish future with the continuation of orthodox culture without subscribing to a Zionist agenda and its implicitly secular aims.

The Landsberg Elections

Within a month of his arrival Heymont thought that Landsberg's residents were ready to hold elections for the camp committee. He suggested that individuals should stand as candidates for specific functions on the committee. The outgoing committee, however, opposed this procedure and favoured a system whereby voters opted for a group or party. The winning group would run the committee and allocate duties as it saw fit. After lengthy negotiations, a compromise was reached between fielding individual candidates and corporate lists. The chairman was to be directly elected from a number of named candidates. In addition, each voter could vote for up to six individuals. The six with the highest number of votes would constitute the new camp committee and, between them, allocate responsibilities.[63]

Not everything went to plan. Despite the agreement to nominate candidates for the chairmanship of the committee, the hustings were based on competing groups, not individuals and the skills they had to offer. To that extent, Heymont's lessons in democracy failed. Yet, the elections themselves worked like a tonic, activating residents and encouraging them to take an interest in their future governance, albeit only within the confines of Landsberg. One of Heymont's officers had even constructed ballot-boxes from scraps of wood and canvas, complete with padlocks to secure them. Another had produced a sign in Yiddish, informing the contestants that all electioneering was forbidden within one hundred yards of the polling booths. Nobody, however, adhered to these unfamiliar rules and competing groups continued to canvass and distribute leaflets right in front of the ballot-boxes. One party celebrated the fact that Jews were making history in Landberg. It hired a truck which cruised the camp, loaded with singing and shouting people who rejoiced because Jews were holding their first free election since liberation in the very town where Hitler had been incarcerated and written *Mein Kampf.* History itself seemed to have turned tables in Landsberg.

This mood that a new era had begun to dawn received a special boost when, on the day of the election, Ben-Gurion, the political leader of the Jews in Palestine,[64] made a surprise visit to Landsberg. To be more precise: the camp committee and the residents had known about the visit but Heymont had not. He first noticed that something unusual was under way when hundreds of people began lining the road leading to Munich, carrying flowers and banners, and when the camp itself suddenly blossomed with all kinds of decorations, sparkling and vibrant as he had never seen it before:

> To the people of the camp, he [Ben-Gurion] is God. It seems that he represents all of their hopes of getting to Palestine. . . . I had quite a long talk with Mr. Ben-Gurion and explained the situation in the camp and our problems. I gave him a straight story without glossing over anything. He could not understand why people were reluctant to move after I explained the overcrowded conditions and our efforts to get them to Föhrenwald. We went on a tour of the camp, and I took him to the worst buildings first. On seeing the overcrowding, he asked some of the people why they did not want to move. After listening to their replies he commented to me, 'It is a long and hard struggle to overcome their psychology' . . . Mr Ben-Gurion seems to be a man with a keen insight and a practical approach to problems. When he left, he commented that he clearly understood our problems and remarked, 'In Palestine, we too have comparable problems. A voyage on a boat does not transform people'.[65]

As for Ben-Gurion, his visit to Germany coincided with the recommendation arising from the Harrison Report that a joint Anglo-American committee should focus on the Palestine issue. The committee was to undertake a fact finding mission in 1946. Ben-Gurion, it seems, wanted to do his own fact finding by meeting with DP leaders, assessing the strength of Zionism and addressing displaced persons to win them for the Zionist cause:

> In the coming struggle you will play a decisive role. You are not only needy persons, you are a political force. You must not regard yourself subjectively but rather from the stand point of the Jewish nation. At this moment – the most crucial in the past two thousand years of our history – strange as it may sound, you can accomplish a great deal. You, the direct emissaries of the suffering of our people, are the driving force.[66]

One month later, yet another fact finding mission into DP camps and provisions for their residents, suggested that Zionist fervour was more patchy than Ben-Gurion assumed or hoped. When a representative of HIAS, the Hebrew Immigrant Aid Society, conducted his own survey in Landsberg in November 1945, he asked 4,976 residents where they would like to emigrate to. With 62 per cent (3,112) Palestine emerged as the top choice, followed by the United States with 18 per cent (884), while six other destinations shared the remaining 20 per cent.[67]

The Second Rescue

One of the first changes Major Heymont had introduced in Landsberg was to abolish the system that residents had to apply to the military for passes if they wanted to leave or enter the camp. Instead of a formal process of admission, people were now treated as free citizens who could come and go as they wished. This liberal approach enabled survivors who moved between camps in search of relatives or who remained undecided about where they wanted to go, to stop over in Landsberg or to live there until a destination emerged or their plans became clearer. The open door policy at Landsberg was particularly helpful to Jews from eastern Europe who had begun to enter Germany in ever increasing numbers. Some had survived in hiding, others returned to Poland and were frightened off by anti-Semitic hostilities, others still were newly displaced after being expelled from the Soviet Union where they had sheltered during the Nazi years. Many of these migrants from the East – officially they were called 'infiltrees' – tried to make their way, legally or illegally, to Palestine. Heymont knew that his camp constituted a stopover on the 'underground railway' from Europe to Palestine. He tried to understand why they came, not intervene:

> People from Poland and other parts of Europe keep drifting in. Many come because of the chaotic economic conditions in Europe and because they believe it will be easier to get to Palestine from a DP camp in the U.S. zone. To most European Jews, Palestine represents the solution to all their problems. This was explained to me by a DP girl who works as a clerk for the camp committee. From the age of 15 to 20, she lived within the confines of a German-guarded ghetto in Lithuania. She was fortunate enough to have escaped the horrors of a concentration camp. In 1944, the ghetto was liberated by the Russians. Once liberated, she married her sweetheart whom she had met in the ghetto. Despairing of earning a livelihood or having a normal family life in Lithuania, she and her husband made their way to the American zone when the war ended. Their method of crossing the American-Russian boundary was very simple: they walked through the woods for five kilometers and thus

went around the border control point. They intend to stay in the camp only until they figure out how they can get to Palestine – and start a new life.[68]

At the end of October 1945, Major Heymont received an order from his headquarters to keep his camp closed to all newcomers from eastern Europe. Although at that time, Landsberg was vastly overcrowded and housed 1,900 more people than its stipulated capacity, he refused to consider turning people away who needed help and were still battling against the destructive effects of the Holocaust on their lives:

> What should be done with the newcomers? They can't just be turned away without destination. In addition to worrying about the Jewish camp, I am responsible for the security of the area. I cannot let people just wander around to starve and be reduced to stealing and plundering.[69]

By way of compromise, he suggested that the army should create additional accommodation in 'transient camps' for newcomers. In a letter to his wife, Heymont argued that the army was wrong to limit its support to survivors who had been liberated in their zone of occupation and that it was wrong to rip families apart who had been reunited after survival. In any case, his experiences with the Landsberg residents had taught him that they would know how to circumvent restrictions, take in newcomers against the rules, share their food with them, and supplement their supplies, if need be, through black market activities.[70]

The issue of accommodating newcomers came to a head in early December 1945. Heymont had already been recalled, and Landsberg handed over to UNRRA.[71] On December 5, he received a call from Regimental Headquarters, ordering him to be present in Landsberg on the following day when a top level delegation of generals, including the Chief of Staff of the United States Forces European Theater (USFET), General Walter Bedell Smith, were to visit the camp.[72] It emerged that one of the UNRRA welfare officers, Leo Scrole, had written a scathing letter to General Smith, announcing his resignation and condemning conditions at the camp as hazardous to human health and utterly deplorable. Apparently, Scrole had intended to draw attention to overcrowding and to the need to open new facilities in order to protect the rehabilitation work that had commenced in Landsberg and, more importantly, to allow Jewish refugees to enter the American zone. The episode ended by Scrole withdrawing his resignation.[73] In turning the spotlight onto the changed realities of displaced living and the unexpected pressures arising from additional Jewish migration from eastern Europe, it forced the army to clarify its approach:

> General Smith made one point very clear. In handling the Jewish DPs, the Army had an initial mission of rescue. By that, he meant getting the DPs clothed, fed, housed, and nursed back to health. The next phase was rehabilitation. The second phase covered schooling, vocational training, and recreation. The rescue phase was just about completed and the rehabilitation phase started when the influx from eastern Europe started.[74]

Between the onset of Jewish migration from the East in late 1945 and the end of the British Mandate in Palestine on May 15, 1948 which removed the largest obstacle to resettlement, Jewish residency in the American zone of Germany rose from around 30,000 to near 160,000 in July 1947. The data compiled in tables 4.1 and 4.2 shows that residency in Jewish displaced persons camps reached a high point in May 1947, with the steepest increase after the pogrom in Kielce in June 1946. Between June and July 1947, an additional 25,000 Jews registered in displaced persons camps in the American zone of Germany. Parallel to increased residency in the camps, numbers living 'out of camp' also rose, but at a more modest pace. On April 21, 1947, the Americans declared DP camps in their zone closed to new arrivals, forcing newcomers to either live there illegally and without registration papers, or to try their luck 'out of camp'. Although Jewish refugees, notably from Romania, continued to arrive, policy had been redefined and the American zone no longer constituted a haven, as it had done before. By contrast, the British occupying powers kept their zone closed to so called 'infiltrees' and the number of Jews living in DP camps remained unchanged at just over 11,000.[75] Newcomers could settle in German communities, but would not be entitled to special help. The second rescue, therefore, took place in the American zone of Germany.

Table 4.1: Residency in Jewish Camps
in the US zone of Germany, January–December 1946[76]

Month	Residents	Month	Residents
January	not listed	July	70,216
February	32,848	August	89,455
March	38,756	September	117,287
April	42,660	October	123,467
May	47,392	November	126,980
June	55,562	December	124,572

Table 4.2 *Jewish Residency in and out of camps, US zone of Germany, 1946-1947*

Date	In Camp	Out of Camp	Total
Dec. 31, 1946	124,272	28,231	152,803
March 27, 1947	124,453	29,243	153,696
May 22, 1947	125,110	32,868	157,978
July 7, 1947	121,954	35,890	157,844
Dec. 23, 1947	111,046	33,627	144,673

At the height of the new migration in 1946, the Americans had established 130 DP camps in their zone, some of them mixed but the majority only for Jews. As numbers increased the social composition of the camp populations changed noticeably since most of the new arrivals migrated in family units or were unaccompanied children who had hidden in forests or among the local population. In January 1946, three hundred Jewish children attended schools in displaced persons camps; at the end of the year, 9,800 did so. Teachers and rabbis among the newcomers began to play an active part in rekindling Jewish culture in their new environment. Marriages and births that had already been on the increase after survivors recovered their health and sought to normalise their lives, rose steeply in the newly enlarged and invigorated communities.[77] At the same time, the relative normalisation of daily life in Germany's displaced persons camps created its own problematic adjustments. Simon Schochet, who lived in Feldafing DP camp after his liberation, reports how an increasing number of Jewish young men formed romantic attachments to German women and how office holders among the displaced Jews began to employ Germans inside the camp because they appeared more disciplined and better qualified that other DPs.[78] The longer Jews remained in Germany, the more impatient they became to leave, and to escape their enforced poverty by engaging in black market activities. Although provisions in displaced persons camps were such that nobody went hungry, and model camps such as Landsberg and Feldafing offered a rich educational and cultural life, Jews waited – some of them despondently, others impatiently – to move on.

Resettlement was slow to take off, and, as we have seen, difficult for Jews. On December 22, 1945, President Truman had issued a special directive aimed at easing immigration restrictions. Rather than revising the national quotas that controlled migration into the United States, the directive decreed that unused quotas could be activated retrospectively. Since German quotas had, indeed, not been filled in previous years, the Truman Directive benefited mainly German Jews. It did not offer new choices of emigration to displaced Jews whose national quotas had been exhausted. In 1948, when the United States revised its immigration legislation, preference was given to agricultural workers and manual or craft skills which few of the displaced Jews could claim to possess. Thus, until emigration to Israel became possible on May 15, 1948, the majority of displaced Jews in Germany had nowhere else to go.

By early April 1948, three million displaced persons had been resettled from Germany, among them just 29,000 Jews.[79] By the end of 1948, 25,000 Jews emigrated legally to Israel; 50,000 left the following year.[80] By late 1949, emigration had slowed considerably, and the United States had overtaken Israel as the preferred destination. The Jewish Agency for Palestine estimated Jewish migration from Germany at 100,000, three quarters of it along legal channels, the remainder illegally. Three years after liberation, the gates of Palestine had finally opened, but so had the gates of several other countries, partly in response to international appeals to end displacement and partly as countries sought to secure additional labour in order to boost their economic reconstruction. Most of the coal miners, farm labourers, nurses and domestic servants who were recruited in 1948 were non-Jewish Balts or Poles. In removing the restrictions to go to Palestine, the year 1948 became a turning point also for Jewish survivors who had regained their health and for refugees who had boosted their numbers, because it offered them, for the first time, a choice whether they wanted to leave Germany or stay there, after all.

5

REMAKING JEWISH LIFE
IN POST-WAR GERMANY

Officially, Nazi Germany had been *Judenrein*, 'cleansed of Jews' by mid-1943. Proclamations to this effect emanated from Joseph Goebbels, the Nazi Minister for People's Enlightenment and Propaganda, and across Germany from cities, towns and villages where Jews had lived or where Jewish communities had existed in the past. When deportations from Nazi Germany began in October 1941, 163,000 German Jews, 30 per cent of those who had lived there in January 1933, remained. Nearly 300,000 had managed to emigrate, 70,000 had died in the intervening years. Most of those who had been unable or unwilling to leave were middle-aged or older, and 60 per cent were women.[1] Initially, forced labour had offered a stay of execution, but racism soon won over economic pragmatism and the last major round of deportations in 1943 emptied Germany's factories of its remaining Jewish workforce. And yet, in 1944, the Reichs Association for Jews in Germany, the state-controlled organization to register and administer all Jews who lived there, reported a membership of 15,028.[2] Who were these Jews? Moreover, deportations of Jews continued until the very edge of defeat, the last one destined for Theresienstadt in March 1945. Who were these Jews who were rounded up on the eve of liberation, and how did they, how did any Jews, survive inside the Third Reich?

Who is a German Jew?

One of the earliest pieces of information on the presence of Jews in Germany after the Second World War originated in Berlin. It suggests that six thousand German and eight hundred displaced Jews lived in the city at the time (table 5.1). It also casts light on the precarious survival some had managed inside the Third Reich since it continues to use Nazi classifications. While Jewish religious law regards a person as Jewish who is born to a Jewish mother, the Nazis decreed that any person with three or more Jewish grandparents was to be classified as *Volljude*, a 'full Jew'. Individuals with fewer Jewish grandparents were deemed to be of mixed race, *Mischlinge*, and referred to as half-Jews, quarter-Jews, one-eighth Jews and so on. Although *Mischlinge* were harassed by discrimination and could become victims of persecution, so called 'full Jews' bore the brunt of the Holocaust. Within this group, individuals who were married to non-Jewish partners could escape deportations. Many of the deportees in 1943 and later belonged to this group and had been protected by their marriage to an 'Aryan' as the Nazis called a person of presumably German descent. Mixed marriages, as table 5.1 documents, fell into two categories. In childless marriages or in a marriage where the children were raised as Jews, the Jewish partner had to wear the Yellow Star. In Nazi terminology, these Jews were *Sternträger*. Marriages where the children had been baptised and were raised as Christians were classified as 'privileged' and the Jewish partner did not have to wear a star. Table 5.1 shows that in September 1945, 60 per cent of the German Jews who were known to live in Berlin had survived inside the Third Reich in mixed marriages because their partners were not Jewish.

Table 5.1 The Jewish population of Berlin in September 1945[3]

Jews by status	Overall	%
'Full Jews'	6,000	88
Of these		
Released from concentration camp	1,155	19.5*
Survived in hiding in Berlin	1,060	18.5
Married to non-Jew and had to wear the Yellow Star	2,000	33
Married to non-Jews whose children were raised as 'Aryans'; did not have to wear the Yellow Star ('privileged')	1,600*	29
Non-German displaced Jews, mostly from Poland	800	12
Total Jewish residency	**6,800**	**100**

* among these, 100 were children under the age of 14

Demographic data such as that presented in table 5.1 highlights two major problems confronting the return of Jewish life to Germany after the Holocaust. The first of these pertains to numbers and the massive destruction of lives and communities that had taken place. The second of these problems pertains to the Jews themselves, their different experiences of survival in the camps or inside the Third Reich and their relative proximity to their German environment as marriage partners on the one hand, with debts of gratitude to the non-Jewish spouse whose refusal to divorce had saved them, and on the other hand as former deportees and concentration camp prisoners, who had lost their liberty. In addition, displaced Jews who found themselves trapped in Germany had their own experiences of the Holocaust and survival, their own assumptions about what it should mean to live as a Jew, and their own reservations about mixed marriages anywhere, especially in Germany. In 1946, when some German Jews began to return from exile, they brought with them yet another package of expectations; how they might live as Jews in Germany again and hopes that after the Holocaust, anti-Semitism might have been relegated to the past once and for all. Whatever Jewish life could be after the Holocaust, it could not restore the communities and culture that had been destroyed, and it was built by very different people – Jews from different backgrounds, with different experiences of survival and a variety of assumptions of 'who was a Jew' and what leading a Jewish life might mean. The return of Jewish life after the war built on a complex mix of experiences and people. As Lutz Niethammer put it:

> It is important to understand the vastly different experiences and biographies of Jews in Germany at the time. I mention only key words: there were the assimilated Jews who had been exposed to persecution while living in mixed marriages. There are emigrants who returned without having themselves suffered persecution. There are Holocaust survivors who, so to speak, narrowly missed the gas chambers by their own wit and survival skills or merely by chance. Most of these are non-Germans, the vast majority Eastern Europeans. There were individuals whose personality has been strengthened by their experiences of survival. And there are others who are completely traumatised and ruined by the experience of survival.[4]

Numbers and Demography

Any attempt to arrive at an accurate picture of how many Jews lived in Germany when the Second World War had ended, is hampered by the fact that, as we have seen earlier, Jews were not identified as such in the statistical records of liberated concentration camps but registered by nationality. This practice only changed in November 1945 and then only in the US zone of occupation as reports began to include a column headed Jews where earlier only Poles, Lithuanians or Germans might have been listed. Although some Jewish communities had been founded – or re-founded – as soon as the war was over, none published detailed statistics, and there was no central agency to collect data. The first general survey was undertaken by the Committee of Liberated Jews in Bavaria. It estimated the number of German Jews as 15,000, of whom 14,000 were thought to have survived inside the Third Reich and 1,000 returned from concentration camps. This survey also revealed that in addition to German Jews, 53,000 displaced Jews lived in Germany at the time, most of them in the US zone of occupation, the rest outside camps in towns and cities (table 5.2). In the French zone, overall numbers were very small, but included a higher proportion of Jews than elsewhere who lived 'out of camp'.

Table 5.2 Jewish Residency in Germany, September 1945[5]

Germany	Assembly Centres	Cities and Towns	Totals
Three Western Zones	34,423	34,046	68,469
US Zone	26,643	27,776	54,419
British Zone	7,400	5,150	12,550
French Zone	380	1,120	1,500

A similar picture emerged from the first full census in post-war Germany. Conducted on October 29, 1946 in all four zones of occupation, it showed that 156,705 Jews were living in the country, 112,013 of them in camps and 44,692 in German society.[6] Of those living 'out of camp', 63 per cent (28,011) were based in the US zone, 14 per cent (6,321) in the British zone, 17 per cent (7,585) in Berlin and 7 per cent (2,275) in the French zone of occupation.[7] As Jewish refugees arrived from eastern Europe, the numerical discrepancy between the US zone that accepted them and the other zones that did not, increased, as did the imbalance of numbers living in camps and out of camps.[8] Only after DP camps were declared closed to new arrivals on April 21, 1947 did refugees also settle in towns and cities. However, as shown earlier, these migration gains in the interim between liberation and resettlement were largely temporary. As resettlement opportunities presented themselves, 60 per cent of German Jews and 80 per cent of displaced Jews who had lived in Germany in the immediate post-war years, left to build a life elsewhere. The mix of German-Jewish and displaced Jewish residency, however, defined the Jewish life that was to emerge inside Germany.

First doubts about a Jewish presence in Germany surfaced early. In its 1945 issue, the *American Jewish Yearbook* recounted the vast destruction that had occurred, but also suggested that the numbers, low as they were, included 'half-Jews' and others whose Jewish credentials might be doubtful:

> Only 8,000 Jews are believed to have remained in the country which had some 224,000 in May 1939 and 525,000 before 1933. In addition, there are several thousand half-Jews living in the larger cities. It is reported that 6,000 Jews, half-Jews and those married to non-Jews, reside in Berlin, some 400 in Munich, 200 in Cologne, 87 in Frankfurt, and smaller numbers in several other cities. Some 265,000 German Jews emigrated before and during the first two years of the war to all parts of the globe.[9]

Despite the presence of some Jews, the devastation of lives and communities was enormous. In Munich, 130 of formerly 12,000 Jews returned. In Frankfurt, 158 Jews survived in mixed marriages and 420 returned from concentration camps. At the end of August 1945, 650 German Jews lived there, down from 30,000 in 1933.[10] In Karlsruhe, 90 German Jews were registered and 20 in nearby Mannheim. In 1933, the Jewish population of Leipzig had numbered 13,030; in May 1945 just 31. The last deportation train with 169 Jews and 'mixed race' persons left Leipzig on February 15, 1945.[11] By the autumn of 1945, the number of German Jews in the city had risen to 86, but no more than 24 of these had belonged to the Jewish community in the past.[12] Who were these Jews and who was a Jew in these uncertain times? Some, as the data on residency suggests, were displaced persons who lived among Germans in German towns. Most, however, were Germans who had survived inside the Third Reich and the handful who had returned from the camps. Nine out of ten German Jews were survivors who had not been deported or imprisoned because they lived in a mixed marriage. Many of them also had their children baptised. By any measure of Jewishness, they led assimilated lives.[13] Many had been turned into Jews by the Nazis but continued to regard themselves as Jews after their liberation. As a group, they played a leading role in founding or relaunching Jewish communities after the Second World War. In his detailed analysis of rebuilt Jewish communities, Harry Maor documented how important these survivors from inside the Third Reich had been in remaking Jewish life in Germany. He also showed how distant from traditional religious practices these founders were with their German spouses and baptised children, and how divided these communities became as displaced Jews disapproved of the assimilation among German Jews, while German Jews tried to obstruct eastern European Jews after they took up formal membership and sought leadership positions and influence in the communities.[14]

Despite their uncertain credentials, Jewish communities played an essential role in supporting German-Jewish concentration camp survivors who returned from the camps and had nowhere to go. Some had been deported at the very end of the war and may have had a home to return to. Most of the other deportees did not. Steffen Held, for instance, expected the Americans to help him when he returned from Buchenwald to Leipzig in May 1945 but was told that, as a German, he should approach the German authorities.[15] With individual and local variations, the same story happened over and over again when German-Jewish concentration camp survivors returned home. In the eyes of the Allied occupiers and their military governments, they were German nationals and no different from the rest of the population. In the first weeks after liberation, some Allied commanders and military government officers arranged special support for Jews. As soon as German administrators had been appointed to replace their Nazi predecessors, all local matters including care arrangements for Jews were placed into German hands. Of course, the wartime Allies had immediately banned all Nazi organizations and manifestations of Nazi ideology. They did not, however, reverse the impoverishment of Jews by rescinding the Nazi laws and decrees that had underpinned it. Therefore, the homes, businesses, financial and personal assets of German Jews remained in the hands of those who had taken them. Bank accounts that had been frozen in the 1930s remained frozen after liberation. Not until the late 1940s and early 1950s, when restitution legislation had been passed, could individuals attempt to reclaim what they had lost. Even then, claims often took years to settle. Priority, it appears, was given to collective restitution as the Israeli and German governments of the day, as well as Jewish organizations, favoured the formula of paying compensation to the Jewish people as a whole, while individuals had to pursue their claims through the courts. When German-Jewish survivors returned, they remained as dispossessed as they had been when they were deported and had to begin again from scratch.

Meanings of Homecoming

As soon as the concentration camps had been liberated, survivors were, in theory at least, free to return home. In practice, several obstacles had to be overcome. Thus, transport had to be arranged. In camps like Buchenwald or Belsen, this was largely left to individuals adept at commandeering lorries or lucky in hitching lifts. Two of the survivors mentioned earlier, Josef Warscher and Anita Lasker-Wallfisch, left their former concentration camps in this way. In Theresienstadt, where most German-Jewish survivors were liberated, applications to join a transport home had to be submitted to the camp committee that was still functioning, although no system existed to assemble transports and bring people home. In some cases, cities dispatched lorries to fetch their citizens, in other cases, Jewish communities sent for them.

Homecomings, like experiences of survival, varied between localities and individuals. Common to all was that it entailed a return to the original place of humiliation. Some, who had families they could rejoin, found the Holocaust experience had created new personal distances that could not be bridged by easy communication. Often, the challenges of survival had distorted behaviour to such an extent that norms and conventions had to be relearned. All German Jews returned impoverished and remained so. It is here that Jewish communities offered a lifeline to survivors who would otherwise have ended up in public hostels for the destitute. This homecoming without welcome compelled survivors once again to draw on the reservoir of personal resilience and determination that had given them strength in the past. The homecoming of German-Jewish survivors was marred by disappointment and daily hardship, interspersed with hope. The four narratives presented below show how these individuals experienced their homecoming. Although every homecoming was personal and unique, each tells a shared story of renewed exclusion and unexpected hardship.

Return to a Different World

Renata Laqueur had been deported together with her husband from Amsterdam, where the family had sought refuge from Germany, to Westerbork concentration camp in Holland on November 3, 1943. On March 15, 1944 she was deported to Bergen-Belsen and liberated in mid-April 1945 from one of the death trains that had been dispatched from there. Although she had nursed her husband through various illnesses, including typhoid and depression during their incarceration in Westerbork and Belsen, she had exhausted her strength just as survival appeared to be within reach:

> I could no longer work at the end of my time in the camp, I was completely drained and was suffering from hunger oedema. The only thing I could manage was to do guard duty at night between the piles of corpses. In return, I received an extra ladle of watery soup.[16]

On the train from Belsen, she fell ill with typhoid and this time, it was her husband who found the strength to nurse her back to health after they had been found and taken to Zeitheim, a former slave labour camp for

Poles near Dresden. She herself attributed her recovery also to her fierce motivation to pull through and return home:

> I did want to stay alive, I wanted to go home. I refused to die at this late stage! I had fought hard to get through everything for too long to die just like that. I had to succeed and live.[17]

Finally, on June 22, 1945, a military truck drove Renata Laqueur and her husband to Holland where they remained for one week in a displaced persons camp operated by the American army. From the camp, she phoned home and was told that everything was fine.[18] The parental home still stood. Her parents and her sister were alive and awaiting her return. Nazi racial classifications had divided the Laqueur family. It had singled out Renata Laqueur for deportation because she was married to a Jewish partner in a childless marriage. Her parents and sister, by contrast, were treated as 'privileged' Jews – possibly since her father was a distinguished scientist. Yet, her brother was deported and perished in the Holocaust. When Renata Laqueur returned to the home of her family, she found no common ground with them and felt as if she belonged to a different world:

> On 26 July 1945, I sat in our house on the large sofa; I sat there in my long brown trousers which I had been wearing day in day out for years and in the brown Hitler Youth shirt I had taken – organized – in Tröbitz. Paul [her husband] asked whether his books and his flute were still there. I asked my sister whether my clothes were still there. No conversation would develop.[19]

Returning to her family and her home, Renata Laqueur realised that her experiences could not be shared and also that she herself had been changed and distorted to such an extent that normal living and daily conventional behaviour had become meaningless. She had internalised too well the skills of survival that had been essential inside the camp. In a normal civic setting, they had lost all validity and amounted to versions of criminality:

> When I returned from the concentration camp, I had to submit myself to some kind of re-education. I needed this therapy because I had become too perfect in 'organizing' things. In the camp and even after liberation, I took what I could get. I was an expert in thieving, in lying and in deceit. In the upside-down world of the concentration camp, the daughter from a good middle class home had to live by the law of survival, and I am proud that I have managed to do this and managed to survive.[20]

The Family is Home

Martha Glass had been deported to Theresienstadt in 1943 and liberated
there in May 1945. She had grown up in Hamburg and trained as a singer
and concert pianist before her marriage in 1903 to Hermann Glass who
owned and ran a clothing store in the city. Martha Glass raised her two
children and worked on a part-time basis testing and demonstrating
Steinway pianos. The couple were deported together, but Hermann Glass
died shortly after arrival. One of the daughters managed to emigrate to the
United States, the other was married to a German and enjoyed the
precarious protection afforded to the Jewish partners in mixed marriages.
Throughout her time in Theresienstadt Martha Glass kept a diary,
recording details of living conditions in the camp and her own experiences
there. As the end of the war drew nearer, she became more and more
impatient for news from her children and oppressed by the monotony of
daily hardship. 'One day is much the same as the next one, spent doing
extremely rough housework and darning socks. It is already the 17th [of
March] and I have heard nothing at all from the children. I am very
concerned.'[21] When fighting stopped, liberation seemed to bypass her and
other German Jews:

> Finally, the killing has ended and we can expect to be liberated after
> two-and-three-quarter years of imprisonment. It seems like a miracle to
> escape from this hell alive. First the French, then the Dutch and then
> the Czechs have been collected to be taken home. The Czechs staged a
> massive parade through the town with flags in their national colours,
> red, blue and white. Their excitement is without limits. We poor
> German Jews are at a big disadvantage and, for the time being, have no
> idea where to turn or where to go. I have to wait for news from the
> children who, I pray to God, are well and I will hear from them soon!!![22]

On May 6, 1945, the Council of Elders published a proclamation to
announce that the International Red Cross had assumed responsibilities for
Theresienstadt. The proclamation also stressed that work remained
compulsory: 'Everyone must continue to work. A person who refuses to do
so will not be assigned to a transport home.'[23] It was an eerie interim. A
few days after the Council's proclamation of 'business as usual', an
American car arrived to collect its chairman, Rabbi Leo Baeck. The US
army had issued instructions to seek out prominent persons and rescue
them immediately.[24] As an ordinary person, Martha Glass enjoyed no such
privileges. Moreover, postal services, although promised by the Council of
Elders, remained non-existent while arrangements to collect survivors were
left to respective governments. For German Jews, the return home had,

therefore, been delegated to a public authority that had ceased to function. Although military governments began to operate in their respective zones of occupation, they focussed on displaced persons whom they found there and did not make provisions for the return home of German Jews. Finally and without co-ordination, transport was sent to fetch Jews back, partly at the behest of Jews who had survived inside the Third Reich and partly in response to pressure from American Jewish chaplains who felt concentration camp survivors should be brought home. Theresienstadt was finally emptied in mid August 1945 when the Czech government reclaimed the town. Martha Glass left there on August 10, 1945. A direct train – the first ever to operate on this route – took her and seven hundred other survivors to Berlin.

Circumstance and coincidence, not choice, determined her place for a new beginning. At the end of June, she had received post from her daughter in Berlin and could have applied to go there. Her mind, however, was made up to return to Hamburg and 'salvage' what she could of her former belongings. Because the promised lorry to Hamburg never materialised, she was left stranded.[25] At this point, she resolved to also register for Berlin and take whatever transport arrived first. About a week before leaving Theresienstadt, Martha Glass heard from her daughter in America. Before returning home, she had learned that her children were well, that her daughter's home in Berlin had not been destroyed and that she, a 'mother blessed by God',[26] might find a new beginning amongst her family, albeit somewhere where she had never lived before.

No Longer a Home Town

Gerty Spiess returned to Munich in August 1945 on one of the last trucks to leave Theresienstadt. Most cities had already sent transport to bring their Jews back. Berlin, Hamburg and Munich were the last to do so. Waiting to be collected for a future that seemed without meaning, she nearly lost hope and felt abandoned. When the lorry finally arrived, her excitement was tinged with anxiety and disappointment:

> Naturally, Munich was Munich – for three years I had boasted about it. Munich would send the best-looking vehicles. I did not find them. No bus anywhere in sight, no company car. She [a woman who told her Munich had sent transport] must have been dreaming last night? I sat down on a turned-over wooden barrel and absentmindedly noticed an old truck, which I had passed several times. Unconcerned, my gaze fixed on its back. I had read its number plate a few times backward and forward. Suddenly, I jumped up: Munich!

What – they had sent such a wreck?! Was that all they could do for us? Not enough that they had cast us out! What did we know of the extent of the destruction at home – Munich was Munich and had to send nice vehicles. What would the others say when they saw – this wreck!

But then the preparations started. I went to the central drugstore and told them that as of today I would no longer come to work. Standing in the door, my boss – a pretty blonde woman from Prague – looked at me: 'Ah, did Munich come?' She embraced me, and we cried together. I made the rounds to all the offices. And in between I packed my few belongings. I did not want to take my two towels, but my boss said: 'Take everything, there is much poverty in your homeland.' She knew better than I; the Czechs had kept in touch with their gendarmes. She mixed a moisturizer for me and gave me a bag of sugar for the way home. Oh, the sugar. I had no idea then that I had a tiny granddaughter waiting at home who had hardly seen sugar since she was born.[27]

It took a few more days until the transport back to Munich was ready to leave Theresienstadt. Very early in the morning, Gerty Spiess made her way to the point of departure, only to find that most of her travel companions had waited there all night – she thought she had heard a lot of noise and shouting – and had claimed their seats. There was no more room. Together with an elderly couple and another latecomer, she seemed destined to be left behind until someone put a ladder to the luggage trailer and urged her and her unexpected companions to climb up and squat among the suitcases. This is how she travelled:

I felt a jolt, those left behind waved and the ones from Berlin shouted 'Have a good trip! Goodbye!' I did not know how I felt. I was on my way.[28]

On the luggage trailer they tried to keep clear of the slipping cases and make the best of an uncomfortable journey. They drove through Prague and, for the first time since her deportation, Gerty Spiess saw a normal city with houses, streetcars, trees and people walking at leisure. When they reached the military checkpoints outside Prague, the Russians, on their side, staged an intensive inspection of travel documents and luggage while the Americans just laughed the transport through – 'keep going'. After a day's travelling, the group arrived in Neustadt on the river Waldnaab, a small town in Bavaria where the Americans had prepared reception facilities and where Gerty Spiess had her first encounter with the normal living conditions that had ended for her three years earlier:

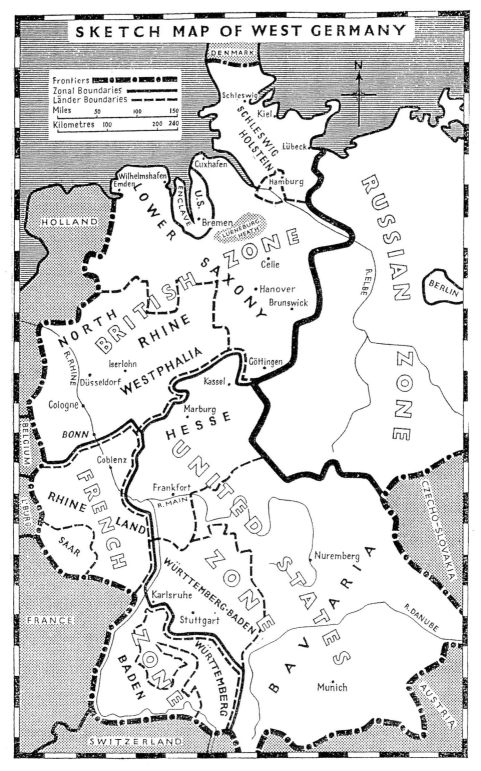

1. Sketch map of occupied Germany and zonal boundaries after August 1945.

2. Death march near
Dachau concentration
camp, April 1945.
The photograph was taken
by German bystanders
when the march passed
through the Nördliche
Münchner Strasse in the
Bavarian village of
Grünwald near Munich.

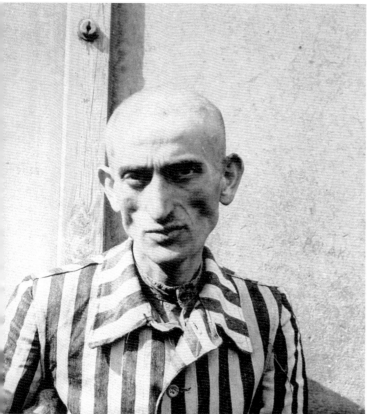

3. A survivor of Dachau
on the day of liberation,
29 April 1945.

4. A group of American editors and publishers on an inspection visit to Dachau at the invitation of General Eisenhower, May 1945.

5. British soldiers stand guard after liberation outside the closed gates of Bergen-Belsen, April 1945.

6. Orphaned child survivors at Bergen-Belsen DP camp with AJDC relief worker Sally Wideroff, after autumn 1945.

7. Joint representatives, including AJDC Executive Vice-Chairman Moses A. Leavitt, visit a clothing workshop in Feldafing DP camp, after 1945.

8. Group portrait of a Talmud Torah, a religious primary school for boys, in Feldafing DP camp, 1946 or 1947.

9. German police preparing a raid against Jewish shops (whose shutters are shown closed) in pursuit of alleged black market activities in Munich, May 1949.

10. Desecration of a Jewish cemetery in Frankfurt am Main, 1947.

11. One of the buildings handed back to the Jewish Community in Frankfurt, 1945.

12. Jewish Police in the DP camp Zeilsheim near Frankfurt.

13. Resettlement from Zeilsheim to Israel, 1948.

14. Passover 1946 or 1947: distribution of *matzot* in Frankfurt.

15. Jewish Kindergarten in Frankfurt, 1948. The boy at the front in the dark pullover is Solomon Korn, who was, at the time of writing, chair of the Jewish Community in Frankfurt and vice-president of the Council for Jews in Germany.

I discovered that the world had not died. Life went on, and it went on inside of me. The thread had not been cut. Americans lifted us out of the truck, they gave us food, we were honoured guests of the city. Indeed, we even sat at tables and carefully showed each other that we had not forgotten how to behave in company. The straw was fresh and clean and the floor on which it was spread, polished. We slept deeply and undisturbed by bugs. Next morning – it was a Sunday – I went down to the small river. A farmer's wife, dressed in peasant dress, passed me, slowly, solemnly, without hurry or fear; she did not turn to look at me, though she must have known – she walked on.[29]

At the stopover, Gerty Spiess and the others in her group were asked to remove the Yellow Star from their outer garments. Although it had been imposed by the Nazis and aimed at humiliating and stigmatising Jews, Gerty Spiess had come to regard it as a 'medal of distinction' and did not see the point of taking it off now, at the very moment in time when it could signal to the outside word which she was about to enter, her Jewish identity and her survival. Despite these reservations, she removed her Yellow Star before continuing on her journey. When her transport reached Munich, she had, outwardly at least, once again become invisible as a Jew:

Now even we latecomers were given a place to sit. We got into the truck. Today it's all the way to Munich! The sun burned mercilessly. My moisturizer made the rounds. There were a few among us who had left Munich only four months ago. One woman assured me that my apartment had still been standing then. It was all the same to me. Apartment, no apartment – how ridiculous! What was wrong with people that they cared about things like that. Old cities, destroyed train stations, endless highways – a glowing sunset – Munich! What was that? Rubble, debris, ruins! Certainly, one had heard all sorts of things. But that it would look like this? . . . And that it could happen to me! And that, perhaps, I did care after all? What did Munich have to do with me? After all, had I not – with a calm heart – reckoned on never seeing it again? And now? [Ibid.]

When they pulled into the Kaulbachstrasse, Gerty Spiess noticed people waving to them. When the truck stopped, it was immediately surrounded. Relatives and friends found and embraced one another. Since she had no family or friends left, nobody had come to greet her. By way of welcome, the group was led to a house and into a dining room where tables were laid and decorated with flowers.[30] Most survivors were too nervous to eat. Everything suggested that they had finally left the camp behind them. The toilets were clean and fitted with locks. Nobody banged against the door trying to get in. The beds were covered with white sheets and there was one bed per person. It was a different world.

Later, Gerty Spiess made no attempt to look for her former home. Her return to normality did not involve going back to the life she had been forced to abandon, but forward to a different life as a writer with a mission to speak of her experiences and of the Holocaust. This personal sense of mission helped her to overcome a new sense of dejection when she realised how well dressed and cared-for the people looked whom she met after her return – the Germans in the street and also the Jews who had survived inside Germany and who now came to listen in horror and grief to the narratives of the survivors. Of the two sets of people, the Germans in their good clothes and solid shoes were more unsettling because she felt the urge to ask them the question that burned inside her: 'Were you one of them?'

Getting Back Without Getting Home

When Hedwig Geng returned from Theresienstadt to Munich, the plethora of paperwork that in 1942 had compelled her to hand over her savings, abandon her possessions and vacate her home, remained in force despite the collapse that had occurred since then.[31] She had nothing to return to. Her daughter lived abroad, and she had no other family in Munich. Like other German-Jewish Holocaust survivors, Hedwig Geng would have been abandoned to public welfare, had it not been for the provisions of food and shelter by the fledgling Jewish communities which, as we shall see in more detail below, extended a lifeline to survivors. After her liberation and return to Munich, Hedwig Geng depended on this lifeline and recorded in her letters the kind of existence it offered.

The transport from Theresienstadt to Munich took Hedwig Geng to the old folks home in the Kaulbachstrasse which served as a reception centre and refuge for survivors. She was just 54 years old when she became a resident. Initially, she shared a room with six other women; after three months, that number was reduced to five, and in February 1946 to four. She craved some privacy, something she had not known since her deportation, but found herself trapped in the hostel-like conditions because life outside seemed impossible without help:

> Week after week I am promised that I shall be allocated a private room without the need to share. The problem, you see, is that if I move out of the old folks home, I have to look after myself. Quite apart from the fact that this would be massively expensive and labour intensive, I would not

even know how to go about it and where to get fuel and heating materials in the winter.[32]

Provisions inside the shared room were sparse. Although each occupant had her own bed, there was no other furniture until December 1945 when one of the beds was moved out and replaced with a table and chair. There was no wardrobe, no chest of drawers or other enclosed space to store any belongings. Six months after her return, an acquaintance lent Hedwig Geng a wardrobe with a full-length mirror door. For the first time in years, she could store her few belongings securely and enjoy some kind of normality. As a special Christmas treat in 1945, she was allowed to borrow a radio that belonged to another resident but was not needed at the time. The sound of the radio attracted neighbours and friends who crowded in to listen, turning Hedwig Geng's room, for a brief moment at least, into a home:

> Christmas passed quietly for me. The warden Dr. Max let me have Thekla's radio after all. We had a very good programme, and it is so uplifting to hear pleasant voices and normal communication. And it seems that we are being offered especially enjoyable treats. Since the country has been so devastated, they are trying hard to guide people's heart and soul into a positive direction. We Jews had our radios taken from us on the Day of Atonement in 1939, they were just grabbed from our homes and never seen again. Therefore, listening to the radio is for us a completely new pleasure. How can I put it? When I turn the radio on in the evening, one by one other residents come along on tip-toe in order to listen a little. Some enter the room, others stay outside the door. At Christmas, all my various friends came in, one after the other, to offer their good wishes and present me with a little gift.[33]

Hedwig Geng accepted, pragmatically and without undue disappointment, the rudimentary living conditions. Theresienstadt had taught her to attach less value to material things and make the best of the new life she had gained. Although the old folks home provided nothing by way of personal comfort, residents were entitled to receive, in addition to heated accommodation and regular meals, parcels containing food, cigarettes, soap and other 'luxuries'. Such parcels were provided from October 1945 onwards by the AJDC.[34] They enabled Hedwig Geng and others like her to upgrade their lifestyle a little. Recipients could, for example, exchange some of the cigarettes or coffee for everyday items such as shoes, warm coats, blankets, clothing that had been taken from them and that money could not buy at the time. While Hedwig Geng appreciated that living in the old folks home protected her from some of the hardship prevailing in contemporary German society, her account also shows that the special provisions fell far short of making up for the losses she and others had incurred at the hands of the Nazis. Although she could offer real coffee by way of hospitality to the friends who visited her in her shared room, she only owned one cup from which they could drink it.

Her sense of relative well-being, compared with the devastated Germany around her, did not extend to the management of the old folks home, and the care taken there of Holocaust survivors. Inside the home, she felt, her needs were ignored and Holocaust survivors expected to put up with intolerable overcrowding and neglect. After several months of requesting improvements, she did what older, frailer and less determined survivors were unable to do: she aired her complaints publicly. In a letter to her family, she recounted what happened:

> At the moment, I am campaigning throughout the home that residents should no longer permit themselves to be exploited by the administration. We concentration camp survivors (*K-Zler*) have become something like a badge of merit that others use to enrich themselves. I have threatened to have photographs taken and the pictures copied and distributed if our rooms are not re-decorated and furnished properly. Miraculously, a couple of photographers turned up the very next day, asked how we were doing, and were horrified about the conditions we had to live in. My room mate Mrs. Schülein came up trumps and did not hold back with complaints. Then the photographers actually took pictures of our room and in particular of my bed. They said the pictures would be used in American films. Everybody is astounded how I make these things happen, like an innocent little white lamb. The administration and the culprits are pulling long faces because they can no longer persist with their diffidence. Bit by bit, I have received all the things I wanted, and I did not even have to bribe anyone with special gifts. The best thing of all is that I do not really care, nothing gets me worked up any more. It is all nothing but theatre.[35]

The Onset of Jewish Communities after the Holocaust

Jewish communities after the Holocaust emerged in a similar mode of self-help, initiated by the German Jews who had survived inside the Third Reich. Buchenwald had only just been liberated the day before when, on April 11, 1945, a group of thirty applied to the Americans who had just taken Cologne, for permission to hold religious services. Two weeks later, they met in the air raid shelter beneath the ruined liberal synagogue and founded post-war Germany's first Jewish community. Similar developments unfolded in other towns where German-Jewish communities had existed before they were destroyed by the Nazis, and where some German Jews remained to venture a new start. It was an anxious start. On the one hand, many believed that Germany 'had been turned into a graveyard where life can never again flourish and where human beings cannot live'.[36] On the other hand, having suffered as Jews, the founders who, for the most part, had not been active in a Jewish community in the past, now accepted the identity that the Nazis had forced upon them. In initiating the return of Jewish communities, they wanted to reinstate the right of holding religious services in public rather than in secret and behind closed doors. They also wanted to shape a public voice for Jews inside the Germany that was to emerge.

Not everyone who had survived inside the Third Reich chose to support a Jewish community afterwards. Based on data collected by the Central Committee for Liberated Jews in the US Zone, Harry Maor shows that six to eight thousand of the 15,000 who constituted the remnant of German Jews in May 1945 took up membership.[37] Jewish men who were married to non-Jewish women were more likely to do so than Jewish women married to non-Jewish men, although according to Jewish religious law, only the offspring of the latter unions would be recognised as Jews.

The German-Jewish founders were joined by survivors of concentration camps, returning exiles and by displaced Jews who preferred to live out of camp. At the end of 1945, ninety Jewish communities existed throughout Germany. Between them they had just over 20,000 members. A handful of communities, such as Weiden or Hof in northern Bavaria, were new ventures that had been founded by displaced Jews in the vicinity of residential camps. The town of Fürth, also in Bavaria, could look back on a distinguished German-Jewish history but the community that re-emerged there in 1945 was run by displaced Jews. In most cases, however, the return of Jewish communities involved German and displaced Jews, the former as founders and initiators, the latter as members in search of a Jewish context for their life outside DP camps.

In 1946 and 1947, when Jewish migration boosted residency numbers temporarily, community life in Germany included an extensive network of Jewish orthodox institutions and facilities, which had no precedence in German history, remained quite separate from the German-Jewish renewal and disappeared in the course of resettlement. Bavaria, the main destination for Jews fleeing from eastern Europe, recorded a larger Jewish population in 1946 than before 1933. The region boasted 59 religious schools for 3,116 pupils up to the age of fourteen, 14 rabbinical seminaries for 1,515 students and a rabbinical assembly of 57 rabbis, all of these supported by Vaad Hatzala. In addition, Vaad Hatzala funded 24 kosher kitchens in towns and cities and supplied religious articles including prayer shawls, prayer books, candles and foodstuff for Jewish festivals.[38]

By and large, the return of Jewish communities after 1945 involved German Jews and displaced Jews. Table 5.3 reviews the situation for March 1949, a time when the main thrust of resettlement had already happened and when the closure of displaced persons camps had persuaded most of their remaining residents to live in German towns which already had a Jewish community they could join.[39] Regional variations were considerable. In Bavaria, more than 90 per cent of community members at the time were displaced Jews. In the Soviet zone, there were none. In Bavaria, Hesse and Württemberg, the regions that were located in the American zone of occupation and whose border had been open for refugees from eastern Europe, displaced Jews outnumbered German Jews. In the other zones of occupation, including Berlin where the borders had remained closed, Jewish communities in March 1949 were predominantly German-Jewish, in the Soviet zone exclusively so. All in all, close to 11,000 of the 21,000 community members at the time were displaced Jews who stayed on.

Table 5.3 German Jews and Displaced Jews in Jewish Communities, by Region[40]

Region	Members	German Jews	%	DP Jews	%
Baden*	600	300	50.0	300	50.0
Bavaria	4,800	300	6.3	4,500	93.7
Berlin	7,000	5,000	71.4	2,000	28.6
Hamburg	1,300	910	70.0	390	30.0
Hesse	2,005	526	29.2	1,479	73.8
Lower Saxony	775	594	76.6	181	23.4
North Rhine-Westfalia	1,907	1,454	86.2	453	23.8
Rhineland Palatinate	373	323	87	50	13
Schleswig-Holstein	295	173	58	122	42
Württemberg*	1,441	265	18.4	1,176	81.6
Soviet Zone	1,149	1,149	100	nil	nil
Overall	21,645	10,994	51	10,651	49

* Prior to the creation of a Land (autonomous region), Baden was located in the French zone, Württemberg in the American zone.

Self-Help and Abandonment

The composition of community membership demonstrates that after the Holocaust, Jewish life in Germany could not replicate or reinstate the German-Jewish culture that had been destroyed. With less than 11,000 German Jews registered as community members compared to half a million in 1933, there could be no continuity. Indeed, only the influx of displaced Jews ensured that some kind of Jewish life could continue at all. Moreover, the German Jews who founded communities again in 1945 were confronted with the unexpected challenge that there was very little material assistance from public bodies, leaving survivors, in particular those who had lost everything, dependent on welfare support. Since German-Jewish survivors were essentially treated as Germans, Jewish communities and their first leaders found themselves in the vanguard of assisting members to alleviate hardship. The Jewish communities that did return were forced to prioritise material survival while religious and cultural aspects took second place.[41] Writing to the newly elected regional prime minister in 1946, the executive of the Jewish community in Dortmund reminded him that Jews felt let down:

> We received no help in rebuilding the Jewish communities and establishing a land organization and only relied on our own strength and initiative. . . . We are sure that you know how difficult it is for people who were broken in body and soul by the past and whose leaders had been murdered, to undertake such a task of reconstruction. We were vastly humiliated to discover, after the collapse, that we together with former political prisoners, had been degraded to benefit recipients. We were liberated from the Nazi yoke by the United Nations. We readily understood that the governments of these nations regarded it as a priority to rescue their own nationals and help them to resume a normal life. We, however, stood completely alone. No German authority, no German organizations took any notice. Nobody acted to fetch us, German citizens of the Jewish faith, from the concentration camps. We had to find our own way. We had to find our own way home.[42]

In a similar mode, Karl Marx, who had returned from exile in order to help rebuild Jewish as well as political life in Germany and came to prominence as editor of the *Jüdisches Gemeindeblatt*, the first German-Jewish newspaper after the Holocaust, recalled that there had been some Allied help after liberation but no help at all from German sources or agencies:

> German Jews were left to their own devices. The only help they did

receive came from Jews who had managed to hide during the Nazi regime. And for a very short period, some Jews who had narrowly escaped death, received preferential treatment in the allocation of housing, in obtaining business permits or in gaining access to public authorities. . . . In Germany, not a single group emerged to help people who had been robbed of everything and who had been the first victims of National Socialism as well as the last. They received not the slightest help in furnishing a home or finding work to rebuild their life. No German body seized the initiative.[43]

Jewish community leaders had to turn themselves into lobbyists, cajolers, and promoters of Jewish concerns. They had to help find housing, secure an adequate allocation of ration cards, help with clothing and other everyday essentials. Communities also operated their own tracing service to locate members' relatives who were still alive, and to verify the date and place of death for Holocaust victims since German authorities did not issue death certificates without this information and German officials refused to pay pensions to bereaved spouses without such certificates.[44] Now and again, community leaders appealed to the military government in their region, but such appeals were usually futile since all local matters, including the allocation of ration cards, domestic fuel and housing, had been delegated to local German administrations almost immediately:

> It would amount to unacceptable hardship if we Jews were put on the same footing with those people who have caused the present situation. Our members, therefore, hope and expect that the military government will support them in their calamity.[45]

More frequent were interventions with German officials on behalf of survivors. Walter Auerbach, for instance, had been imprisoned in a Gestapo camp for Jews in mixed marriages. In the 1930s, the Nazis forced him to sell his business and seized his possessions. When he returned to Dortmund after liberation, he was unable to obtain a residency permit and ordered to move to a village where bomb damage had been less severe. Despite poor health, he rejoined his former company as an employee, travelling to Dortmund on a daily basis. Repeated applications to be rehoused were unsuccessful. When he finally located a flat that used to belong to a Jewish family and whose tenant was about to move out, the landlord accepted another, non-Jewish occupant, although he should have been obliged, according to military government law, to give preference to a Jewish survivor. Siegfried Heimberg appealed repeatedly on behalf of Walter Auerbach, but to no avail.[46]

In a similar vein, the Jewish community spoke up for Max Stern, a

Holocaust survivor, who said that he had been excluded from a distribution of furniture to which he believed himself entitled. In this case, the city's Economic Department (*Wirtschaftsabteilung*) replied, detailing what Stern had received earlier and indicating that, in their view, he had already been treated better than he deserved. What, then, did Max Stern receive that he should have appeared so favoured?

> Ration cards for the following textiles were issued to Mr. Max Stern, born on 1 April 1879:
> 26. 6. 45: 2 shirts, one piece of head gear, 2 pairs of socks, 2 pairs of underpants, 2 vests
> 13. 8. 45: 1 jacket
> 5. 10. 46: 1 suit, one piece of head gear, 4 handkerchiefs
> 7. 11. 46: 1 winter coat, 1 suit, 1 shirt
> 9. 1. 1947: 2 pairs of socks
>
> Footwear:
> 24. 6. 46: 1 pair of shoes
> 7. 11. 46: 1 pair of shoes
> 28 12. 46: 1 pair of slippers, 1 pair of rubber boots[47]

By mid-1947, when Max Stern received his reprimand, matters had already begun to improve. The Jewish community in Dortmund had been offered some Care parcels to distribute among its most needy members, and an offer of help from the United States.[48] Most importantly, aid from the Joint Distribution Committee had finally kicked in. It consisted of a contribution of 2,500 Reichsmark per month to run the land organization in Westfalia and distribute to affiliated communities.[49] Earlier, money had to be raised through street collections and special appeals to the regional government, most of it required to supplement the very low benefit payments of most Jews. The Joint Distribution Committee aid also consisted of *Betreuung*, a system of distributing food, clothing, personal hygiene items such as toothbrushes and soap and other goods for everyday living which could include coffee or cigarettes. These two ingredients of the packages were more valuable than money at this time and could be exchanged for much needed things like furniture.

The system of distribution, however, disadvantaged German Jews and their communities. The American Joint Distribution Committee did not send its aid directly to local or regional organizations, but used the Central Committees of Liberated Jews as agents and distributors. These committees, as shown earlier, were based in the American and British zone respectively – attempts to create a unified organization had failed in July 1945 – and represented displaced Jews. In the British zone, where

Dortmund was situated, the Central Committee of Liberated Jews was based in Belsen and in charge of distributing 15 per cent of the Joint aid destined for Germany. Rather than dealing with Jewish communities directly, the Belsen committee worked only with the *Verband der jüdischen Gemeinden Nordwestdeutschland,* the Association of Jewish Communities in Northwest Germany, which, in turn, would redistribute aid to member communities. The *Verband* was headed by Norbert Wollheim, a Holocaust survivor who had met Josef Rosensaft, the chairman of the Committee of Liberated Jews, in Belsen after their liberation and continued to work closely together. For Jewish communities in the British zone, this double bureaucracy at the centre of aid distribution produced a cumbersome and obscure system. In applying for support, communities had to complete a separate application form for each member requiring help and then get it approved by the relevant land organization before they could send it to Wollheim who would make the decision. Needless to stay, this procedure was slow, and many applications fell by the wayside. In effect, Norbert Wollheim controlled how AJDC support was allocated to German Jews in the British zone.[50] Other obstacles originated directly in Belsen. On February 10, 1947, the Central Committee informed all Jewish communities in the British zone by way of circular that it had decided to distribute Joint aid packages only to Jews who could produce a medical note from their doctor together with an X-ray certificate to prove that they were in poor health.[51] At the time, it was virtually impossible to obtain X-rays for all but the most seriously ill patients. The innocuous sounding requirement meant that many German Jews found themselves excluded from aid they continued to need.

Despite the cumbersome bureaucracy, Jewish communities secured and distributed additional help for their members. Packages normally arrived once a month, and members were notified in the local newsletter or by circular of the date and the goods that were expected for distribution. Predictably, not all wishes were met, and some members felt left out or suspected that they had been cheated. Blame usually fell on community leaders at local level. In July 1948, for instance, Ernst Huldschinsky complained directly to the Central Committee of Liberated Jews in Belsen:

> I am a Jew who was born in Breslau and I now live, together with a small group of the same faith, in a remote village, and we are being cared for by the land organization of Westfalen in Dortmund. You have stated that distributions take place once a month, but it seems that different distribution centres follow different patterns. I noticed this in particular when I visited Hamburg ten days ago. There, the last two distributions included eighty cigarettes, and the same applied in Lübeck while we received only sixty in the last-but-one distribution and merely

forty in the most recent one, and were told that the difference was needed to support Palestine. Whether this is true and whether this can actually be implemented in terms of transport, I cannot say, but for other items similar differences exist. . . . I should also like to mention the problem of clothing that is being distributed in addition to food. In our area, much could be said about this. During all these years, I, as a man, have only once received a sport shirt and when such shirts were distributed the last time, the distributor overlooked me, allegedly because one of the three shirts allocated for our area was for a boy, and a boy received it. When I asked in Dortmund some two months ago whether they did not, after all, have a such a shirt for me which I, as a refugee from the east, need urgently, I did not even receive a reply. The things which arrive here from Dortmund are shoes, rubber galoshes, slippers and ties, nothing else for men, and these things are torn and totally dirty. I have concluded that Dortmund keeps all usable things for its own people and sends only useless stuff to us, unless they received nothing better which, however, I do not believe. It is nearly as bad with women's clothing and I should be most grateful to you if you could let me know what, how often and in which condition you receive material by way of clothing and distribute it, in order to ensure that we in this godforsaken village may receive some, albeit modest, help.[52]

For the Jewish community in Dortmund and the land organization in Westfalia, Siegfried Heimberg refuted all these allegations. Joint aid in his area of responsibility arrived at a central location where local distributors collected the goods intended for their community. If errors had occurred, the distributors, not the community leaders, were to blame. On the other hand, Huldschinsky's letter alerted Heimberg to the fact that Jews in Hamburg and Lübeck had been unfairly advantaged by receiving a larger allocation of cigarettes than those in the Dortmund region. Cheating, it seemed, happened at the top, where it counted for nothing that his communities had actually used 20 per cent of the cigarette allocation to support the Jewish underground movement in Palestine. As for Huld-schinsky, Heimberg had nothing but contempt for someone who passed himself off as Jewish, but whose credentials as a Jew were more than doubtful:

To date, our land organization had never received a complaint of this kind. It has been left to Mr. Huldschinsky to become the first person to voice such a complaint. I should like to stress that Mr. Huldschinsky has approached us with a great many requests and has always been helped to the best of our ability with the allocation of numerous coupons for furniture, for instance. It might be worth mentioning that we have been told by several refugees who knew him in eastern Germany, although we cannot guarantee the accuracy of this information, that in the past Mr. Huldschinsky did not belong to the Jewish but to another religious faith.[53]

A Problematic Normalisation

As economic conditions began to improve in Germany and the currency reform of 1948 restored the value of money, the AJDC switched its policy from the distribution of parcels to financial aid to top-up low incomes. This turned out to be a problematic normalisation. Payments were means-tested, given only to the poorest and reassessed on a regular basis. They were, however, set at such a low level that recipients were unable to come out of poverty.[54] In the British zone, where the administration of Joint aid remained unchanged even after the distribution of parcels was discontinued, recipients of even the smallest payments were obliged to sign a declaration (*Abtretungserklärung*). It bound them to repay the sum received as soon as any restitution had been paid to them.[55] This rule meant that Holocaust survivors, who lived in poverty and therefore qualified for income supplements from the Jewish community, accumulated a debt against their former belongings.

German-Jewish survivors who found themselves dependent on benefit already felt humiliated by the magnitude of their deprivation and disappointed in the reluctance of German public bodies to provide the support they needed to lead dignified lives. In addition to these disheartening conditions, survivors who had been unable to shake off the poverty imposed by the Nazis found themselves trapped in debt agreements for the Jewish help they received, blunting any promise that restitution, if it ever arrived, might mean a better life and future.

A good many could never find a normal life inside Germany. Jewish community files from the late 1940s onwards are full of reports of transient Jews and warnings against offering them financial assistance because they might apply, under a pretext, to several sources. An elaborate system emerged to circulate lists of named scroungers or 'schnorrers' and brief descriptions of how they tricked community officials into parting with money:

> Attention! Remember that with the money that you are giving to professional scroungers and vagrants you could, much better, help Jews who are living in poverty.[56]

A certain Michael Fessel, aged 19, pesters Jewish communities in order to obtain financial help. He behaves rudely and appears to be an asocial element. We are warning against this professional scrounger. As an example we would like to mention that he called at the Jewish community in Mönchen-Gladbach and was already drunk at 10 o'clock in the morning.[57]

No less dire were warnings circulated about Jews who had returned to Germany despite having accepted resettlement earlier. They were deemed illegal immigrants, arrived penniless and, according to the 'Bayrisches Hilfswerk', constituted a menace to Jewish communities:

> We are once again issuing an urgent warning [to Swiss communities used as transit points] not to send illegal returners to Germany! They are living in extremely cramped conditions, often with many children, unimaginably primitive! Some of the children have already fallen ill. The police will deport all illegal immigrants. It is, therefore, irresponsible to supply these people with money to pay for their journey to Germany.[58]

Despite misgivings, Jewish communities in Dortmund and elsewhere once again assumed the care function at the heart of their post-war activities and provided – albeit begrudgingly and under protest – financial help and membership rights to the unexpected newcomers. Like the Jewish refugees from eastern Europe before them, returners arrived as families and with children. By the mid 1950s, six thousand returned from Israel, another three thousand from other countries of emigration or attempted resettlement. The returners spread across all age groups, although more than half were over 50 years old. One in six, however, were children under the age of fifteen.[59] Their arrival, as we shall see, shifted the care function of the Jewish community from clearing up the legacies of the Nazi past to focussing on a possible future.

The Remaking of the Jewish Community in Frankfurt am Main: A Case Study

On March 29, 1945, the Americans took control of Frankfurt am Main. On April 1, 1945, Lt. Col. Howard D. Criswell, the officer in charge of putting in place a new German administration in the city, ordered the establishment of a *Jüdische Betreuungsstelle*, a Centre for Jewish Care. He also appointed August Adelsberger, one of the Jewish survivors from inside the Third Reich, to run it. Moreover, Criswell ordered the return of three former Jewish community buildings and appointed Fritz Stein, an employee of the *Reichsvereinigung der Juden in Deutschland* and before that of the Jewish community, to look after them and also attend to the Jewish cemeteries in the city. In time, these three buildings were to house the community office, a synagogue, a hostel and an old folks home, and constitute the cornerstone of post-war Jewish life in Frankfurt.[60]

Also on April 1, a small group held a first prayer meeting. Six weeks later, regular services commenced, and a room was consecrated for use as a synagogue. In June 1945, a military government official suggested the creation of a Jewish community but it took until August until Frankfurt's Jews decided on a temporary executive. Elections were only held in November 1945 when the Jewish community was formally instituted.

Jewish Care: Achievements and Limitations

When military government in Frankfurt created the Centre for Jewish Care as an agency of local government and nominated August Adelsberger as its head, just 158 Jews remained in the city. Most had escaped deportation because they were married to non-Jewish partners; some had been classified as of 'mixed race', a handful had survived in hiding. All, however, had suffered persecution under the Nazis and had narrowly escaped deportation. The last deportation train took 300 Jews from Frankfurt to Theresienstadt on February 16, 1945. This last transport also included two children. Overall, the Gestapo deported 9,715 Jews from Frankfurt itself and a further 10,000 from the surrounding area.[61]

As head of Jewish Care, Adelsberger tried immediately to undo the material hardship imposed on Jews during the Nazi years. The beneficiaries of these efforts were people who, like himself, lived in Frankfurt when the city was liberated. Within weeks, he had secured and reallocated 130 apartments that had been confiscated by military government from so called Nazi activists. A start-up budget of 35,000 Reichsmark enabled Jewish Care to assist with obtaining furniture, clothing or employment and provide small business loans.[62]

> Dr. Adelsberger arranged for the production of bedroom suites and kitchen furniture and prepared a distribution plan stipulating that people should receive goods in the order of their entry on the list. This arrangement does not reflect actual requirements since any distribution of goods has to be determined by need alone.[63]

Yet, it had also been Adelsberger who raised 134,000 Reichsmark to bring Frankfurt's Jews home from Theresienstadt. As mentioned earlier in this chapter, German Jews had to remain there until their home towns sent transport. The Russians made no such arrangement, while the Americans sent Jeeps in early May 1945, but only to collect a few well-known individuals. Most survivors did not fall into this category. By the end of May, Adelsberger had found enough money to arrange for the return home, but it was to take another six weeks for the first lorry to be dispatched. About three thousand had been deported from Frankfurt to Theresienstadt; 362 came back.[64] The last group, all of them bedridden, left on August 17, 1945 as the closure of the camp was imminent. In a letter to the Jewish community in Frankfurt, the transport office in Theresienstadt explained:

> Today, we are sending 12 persons to you by train and hope that they will arrive safely. The furnishings of the waggons, tables, chairs, mattresses, bed linen etc. are reportedly the property of the Jewish community in Frankfurt. There are no more Jews from southern and western Germany in Theresienstadt. The former Ghetto will be closed in a few days.[65]

The Return of Frankfurt's Jews from Theresienstadt

For many, it was a troubled homecoming. While military government had confiscated flats and buildings immediately after liberation, by the summer of 1945 local matters were in the hands of German officials. The return of Holocaust survivors from Theresienstadt constituted such a local matter. German city officials, not military government or army personnel, were in charge of arrangements. Frankfurt's administrators felt little urgency or no need to make special provisions to care for concentration camp survivors. In May and June 1945, when survivors from Buchenwald, Dachau and other concentration camps arrived in the city – no more than 60 in all – only one of the Jewish buildings was fit to offer temporary accommodation for 25 people. The others had to find a bed in one of the city's emergency shelters.[66] When Fritz Stein sent more homeless returners than he was supposed to, he received a stiff reprimand:

> As you know, we have offered 25 beds to accommodate people who have been released from concentration camps. You, however, have already sent 36 persons to us. We ask you to ensure that the excess of eleven persons is accommodated elsewhere. When referring people to our hostel, would you kindly make sure to issue them with the required referral documents.[67]

Two weeks later, another and even sterner letter followed:

We have asked you repeatedly to call at this office in person in order to discuss various matters. We had pointed out in particular that beds are already in short supply in our transit camp. Nevertheless, again and again, returners from concentration camps are sent to us. In the interest of the concentration camp inmates (*Insassen*) in your care, we must insist that you, for the time being, do not send anybody else.[68]

To accommodate the much larger group from Theresienstadt, August Adelsberger and Fritz Stein tried desperately to get the roofs of the buildings repaired that had been returned to Jews in the city, and to fit them out as temporary accommodation. They had even located a supplier of building materials but could not get any work done because the city's Transport Department blocked them. Although military government had provided a vehicle, city officials refused to issue the required permit to obtain petrol on the grounds that they could not consent to transporting religious items such as prayer books. The real reason the vehicle was needed seems to have been ignored. On May 19, 1945, Adelsberger protested:

Would the Vehicle Office please take note that the vehicle registered in our name will not be used for religious purposes such as transporting prayer books or ritual items, but is required to move building materials in order to repair as fast as possible the buildings that have been assigned to us by the Lord Mayor. This work is essential so that the returners from concentration camps and holding camps who are shortly expected to arrive here, may be accommodated and find a home. It is a duty of honour for every administrative department and economic division to do their utmost that this labour of love of helping unfortunate people without reserve can be accomplished. I therefore ask you to rescind the ban on the use of our vehicle.[69]

One of the buildings, 'Sandweg no.7', had been a Jewish residential home in the 1930s and was to be kitted out as a short-stay hostel. Fritz Stein, who was in charge of administering the buildings and overseeing the repairs, also found himself stonewalled by officialdom. In a letter to Adelsberger he voiced his frustration and also his concern that the returners might blame him if they had nowhere to live:

I have been unable to obtain a permit for the vehicle, and once again received a rejection without being given a reason. . . . These obstacles make all activity impossible, and I have to remind you of the consequences. I know that you have tried to get things moving and have not succeeded, but I should like to point out to you that when the people from Theresienstadt will return and find conditions as they are now, accusations and complaints will be raised. They will think both of us guilty and we will not be able to prevent it. I have no intention of becoming anyone's whipping boy and, if no last minute change can be achieved, I think it better to resign. Will you, kindly, bring these impossible conditions to the attention of the relevant authorities, since the problem is too pressing to allow further delay.[70]

German Bureaucracy and the Special Needs of Survivors

Little more than the bare numbers are known about the Jews who returned from Theresienstadt to Frankfurt. Of the 362 who did, most had been on the last transport from the city in February 1945. Until their deportation, they would have lived in mixed marriages. After their return, this group might have had a home to go to. Those who had been deported earlier and whose homes, families and contexts had been destroyed, depended desperately on help. They numbered less than one hundred. A Jewish hostel with 31 places was not yet ready.[71] The Jewish old folks home opened only in November 1945, accommodating 55 residents. In July and August 1945, when the Theresienstadt survivors actually arrived in Frankfurt, nothing was in place. Emergency shelters in the city were fully occupied. At the last minute, Fritz Stein managed to book a couple of rooms in local hotels to ensure that returners had, for the moment at least, a roof over their heads and the city administration provided a dozen hospital beds in nearby Köppern.[72] German officials, it seems, stuck to established practices and refused to regard concentration camp returners as special cases. Holocaust survivors, like everybody else, were entitled to ration cards totalling 1,100 calories per day.[73] Housing officers made no emergency provisions and even refused to intervene when German landlords accepted non-Jewish tenants, although the housing department had already given the go-ahead to a Holocaust survivor.[74]

In October 1945, one of the returners, Leopold Neuhaus, recorded his sense of outrage at their virtual abandonment to an impenetrable and even hostile bureaucracy. Before his deportation in September 1942, Neuhaus had worked in Frankfurt as a teacher at the Jewish Grammar School and later served as the city's last rabbi. After coming back from Theresienstadt in July 1945, he succeeded Adelsberger as head of Jewish Care. Adelsberger had been dismissed for accusing his military government sponsors of disadvantaging Jews a second time over by treating them no different from Germans.[75] As we have seen, military government had already handed responsibilities to German officials when Neuhaus took over. In addition to heading Jewish Care, he also became the first rabbi and the first chairman of the Jewish community that emerged in Frankfurt after the Holocaust. In October 1945, he recalled in an open letter to a local newspaper how little was done to help Theresienstadt survivors:

> Among the small number of Jews who returned from concentration camps were very few who required housing. Nevertheless, they had to undertake countless treks to the housing department and were often given unsuitable accommodation. Clearly, nobody cares to understand the years of suffering they had endured or what it means having to sleep on straw without beds, on the floor, and living cramped together with many others. . . . Without possessions, without proper clothing, without warm wraps for the winter (as we know, Jews were forced to hand over all their furs and woollens), after years of hunger, deprivation and emotional as well as physical suffering, strength needs to be given to these people from the outside, in the shape of a furnished home that may be small but should be comfortable, in the shape of proper shoes and of warm, good quality clothing. It is not enough to issue ration coupons which, in any case, cannot be exchanged for goods and which are so low in value that they amount to no more than alms thrown to a pauper.[76]

The mismatch of an inflexible German bureaucracy and the special needs of Jews after the Holocaust manifested itself in many different ways. For instance, only persons who originated in Frankfurt were entitled to receive regular ration cards. For others, a stay in the city was assumed to be limited, and supported only temporarily by food coupons to sustain them during their journey. Among the twelve bedridden survivors who were dispatched from Theresienstadt on August 17, 1945 were some who arrived in Frankfurt because their home towns had not made arrangements to take them back and who were not well enough to travel unaided. Miss Durlacher was one such person. Born in 1877, she was 78 years old at the time. In Frankfurt, she was initially assigned a straw sack in a hostel but within two weeks had to be admitted to hospital. When the hospital requested her ration cards in order to provide food, it emerged that she had none. Fritz Stein who signed himself as 'in charge of reconstruction and administration of the buildings and the cemeteries of the Jewish community in Frankfurt' explained the difficulties:

> We herewith acknowledge that Miss Mathilde Durlacher came to us from Theresienstadt and is a temporary resident in our hostel in Sandweg 7. Up to now, she had been fed by means of travel ration coupons, allocated to her by the Office of Food in Frankfurt. Our residents change often and all receive travel rations. We in turn provide

communal meals. We are not in a position to issue a certificate detailing her regular ration entitlements. Please find enclosed Miss Durlacher's remaining travel ration coupons.[77]

The list of obstacles to everyday survival, let alone normalisation after liberation, seemed endless. Everything from housing or food to furniture, shoes or clothing could only be obtained if the relevant coupons had been allocated. Frequently, even coupons did not enable their holders to purchase the required goods. Forcing Jews to depend on a system devised for and operated by Germans was in itself an injustice. Not only had Jews in Germany endured persecution and been robbed of belongings and assets by the Nazi state and its beneficiaries, those who returned from concentration camps possessed little more than their life and the clothes they were wearing. The system of coupons (*Bezugsscheine*) and official allocations did not allow them to rebuild any kind of normality but extended the deprivation and impoverishment they had suffered into the post-war era.

On the face of it, Jewish Care offered privileged treatment to Jews who had been persecuted and possessed an identity card to prove it.[78] In reality, securing actual provisions was a constant struggle for individuals as well as for Jewish Care. In August 1945, Neuhaus had managed to obtain improved rations of two thousand calories for concentration camp survivors, but these came to an end after a few weeks. Rumours that a similar allocation of milk might be available turned out to be false. Responding to an enquiry by Rabbi Neuhaus, the head of Frankfurt's Department for Special Care (*Sonderbetreuung*), Beckmann, left no doubt that in the eyes of the public authorities of the day – Allied as well as German – special provision for Jews was not necessary:

> Your letter of 20 August in which you ask me to confirm that all concentration camp prisoners are to receive one litre of milk per day, has been passed on to military government and been answered there as follows: 'The contents of the inquiry does not tally with the facts, but concentration camp prisoners may, on presentation of a medical certificate, receive an allocation of milk in exactly the same way as the rest of the population'.[79]

Lore Geminder was 19 years old when she survived several concentration camps including Auschwitz and returned to her home town of Frankfurt. City officials in charge of allocating clothing coupons apparently decided that she was eligible to receive help. In a letter to a local newspaper, she recorded her experiences:

We were very cold in the concentration camp, and we are certainly hardened. When we arrived in Auschwitz in the winter of 1944, after languishing for four years in other camps, a rag was thrown at us which was supposed to be a dress. Everything else was taken from us. We had nothing underneath and nothing on top of it, only a pair of wooden clogs. (Why give us more, since we were destined for the gas chambers?) Chance and luck would have it that my mother, my sister and I escaped this fate. My father was shot. Now we are again in Frankfurt and we thought that, for this winter, we shall finally have warm clothing. When we voiced our request in the Economic Department we were told that we had to present a medical certificate that we were ill. Otherwise, no coupon for a winter coat could be issued, not even for concentration camp prisoners. Take note, not even a coupon, and it is by no means clear that possession of a coupon results in obtaining a winter coat. With coupons for other items, i.e. a vest, one pair of knickers, a slip and two pairs of stockings per person, we had no luck so far.[80]

After the initial flurry of goodwill in March and April 1945, military government remained aloof and left the care of Jews to the Care Centre and the German authorities it had installed in the city. Yet, it was on military government orders that repairs were carried out to Frankfurt's largest synagogue in time to hold High Holiday services there. In September 1945, the first Jewish New Year services after liberation were celebrated in the Westend Synagogue and conducted jointly by George Vida, a US Army Chaplain based in Frankfurt who spoke in English, and Leopold Neuhaus, Frankfurt's own rabbi, who spoke in German. Two thousand worshippers shared in the experience, most of them American service personnel.[81] For those who were present, the event served as a stark reminder of the destruction inflicted upon Jews in Frankfurt and throughout Europe:

This was the most moving hour since the arrival of the Americans. In the burnt-out, hastily repaired synagogue in the Freiherr-von-Stein-Strasse gathered what remained of the large and famous Jewish community of Frankfurt, this community that was known the world over for its high culture, scholarship and hundreds of charitable foundations. Now the remainder of this community sat in the last Jewish house of God in this city that had not been totally devastated by animal-like hatred. In a room that no longer had an organ or the old seating but was lit comfortably by candles, sat the last ones remaining of 35,000 people, the survivors of extermination camps, those who had been saved from the gas chambers, a heart-stoppingly low number. They sat between many American soldiers who had come from

Frankfurt and the surrounding region. It was difficult, not to shed tears in this hour.[82]

The first Jewish New Year service since liberation and the re-opening of a synagogue that had been destroyed in November 1938 signalled the onset of an era when Jews were again free to live as Jews. As German Jews worshipped alongside American Jews stationed in Germany, the isolation and abandonment of the persecution years seemed truly at an end. For Rabbi Neuhaus, however, who officiated at the service and spoke as the voice of German-Jewish survivors, unanswered questions loomed because nobody tried to understand Jewish experiences and needs:

Nearly 34,000 Jews lived in Frankfurt am Main at the beginning of the Nazi regime and today, a pitiful 600 people are remaining. One of the most distinguished communities with magnificent synagogues at the Börneplatz, in the Freiherr-von-Stein-Strasse – today miserably repaired – in the Börnestrasse and in the Friedberger Anlage, presenting themselves today as places destroyed and levelled to the ground. Can there ever be restitution, can there ever be restoration? 'Soul, can you ever forget?' People today must understand that we Jews can no longer trust notions such as mankind and human kind, humanity and education, and so we keep asking fate to answer this one question: How is it possible that German people were turned into animals, that they could destroy the things that were the holiest to others? This question stands, this question remains! Who will answer it?[83]

At the more pragmatic level of daily living, answers were unsatisfactory or non-existent. Jews who had been liberated in Frankfurt or returned there from concentration camps found themselves, at the end of 1945, regarded as Germans without recognition of any special needs that might have arisen from the impoverishment they had endured at the hands of the Nazis. The service to celebrate the Jewish New Year in September 1945 may have attracted a huge congregation and seemed to signal a new alliance between German and American Jews, but it remained a symbolic act, detached from reality:

The food allocation to the Jewish population in Frankfurt is exactly the same as that to the general population, although the camp inmates and the star-wearing Jews (*Sternträger*) had been, over several years, disadvantaged significantly with regard to food and nothing has been done yet to redress this imbalance. We are particularly disappointed that we have not received any kind of assistance or food from the big

American aid organizations such as the Joint or UNRRA, because we had looked towards them with high hopes.[84]

Material Hardship as Jewish Experience

The persistent material hardship after liberation prolonged the racial classifications and divides that had been imposed by the Nazis and that now served to lodge or deny claims for support. Terms such as 'Full Jew', 'Half-Jew', 'Faith Jews' or 'Race Jew' became a kind of shorthand for the degree of material and personal destruction endured between 1933 and 1945. The continued dependency and impoverishment of groups of Jews created new hardship and new rivalries.

In Frankfurt, non-Aryan Christians and so called 'Race Jews' (*Rasseju-den*) complained that so called 'Faith Jews' (*Glaubensjuden*) received preferential treatment by Jewish Care. The former group consisted of persons who had been defined and treated as Jews by the Nazis on account of their parentage. In the same terminology, *Glaubensjuden* were deemed to be Jewish by both origin and faith. After months of discontent, the representatives of the non-Aryan Christians resigned from the advisory council of Jewish Care and set up their own agency in the former offices of the *Reichsvereinigung der Juden*.[85] Others tried to pass themselves off as Jewish in order to receive any support that might be on offer.

How difficult it was at the time to determine whose claim to be Jewish should be dismissed and whose accepted as genuine is evident from a letter by Rabbi Neuhaus in his capacity as head of Jewish Care to the administrator of the fledgling Jewish community:

> Dear Mr. Stein, I just learned from my staff in the distribution centre that people are sent here with certificates issued by you, stating that they are Jews while the distribution staff as well as myself established without doubt that they are not. I have to ask you politely and urgently to adhere strictly to the questionnaire and refrain from issuing certificates to people who want to be Jews for the sake of a tin of milk or a package of Ovaltine. We do not hand out certificates to so called Jews in exchange for milk or Ovaltine.[86]

Sometimes, it was the turn of Jewish Care to be attacked for being too lenient in assessing entitlements and for serving the wrong clientele. Thus, the head of Frankfurt's department for domestic fuel (*Hausbrand*), himself a Jew, berated Neuhaus for failing to distinguish between privileged and non-privileged Jews and, even worse, for issuing fuel coupons to so called 'Half-Jews'.[87] Neuhaus retorted that people were freezing, regardless of their classification. As an agency of the city, he argued, Jewish Care had to be inclusive and help all persons who had suffered under the Nazis because they were Jews:

> The centre for Jewish Care does, to the best of our ability, provide practical support and advice to all Jews and Half-Jews. This support does, of course, extend to offering financial help, finding employment opportunities for people in our care, assisting with housing or the acquisition of furniture, all of it from confiscated apartments of former Nazi functionaries. We also operate a successful tracing system, based on lists of displaced persons and of inmates from various concentration camps.[88]

Given its status as an agency of local government, Jewish Care aimed to be inclusive. The Jewish community, which Leopold Neuhaus also headed, was not. In October 1945, Jewish Care had 1,200 individuals on its books of whom just six hundred were members of the community. In April 1946, Neuhaus published a further report. Again, he stated that 1,200 were receiving assistance, six hundred of them outside the Jewish community. Just 20 had been found employment while 75 remained totally dependent on assistance for their daily survival. By this time, however, the future of Jewish Care itself was in doubt as the city administration had slashed its budget to 15,000 Reichsmark and resolved to extend its remit to serving all former persecutees.[89] Jews would be represented on the steering committee but no longer head the redefined body. In response, the Jewish community insisted on retaining and staffing its own Care Centre because the civic facilities might not meet Jewish needs. Who, then, were the six hundred Jewish residents of Frankfurt who, in April 1946, did not belong to its Jewish community?

Leaving aside the inner-Jewish divides arising from Nazi classifications and their perverse arithmetic, the Jewish population of Frankfurt after liberation consisted of two broad groups: firstly German Jews who had either survived there or returned and, secondly, displaced Jewish Holocaust survivors from eastern Europe who had arrived in Frankfurt because they did not wish to live in a displaced persons camp and also because they regarded the city as a jumping-off point for emigration to Palestine, the United States or other destinations. By September 1945, the number of displaced Jews in Frankfurt had risen to over one thousand, prompting military government to establish a new displaced persons camp in nearby Zeilsheim. Designed for 1,200, Zeilsheim was soon home to some three thousand.[90] From 1946 onwards new arrivals included Jews who had fled from Poland and other eastern European countries after their liberation, as renewed anti-Semitism erupted there. Since the American zone of occupation kept its borders open and offered recognition to displaced Jews, it became a haven for such newcomers. Bavaria took the brunt of this new migration, but Hesse and Frankfurt also played an important part.[91]

Not all displaced Jews and newcomers from eastern Europe chose to live in camps. In Frankfurt, therefore, the Jewish population included German Jews who had survived inside the Third Reich or who had returned there from concentration camps. It also included eastern European Jews who had been liberated inside Germany or who arrived there subsequently.

The Jewish community that emerged in Frankfurt after 1945 did not wish to embrace this new diversity but to continue distinguished, albeit shattered, German–Jewish traditions. Writing in June 1946 to the newly appointed State Commissioner for Jews, Curt Epstein, Rabbi Neuhaus explained:

> I am convinced that you know what the Jewish community in Frankfurt once meant for the world. Although it has become much smaller and in no way resembles the old Frankfurt community, I nevertheless wish to – and you will understand this – ensure that the Jewish tradition of this community will be preserved.[92]

Displaced Jews and German Jews – Diversities of Needs and Cultures

Foreign Jews had no place in this German–Jewish project despite their presence in the city. The old folks home only considered applications from Jews who had formerly lived in Frankfurt and remained closed even to German 'outsiders'. The Jewish hostel had been intended for German Jews. When eastern European Jews began to arrive in larger numbers, provisions were less than adequate. A report in June 1946 noted:

> We have inspected the rooms and found that the straw sacks are in a bad state and need to be filled again. We also concluded that a further 200 straw sacks are required. The toilet facilities are totally inadequate. Therefore, the travellers do their business just about anywhere in the most impossible places in the building. . . . There is a large room that could be used as a day room and dining room. About 50 tables and some 300 stools would have to be secured, in order to make it easier to keep the dormitories clean and to enable people to eat in a dignified manner sitting at a table.[93]

Faced with the new migration from eastern Europe, the Jewish community in Frankfurt was willing to provide hostel facilities but took the view that these were displaced persons whose care should be the responsibility of UNRRA. 'Processing the imminent mass transports' could not be expected from the Jewish community and its scarce human and financial resources.[94] Less pragmatically anchored were cultural divides. When several Hungarian Jews tried to attach themselves to the local synagogue and attend religious services there, they were asked to leave because their mode of prayer was deemed incompatible with German-Jewish practices. By April 1946, cultural divides had become institutionalised with east European Jews establishing their own synagogue. This bifurcation of Jewish culture replicated past distances between German Jews and *Ostjuden*. It also arose from a stifling sense that the Jewish community in Frankfurt had to preserve hallowed traditions after the unimaginable destruction inflicted upon it.

Such divides between German and eastern European Jews contradicted the belief that the Holocaust had created a new unity among Jews and lent new weight to community membership. These sentiments inspired Neuhaus in his dual commitment to Jewish Care and Jewish community organization. They were also at the heart of a mission statement, written by his wife Cilly for the first issue of the *Jüdisches Mitteilungsblatt*. Essentially a newsletter published by Leopold Neuhaus and depending heavily on contributions by him and his wife, the *Mitteilungsblatt* intended to inform Jews in Frankfurt and elsewhere about emigration, residency permits and arrangements for Jewish care but also addressed, now and again, more fundamental problems of a new beginning:

> Beginning means creating something new, moving forwards, wishing to think in the present and towards the future. The community protects and carries the individual, helps him in need and offers him support and stability in building his life. Anyone who does not recognise these positive aspects and only sees the negative, has learnt nothing from the fate of the last years, from the years that taught us that nobody but our God accepted us in the world. . . . Do not segregate yourself from the community – this is an old Jewish saying that has always shown itself to be true. . . . Support and promote community life by attending religious services, be interested in and well inclined towards everything that is intended to strengthen the community again. Show your gratitude for your salvation from danger in this way, do not denigrate the miracle of your life which should be filled with new meaning for yourself and for your children. The suffering of the last years has ennobled us all![95]

To the displaced Jews, matters looked very different. As the headquarters of American military government and, increasingly, as a location for consulates, the Jewish Agency, HIAS, the American Joint Distribution

Committee and other political or aid organizations, Frankfurt was perceived as a key staging post for leaving Germany and obtaining the relevant documents. After the Truman Directive of December 22, 1945 which freed immigration quotas for Germans, German Jews who had family or other sponsors in the United States were able to apply for visas. Leopold and Cilly Neuhaus were among a group of twenty who left Frankfurt for the United States on one of the first ships in 1946. Two out of three German-Jewish survivors chose to leave as soon as possible, many of them leaders of the first hour who had briefly helped to rekindle Jewish life in Germany after liberation.[96]

Those who stayed tended to be elderly, sick, infirm, unable to obtain the required papers. Many were more firmly rooted in Germany than other survivors and less familiar with Jewish religious and cultural traditions because they were married to non-Jewish partners. After the first wave of German-Jewish emigration in 1946-7, eight out of ten members of the Jewish community in Frankfurt belonged to this group.

Displaced Jews living in the city did not benefit significantly from the Truman Directive or find other countries willing to accept them. No additional national quotas had been freed and applicants would have had to reside in the American zone prior to December 22, 1945, a condition that excluded most Jews who had arrived from eastern Europe or elsewhere in Germany after that date. Access to Palestine, the preferred destination, remained regulated by Palestine Certificates. At the time, these were unobtainable in the American zone.[97] Destination Frankfurt, therefore, was a location to wait for opportunities, to live in transit until an unspecified date of departure and an unknown new beginning. Since departure was not imminent, the interim acquired a problematic permanence and it mattered more that local Jews appeared to have closed ranks against the newcomers.

The intervention of the American Joint Distribution Committee changed all that. In September 1945, a representative, Sadie Sender, arrived in Frankfurt. It took her until February 1946 to set up an office and there is no evidence that German or displaced Jews in the city received any aid earlier. One month after opening her office, Sadie Sender initiated the creation of a Jewish Committee in Frankfurt, parallel and in competition to the Jewish community. In her account of events, Sadie Sender claimed that displaced Jews had been left destitute and needed help:

When I arrived at my station in Frankfurt last September, I found the German community (*Jüdische Gemeinde*) already set up. At that time, there were very few DPs living in Frankfurt. Since the function of the Joint in Germany is to work through communities because our personnel is too small to handle individuals, I recognized the German community and its leadership. The Joint made monthly financial contributions as well as supplied the community with supplementary food and clothing. Later, when the DPs began to settle in Frankfurt, the leader of the Jewish community refused to admit these arrivals to his community organization. Since, in a short time, there were about 550 DPs in Frankfurt, it was necessary to have them organized in order that the Joint could service these people. The Committee of Liberated Jews in Frankfurt was instituted.[98]

Jewish Committee versus Jewish Community

Committees of Liberated Jews in the US zone dated back to the summer of 1945, when the Central Committee was created in Munich, followed by a network of regional and local committees to give organizational cohesion and a public voice to displaced Jews. In June 1945 the AJDC, which had only just sent a first representative to Germany and had not began actual aid work, authorised the Central Committee of Liberated Jews to function as a distribution agency on its behalf.[99]

In using Jewish committees in this way, the Joint sidelined the re-emerging Jewish communities and German Jews. Jewish committees were normally based in displaced persons camps. In some places, however, displaced Jews who had chosen to live 'out of camp' also organized themselves as committees, not communities. Frankfurt was such a location.

The Jewish Committee of Liberated Jews in Frankfurt was founded on March 26, 1946 by a group of twelve and consolidated in follow-on meetings during the next two days that involved up to two hundred founder-members. They installed an executive consisting of a chairman, secretary and treasurer and also set up an 'Economic Office', an 'Organizational Office' and a 'Cultural Office', each with a broad brief for action and a designated head. The stated aim of the Jewish Committee was:

> to provide good accommodation and adequate food to those who come from Poland and other German zones and who are staying in Frankfurt on their way to elsewhere.[100]

The first public announcement struck a somewhat different note. It presented the Committee as the sole agency for Jewish support in the city, not merely for short-term and displaced residents. Between March 28 and April 4, the Committee used local radio and the press to inform all Jews living in Frankfurt that they had to register at its offices by April 5 in order to be included in aid distributions.[101] Additional advertisements announced that food distributions would be held on the twentieth of every month although this timetable was never adhered to.

Clearly, the Committee purported to speak for all Jews, not only for displaced Jews waiting for travel documents or resettlement opportunities. Of course, the Jewish community protested and informed the Committee by letter that the call for registration could not possibly apply to its own members because their care, now as always, lay in the hands of Rabbi Neuhaus.[102] In reality, the Jewish community had already been wrong-footed by developments: control over Jewish aid beyond the pitiful German rations and coupons had been lodged with the Committee and its new executive. The storeroom and designated distribution point for aid was administered by the Committee's Economics Office while the Organizational Office compiled the membership lists that were submitted to the Central Committee in Munich and determined how much aid would be sent from there.

In June 1946, Sadie Sender tried to broker an agreement between the two sides in order to ensure that German Jews would receive a fair share of the AJDC supplies. A Council of Five was set up to oversee co-operation. It left both parties dissatisfied. The Jewish community was limited to two representatives and always felt outnumbered and overruled. The Committee representatives, on the other hand, never warmed to the co-operation imposed on them. After six months of disagreement and mutual recriminations, the Council of Five ceased to function. A proposal to simply allocate 45 per cent of Joint aid to the community and 55 per cent to the Committee was never implemented.[103] In any case, implementation could not have been monitored since the Committee ran the depot and did not supply accurate membership data. In May 1948, an audit remonstrated:

> Although it had been decided at the first meeting of the executive that a comprehensive membership list should be compiled as a matter of urgency, this decision has not been carried out to this day. The absence of proper records prevents accurate checks of the distribution system and also makes it impossible to defend the rights of actual members vis-a-vis other bodies. Furthermore, no economic planning of any kind can be carried out since it is not known how many members really exist. A card index recommends itself as the most practical means of establishing statistics and gaining an overview.[104]

Committee officials produced list after list with membership figures and recipients of support. None of them tallied with estimates of the displaced Jewish population in Frankfurt or with AJDC distributions; however, the lists are indicative of the social composition of the membership and also allow some comparisons between Committee and community. In the three years between March 1946 and March 1949, the membership of the Jewish Committee rose from around six hundred to well over one thousand. A slight increase of Jewish community membership over the same period from six hundred to six hundred and fifty suggests a false stability since losses through the emigration of German Jews in 1946–7 and modest gains balanced each other out.

In September 1947, the Committee listed 906 members. Most were young, two thirds were men and just 14 individuals aged fifty-five or over. Among its members, the Committee included 60 children under the age of seventeen, 36 of them babies under one year old. Nine women were pregnant at the time.[105] In the Jewish community, members were older and included more women.[106] A list dating from February 1947 also mentioned nearly sixty children under eighteen and one baby.[107] This list named all individuals who were entitled to Jewish care at the time and was compiled after the Joint had agreed to extend its support to non-Jewish spouses in mixed marriages. An executive minute on this topic stated dryly:

> As a matter of principle, every Full Jew and his wife, provided she lived with him during the Nazi years, are entitled to hold a care certificate (*Betreuungsschein*).[108]

Like the population of Jewish DP camps, the displaced Jewish population in Frankfurt was predominantly young, while the average age of the German-Jewish population was much higher, in particular for German-Jewish Holocaust survivors. Most of the few children listed as members of the Jewish community were the offspring of mixed marriages, had non-Jewish mothers, and most would have been baptised to protect their life during the Nazi years. In open conflict with religious laws and traditions, the Jewish community in Frankfurt – not unlike other Jewish communities in Germany in the aftermath of the Nazi years – defined membership pragmatically by personal affiliation and material need.[109] This definition of 'Who is a Jew?' and the presence of non-Jewish marriage partners were unknown among the membership of the Committee and not accepted by its religious leaders.

The Committee faced different uncertainties arising, above all, from the transient nature of its membership. Officially at least, displaced Jews were permitted to live in Frankfurt while waiting for papers to move on. In reality, the Committee executive was very effective in securing repeated extensions of temporary permits, often over several years. There did not appear to be a procedure to end registration with the Committee when individuals left Frankfurt, nor did the AJDC or other Jewish agencies who assisted with such moves notify the Committee of any changes. Thus, lists were not updated and amended when members of the Committee left the city.

Even more complex was the link with Zeilsheim, the nearby displaced persons camp.[110] The Committee openly encouraged Zeilsheim residents to move to Frankfurt in order to make room for newcomers inside the camp, where they would receive UNRRA care. This approach was particularly relevant at the height of the post-Holocaust migration from eastern Europe which brought at least 160,000 new residents into the American zone, all in need of food, shelter, clothing and other help. In 1947, when the US military government declared displaced persons camps in the American zone closed to new arrivals, Zeilsheim lost its function as a stopover. Yet, a link remained because a substantial number of displaced Jews were registered in both locations, drawing support from UNRRA inside the DP camp and from the Joint Distribution Committee via the Jewish Committee in Frankfurt. Ignoring the complexities of its membership, the Committee used existing address lists and pre-printed postcards to notify individuals that supplies had arrived. A significant number of these could not be delivered and were returned because the recipients had moved on. A typical postcard would read:

> An allocation of food/ clothing/ Pesach/ Religious Holidays/ Champagne/ Children's goods (underlined as applicable) has arrived. Please collect immediately from the offices of the Jewish Committee.[111]

Contrary to its own printed instructions, the Committee appeared to have dispensed with the requirement that recipients of aid should sign for their packages.[112] This lax administrative practice contrasted with the Jewish community where everyone was required to appear in person to collect and sign for any goods. Nevertheless, when the Regional Committee audited the distribution procedures in November 1947, it also accused the Jewish community of poor record keeping.[113]

From the outset, provisions for the Jewish community and its office holders fell behind those for the Jewish Committee, giving rise to a steady but futile stream of complaints. When the Joint imposed cuts in 1947 – on top of cuts for German rations – food and clothing for community members became so inadequate as to reach crisis point. Ignoring objections by the executive, a group of women in the Jewish community took matters into their own hands and contacted Jewish women's organizations in the United States in order to alert them to the continued hardship endured by German Jews in Frankfurt and seek their help. In response, the women received so many parcels that they could satisfy the needs of all community members and even offer some for distribution among members of the Jewish Committee.[114]

The persistent hardship of Jews living in Frankfurt and their continued dependency on material aid turned foodstuffs and prized items such as cigarettes or coffee from facets of daily survival into implements of power. The Committee executive seemed particularly adept in accumulating goods to fund other aspects of their work or to bribe German officials.[115] In some cases, self-interest appears to have been the dominant motive. For example, when five complete sets of Passover dishes were donated to the Jewish Committee, members of its executive retained four for their own use.[116] When wine, champagne, chocolate or cigarettes arrived in the aid packages or as special donations, office holders of the Committee as well as the community received the lion's share. On one occasion, a consignment also contained chewing gum. The Committee decided to present it to the children as a treat. In the Jewish community, the treat was claimed by and distributed among the executive.[117]

While hierarchies of entitlement within Committee and community can be linked to the negative impact of persistent scarcity of material goods, the AJDC practice of designating certain office holders as American employees who received American-style salaries in addition to preferential allocations of aid supplies created additional divides. While the executive of the Jewish Committee enjoyed these additional benefits, the executive of the Jewish community did not. Payments for Joint officials could be forty or fifty times higher than payments for other employees, not to mention the fact that most Jews were unable to generate income through employment or, in the case of many displaced Jews, did not wish to do so as part of the German economy.[118]

The Committee's Role in Remaking Jewish Life

Problems of aid distribution and record keeping should not obscure the contribution of the Jewish Committee as the louder, more assertive and more demanding of Frankfurt's two Jewish voices. From the very beginning, it went to the highest authority at any given opportunity to enlist help or complain about poor provisions. Frankfurt's Lord Mayor was persuaded to offer one hundred apartments to displaced Jews at a time of extreme housing shortage in the city.[119] With the help of Curt Epstein, the Committee executive also secured residency permits and hundreds of extensions although, officially, Frankfurt was closed to new arrivals.[120] When new regulations purported to cancel all temporary residency permits and threaten displaced Jews with eviction from the city, the Committee put pressure on the regional minister to exempt Jews.[121] In a letter to the Committee, Epstein wrote reassuringly: 'I believe, I can state with certainty that all eviction orders have been completely overturned.'[122] The

Jewish community, by contrast, tended to accept the restrictions as insurmountable and publish warnings in its newsletter that housing and residency in the city were unobtainable even for former Jewish inhabitants of Frankfurt. The Committee exercised no such caution.

In order to obtain clothing, furniture and other essentials which AJDC distributions did not normally contain, the Jewish Committee identified producers and then sought to persuade the relevant public authorities that they should allocate the necessary raw materials and permits. In order to persuade German officials to decide in their favour, the members of the Committee executive stressed without hesitation the past suffering and the present needs of the intended beneficiaries:

> The members for whom we care are Jews who returned from concentration camps or were deported. After years of incarceration and dislocation they require the most essential footwear. The shoe factory Salamander in Frankfurt has agreed to produce these shoes for our people. It now needs the required raw materials in order to deliver the shoes to our people who will obtain them in exchange for ration coupons. Since we are talking here about a life saving acquisition for the people in our care, we beg you to supply the above named company with the raw materials it requires in order to undertake production against payment.[123]

A virtually identical letter was sent to the textile department of the region's Economic Office to authorise the production of clothing for 'the people in our care'.[124]

Other initiatives seemed even more audacious, although less certain in their outcome. In September 1946, the Committee executive proposed to the state government in Wiesbaden that it should hand over closed or ailing businesses that had formerly been owned by Jews and allow displaced Jewish members of the Committee to run them. The list of suitable businesses included tailoring and laundry services, the manufacture and retailing of textiles, leather goods and cosmetics as well as printing works, farms and all kind of asset management.[125] In order to address the contradiction that Jews who were said to stay only temporarily in Frankfurt should wish to run a business there, the Committee proposed that all proceeds and earnings should be paid into a special fund and used as start-up capital by the would-be entrepreneurs after resettlement. Some months later, the Central Committee for Liberated Jews in the American Zone proposed a more elaborate scheme of factories, workshops and agricultural enterprises employing 40,000 Jews. Goods and produce would be exported or sold to US forces. Funded by the Joint Distribution Committee, this Jewish economy would remain completely separate from the German setting in which it existed. Since the Joint refused support, nothing came of this project.[126] In Frankfurt, the proposals to create enterprises for displaced Jews also never left the drawing board. Their very existence, however, suggests that, for some members of the Committee and its executive, Frankfurt may have constituted a more permanent place of residence than they could or would admit at the time.

In its self-styled role as the voice for all Jews in Frankfurt, the Committee threw itself energetically into rebuilding and developing Jewish life in the city. This entailed pursuing issues as disparate as carrying out repairs to Frankfurt's synagogues, reclaiming the use of the former Jewish grammar school for staging cultural events, setting up a kindergarten, starting a Jewish day school as well as a religion school served by two full-time Jewish teachers. While the Jewish community barely had desks and chairs in its office, the Jewish Committee furnished theirs with everything that might be required, including mocha cups and a piano. When ordered to return the piano to the German authorities, it immediately demanded an *Ersatzklavier* as a replacement.[127]

Early successes also included establishing an additional synagogue (Friedrichstrasse) with its own rabbi and rabbinical assistant where orthodox religious services were held daily although some members of the Committee also attended services in the synagogue run by the Jewish community. Here, they often helped to make up a *minyan*, the ten men required for prayers. The Jewish burial society, *Chewra Chadisha*, depended entirely on members of the Jewish Committee. Within months after its inauguration, the Jewish Committee had also constructed and opened a *Mikvah* – a ritual bath for the purification of women.

It took somewhat longer to open a kosher kitchen. Although proposed in one of its first executive meetings, the People's Kitchen, as it was called, finally opened in the autumn of 1947. There were several reasons for the delay. The Joint and the Central Committee for Liberated Jews in Munich had initially refused to provide funding and food supplies because the venture did not fit into their established system of allocation. While the Jewish community authorised the use of a building as a communal kitchen, the executive resolved to see 'if a clear and orderly basis can be established for this enterprise' before getting involved further.[128] With the help of its own rabbi, the Committee found other sponsors. The ultra-orthodox Vaad Hatzalah paid 20,000 Reichsmark towards the kitchen in order to provide every Jew in Frankfurt who wanted them with kosher meals. In addition, Hesse's State Commissioner for Jews donated 5,000 Reichsmark.[129] Once the kitchen had actually opened, the Joint withdrew its objections and allowed the use of food allocations to run it. Situated next door to the warehouse and food stores of the Jewish Committee, and run by a kitchen sub-committee, the Jewish People's Kitchen fed about sixty people every

177

day. Although soup kitchens for the needy had operated in Frankfurt since liberation, this was the first to cater specifically for Jews by offering kosher food.[130] Yet, the kitchen also attracted a stream of criticism from the Jewish community and the Regional and Central Committees of Liberated Jews for inefficient organization and for alleged misuse of Joint supplies.[131]

After a similarly slow start, the Committee's cultural department organized a fortnightly programme of events including theatrical performances and musical evenings, aimed in particular at attracting younger members. Frankfurt's Lord Mayor provided funding. An English language course proved less attractive and closed within weeks.[132] On a more sombre note, the committee's secretary, Emil Wulkan, organized an extensive tracing service. He had grown up in Breslau and returned there after surviving deportation and several concentration camps. Before arriving in Frankfurt in February 1946, he had compiled lists of Breslau's Jews.[133] Containing about two thousand names, these lists enabled Wulkan to answer a stream of enquiries after individuals and families who were feared dead and whose whereabouts after liberation remained unknown.[134]

Promises and Setbacks

Not all promises were met and unexpected difficulties surfaced. In November 1946, only twenty-five of the hundred flats that had been pledged in April that year had actually been allocated.[135] Even more alarming had been the threat to withhold short-term residency permits from displaced Jews. With the help of State Commissioner Epstein, this threat could be averted. As one fear had been soothed, others sprang up. The German environment in which they lived was less and less inclined to consider Jews in need of special help. In January 1947, the City of Frankfurt introduced new regulations, requiring evidence of employment for all men between the ages of fourteen and sixty-five and all women between the ages of fourteen and fifty before issuing ration cards.[136] Nobody, including Jews, was to be exempt from these regulations. On behalf of Frankfurt's displaced Jews, the Committee again asked Curt Epstein to intervene:

> Our members are greatly concerned about the new law about employment and making the allocation of food dependent on it. We require help to persuade higher authorities to pass a decree that Jews who wish to work but are unable to find work, will not encounter problems at the labour exchange. Our Committee now has 700 members, and most of these are people who have signed up to emigrate as soon as possible and will, therefore, stay no more than a few weeks in

the Frankfurt area. In spite of these circumstances, these people are prepared to participate in the labour process during the period of waiting. Despite having to overcome various obstacles, the work of our committee in the last two months has been successful. . . . Our contribution to the situation of Jews has been entirely positive and we ask for your valued support to help us extend our work further and to secure improved recognition for us from military government.[137]

Daily obstacles came in many guises. In November 1946, for instance, the Frankfurt Gas Works suddenly cut off supply to a communal kitchen belonging to the Committee and to the flat above it. When Sadie Sender, the Joint representative, remonstrated with the local gas works that a supply was required to operate the kitchen she was told that the Jewish tenants had 'no right to gas'.[138] In a similar incident, the gas works disconnected supplies to a flat occupied by two members of the Committee executive. The letter of protest stressed their special status as Jews and also as 'American officials':

The flat is inhabited by two of our leaders who also belong to the American organization [Joint], and they require a gas cooking point. We are utterly astounded that a Jewish body, let alone one which consists of American officials, should encounter difficulties with your office.[139]

The Committee never hesitated to emphasise the persecution history and special needs of its members. In December 1946, for instance, Heinrich Blau, a member of the Committee, reported that someone had stolen a leather coat, two suits with important papers, nine hundred Reichsmark, two pairs of trousers and a jacket from his bedsit. In his letter to the German police, the chairman of the Committee, David Werba, left no doubt that this was no ordinary case:

We ask for your valued help, because the matter concerns a former concentration camp prisoner who is a member of our Committee and who, in any case, has been robbed of everything during the Nazi years. We request to be notified by telephone [here the number is cited, E.K.] as soon as you have positive results.[140]

As the voice of displaced Jews in Frankfurt, the Jewish Committee also sought to remedy perceived injustices, albeit with limited success. For example, the Committee asked Curt Epstein to use his powers as State Commissioner by ordering German police at Frankfurt's railway station to stop harassing Jews. Apparently, police tended to stop and search arriving passengers, subjecting Jews in particular to body searches. There is no evidence that Epstein complied. The Committee also failed to enlist the help of the AJDC, Epstein and a US Army chaplain in persuading General McNarney that Jewish Displaced Persons who were serving prison sentences in Germany – usually for black market activities – should be included in his 1946 amnesty.[141] A campaign to extend Joint aid to displaced Jews in prison and to set up a programme of regular prison visits fizzled out without result. For a short time, however, the Committee seemed to seize the initiative in all things Jewish inside Frankfurt and upstage the community as the Jewish voice after liberation.

The Eclipse of the Jewish Committee

The creation of the Jewish Committee in 1946 as a distinct tier of support for displaced Jews reflected and extended the divide between this group and the emergent Jewish community in the city. One year on, the parameters had begun to change. As post-war Germany reinvented its economic and political system, Jews faced the challenge of locating themselves in this new context.

While survival after liberation had been dominated by material issues and the needs arising from years of maltreatment, ill health and impoverishment, the reinvented political order and the transfer of control from Allied to German agencies added the new priority that Jews in Germany required effective organizations in order to support their culture, and also to meet their claims for restitution at local, regional and national level. Jewish Committees and their clientele of displaced Jews were excluded from these developments. When a Regional Association of Jewish Communities (*Landesverband der Jüdischen Gemeinden*) was constituted in Hesse in 1948, the Committee in Frankfurt received an invitation to the inaugural meeting but found itself ineligible to secure actual representation because it existed 'outside the Jewish Community as a separate entity'.[142] In July 1947 already, the Jewish community in Frankfurt was advised by an official in the Ministry of Culture that the State of Hesse would allocate 40,000 Reichsmark to the planned Regional Association for distribution to member communities. The Frankfurt community had no doubt who should benefit from these funds:

> There is general agreement that only the so-called German Jewish communities are entitled to receive these funds, not associations that belong and are answerable to the Regional Committee, since these associations are already funded by foreign organizations.[143]

Not surprisingly, the Association of Jewish Communities in Hesse regarded a merger between the Committee and the community in Frankfurt as a foregone conclusion. A letter to the Committee did not mince words:

> You do not appear to have understood what is at stake. The merger consists of nothing more than to rectify a regrettable error of the recent past and to underline the unity within one community of all Jews who live in Frankfurt. This merger cannot be judged by the criteria of a good or a bad mood or depend on who dislikes whom. The merger is a more fundamental requirement and it will come, regardless of the reasons why the leaders of one or the other group may oppose it.[144]

When the merger finally did occur, in April 1949, members of the Jewish Committee were required to submit individual membership applications to the Jewish community. More than eight hundred, two thirds of the registered total, actually did so. At the time, Jewish community membership stood at 516. An agreement about procedure had stipulated that the Committee would be entitled to one seat on the new executive for every two hundred members who joined. Of an elected executive of nine members, four had belonged to the Committee. Although displaced Jews outnumbered German Jews by more than 50 per cent in the unified membership, the Committee had been taken over, not joined as an equal. Indeed, since August 1948, the Jewish Committee had been defunct in all but name. Its executive, which had been so eager and active at the outset, met only occasionally and most cultural activities had ground to a halt. Only the kitchen remained open, not least since the Jewish community had assumed a more prominent role in running it.

A major factor in the collapse of the Jewish Committee in Frankfurt was the onset of resettlement in 1948. Resettlement enabled displaced Jews to leave Germany and enact, in the majority of cases, the Zionist option. Inside Germany, the advent of resettlement recast the parameters of everyday living. As soon as the State of Israel was founded in May 1948, Jews under the age of thirty-five were barred from belonging to the Jewish Committee while the AJDC refused to support anyone who had not registered to leave Germany.[145] 1948, therefore, constituted a turning point between staying and going. For the Committee, resettlement posed the question of its own future. In January 1949, the executive minuted the end:

> Since emigration has assumed such massive proportions we have arrived at the conclusion that we should now actively pursue the issue of a merger, not least since the Jewish Agency is increasing the pressure to speed up emigration to Israel.[146]

Other factors also contributed to the paralysis and collapse. As displaced Jews in Germany were encouraged and even urged to commit themselves to the Zionist option, the Jewish Committee in Frankfurt became a base for displaced Jews who had no plans to leave. The closure of the DP camps consolidated this new focus. As the Jewish Committee lost members through resettlement and emigration, it gained new ones by defying German as well as American objections and assisting several hundred former residents of Zeilsheim to remain in Frankfurt. Compared with its founding period, however, the Committee could offer little material help. The Joint had already reduced provisions and moved to demanding that recipients produce medical certificates to document their need. American Joint Distribution Committee representation in Frankfurt had also changed from the heyday of Miss Sender. Her successor, Mrs. Preiser, arrived in 1947 and worked more closely with the Jewish community.[147] When Rose Gandel, the third representative in as many years, took over in 1948, she intensified controls and insisted on being present when distributions took place. A stencilled letter announced her visits:

> I shall be visiting your town/city on (date) in order to assist you with the distribution of Joint aid. I shall bring with me the products that will be distributed.[148]

This letter was accompanied by a list of eligible recipients who had to appear in person. If the recipients were children, at least one parent had to be present. The olden days of bulk deliveries, handwritten store records and distributions without signatures or names were well and truly over. They ended for good on August 15, 1948 when the Economic Office of the Jewish Committee emptied its storerooms and transferred the remaining contents to the Jewish community. An explanatory note suggested that these constituted the food allocation for May 1948 but had only just been received in Frankfurt.[149]

Social Normalisation, Poverty and the Remade Jewish Community in Frankfurt am Main

The collapse of the Jewish Committee as a voice and an agency of Jewish support was hastened by the emergence of German-Jewish organizations, by the onset of large-scale resettlement that reduced the overall number of Jews in Germany from about 200,000 in 1946–7 to just 20,000, and by the shift of AJDC support from food and other material aid to funding Jewish organizations. While all three developments undermined the function of the Jewish Committee, it was left to the Currency Reform of June 1948 to strike the mortal blow. One month before, the Committee had already run out of money, since the Central Committee had halted all transfers and banks refused to arrange emergency loans. In early June, the executive decided to pay the outstanding salaries of office holders and employees by using up all reserves.[150] Other channels of support had also dried up.[151] When presented with a list of expenditure incurred to run its office, State Commissioner Epstein, who had been so amenable earlier, declared that the Committee was 'not entitled to any money'. As a gesture of goodwill, he offered 5,000 Deutschmark to pay outstanding bills, and referred to the sum as a gift that could not be repeated.[152]

For the Jewish Committee and its members, the Currency Reform changed more than the legal tender in circulation: it changed a world and a way of life. The Committee had emerged and enjoyed public backing at a time when money had no value in Germany. Jewish survival after liberation had emerged under distorted conditions, in an economic and social context where earned income, even if it had been accessible, was overshadowed by the value of goods as a second, more potent currency. Deprived of their belongings and possessions, displaced as well as German Jews would have faced renewed starvation and further impoverishment but for the food and other material goods distributed to them by humanitarian aid agencies and above all by the Joint. In the barter economy of the immediate post-war years, some of the items in these aid packages could be sold or traded. Cigarettes could be turned into winter coats, packages of coffee into shoes or blankets.

Although barter of this kind pervaded German society between 1945 and the Currency Reform in June 1948, Jews – and above all displaced Jews – depended on it to rebuild their everyday lives; but found themselves vilified as black-marketeers. The critics, most of them Germans but some of them Americans or other Jews, made no mention of the forced and prolonged impoverishment or the inability to regain any kind of normality on the basis of German ration coupons for goods that were unobtainable.[153] In the distorted economy of survival after the Holocaust, Jews had to find their own means of obtaining toilet soap, underwear and overcoats, of eating fresh fruit, drinking milk or dressing their newborns in baby clothes.

Overnight, as the Currency Reform restored the value of money, goods lost their value as currency, and barter became obsolete. Overnight, therefore, Jews lost the precarious balance they had constructed in their daily lives and faced renewed poverty. In principle, of course, the Currency Reform treated everybody the same. On presentation of a passport or a valid identity card, each person was entitled to receive DM 40, the so-called '*Kopfgeld*', Head-Money. Not all displaced Jews possessed the required documents to claim the money. Even for those who could, the

40 Deutschmark in hand were all they had. Displaced Jews, unlike most Germans, did not hold additional money in savings accounts, let alone shares. German Jews found themselves doubly dispossessed because their bank accounts and other assets remained frozen and inaccessible. Moreover, as political normalisation gathered pace, German civic authorities demanded that housing and furniture that had earlier been allocated to Jews from confiscated ex-Nazi stock, should be returned to their rightful owners. Jewish survivors had no right to keep what they had been given after 1945. On the other hand, they also had no right to reclaim their former belongings and reverse the Nazi confiscations and injustices.

The apparent normalisation in the wake of the Currency Reform entailed a renewed threat of poverty for Jews. In Frankfurt, this threat of poverty was particularly pressing for German-Jewish Holocaust survivors who were too old or too infirm to rebuild independent lives, and for displaced Jews who had no chance to do so. Some residents of Frankfurt's old folks home could no longer afford to pay the DM 120 per month it cost to stay there without additional welfare support; others saw their application for a place turned down because their income was too low. In most cases, the hardship arose because pension entitlements had not been agreed by the German authorities, leaving Jewish Holocaust survivors impoverished and dependent on charity.

Displaced Jews turned to the Committee for financial help. Their requests show how severely the Currency Reform had unhinged everyday lives. In July 1948, for instance, Erwin Dimst asked for help because he was unable to pay his rent of DM 47 'in the new money'.[154] Hermann Ackermann feared eviction from a rented bedsit costing DM 25 a month. Elisabeth Stein was without employment or income and hoped to be considered in 'a future distribution of money'. Sander and Magda Lustig begged for 'monetary support', since they had 'no money at all or any kind of salary due to the currency reform'.[155]

Others directed their call for help to the Care Centre in Frankfurt whose clientele now included all victims of National Socialism. The Jews among the petitioners had all endured imprisonment in concentration camps. Horst Geuder cared for his sick mother and did not have enough money to buy clothes. He was given DM 100. Anna Fölsing requested DM 500 to carry out repairs to her flat but 'in view of the shortage of funds' received only DM 200. Käte Grau, another Jewish Holocaust survivor, did not have enough money to pay DM 33.50 for dental treatment. Rosa Hassel had returned from Theresienstadt and needed money to buy a mattress, a radio and other household items. She had asked for DM 300 and was allocated DM 100. In its August sessions, the Care Centre in Frankfurt distributed DM 9,000 to over seventy applicants, half of them Jewish concentration camp survivors.[156]

This new poverty did not strike without warning. In June 1948, the Regional Association of Jewish Communities in Hesse had alerted the state government of the imminent hardship, and secured an agreement that help would be provided from public funds under the broad heading of 'restitution'. Setting out the terms of the agreement, it informed the Jewish Committee that a total of one hundred recipients could be supported in Hesse as a whole with sums of up to 80 Deutschmark for a single person, 120 for a married couple and 140 for a couple with children. In order to submit a claim, the Committee was instructed to compile and send a complete list of names, stating in each case the type of hardship and the reasons for it. The list had to reach the minister in charge by July 1, 1948. In June 1948, the office of State Commissioner for Jews had been closed and its functions absorbed by the Ministry for Political Liberation. When the new poverty struck, the Committee no longer enjoyed a direct and personal link to the relevant decision maker or ministry. In accordance with instructions but disregarding the numerical limits that had been set, the Jewish Committee submitted a list of 337 names, more than three times the maximum suggested for the whole region.[157] The extensive list could be read as a sign that the Committee had retained some of its earlier fighting spirit even in decline. It might be more accurate to read it as evidence of the extent to which displaced Jews in Frankfurt had become exposed to poverty and were again desperately in need of help.

When eight hundred members of the Jewish Committee joined the Jewish community in Frankfurt in April 1949, many had seen the precarious everyday survival collapse that they had constructed for themselves after liberation. Under changed conditions, they were forced to start again. So many continued to need help and so few found employment that the AJDC restarted a limited financial aid programme to assist individuals. On the other hand, the momentum of post-war German economic reconstruction also improved the life-chances of Jews who had opted to stay or who returned in the 1950s after failed attempts at resettlement.

In Frankfurt, the merger of community and Committee rejuvenated Jewish culture even before social and economic conditions improved. The Jewish Committee, as displaced Jewish populations elsewhere, had included more members under forty, more families with children, more babies and far fewer people over fifty-five than the Jewish community where most members were older, where families – if they did exist – normally included a non-Jewish parent, and where very few of the children were Jewish. After the merger, the Jewish community established its own kindergarten, set up a Jewish school and organized its own cultural programmes. Caring for ageing and ailing members remained a significant challenge, although mellowed by the presence of young people and a new generation whose future lay ahead of them and would begin in Germany, even if they chose to settle elsewhere later. The merger with the Committee gave the Jewish community a new lease of life and a new relevance for the future.

6

JEWS AND GERMANS:
DISTANCE, DISTRUST AND
NEW BEGINNINGS

Perceptions of Jews and Germans

In February 1946, when Simon Rifkind prepared his report as Jewish Advisor after five months in Germany, he concluded that all Jews there were displaced and ready to leave as soon as possible.[1] Where Jewish life had existed in the past, none could be expected in the future. As for Germans, he believed them tarnished by the Holocaust, without a sense of guilt for what the survivors had endured and unwilling to help:

> The Jews who are today provisionally in Germany and Austria are small in numbers; approximately 100,000 of them are living in all zones of these countries; family life is practically unknown among them – the members of their families are dead; they are destitute – the Germans stripped them of everything; a child is a rare treasure among them – extermination of the young was a Nazi priority; they suffer from psychological and physiological ills as a result of life in the concentration camps and the experiences they have endured. Their civilization, so laboriously created over the centuries, has been brought low; its leadership is dead; its institutions – economic, social, religious and scholarly – are demolished. The one thing that Hitler failed to take from these people was their spirit.[2]

As he visited displaced persons camps and fledgling Jewish communities, he could not but notice that life was far from normal. Most Jews were housed in camps or hostels 'while the Germans live in civilian homes'. Most possessed very little clothing and often no shoes, and were disappointed when help consisted of cast-off clothing collected in

American salvage drives. In Deggendorf, a DP camp where two-thirds of the residents were German-Jewish survivors from Theresienstadt who had opted to wait there for resettlement rather than returning to former home towns that had forced them out, recipients were so disgusted at the low quality clothes they were sent from the United States that they staged a collection of their own to send clothes to their obviously impoverished donors.[3] As far as Rifkind was concerned, Americans had a duty to 'satisfy the needs of these Jews',[4] and a duty to ensure that Germans contributed their share. He regarded it as a central aspect of his mission in Germany to hold the local population accountable and refused to accept the view that Germans themselves were too dislocated by the extent of bomb damage, food shortages and general hardship to concern themselves with the plight of Jews. In spirit, he stuck to Memorandum 39 and its notion that the needs of displaced persons and persecutees should be met from German resources even if this meant moving Germans into former concentration camps.[5] He was irritated by complaints about the housing shortage in Germany's bombed-out cities and angered by the false arithmetic that there were not enough houses left to accommodate Jews:

> Assuming the highest reported proportion of destruction of housing, the Germans are still trespassers in the aggregate when they house 100,000 Jewish displaced persons in all zones where 600,000 Jews lived before.[6]

In reality, of course, most liberated Jews lived in camps that had been set up in former slave labour compounds or concentration camps, disused military barracks and, occasionally, in residential settings. The Germans who lived near these installations remained aloof or were outright hostile. The same population who claimed not to have noticed that they had lived cheek-by-jowl with a camp and its prisoners during the Nazi era, resented their new neighbours. Until shortly before Rifkind's arrival, camps had been surrounded by barbed wire fences, keeping the liberated Jews inside and segregated by armed guards from the German population. When the former prisoners were finally permitted to move freely like other civilians, Rifkind found them vilified as undesirable elements:

> The calumny has been uttered that the displaced Jews constitute the dregs of the East European ghettos. Sometimes I wonder who in this wide world has the moral right to judge them. But, if judge we will, the truth is that whether they be dregs or cream of the crop, they surpass the vintage wines of the Rhineland. I shall never forget that one of the first requests of the so-called de-nazified civil governments of Germany to the Allied Control Council was that the rations of the displaced

persons should be reduced. That is a measure of the German confession of guilt; that is an index to the level of character that today prevails among the Germans.[7]

Judge Rifkind's successor as Jewish Advisor, Philip Bernstein, arrived in Germany in May 1946 and served until August 1947 through what he called 'a stampede out of Poland'.[8] At its height in August 1946, nearly four thousand Jews crossed from Czechoslovakia into the US zone in one night alone. From a German perspective, the influx occurred at a time when local populations were experiencing unprecedented food shortages because farmers shunned normal retail channels and preferred instead to barter in exchange for other goods and valuables. Inside displaced persons camps, food and other essentials were supplied by the military, distributed by UNRRA aid workers and supplemented by the Joint Distribution Committee who also provided religious articles. By way of exception to this separate and parallel system, German farmers were supposed to supply fresh milk and vegetables, although they never did so without objections. During his assignment in Germany, Bernstein noticed, as his predecessor had done, a lack of remorse among Germans for the past. Instead, they tended to blame their own shortages on the presence of Jews and the provisions they required:

> It is the opinion of most observers, confirmed by my own experience, that the Germans bitterly resent the presence of Displaced Jews in their midst. Only a student of abnormal psychiatry could explain the perverse convolutions in the minds of the Germans who, after having decimated the Jews, stolen and destroyed their possessions, deprived them of their rights, driven them from their homes, now blame them for the Germans' privations. Nevertheless, it is a fact that the Germans do blame the Jewish DPs for the current shortages of housing, food, clothing and fuel. That this has no basis in fact does not disturb those who again are seeking a scapegoat.[9]

Given the shortages that pervaded Germany after the Second World War, resentments ran high that the wrong people were obtaining unfair advantages. These resentments did not stop at Jews, nor were they exclusively aimed at them. Fingers of blame pointed especially at former Nazis who, it was rumoured, managed to hoard provisions when they were in charge and who could now draw on these while most other people had nothing. A house that had been confiscated from a Nazi and allocated to a former victim yielded crates of cigarettes, tobacco, raisins, wine and liqueur from under the floor boards.[10] In a similar vein, Kurt Brode, a former political detainee, alleged that Nazis had enriched themselves and remained advantaged:

> We, who were racially and politically persecuted and incarcerated in prisons and concentration camps, find denazification far too slow. This is all the more regrettable, since the Nazis are, meanwhile, trading their stock of goods on the black market, live the life of Riley and have absolutely everything while the decent people have nothing. Who were the owners of most businesses and factories? The Nazis! Who was able, at the time, to move their belongings to secure locations? The Nazis! The rest of the population had no chance at all to find apartments where to hide their stuff or obtain the use of cars to transport it. Who kept most of their assets and valuables? Who were among the first when car licences were issued again? The Nazis! Who was, therefore, in a position to get to the goods they had stored elsewhere und use their cars and their stock of goods to tour the countryside obtaining food? The Nazis! Of course we all know today that the Nazis have never been Nazis, but they all know one another, they all stick together, support each other and do deals between themselves. This underground organization has to be smashed before anything will change.[11]

Problems of Return and Daily Living

In the aftermath of the Second World War, misgivings about unfair treatment were not merely directed against displaced Jews in their camps or at former Nazis in their presumed lairs packed with loot, but permeated the social fabric closer to home. Germans complained that they were losing out to Jews while German Jews complained that virtually nothing had been done for them after the Nazi era ended. A poignant occasion to bring these conflicting views into the public arena was the official address delivered by Walter Kolb, the newly elected Lord Mayor of Frankfurt am Main, on New Year's Day 1947. In it, he celebrated the fact that his city had been chosen as the administrative centre of the Bi-Zone, the union of the American and British zones of occupations and forerunner of a new Germany. Given the extent of destruction and the scope of renewal that had to be accomplished, this Germany and Frankfurt in particular depended, in the Lord Mayor's view, on the input and active contribution of the Jews who had been driven out under the Nazis. He therefore called on Jewish exiles to return to their former home town and make it rise again, as they had done in the past:

> We all know that Frankfurt became wealthy and big, not least through

the achievements and the work of its Jewish fellow-citizens who exerted an immeasurably beneficial influence and were a blessing to the city's development. And I can simply do no more than express the hope and voice the request that those Old Frankfurters of the Jewish faith who, surely, have remained citizens of their hometown in their hearts, should seriously consider whether they can return – despite all the hardship and mistrust. We promise with all our heart that we shall accept them, and we promise solemnly that we shall do our best to make them feel comfortable in their old home region (*Heimat*).[12]

Appeals to exiles to return were not altogether new. In October 1945, Dr. Blaum, Walter Kolb's predecessor who had been appointed by the Americans to serve until elections were held in 1946, corresponded with several eminent exiles, not all of them Jewish.[13] In his letter to Ferdinand Blum, a former university professor and distinguished scientist, the Lord Mayor wrote:

I would be extremely gratified if you would return to our city and continue your research work here. I need not mention to you that you will receive the full support of the local government administration in Frankfurt upon your return. It is a duty of honour and a guilt of thanks (*Dankesschuld*) which we would like to perform towards you.[14]

The appeal of January 1, 1947, by contrast, was not directed at known or prominent individuals but at Jewish exiles in general, albeit those with the assets and acumen to contribute to Frankfurt's reconstruction. However, when some ordinary and impoverished exiles wrote to ask for help with settling in Frankfurt, such help was not forthcoming. Responding to a 61-year-old refugee who had escaped to Shanghai, Walter Kolb turned him down, ostensibly because bomb damage made it impossible to provide housing but also because the man had lived in Berlin, not Frankfurt, when he fled Germany, and had been no more than a humble employee in a Jewish publishing house:

It will be difficult to assist you with living in reasonable comfort here because the City of Frankfurt am Main has, as you will know, been damaged to more than 50 per cent by bombs.[15]

When Leopold and Anna Hanauer-Seyd who had lived in Frankfurt wrote from Belgium asking 'to be given the chance and permission to return to our home town', they were accepted in principle, but also not made as welcome as the New Year's Address had intimated:

Frankfurt is currently experiencing a housing shortage of catastrophic proportions. . . . Under these conditions, the city cannot assume the responsibility of providing accommodation within the next couple of months.[16]

The appeal of January 1, 1947 did not reverse German-Jewish migration at the time although in the early 1950s, several prominent Jewish exiles such as Theodor W. Adorno and Max Horkheimer, the founders of the Institute of Social Research at Frankfurt's university, settled again in the city. Inside Frankfurt, however, Walter Kolb's New Year's Address elicited gasps of disbelief and very little acclamation. The letters page of the *Frankfurter Rundschau* served as a public forum to a variety of responses. Jews tended to put pen to paper to voice their outrage at the assumption that all Jews were wealthy although the Nazis had robbed them, including exiles, of everything. Based on her own experiences, Maria Fulda warned that Jews could not expect any help:

After all my relatives have been completely exterminated, I am the last member of a family that had lived in Frankfurt for more than 300 years. I was ordered on five separate occasions to prepare for transport to Poland, Estonia and so on, and I have only been saved by a miracle. When you, Mr. Lord Mayor, ask the Jewish citizens of Frankfurt who now live abroad to return, I can only surmise that you have no idea about the bad living conditions of Jews in Frankfurt today. To welcome human beings who have been driven in shame and humiliation from their homes and their livelihoods and who managed with great difficulties to rebuild some kind of life abroad, to greet these people with nothing more than a 'joyous heart' amounts to reopening the wounds of the past, not healing them. How could you possibly seek to heal these wounds, Mr. Lord Mayor when, at this very moment, Jewish citizens of Frankfurt are completely dependent on public welfare and receive no more than 70.50 Reichsmark a month?[17]

Regarding her personal situation, she reported to have tried and failed repeatedly to obtain a business licence from the German authorities to open an antiques shop. Frankfurt's Benefit Office let it be known that in addition to her welfare cheques, Maria Fulda had received two special payments totalling over RM 1,000. While alleging that she had not been telling the truth, nothing was said about forcing her into benefit dependency by refusing to issue a business licence.[18] Another correspondent, Heinrich Meyer, told a similar story. He had tried for several months to help a Jewish survivor open a shop in Frankfurt but could not get the German authorities to issue the required permit. Disheartened, the potential businessman left Germany for America. In another case, he tried to assist a Jewish woman in a small town near Frankfurt to open a textile shop. The local administrators assigned a dank room as premises but ordered her to cease trading almost immediately because the room could not be heated. On the basis of his experiences, Heinrich Meyer concluded, Germans did not want Jews to live in their society:

> I listened with deep interest to your New Year's message, and I am convinced that you personally will do everything you can to make the return of Jews possible and ensure that they receive a warm welcome. Your intentions, however, transcend your influence. The German people in its majority remains anti-Jewish, and even the newly appointed civil servants are reluctant to assist Jews. The standard reply is that there are no laws to make special provisions, and that nothing can be taken back from those who enriched themselves at the expense of Jews during the Third Reich.[19]

Fritz Uhlmann, who referred to himself as 'one of the few German Jews who have returned from abroad despite the murder of their relatives' used the occasion of Walter Kolb's appeal to highlight how little help he had received and how unwelcoming his former home town had been. He could only warn others against coming back:

> As long as German Jews who survived the horrors of the Nazi period are not compensated properly, as long as their Nazi torturers enjoy better living conditions than those who returned, as long as the few who did come home are not even allocated a half-decent flat or, as happened to me and my wife, are given no more than a rickety bed, an unusable wardrobe and a wobbling table . . . as long as things are like this, I have to warn all Jews who escaped from the Nazi regime strongly against coming back.[20]

Like all Jewish complainants, Fritz Uhlmann was invited to attend a personal consultation with the Lord Mayor or his personal assistant. A handwritten note in the margin of the file copy warned, however, that Uhlmann was a member of the Communist Party whose complaints might be ideologically motivated and politically hostile. Although German officials appear to have harboured and voiced misgivings about the critical comments voiced by Jews such as Maria Fulda and Fritz Uhlmann, Walter Kolb at least listened to their grievances. He was less easily persuaded to heed objections voiced by Germans about his approach towards Jews. A case in point is his response to Karl Enck whose letter stressed that he, a genuine citizen of Frankfurt, had to live in an out-of-town pre-fab without being invited back:

> Although we 'little people' are not such 'fat' tax payers as the Jews and former inhabitants of Frankfurt who are now invited to return (because I believe that most of the returners must be Jews), we were also former inhabitants of Frankfurt and tax payers.[21]

Walter Kolb replied that, in his view, Jews had to be treated differently from Germans because they had been treated differently by the Nazis:

> If you look at matters objectively you must admit that of all people, Jews had been stripped of their possessions long before the outbreak of the war, and forced to flee into the unknown. . . . Injustice has been committed and needs to be rectified.[22]

Other communications from local Germans that arrived in Walter Kolb's office in response to his New Year appeal expressed more forcefully why Jews would not be welcome. A group calling itself 'Elderly Citizens of Frankfurt' suggested that the 'Jewish problem' should be shelved for several years. They claimed to know that Jews would not contribute their share towards clearing the rubble in Germany despite being 'largely responsible' for it. By way of evidence, the letter writers referred to alleged wheeler-dealer activities in Zeilsheim, the DP camp on the edge of Frankfurt. There, they argued, everyone could see that Jews lived by shunning work and by enriching themselves at the expense of others.[23] In another letter, one of Frankfurt's German inhabitants objected that if Jews were to return, Germans would have to make do with less:

> We heard your New Year's Address and your wishes for the new year with pleasure, except the bit about Jews. We did not expect from you that you would invite the Jews back. Jews demand their advantages, and you would have to take those from us. Jews are crooks, and I can prove this. They arrive here without anything to their name, and how many of them have hundreds of thousands of marks, where do they get it from if they are not crooks? And there you go and call the Jews at a time when there are already so many Jews in Frankfurt![24]

As for the Jewish community, its leaders hoped that perhaps the city might assist them with the return of exiles from Shanghai.[25] Contrary to individual Jews who had aired their discontent, the community's official response welcomed Walter Kolb's remarks as endorsement from the political leadership of the day of a Jewish residency in Germany, an endorsement that seemed to elicit nothing but gratitude:

> We do not want to be amiss in thanking you whole heartedly for your words which were inspired by a genuine sense of moral responsibility. As the first ever invitation by a party conscious of its responsibilities, the head of the ancient and tradition-rich city of Frankfurt, this call was most effective. It gave all Jews who live here or abroad hope for a better and more blessed future in a democratic Germany.[26]

Anti-Semitism in Germany after the Holocaust

Officially, military government had stamped out Nazism and its ideology in Germany by banning Nazi organizations, imposing censorship on publications and removing known Nazis from public office. Together, these measures were designed to remove anti-democratic and racist practices and the people who had implemented them. Attitudes and assumptions, however, were not as easily dislodged, and anti-Semitism constituted a case in point. Within months of establishing military government in Germany and promoting re-education, American officials were eager to gauge the success of their approach and ascertain the prospects for creating a democratic political culture in the parts of Germany that they occupied. The Office of the Military Government in the US zone, OMGUS, used opinion polls to find out how Germans saw their past and imagined their future.[27] Most of the questions focussed on preferred systems of government, but some tried to establish what respondents thought of Jews. The first survey was published in 1946. It found that 80 per cent of the German population viewed Jews negatively, half even characterised themselves, with a certain degree of pride, as ardent anti-Semites.[28] Just 20 per cent of respondents seemed free of anti-Semitic prejudices. Two years later, a similar survey yielded similar results. Replica studies in 1949 and 1952 showed that fewer people chose to identify themselves as anti-Semites but a much larger number refused to engage with the question and claimed to have no views on the matter of Jews.

Surveys and Manifestations

German anti-Semitism in the wake of the Holocaust manifested itself in several ways. At its most direct, it consisted of violence and verbal abuse. In Bavaria, local mayors evicted Jews from their homes in order to accommodate Germans waiting to be denazified. Jews who travelled on trains or trams risked being beaten up. In one case, a German railway guard had tried to throw an Auschwitz survivor from a moving train.[29] When cinema newsreels reported that a synagogue had been reopened in Munich, members of the audience shouted: 'Not enough Jews were killed'.[30] In various localities, Jewish shops, and buildings thought to be used by Jews, were vandalised or daubed with Nazi slogans. Year on year, anti-Semites ransacked a dozen or more Jewish cemeteries.[31] In 1947, 27 Jewish cemeteries were attacked in the British zone alone.[32] The Bavarian State Commissioner for Victims of Racism, Philip Auerbach, himself a survivor of Auschwitz and Buchenwald, received hundreds of threatening letters every day and was called upon to defend Jews against innumerable acts of everyday discrimination.[33]

Non-Jewish observers tended to dismiss anti-Semitism as the work of hooligans who moved on the fringes of society and responded to what they perceived as a provocative Jewish presence. This kind of response was wrong, but, as the *Ruhr Zeitung* explained to its readers, a product of difficult times and provoked by the behaviour of Jews themselves:

> After the capitulation in 1945, there were waves of anti-Semitism. In all these cases, it could be shown that the perpetrators of these campaigns were small organized groups. Anti-Semitism, however, has been reinforced by the influence of demoralised Jewish DPs. In the interest of German Jews and of World Jewry as a whole, the relevant authorities have, therefore, done their utmost to assist these people with emigration.[34]

The British Foreign Office adopted a similar position and belittled violent incidents against Jews as 'statements of individuals or very small groups'.[35] A decade on, the West German government was to use the same arguments to deny that a wave of anti-Semitic incidents in 1959–60 pointed to a presence or resurgence of National Socialist orientations in the country.[36] After the Second World War, resentments against Jews remained lodged in the minds that had been indoctrinated without questioning whether the doctrine should be followed. In addition, the widespread dislocation caused substantial sections of the German population to perceive and resent Jews as a presumably privileged group. Germans saw themselves as having been crushed by defeat and, through no fault of their own, exposed to hardship and uncertainty. In his report as Jewish Advisor, Philip Bernstein noted that anti-Semitism manifested itself differently from the past but seemed as strong as ever:

Recent Army studies of German attitudes indicate that six out of every ten Germans would condone overt acts against Jews. Until the present time the Army has pretty well kept such acts under control. But in the camps and cities, Jews are reporting sharper tensions, abuse in public places, snatches of Nazi songs, an occasional rock thrown in the windows of a Jewish home. With the utmost sobriety, I predict that the withdrawal of the American forces would again lead to pogroms. There must be no withdrawal until the Jewish DPs leave Germany, as all of them wish to do. It is perfectly clear that their early removal is imperative.[37]

Following a similar line of thought, Lucius D. Clay, the military governor for the US zone, argued before the Anglo–American Commission on the Future of Palestine that displaced Jews could not be expected to remain in Germany and find employment there without creating a backlash of intensified anti-Semitism.[38] Despite such misgivings, military governments in the western zones of occupation were already preparing by 1947 to turn their sections of Germany into a political and economic ally of the western world. While American and other Allied forces might remain in the country, the actual government and the organization of society would be left to Germans and their chosen representatives. From 1946 onwards, elected regional governments had replaced the appointees of the first hour, while military government influence receded to supervising the political and economic framework of the emerging German democracy without running matters in detail. In this set-up, there was no permanent place, as Bernstein had postulated, for the US or any other army as a buffer between Germans and Jews. When General Clay was approached to appoint some kind of guardian or commissioner to protect Jews in Germany from hostilities, he refused. Indeed, the military had already reduced its personnel in Germany and begun to retreat from its governing function. These developments meant that manifestations of anti-Semitism could not be controlled from the outside but had to be tackled from within.

How did the problematic relationship between Germans and Jews manifest itself? This was the central question addressed in an OMGUS report of July 1, 1947.[39] It concluded that American service personnel had learned about the Holocaust after the discovery of the concentration camps and responded with outrage to the mountains of corpses and the pitifully weakened survivors they had seen. Germans, by contrast, were inclined to keep their distance. They did not visit the liberated camps unless forced to do so by a military unit who had taken control of their area. Even then, few showed 'genuine revulsion'. They distanced themselves from what happened by referring to the Holocaust as 'a mistake' while part-endorsing National Socialism as 'a good idea that was carried out badly'. After the defeat and under the watchful eye of the military occupiers, Germans kept their anti-Semitic views hidden.[40] Within a year, however, they surfaced again, this time in the guise of isolated incidents of violence against Jews, administrative sabotage in allotting to persecuted Jews the privileges to which they were entitled, desecration of Jewish cemeteries, threats, anonymous letters vilifying Jews sent to newspapers and individuals.[41]

Under the changed conditions of the post-war world, anti-Semitism was no longer perpetrated or promoted by the state. On the contrary, it was deemed unacceptable or classified as a criminal offence. Banned from public manifestations, anti-Semitism went into hiding and sought less blatant outlets. An article in *Der Aufbau*, the German-language journal published in America for and by German-Jewish refugees, explained:

> Anti-Semitism in Germany does not, at present, manifest itself through aggression – obviously, the 'boiling soul of the people' that had been organized from above in the Nazi years is no longer there – but in a more latent form. Having said this, there have been repeated acts of violence such as the destruction of Jewish cemeteries, the smashing of display windows of Jewish shops etc. The fact that the number of such offences has remained small, should not give rise to premature conclusions. The German population knows full well that the occupying powers will not tolerate any anti-Semitic hostilities and actions. In addition, Jews today and in particular displaced Jews no longer allow themselves to be mistreated but are hitting back hard. It is impossible to predict what will happen on the day when the occupying powers are leaving Germany. That much is certain: the Jews fear that anti-Semitic excesses will occur, provided that any Jews and especially DPs remain there.[42]

Pointing a Finger at Jewish Behaviour

During the war, Germans had experienced comparatively few food shortages since the ruthless exploitation of all occupied areas and their inhabitants to the benefit of the German population constituted a core aspect of Nazi policy and practice. When food shortages did strike after the war, they were blamed on the occupying powers and on formerly persecuted groups who appeared to receive unfair privileges, notably Jews. Some held that Jews themselves invited hostilities by their behaviour. OMGUS tried to explain what was happening between Germans and Jews:

> The population is highly envious because of its own unsatisfactory

living conditions, resents what it considers special privileges granted to Jews in matters of rations and dwellings. It appears, however, that the privileges granted to victims of Fascism are generally overrated. The behaviour of some Jewish DPs and their alleged black market activities provide an opportunity for the overt expression of anti-Semitic tendencies. Often, this type of race prejudice is cloaked in the profession of a friendly attitude towards 'our' [German] Jews as compared to Polish Jews etc. The behaviour of DPs aggravates rather than causes anti-Semitism and makes it more difficult to counteract.[43]

Generally speaking, German political leaders did not confront the issue of anti-Semitism head-on, or make public pronouncements about how Jews should be treated. In his plea that Jews should return from exile, Walter Kolb was something of an exception to this rule, although even he did not cut red tape and make provisions for Jews over and above what the relevant departments in his administration were inclined to offer. While many individual needs remained unmet after survival and liberation, the political consensus at the time and the public discourse no longer included anti-Jewish references. They also did not include explicit reference to Jews although occasionally, the Holocaust was condemned explicitly as 'a horrendous past whose terror was too great' to be mentioned in detail.[44] After seventeen months of military government in the American zone of occupation, General Joseph T. McNarney concluded:

A certain degree of anti-Semitism continues to exist in Germany among those people who have not yet grasped the new spirit of the age and who do not want a new and free Germany.[45]

As far as he was concerned, he had not found a single German public authority that supported any kind of anti-Semitic tendencies. This acceptable face of official politics contrasted with the less benign demeanour of ordinary Germans.

This would not have been apparent to an American top general, but it troubled Jews who lived inside German society and who felt more hostility and much less acceptance than seemed evident at the political and institutional level. In 1947, Ralph Giordano, a Jewish journalist, described what was going on between Germans and Jews at the informal level of assumptions and perceptions:

When the average German hears of the millions of graves in Treblinka, of the electric barbed wire of Buchenwald, of the murdered inhabitants of Oradour-sur-Glance or of the ditches filled with corpses at Babi Yar, he launches himself – as grotesque as it may sound – into his counter-arithmetic. With a threatening gesture he points to his stomach, demanding to know: 'And what about this?' In all earnest, he equates his empty stomach, that is to say an immediate consequence of the policy of criminality which he, following 'higher orders' had defended until five minutes past twelve, with the monster crimes of Auschwitz, Lidice, Vercors and Maidanek. He also displays a frightening lack of understanding that other peoples after their bloody experiences and after millions of murders and billions of tears, do not wish to tolerate Germans who caused all this horror, within their borders.[46]

American military government did not share such misgivings but believed that economic normalisation would, over time, normalise social conditions and ease tensions between Germans and Jews.[47] By way of conclusion, the OMGUS report on anti-Semitism formulated a number of recommendations. All of them were aimed at 'closing the gap' between Germans and Jews. Some pertained to developing interdenominational contacts in order to 'combat the social isolation of individuals'.[48] Others focussed directly on Jews who were urged to conform more emphatically and to integrate if they wanted to combat anti-Semitism. To achieve this, Jews had to change their ways and appease the Germans among whom they lived:

> Wherever possible, targets of prejudice (Jews in this case) should take measures to limit activities (black marketeering, etc.) which aggravate feeling against them. . . . The minority group should, in so far as possible, be encouraged to adapt itself to the predominant group, to respect its customs and traditions, to seek its friendship and cooperation.[49]

Jews and the Black Market: Assumptions and Realities

The Jews who lived in Germany could not forget the fear driven into them by the Gestapo, the SS and its auxiliary forces during the Nazi years, and continued to equate the German police with its racist predecessors. Although the police, like other public bodies, had been hastily reconstituted by military governments to eliminate their Nazified leadership, Jews could not but associate uniformed German police officers with round-ups and maltreatment.[50] For their part, the German police regarded Jews, by and large, as black market operators and criminals. These assumptions also prevailed within the American military police. While military government aimed to protect German and displaced Jews and facilitate a new beginning for these groups, American military police tended to perceive Jews, not unlike their German colleagues, as potential or actual black-marketeers whose activities had to be curtailed. In the prolonged interim between liberation and resettlement or staying on, German and military police staged a number of raids. Revisiting some of these can illuminate the mixture of fear and resentment that prevailed among Jews at the time and also show how fragile the place of Jews remained inside Germany after the Holocaust.

The Stuttgart Raid

On April 1, 1946, Emmanuel Celler, the representative for New York, voiced his outrage in the US Senate that German police had raided a Jewish camp with 'Nazi arrogance' and 'smashed their victims with rubber truncheons'.[51] The incident took place on March 29, 1946 in Stuttgart where a number of apartment buildings had been assigned to displaced Jews and designated as an UNRRA camp.[52] When 230 German police arrived with dogs and loudhailers, the camp director, Harry Lerner, had not been forewarned. By the time he arrived at the scene, one person, Szmul Danzyger, had been shot dead and hundreds wounded, four of them seriously. Unexpectedly, the Jews had fought back when they were rounded up and their homes searched for allegedly concealed black market merchandise and stolen goods. In line with regulations, the German police had been accompanied by a small contingent of eight US soldiers. They remained in the background and later claimed that they had not been informed of what was going to happen. A report on the incident by the chief of police in Stuttgart alleged, however, that military government had authorised German police and even set the date:

> ... to send 120 officers armed with rifles and a further 100 detectives armed with pistols in order to search a number of apartment blocks in the *Obere Reinsburgstrasse*.[53]

In the eyes of the German chief of police, the displaced Jews were felons and his men did no more than uphold law and order. Casualties arose only when the suspects resisted arrest because, he surmised, they had something to hide:

> In reality, the German police is convinced, on the basis of information gathered at the scene, that the reason for organizing collective resistance was that several Poles were interested to prevent, under any circumstances, a search of their houses because such a search would have exposed them without any doubt as illegal traders and as criminals and their

massive stocks of black market merchandise would have been taken from them.[54]

For Harry Lerner, the raid shattered a promising career as an UNRRA administrator. Having arrived in Germany in September 1945, the camp in Stuttgart had been his first placement. In March 1946, he was promoted to the position of director and felt that his efforts were bearing fruit because 'our fellow Jews are gradually beginning to be more like people'.[55] Confident that normality had begun to emerge and also certain of the hiatus that continued to separate him from his charges, he had moved his office and private dwellings to a location one mile away from the camp, one of the reasons why he could be caught so completely off guard. When Lerner confronted Arnulf Klett, the Lord Mayor of Stuttgart, to challenge the manner in which the German police had been deployed, he was surprised to find 'a very nice man'. Without hesitation he accepted the explanation proffered to him, that in peace time, the Mayor's office would, of course, have been free to 'select' police and determine their activities but could not do so while Germany was under military occupation.[56] Yet, it was the same Lord Mayor who did his very best to present displaced Jews and their activities in Stuttgart in a negative light during his regular meetings with military government officials, and who favoured their forcible removal from the city and from Germany.[57] As for Harry Lerner, he was cleared of all wrongdoing by an internal UNRRA enquiry, but nevertheless transferred against his will to a transit camp for eastern European Jews in northern Bavaria near the Czech border. A few months later, and disillusioned by the treatment he had received, he quit UNRRA and his work with displaced Jews.

At the macro-level of policing Jewish camps inside Germany, the Stuttgart raid had more momentous consequences. Army directives were sharpened to redefine and restrict German police powers. From now on, German police were not permitted to enter any Jewish DP camp unless they were accompanied by military police and had obtained advance permission from the local camp director.[58] Once inside, they were forbidden to carry arms.[59] Effectively, German police power after the Stuttgart raid came to a halt at the perimeter fence or boundary of a Jewish camp.

Policing Jews in Germany

Although the new rules ascribed a restraining influence to the US military police in order to shield displaced Jews from unfair treatment at the hands of the German police, misgivings were ripe among US soldiers about the displaced Jews they were supposed to protect. The liberators of the first hour, who had witnessed the destruction of human lives in the concentration camps, had been more sympathetic in dealing with their survivors. They knew that normal behaviour had frequently been destroyed by dehumanising treatment and had to be recovered over time. This cohort, however, had long returned home and been replaced by personnel without first-hand experience as liberators and concomitant sympathies. From their vantage point, working with Germans seemed more straightforward than working with displaced Jews whose attitudes and behaviour they disliked:

> It is suggested that assuming the police are not at fault and properly perform their duties, the fault for the disturbances is in the mental attitude of the DPs themselves. The legitimate DPs were long-suffering under the Nazis because of mistreatment and discrimination. When they were liberated, a policy of pampering, protection, and privilege was adopted in regard to these people, resulting in a mental attitude that they were above and outside of the jurisdiction of law enforcement and especially that imposed by the German authorities. Couple this dangerous attitude with the newsvalue [*sic*] headline reading 'Germans Again Persecute Jewish DPs' and you arrive at a situation where the legitimate manhandling of a resisting operator of a printing press making counterfeit ration coupons will be termed 'Persecution' and the law enforcement involved glossed over in favor of a sensational headline.[60]

As far as the US army was concerned, displaced Jews did not keep their side of the bargain. Rather than quietly accepting whatever food or clothing were handed out to them and gratefully waiting for resettlement, they complained about the poor quality of provisions, resented the monotony of having to eat pea soup, potatoes and other starches day after day, and did not even try to find out how to cook with the oatmeal or corn contained in aid parcels, foodstuffs that Americans regarded as a normal part of their diet but that were unknown to the parcels' recipients. The Public Safety Branch of military government shared German assumptions about displaced persons as would-be criminals and regarded their camps as 'open trading centers'.[61] Some observers argued that individuals were forced into the black market because they lacked so many items of daily living and were unable to buy them in a regular way. Thus, Arno Rudert, a journalist writing in the *Frankfurter Rundschau*, admits that some Jews, while waiting to leave for Palestine, were engaged in black market trading, but they would neither be displaced nor impoverished the way they were if the Nazis had not turned against them:

Today, everyday living is a challenge, and within everyday living, the black market is a challenge. Everywhere in Germany where camps for displaced persons are located, certain Germans are inclined to point an accusing finger at these camps and to identify the names of these camps seamlessly and simply with the black market, a very comfortable method to avoid having to think about things. Is it really so difficult to understand the desire for a good suit or a well-fitting shoe?[62]

When the chief Jewish military chaplain, Rabbi Barnett Brickner, visited Germany in 1947, the newspaper of the US armed forces, *Stars and Stripes*, reported his appeal to understand rather than condemn displaced Jews, possibly in order to counteract negative views held by American servicemen:

> He found DPs in almost every camp shivering in unheated rooms. What food they do get, he said, is 'monotonous, the same day after day'. He described how two and three families lived crowded together in a single room 'without privacy even for their love-making'. The rabbi explained the rampant black market, which has become closely affiliated with DP camps, as a result of Jews having too little food, clothing and the necessities of life. He added that those Jews who engaged in black marketeering for the most part only served as middlemen between the Germans and the military.[63]

The Public Safety Branch of US military government shared none of these sentiments but associated displaced Jews and their camps with criminality. Although apportioning some blame to the German police for failing to 'exercise control over the illegal activities outside of displaced persons camps',[64] there was a widespread consensus that Jews as a group engaged in black market activities and all Jewish DP camps functioned as 'sanctuaries' because the German police could not enter them.[65] Despite pressures from inside the US military to open displaced persons camps to German police, the ban remained in place:

> If it appears that the presence of German police in a camp will be a source of disturbance regardless of the number of troops assigned to the operation, permission for the entry will not under any circumstances be authorized.[66]

Directives, however, did little to calm tempers and assuage distrust between Germans and Jews or between Jews and the US military police. On April 29, 1946, for instance, rumours in Landsberg that two of their number had been kidnapped, caused nine hundred Jewish residents to attack German civilians in the proximity of their camp. When military police tried to restore order and make arrests, they were rushed by up to five thousand DPs who freed the detainees and then marched through the town 'indiscriminately assaulting German civilians in the street. As a result, eighteen German civilians were hospitalized with stab wounds, lacerations and bleeding'.[67] In the small town of Uffenheim, also in Bavaria, about 150 Jewish DPs surrounded the house of a US military guard who had earlier rebuffed an attack by a group of three. To disperse the crowd, shots were fired:

> The mob refused to leave and threatened the American personnel with violence. The Americans were forced to use their weapons, firing a total of 18 shots into the air and then directly at the attacking DPs. The mob then dispersed. One member of the mob is believed to have been wounded.[68]

In Turkheim, a quarrel between a German householder and four Jews attracted 250 others to join in, threatening violence. The Bavarian Rural Police summoned help from the military. The crowd only dispersed after a 'light tank' was deployed and fired several shots 'into the mob'.[69]

These flare-ups and clashes were typical of the kind of trouble involving Jews, Germans and police in the mid-1940s. It was often ignited by exaggerated fears and overreaction on the part of the Jews. In defending themselves against perceived threats they did not shy away from aggression. Moreover, other Jews would rally in great numbers to the defence of individuals who would always be seen as innocent victims of maltreatment. This explosive mixture of resentment and aggression alienated the US military and persuaded their police and public safety personnel that displaced Jews were disorderly and often dangerous. This negative evaluation mirrored the view held by the German police that displaced persons were particularly prone to commit crimes.

Unfounded Accusations

However, the data produced at the time to point an accusatory finger at Jews proved, on closer inspection, that black market trading and similar criminality were more widespread among Germans. Thus, a detailed compilation of crime statistics for Bavaria argued that in the course of 1947, 'foreigners' in the region committed 17.5 per cent of all criminal offences but constituted just 4 per cent of the population.[70] The data also showed that the crime rate among Germans doubled in 1947 while that of non-Germans had peaked in July, and then fell from nearly 7,000 to 1,800 per month in December.[71] A similar survey prepared by the Bavarian Rural Police in January 1948 alleged that most unsolved crimes had been committed by displaced persons but showed the number of convictions to be in line with their share of the population.[72] When military government in Bavaria compiled their own data, no evidence was found that displaced persons dominated criminal activity. Crime statistics showed that Germans were twice as likely as displaced persons to be convicted for black market offences.[73]

Statistical evidence had no bearing on assumptions. In the eyes of the German police and the German population, the very presence of displaced Jews impeded their personal and public safety. In November 1945, the chief of police for Stuttgart painted a disturbing picture of presumed threats to public safety in a report to the military government:

> In the population, complaints are rife on the increased flooding of the city with inferior foreign elements. At Castle Square, the goings-on of these elements are at various times so outrageous that one has the impression that it would take no more than an unguarded word to incite these lay-about lads and men into assaulting the German population. Increasingly, fears are being voiced that in winter and with increasing darkness, security conditions in the city will become precarious. The population draws such conclusions from the fact that, in certain areas of the city, whole apartment blocks have been allocated to foreign elements of doubtful origin, among them also criminals, and that frequently acts of theft, looting and mugging have occurred in the immediate and more distant vicinity.[74]

The German police, in their submissions to military government, also portrayed 'Jewish camps' as hideouts for criminals who forged identity papers and ration cards, slaughtered animals illegally, and traded in all kinds of 'robbed or stolen property'. The Rural Police in Bavaria even sent a memorandum in English to the region's military government in order to voice their concerns:

> It has been proved by evidence that wanted criminals among the DPs time and again submerge in authorized camps, for there they are protected from the German police because these camps . . . can be entered only with an escort of US personnel. . . . About 500 pursuits of DPs surprised at the very scene of crime had to be discontinued in the last three months because the perpetrators submerged in DP-camps and rural policemen were not allowed to enter them immediately. Criminals have the possibility to remove traces of their crimes and can recover within the camps in the event they were wounded. Robbed or stolen

property they are able to hide or sell in the camps without difficulties. Many camp commanders and camp police chiefs refuse cooperation with the German police although the Rural Police strove for an effective cooperation. They allow that robbed or stolen goods are traded within their camps, and black market goods often offered for sale in open stalls. Current black slaughters [i.e. the illegal slaughter of animals for human consumption] considerably jeopardize the food situation. At almost all camps, supervision of visitors at accesses and exits is very bad. Cooperation with the Rural Police in most cases proved to be inexpedient because DPs wanted by the German police were warned by the camp police who even cooperate with the perpetrators. An extremely small number of them has such a character as policemen should have.[75]

With the onset of resettlement, the German police turned their attention from camps and places of residency to the baggage that individuals intended to take out of the country. They assumed that Jews who left Germany could not have belongings that were legally obtained and used their powers of control at ports and border crossings to confiscate at will. It took the best efforts of the Jewish Advisor, William Haber, to persuade the American military that Jews were entitled to take with them sewing machines and other tools of trade, household goods and various items for personal use. Only by dispatching Jewish baggage along military channels could German police powers to search and confiscate be halted.[76]

Round-ups and Searches

Directives and controls could monitor and curtail German police powers but could not alter established practices. Time and again, the German police staged massive and spectacular raids. They always involved large detachments including armed officers and police dogs. These round-ups were not specifically aimed at Jews but targeted places where black market ventures were thought to occur. The normal format consisted of throwing a police cordon to seal off an area and arrest offenders suspected. One of the most spectacular raids of this type took place in Frankfurt am Main when, on February 3, 1947 the main railway station was sealed off and five thousand people searched. The station was supposed to be a hotbed of black market activities of Germans and displaced persons, especially Jews who were thought to arrive there from elsewhere in Germany to engage in illegal trading. An American journalist who found himself caught up in the raid, which also netted US servicemen who used the station to meet German girls, described the scene:

While the German police kept several thousand civilians corralled, barriers were set up. At each exit, American and German policemen together with interpreters and detectives began to screen individuals. They had to show their various identity cards, ration books and other papers required for existence in this upside-down world of Germany. All the luggage was also opened, and almost every one carried at least a knapsack. Nobody could talk back. Who can argue with a German policeman armed with a thirty caliber American carbine, backed up by a GI-MP armed with a forty-five caliber Colt automatic? . . . Those who carried excessive food rations, usually a circumstantial evidence of black marketeering operations (even for the benefit of the purchaser's own stomach), unposted mail, or whose cards were out of order were weeded out for further examination at the local police presidium. When a reporter pointed out that there exist many types of valid identification cards in Germany today that did not match the required ones in the Frankfurt Bahnhof roundup, a bustling junior officer commented, 'All the honest guys stay at home at night'. . . . In the war-gutted Germany of today the police power is the supreme arbiter. The war was fought to destroy this form of personalised uncontrolled inquisition of ordinary people. Professional policemen, Americans as well as Germans, will explain the need of a constant psychological warfare against the masses to keep them docile. But there is one inescapable conclusion: Nazi Germany, which lost a police state on May 8, 1945, inherited another. It is a bit difficult under the circumstances to make preachings for 'Democracy' stick in the mind of the ordinary German commuter who missed his train last night.[77]

The official police report on the Frankfurt raid included the list of goods that had been confiscated. It was a pitiful haul, consisting of 20 lbs of butter, 3 cans of lard, 20 lbs of bacon, $\frac{1}{2}$ lbs of coffee and 770 lbs of fresh meat. Only eight men were arrested. Clearly, the scale of the raid bore no relation to the assumptions about the scale of black market offences that had informed it or the actual offences that had been detected.[78] A similarly vast raid took place in Zeilsheim, a suburb of Frankfurt, where several houses and apartment buildings in a residential neighbourhood had been allocated to displaced Jews. Locally, however, these Jewish neighbours were never accepted as refugees or survivors in need of help but rejected as a *Landplage*, an infestation of the country:

Not only were the German inhabitants thrown out of their homes when this colony was established, now five families share two rooms, sometimes only one room. When a person in Zeilsheim dies, they just move into their flat and take it over. The camp inmates no longer want to live in a camp, they want to live in proper homes. They are spreading themselves about everywhere, the people are not even dead and others already settle in their place.[79]

In line with such misgivings, Zeilsheim was vilified as a black market capital where food and other goods, all of them allegedly stolen, were traded at will. The German inhabitants of the suburb had demanded for some time that a police raid be staged to flush out the supposed criminals. Since Zeilsheim was classified as a displaced persons camp, such a raid had to be carried out by military police, a practical detail that the German complainants had not known about or expected. On March 24, 1948, American military police conducted a six hour raid on Zeilsheim. It failed to accomplish what Germans had expected from it:

This raid which has long been demanded by the just and sound thinking part of the people resulted, after it had been carried out, in a reaction that could hardly have been worse. The reason being the conduct of the American troops who carried out this raid in a manner that cannot be imagined more disgraceful of a cultured people. According to the statements of inhabitants of Zeilsheim, the troops showed a behaviour during this raid that puts the well-known plunderings of Russian soldiers during the last days of the war considerably in the shade. They speak of bodily maltreatment of women and children, of thefts of jewellery and valuables as well as of the destruction of household goods and furniture.[80]

Hundreds of locals lodged complaints with the German police about the American raid, 23 pressed charges. They were particularly incensed that the military police had entered German homes and included Germans in their black market suspicions. They also alleged that only American goods were confiscated while other goods were ignored as if they were legal possessions. Jews resented the raid as a violation of their homes; Germans resented it because it failed to change anything:

Black market goods of non–American origin were returned to the Jewish DPs. Informers report that one hour after the end of the raid, black market activities were again in progress.[81]

Because German police were not permitted to enter displaced persons camps they regarded them as detrimental to public safety. Report after report conjured up the image of Jewish black-marketeers undermining the already precarious economic and social fabric of Germany by producing and circulating counterfeit money, by trading illegal or stolen goods in shops, cafes or on street corners, by forging identity papers and ration cards and especially by slaughtering animals illegally and in large quantities to reap huge profits from the sale of meat. Black-marketeers appeared to enrich themselves at the expense of honest people and even more reprehensibly, undermine the efforts of German public authorities to provide for everyone through the ration card and distribution system.

Outside displaced persons camps, German police forces could operate in accordance with their own regulations and without the need to co-ordinate activities with the military police in their region. In early 1949, military government officers in the American zone of occupation noted with concern that police practice in Germany did not appear to comply with their expectations because it did not preclude entering and searching premises without a warrant. In the United States, police had to obtain a warrant before a search could be conducted. In Germany, police regulations stated that searches could be conducted without a warrant if a delay was likely to obstruct detection of a crime and aid the criminal. When the German police had been reconstituted in a democratic manner after the Second World War, police regulation had been rewritten. The offending clause had been commonplace in German police practice even before the Nazi era and was not perceived as controversial. When American military government officials noticed it, having overlooked it before, they interpreted it as undermining the democratic project they had set in motion in post-war Germany:

> The inviolability of the home becomes a meaningless phrase, since police officials may invade the homes of private individuals at their discretion, no court being able to determine that they acted arbitrarily and without jurisdiction so long as they claim that in their opinion an imminent danger existed at the time of the search. . . . The police practice of search without warrant has become so routine that the police conduct searches without even pretense of claiming imminent danger.[82]

Apparently, German police frequently conducted searches without a warrant in response to unsubstantiated allegations made in anonymous letters or in denunciations originating within neighbourhoods.[83] They were part of normal police activity. In Württemberg-Baden, over 10,000 private homes had been searched over a nine month period.[84] Only in 81 cases did police obtain a warrant.[85] In Bavaria, 50,033 homes were searched in the course of 1948, 85 per cent of them without a warrant, a percentage rising to well over 90 per cent in towns with large populations of displaced Jews, notably Landsberg, Rosenheim, Fürth, Bayreuth and Munich.[86] The American response to their discovery shortly before 'the reinvented West German state came into being'[87] was to fear for its democratic governance.

History has shown that these fears were exaggerated. It has also shown that Germany remained a troubling environment for the Jews who, for whatever reason, chose to stay there.

A Future for Jews in Germany?

After an official inspection tour as Jewish Advisor in the British zone of occupation, Col. Robert Solomon was in no doubt that Jews in Germany could be divided into stayers and goers, and that the stayers had a future there. His visit in October 1947 had taken him to places where German and displaced Jews lived in private houses inside German society and had begun to build communities, and it took him to Belsen where residents were impatient to leave for Palestine. His report served a straightforward purpose:

> Objective: To encourage German Jews to remain in Germany and facilitate the return to Germany of German–Jewish exiles who are desirous of taking this step. Method: by Reconstituting the basis of German Jewish life.[88]

In line with British policy, Solomon did not regard Jews as a national group who might deserve special consideration. Jews living in German towns and cities, therefore, became German Jews. Jews in camps counted as foreign nationals although the Central Committee of Liberated Jews in Belsen had, from the outset, demanded that they be treated as a national (Jewish) group. Under the leadership of its chairman, Josef Rosensaft, Belsen had not merely been turned into a Zionist stronghold but also into a stronghold of warnings against staying in Germany:

> Do not believe it when you are told that a new Germany is coming into being, or that a new democratic Germany is springing up. . . . Jews in Germany will tell you that anti–Semitism in Germany is just as rife today as in 1933, 1935 or 1939, and no one can be certain that, if given the least power, the 'herrenvolk' will not revert to the dastardly deeds which they then perpetrated against Jews.[89]

Stayers and Goers

Col. Robert Solomon did not share these concerns about a future Germany or the negative sentiments of the group he called 'goers'. His report made no mention of anti–Semitism or a potential threat to Jews from Nazi tendencies in the present or the future. It also did not probe into the strength of Zionism in the British zone and the taboo subject of Jewish settlement in Palestine.[90] He even remained silent about the wave of protests that had been sparked off among displaced Jews when the *Exodus*, a ship laden with several thousand illegals, had been turned back by the British after reaching the port of Haifa in July 1947. In September, its luckless passengers were forcibly returned to Germany and accommodated in special camps in the British zone.[91] Without allowing himself to be distracted by the disquiet among displaced Jews in his area of responsibility, Robert Solomon held that a new beginning for Jews in Germany was possible and desirable, a beginning by German Jews for German Jews who chose to stay.

When Col. Solomon conducted his fact-finding tour with a view of aiding the 'stayers', the British zone of occupation included 37 Jewish communities with a membership of five thousand. His headcount, however, included only Jews who were German by nationality. Displaced Jews who lived in German towns and were affiliated to German communities there, seemed to be omitted from Solomon's list. A survey of March 1948 showed at least three thousand displaced Jews in the British zone living in private housing and not in camps.[92] Moreover, German towns included Germans who had been classified and persecuted as Jews but whom communities did not recognise as Jews and accept as members or who chose not to join.[93] In Hamburg, for instance, nine thousand individuals had been treated and persecuted as Jews while just 1,400 belonged to the Jewish community. This group and German Jews generally, Solomon argued, had been disadvantaged after liberation compared with displaced Jews. They now needed 'their special case recognised' in order to enable them to stay in Germany:

> German Jews have naturally not yet recovered from the tremendous shock of persecution and view with distrust a future which seems to be going to bind them to the German economy without safeguards. Hence, they are vacillating regarding their intentions. With a little encouragement, many would determine to remain in Germany, but as things stand at present, they are easily influenced by vigorous leaders of the Foreign Jews who are absolutely determined that Germany is not a safe or proper place within which a Jew can be advised to begin his life anew.[94]

Solomon had no doubt that Jews could live in the remade Germany without problems or disadvantage. Convinced of a Jewish future, he sided with the 'stayers'. The 'goers', he felt, had always been better organized, enjoyed a more vociferous representation of their views and did not need encouragement. German Jews, by contrast, had their lives shattered by persecution and remained unsure where and how to rebuild them. For foreign Jews – the 'goers' – Palestine had become the dominant and virtually uncontested choice. German Jews – the stayers – lacked such a clearly defined perspective. It was here that Solomon tried to make an impact as Jewish Advisor by persuading British-Jewish organizations to channel aid to German Jews and their organizations.[95]

As a direct consequence of Solomon's report, the British Jewish Relief Unit (JRU) stepped up its involvement in Germany and deployed additional personnel, partly to advise 'goers' in matters of resettlement, but especially to promote community membership among actual or potential 'stayers':

> It is strongly recommended that the *Jüdische Gemeinden* (Jewish communities) should be encouraged. To accomplish this the *Gemeinden* should have restored to them their legal status. In the meantime, a chosen representative of the *Gemeinden* should represent the German Jews and steer the *Gemeinden* during the initial stages of their legal resuscitation. It is recommended that the Stayers (who are for the most part likely to be German Jews) shall be given more encouragement and that the Goers, if German Jews, shall nevertheless, be encouraged to enrol with the *Gemeinden* instead of tending towards the Committee. This again can only be accomplished, for the time being at any rate, if German Jews are allowed to feel that, notwithstanding their nationality, their recent history is taken into account.[96]

'There are Jews who live in this land': Facing Reality

In the American zone, successive Jewish Advisors had regarded displaced Jews as the dominant Jewish population and assumed that all Jews in Germany were in transit. Once resettlement had been accomplished, Germany would become a country without Jews although an estimated 2,700 individuals might be forced to stay behind because they were too ill, too old and frail, or too mentally disturbed after their Holocaust experiences to meet the immigration criteria of another country.[97] Nobody else, it was assumed, would choose to stay and 'any Jew who considered remaining in Germany ought to have his head examined'.[98]

When Harry Greenstein, the last Jewish Advisor to be appointed in the American zone of occupation, arrived in March 1949, he assumed that his duties would consist of clearing up and overseeing departures. The displaced persons camps had begun to close. Where 130 camps had accommodated Jews, only four remained. After a slow start in 1948, resettlement had gained momentum as several thousand Jews left Germany every month. As soon as he arrived in Germany, he was proved wrong on two counts. Firstly, Germany did include a small number of Jewish residents who had founded communities and seemed intent on staying. Secondly, the assumption had been mistaken that all but 2,700 of the displaced Jews would be leaving. Between 12,000 and 20,000 displaced Jews appeared set to stay on. Responding to this unexpected scenario, Greenstein convened a conference in Heidelberg. Its agenda is contained in its title: 'The Future of Jews in Germany'. The aim was to bring together representatives from all facets of Jewish life existing in Germany at the time, and consider whether a future might be possible there for Jews and what it might look like. The delegates included German-Jewish community leaders, chairmen of Jewish committees as representatives of displaced Jews, as well as rabbis, army chaplains, organizers of Jewish charities and spokesmen of other aid organizations. Under the chairmanship of Harry Greenstein, the Heidelberg Conference set out to probe into the quality of Jewish life that had begun to emerge in German communities and establish a consensus on how it should be organized, given that none had been expected to persist.[99] The timing of the Heidelberg Conference was also determined by the pace of political reconstruction. On May 23, 1949, the contours of a democratic post-war German state had been defined when the regional parliaments ratified its constitution, the Basic Law prepared the ground for national elections to be held in August and a new government to commence work in September 1949.[100] The emergence of a post-war state signalled the end of military government and its involvement in assisting Jews. From now on, Jews in Germany had to rely on their own organizations to pursue their interests and locate themselves in the new setting.

The immediate purpose of the Heidelberg Conference was to agree the creation of a central and unified body as the organizational and authoritative voice for all Jews in Germany. Greenstein envisaged that such a body should represent communities as well as committees, drawing on German and displaced Jews as its distinct constituencies. While the idea of a central organization found favour with most delegates, the explicit inclusion of committees and displaced Jews did not. One year later, when the Central Council of Jews in Germany was founded, the name left no doubt that its members were Jews who happened to live in Germany, not Jews who were German by nationality or culture. It also left no doubt that they spoke with one voice, through one organization and as emissaries of the Jewish culture that existed in Germany, not as a replica of German-Jewish culture but in its remade, weakened and much-altered form. Greenstein had wrongly assumed that German and displaced Jews would retain separate identities and organizations. Instead, committees inside and out of camp closed down as soon as dedicated support for them dried up. As shown earlier for Frankfurt am Main, displaced Jews joined existing communities which developed an unexpected internal diversity.[101] In the rebuilt communities, at least one in three members – and frequently many more – originated from a country other than Germany and from a different Jewish culture. The balance between German Jews and displaced Jews varied between localities and regions with a larger number of displaced Jews in the American zone of occupation than in the other parts of Germany.[102] Everywhere, however, displaced Jews became submerged into a German-Jewish setting in terms of organization and representation. This mix created its own tensions. Where displaced Jews constituted a majority among community members, German Jews frequently tried to restrict their voting rights and access to executive positions.[103]

For the delegates at the Heidelberg Conference, this new Jewish diversity in Germany did not elicit hope but raised serious doubts about the quality of person who would choose to stay and the kind of cultural and religious life that passed for Jewish. In July 1949, when the Heidelberg Conference took stock, there were barely 20,000 Jews in Germany, scattered across one hundred communities (see the overview table in the Appendix). Only a handful of these communities had more than one hundred members. Most counted their members in double figures. With the exception of Berlin whose members numbered several thousand, most Jewish communities did not appear viable and were too small to attract, on a regular basis at least, the required ten men (*minyan*) to conduct religious services. Moreover, at least half the community members lived in mixed marriages. In Berlin, Hanover, Düsseldorf, Kiel and Hamburg the proportion was as high as 75 per cent. In Frankfurt, Wiesbaden or Cologne, some non-Jewish spouses had converted to Judaism, especially in marriages involving displaced Jews. As a rule, however, eight out of ten non-Jewish partners did not attempt to join the Jewish faith.

Other reservations concerned the displaced Jews who stayed in Germany. Their blueprint for a new beginning had involved resettlement, not residency. Those who ignored this blueprint seemed doubtful characters, a contemptible hard-core of quasi criminals and economic opportunists.[104] Furthermore, had not the best of the German Jews seized the chance to abandon the country of the perpetrators and begin a new life elsewhere?[105] Despite these misgivings about a Jewish presence in Germany and the personal qualities of the individuals involved, the Heidelberg Conference addressed the indisputable fact that Jews continued to live in Germany and that they needed help to do so:

The premise upon which the proceeding of this conference was based was the reality of today – the fact that there are Jews who live in this land. This fact and not the question as to whether or not those Jews ought to leave or ought to stay here is our starting point. The recognition of this reality at the very outset ruled out any question as to the wisdom of those who had elected to remain in this wounded country. If we think in terms of planning we must plan with no time limit and with no kind of adulation in anybody's mind but with a clear understanding that as long as there are and will be Jews in Germany, we shall serve them in whatever capacity they wish us. We shall be at their disposal and help them to live a life of pride, self-respect and dignity, to the extent that such a life is possible in a country torn asunder by so many problems and conflictions [*sic*]. We are living in a strange Jewish world. We ought to be careful in our use of terms that are applicable only to a vital Jewish community. German Jewish life has nothing of the glory and the splendor of a real living Jewish organism. Although Jewish history has been written in this country, the community itself is in its present level, number, and content, no longer anything but the echo and the reflection of what once was a noble reality.[106]

The plea to accept the Jewish presence in Germany because it had occurred did not, however, reassure conference delegates that the communities that had re-emerged could be regarded as Jewish by religion and culture. Was it not true that very few of them employed a rabbi, cantor or religion teacher? Only three – Frankfurt, Wiesbaden and Berlin – held daily prayers, although elsewhere regular Friday evening and Saturday services took place.[107] Provisions for religious instruction were patchy. Jewish children attended German schools and many were even baptised. Most communities had a library, but other cultural programmes such as lectures, courses in Hebrew, concerts or special events barely existed. There were virtually no kosher butchers or suppliers of other kosher food. The stocktaking of Jewish culture in Germany in 1949 revealed extensive deficiencies and none of the strengths that should accompany a new beginning:

> The number of children eligible for religious instruction is very small. Properly trained educators are unavailable. . . . Unless rabbis and teachers come from other countries and rotate among the small communities, Judaism will have a difficult time to survive. The percentage of inter-marriage is high. Jewish religious and cultural life is very weak. The future of these communities is not bright. Assimilation and peripheral Jewish living rather than an integrated Jewish life are the prospects.[108]

'As long as conditions in Germany are not unfavourable': Reasons for Staying

After liberation, it had seemed that virtually all Jews except the very ill, old and feeble were longing to leave. With nowhere to go, Germany became an interim, a waiting room, a staging post between past and future. When Earl Harrison collected his information on their living conditions in 1945, he had found most Jews impatient for resettlement. Palestine was the preferred option, followed by the United States. It took until 1948 for barriers to resettlement to come down and until 1950 before all Jews who wanted to leave Germany could in fact do so.

Less than one year after the State of Israel had been founded, migration there had slowed to 50 per month. Increasingly, potential leavers had second thoughts when news reached them about poor housing – many had to live in tents – and general hardship that was exacerbated by war in the region. At the Heidelberg Conference, AJDC representatives reported that another 10 per cent of Jewish community members intended to settle in Israel although few had made actual arrangements to do so, citing family reasons or business commitments why they were not yet ready to leave.[109] By the summer of 1949, 25 per cent had definitely decided to stay, the remainder could not or would not declare their intentions. Across Jewish communities, preferences varied. In Mannheim, 85 per cent had made up their minds to 'stay as long as conditions in Germany are favourable'. In Frankfurt and Berlin, half the Jewish population did not know where they might want to live in the long term. This tentative and conditional approach to remaining in Germany generated an image of Jews sitting on their packed suitcases, dreading renewed persecution but also ready to flee and save themselves when the need arose. The inability of Holocaust survivors and displaced Jews to admit that they had in fact decided to remain in Germany is reminiscent of labour migrants who never intended to settle in Germany and found themselves unable or unwilling to admit that they had already chosen to do so.[110]

From the vantage point of Jews who stayed, living in Germany amounted to a problematic and uncomfortable option. The Holocaust continued to overshadow the devastated communities as well as individual efforts at rebuilding lives. Until the early 1950s, when rapid economic growth and a general improvement in material conditions transformed living standards in West Germany from post-war deprivation to unknown levels of affluence, Jews found themselves more often in poverty than the German population. Many had been unable to regain their health after the Holocaust, among German Jews, a majority were of or near retirement age, and among younger ones, unemployment or unemployability constituted persistent problems. Living conditions among Jews in Germany were so bad that the AJDC was forced to resume a programme of material support after it had already been halted. In 1950, when most of the DP camps had already closed and Germany's Jews begun to settle, half the Jewish community members in the former British zone and one in three in the former American zone were too poor to manage without additional benefit from the Joint (table 6.1).

Table 6.1 Jews in Germany by Residency and AJDC Support, September 1950[111]

Jewish Population	US Zone	British Zone	French Zone	Russian Zone	Berlin (all sectors	TOTAL
1. CAMPS						
No. of camps	4	1	nil	nil	nil	5
Population	10,784	700	nil	nil	nil	11,484
Assisted Pop.	5,366	450	nil	nil	nil	5,816
Non-assisted Pop.	5,418	250	nil	nil	nil	5,668
2. COMMUNITIES						
Population	12,898	4,274	375	1,188	6,757	25,465
Assisted Pop.	2,155	1,750	nil	nil	nil	3,905
Non-assisted Pop.	10,743	2,497	375	1,188	6,757	21,560
3. TOTAL JEWISH POPULATION	23,682	4,947	375	1,188	6,757	39,949
TOTAL ASSISTED POPULATION	7,521	2,200	nil	nil	nil	9,721

In the course of the 1950s, economic reconstruction and growth also created new opportunities of social integration for Jews and improved their living conditions. Prolonged poverty, however, 'extended the years of suffering'[112] because restitution was slow to come. The military governments in the US and French zones had legislated on the issue in 1947, followed by their counterpart in the British zone. These first restitution laws stipulated that compensation could be paid for each day of imprisonment, and property be returned. Yet, nothing could happen until the German Länder translated the new laws into bureaucratic procedures and agreed practices.[113] In some regions, notably in Bavaria, this was attempted at speed since Philip Auerbach, the State Commissioner for Restitution, saw to it. He had advised military government on the preparation of the law, and lost no time to publicise its contents and who the beneficiaries might be.[114] Despite Auerbach's zeal, this first restitution law was rejected by the *Länderrat*, the council of regional governments in the US zone. Since German administrations had been democratically elected and could not be dictated to by military government, the latter had to resume the initiative by passing new legislation, Law No. 59, hoping this would be ratified by the regional council. The revised law confined its remit to the restoration of goods and property without aiming at compensation for loss of liberty.[115] The German Länder took until 1949 to agree procedures for implementing it although some payments had already been made from a Special Fund in anticipation of later, justified claims.

For many Jews, however, these delays meant that compensation did not commence in earnest until after Allied control in Germany had ended and the Federal Republic of Germany taken shape as a state. Given the unfavourable age structure of the German-Jewish population, many Holocaust survivors could never resume any kind of normal life after liberation. Many remained frail, confined to old people's homes and lived impoverished for years until their restitution claims were heard. Others died before their restitution had been considered and without regaining any of the possessions they had lost.

All in all, however, the 1950s addressed the neglected issue of restitution, enabling individuals to prepare claims, usually with assistance from their Jewish communities and from specialist lawyers, frequently Jews who had returned from exile to concentrate on this work. At the collective level, the German and Israeli governments negotiated an agreement whereby Germany paid monies to the new Jewish state in lieu of the Holocaust victims and the Jewish people as a whole. Signed in 1952 and secured against strong opposition by Germany's first post-war chancellor, Konrad Adenauer, the agreement constituted an official and formal recognition that Jews had been victims of crimes perpetrated by Nazi Germany, and that its successor state, the Federal Republic, assumed responsibility for its recent past.[116] Before the Bundestag decided on the issue, the Federal Government issued a statement explaining why restitution would have to be undertaken:

The Federal Government and the majority of the German people know about the immense suffering that was brought upon the Jews in Germany and in areas occupied by Germany during the Nazi period. The German people, in its overwhelming majority, condemned the crimes committed against the Jews and did not take part in them. During the Nazi years, many members of the German people, at the risk of their own safety, helped their Jewish fellow-citizens, be it for religious reasons, be it because they were ashamed at seeing Germany's good name defiled. In the name of the German people, unspeakable crimes have been committed which demand moral and material restitution, both with regard to individual losses suffered by Jews and with regard to Jewish property where heirs may no longer exist. In this area, first steps have been undertaken although much needs to be done. The federal government will legislate without delay on restitution and its fair implementation. Some Jewish property has already been given back. Further restitution will follow.[117]

As Jews in Germany constructed their history after the Holocaust and learned how to relate to a country and government whose intentions remained untested, they came to regard Konrad Adenauer's decisive role in formulating and implementing a restitution law as 'something positive', a landmark of change for the better.[118] On the other hand, many question marks remained. Why was there no special help for Jews who needed employment? In 1946, when denazification panels required staff, Jews were offered positions but these were temporary. In the longer term, they also put their holders on the wrong side of public opinion and political development. When the new West German state created its administration, it gave preference to former Nazis who had been dismissed from their posts in the course of denazification. In 1951, 24 per cent of the West German civil service consisted of former active and implicated Nazis. In some ministries, the percentage of ex-Nazis was even higher. As the new state consolidated its structures, it operated a policy of positive discrimination towards so-called '131ers', named after the reference number of the federal law that regulated the preferential appointment of former Nazis who had been dismissed from civil service positions they had held in Nazi Germany.[119] Germany's Jews did not enjoy such protection. Many were concerned about developments that appeared to reinstate Nazi activists. On the other hand, they felt reassured by the fact that official policy had detached itself from Nazi principles, although the break with the past was murky and lacked decisiveness.

An Identity 'Between All Chairs'

Living in Germany, therefore, confronted Jews with the challenge of squaring their Holocaust experiences with the social and political reality of an environment that could neither be trusted nor condemned outright. It also confronted them with hostile verdicts about their choice of residency from other Jews. 'We Jews in Germany are sitting between all chairs.'[120] Addressing potential returners, Hendrik van Dam, the first chairman of the Central Council for Jews in Germany, who had himself returned from exile in England after the war, outlined some of the difficulties and misgivings:

Germany is not a country into which one could encourage Jews who emigrated after 1933 to return. Jewish communities, however, have a right to exist there. He [van Dam] does, under no circumstances, agree with the position of many Jews throughout the world as well as in Israel, who have tended to regard every Jew who returned to Germany, as a traitor to the Jewish cause. But he also warns of a rash return to Germany.... Dr. van Dam thinks that people should not attempt to come back who cannot free themselves of resentments that might have been understandable in 1945 or 1946, but which today are no longer appropriate.[121]

Zionist organizations, their spokesmen and followers, had always been unequivocally negative about a continued presence of Jews in Germany.[122] In September 1950, the Jewish Agency, who administered and co-ordinated the resettlement to Israel, closed the last of its offices in Germany and vilified Jews who remained there for their failure to leave. From a Zionist vantage point, the remade German state should be forced to pay restitution but could not be condoned as home to Jews. The Central Council held its ground in defending Jews in Germany against their detractors:

It obviously has been overlooked that, in addition to displaced Jews, there are Jews in Germany who have lived there in the past, who expect to have their property and assets returned to them and who, in most cases, are too old to emigrate. This situation would have demanded special consideration. That no such consideration has been forthcoming can be interpreted in many different ways. There is no doubt, however, that this lack of consideration amounted to discrimination against those Jews who continue to live in Germany.[123]

Jews in Germany and their leaders adopted a complex answer to the question of where Jews should live. The generation who had refounded communities after 1945 and done so despite their experiences of persecution and the Holocaust, insisted that theirs had been the right course of action. They believed that their presence in Germany was required to demand restitution and achieve public remembrance for the Jewish victims of the Holocaust. For the next generation, however, they advocated emigration to Israel, a frontier country built on a forceful will to live. Young people, they argued, could not cope with being wedged between past and present, between Holocaust and a future in Germany. The generation of survivors had mastered these challenges and learnt to live with them. The young ones should leave and serve a less burdened, emerging society. The older people should stay because only they could take Germany to account. As places of residency, therefore, Israel and Germany stood side by side, albeit for different groups and contrasting purposes:

At a time when Judaism in the State of Israel is challenged to pass the test of fire of its rekindled national sentiments, Jews in the communities in Germany must not stand aside and watch in a disinterested or sceptical manner when news of the fighting in the struggle for the Jewish state arrives daily. Nobody has the right to decide on behalf of the young people who already went there. Who can predict whether these young people would have the strength to enter into a fruitful symbiosis with today's Germany? What is clear however, is that these young people do have the strength to link up with the rejuvenated Judaism in Israel. Jewish communities must not hold these young people back if they are at all serious with their call for 'living Judaism' which ultimately aims at creating a nation and community. Is it really true that those who stayed behind would be 'superfluous' if the young were to leave?[124]

Jews in Germany maintained that support for Israel as a state and for Zionism as a belief could exist side by side with the fact that they, individually and collectively, did not live by its prescriptions. In their view, the imperative for a Jewish state arose from the Holocaust that would not have trapped so many Jews had their own state been able to take them in. It also arose from the experiences of liberation that left Jews trapped once again. An article in the *Jüdisches Gemeindeblatt*, published in the interim between liberation and resettlement, explained how to square the circle of supporting a Jewish state while living in Germany. While the 'broken people' could not possibly be expected to leave again, Jews had a duty 'to hold out here in Germany and to build up again what had been taken from us'. Complementing this special mission inside Germany, a Jewish State was perceived as a necessary safeguard where Jews could find refuge should history in Germany repeat itself:

We want to be citizens of a country that offers us rights and protection, and it should never again be as it had been after the liberation by the Allies. When the Americans and the British liberated the concentration camps, the Belgians came to fetch their people home, so did the French, the Dutch, the Hungarians and many other states. The Jews were left behind, without rights and protection and dependent on the compassion and pity of the Allies. If we would have had a Jewish state at that time we would have had somewhere to turn.[125]

'Fruitful Symbiosis' or Disillusionment? Jewish Experiences with Post-war Germany

The Central Council of Jews in Germany believed that Jews could live in a 'fruitful symbiosis' with the German environment. Although it encouraged emigration and assisted those who had opted for it, it also encouraged those 'who wished to return to Germany'.[126] The *Jüdische Allgemeine Wochenzeitung*, published under the auspices of the Central Council, popular supplements and picture magazines as well as local newsletters took pride in reporting in detail when German political leaders and contemporary dignitaries had attended Jewish public events. Such events ranged from unveiling memorial sites for synagogues or whole communities that had been destroyed by the Nazis, to the festive opening and consecration of new or restored community facilities and prayer halls. Although nationalism and anti-Semitism had not been erased, the new political leaders seemed to support a 'fruitful symbiosis' with the Jews in Germany and their communities. What was meant by such a symbiosis is evident in the account of a memorial event in the town of Fulda near Frankfurt published by a Jewish community paper:

> In a ceremony to unveil a memorial stone in the former Jewish cemetery in Fulda the member of the Bundestag, Jakob Altmaier stressed that Jews refer to a cemetery as 'the good place' where 'no word of hatred shall be spoken'. The event was attended, on behalf of the town of Fulda, by the city executive headed by the Lord Mayor, Dr. Raabe and by mayor Heinrich Gellner and many members of the local assembly. For the churches, Dr. Abel from the cathedral and deacon Dr. Schuster were present. . . . The rabbi for the region of Hesse greeted the guests of honour and the good many people who attended the ceremony, with the words: 'We are here in order to draw a concluding line under a development that everyone regrets'. He stressed that in Fulda not only a cemetery had been destroyed but also a large Jewish community. But all of this now belonged to the past. Where injustice has occurred, it cannot be that those who have suffered it constantly remind those who perpetrated it of what they have done.[127]

Instead of revisiting the past, Rabbi Lichtigfeld expressed his belief in peace. Official occasions such as unveiling the memorial stone in Fulda allowed Jews in Germany and their leading representatives to rub shoulders with German political and cultural leaders who condemned, by their presence and in their speeches, the treatment of Jews under the Nazis and signalled acceptance of Jews in the new Germany. Jewish leaders, in turn, signalled that their confidence in a new beginning was justified since anti-Semitic dangers, if they did exist, would be thwarted by a remade political will.

In the 1950s, official occasions such as the consecration of synagogues or the opening of old folks homes became more frequent after the property rights of communities had been clarified. In 1949, a restitution formula had been advanced by the JRSO, the Jewish Restitution Successor Organization, forcing Jewish communities in Germany to hand over redundant or ownerless properties.[128] These adjustments raised much opposition at local level and German community leaders enraged the JRSO and the American Joint Distribution Committee by demanding exorbitant sums of money in support of their activities and attracted criticism for adopting an 'arrogant' and uncooperative tone.[129] Despite these rifts and despite prolonged resistence by communities such as Fürth or Frankfurt to the JRSO formula, the restitution formula enjoyed the backing of the Central Council of Jews in Germany and thus of the Jewish leadership. Indeed, before his election as chairman of the Central Council, Hendrik van Dam had worked for the Jewish Relief Unit (JRU) as a legal advisor on restitution and regarded restitution as the defining mission of the organization he headed.[130] By the mid-1950s, all remaining Jewish communities had agreed a financial compensation package that allowed them to focus on upgrading their remaining buildings or selling those surplus to their requirements at that time.

At the public level of institutions and ceremonial events, a 'fruitful symbiosis' between Jews in Germany and the new German state had emerged. Like Rabbi Lichtigfeld, Jews tended to refrain from opening wounds during these occasions and accepted an unwritten agenda that despite the Nazi past, the West German state and its leadership shared a commitment to democracy and a better, peaceful future with the Jews who lived there. Jewish life appeared to be integrated and its leadership at ease with the German establishment. As symbolic and ceremonial Jewish events included representatives of the remade Germany, symbolic and ceremonial events of this Germany included representatives of its Jewish inhabitants.

At the private level of daily living, unease and a sense of distance were less readily dispelled. Jews from all walks of life – returners, survivors, refugees from eastern Europe and those who had escaped deportation inside the Third Reich – shared the shock experience that Germans appeared to subscribed to something like collective amnesia: nobody admitted to having known anything or to having been involved in any aspect of the killing machine. No German admitted to ever having been a Nazi. When Peter Prager, who had left Germany for England on a *Kindertransport* in 1939, returned to Germany in September 1945, he was shocked to find Jews classified as 'enemies' and 'Auschwitz' dismissed as Russian propaganda.[131] Karl Marx, who made his mark as editor of the

Allgemeine Jüdische Wochenzeitung, had left exile in England for Germany in 1946 in the hope of contributing to 'building a really democratic Germany'. At the personal level, disillusionment loomed large:

> I had assumed that, so soon after National Socialism, there would be people in Germany courageous enough to remember what had been done to the Jews because they had themselves been eye witnesses, and to profess publicly: 'We have a sacred duty to make some amends to the remaining Jews.' When I arrived in Germany, I was bitterly disappointed. During the first few months, I had hundreds of conversations with hundreds of people but could not find a single one who had been a National Socialist. To this very day, I have been unable to detect anyone willing to confess: 'Yes, I took part and I have worked against Jews. Today, I am not merely disappointed, but I have learned something.' I personally only met Germans who told me that they had no idea what was happening to the Jews.[132]

In the recollection of Germans about National Socialism and the war years, Jewish neighbours or local shopkeepers suddenly 'disappeared', presumably for good reasons. When some Jews – unexpectedly – remained or returned, Germans resented restitution payments that seemed to enable Jews to buy a fancy 'Borgward' car, a five-ton truck or a large house while they had to wrestle with poverty and hunger.[133] In 1952, 37 per cent of the German population did not want Jews to live in their country while a further 44 per cent masked their reservations by declaring themselves undecided about the issue.[134] The German vision of normality and a new beginning focussed on economic and political reconstruction. Jews and their presence in society had no special relevance for this vision of a rebuilt Germany. On the contrary, they were perceived negatively as unwelcome reminders of a best-forgotten past.

Scenarios for a Jewish Future

In this uneasy German setting, Jews constructed Israel as a counter-world where a new beginning was possible. In 1946, the *Jüdisches Gemeindeblatt* looked back at the Holocaust and the continued displacement after liberation to argue that a Jewish state was needed because Jews needed a safety net. Now, the actual state that had begun to take shape was perceived in more personal terms as a promising, even vibrant environment. The contrast to Jewish life in Germany could not have been starker. In the emerging Jewish state, inhabitants seemed young, confident, unburdened by experiences of ghetto, persecution and slave labour. Jewish magazines used their cover pages and extensive pictorial reports to show what the new life was like: the smiling faces of young men and women in uniform, all carrying arms and ready to defend their fledgling country; bulldozers and heavy machinery carving new roads into the barren rocks; work gangs constructing apartment blocks to house newcomers with all modern comforts; Jewish men tilling the soil and tending crops; Jewish women caring for the children in the communal nurseries of collective agricultural settlements and village cooperatives.[135] For Jews in Germany, Israel signified more than the challenges and successes of building a new state. It signified the arrival of a new kind of Jew and the promise of a new kind of Jewish future.

In March 1953, the popular supplement of the *Allgemeine Jüdische Wochenzeitung* used its title photo to present a glimpse of this Jewish future. The picture showed two small boys sitting in front of a tent in one of the temporary camps for recent immigrants. Many would-be leavers in Germany had been persuaded by the existence of such tent cities that provisions in Israel were far from adequate to risk a new beginning there. The picture sought to deliver a different message. Its caption read:

> Two Children – One Heart. The two children, a small boy from Germany and another from an oriental country arrived from far away in their new homeland, the Promised Land. Both differ with regard to upbringing and skin colour. But in their chest beats the heart of a child and this overcomes all barriers.[136]

Inside Germany, inner-Jewish diversity and the new mix of German and displaced Jews had not been celebrated. At best, it had been borne grudgingly because without the influx of 12–15,000 former DPs communities would have been too small to sustain any kind of Jewish cultural and religious life. In the 1950s, when about five thousand Jews returned after exile or resettlement had failed, Jewish communities felt uneasy about including people who did not share their assumptions about Jewish life in Germany. Most had been driven back by poverty and the prospect of obtaining 5,000 DM as an immediate advance on restitution payments. Many arrived with children who were born abroad and had never known Germany and its troubled German–Jewish relations. In Germany, diversity bordered on division and was perceived as a negative, even destructive factor. In Israel, where everybody was Jewish, diversity took on the positive sheen of innovation and future promise because it seemed to point towards a stronger future for Jews as a people. In Germany, the overall number of Jews was so small that diversity translated into diffusion and decline. In a deliberate bid to stem such decline through diversity, the Central Council for Jews and the Jewish communities insisted on the

Einheitsgemeinden, a unified format of Jewish observance and an organizational framework where local and regional managers, not rabbis or clerics, were in charge.

Over time, social and political realities in post-war Germany set their own agendas and new challenges for the country's Jews. In 1953, anti-Semitic tendencies in the German Democratic Republic and the onset of show trials persuaded Heinz Galinski, the head of Germany's largest Jewish community in Berlin, to encourage East German Jews to escape to the West. He also promised that his community would help with finding accommodation and obtaining all necessary documents to venture a new beginning. About one thousand East German Jews, one third of the total, fled to Berlin or via the city to West Germany. Without official declarations or policy pronouncements, Jewish communities in Germany had found a new mission, the mission of receiving Jewish refugees and helping them to start a new life in the very place where none had been expected to remain:

> Judaism in Germany today is in a position to assist all Jews who are willing to come to us. . . . Human beings who are in danger can be helped. Let us be fully aware of the size of this task. Everybody has to try and contribute to it in order to do his duty as a Jew.[137]

EPILOGUE

Refuge Germany

The remade communities in Germany did indeed become places of refuge. After the Holocaust, they provided material support, shelter, and advice to Jews who had been impoverished and humiliated inside the Third Reich or in its concentration camps. These founders were soon joined by displaced Jews who had not intended to settle in Germany but ended up there because emigration or resettlement took so long to arrive. Most had ventured to rebuild their lives inside German society, a small number had been waiting in camps, unable to decide where they should go. In the late 1940s, the majority became community members. Although largely secular and falling short of religious expectations, the remade communities offered a context and the company of other Jews that is required for religious observance. They also offered practical support with finding a foothold in Germany and with fighting for compensation or restitution in the wake of the Holocaust. On the cusp of statehood, in 1949, the remade communities in the western zones of occupation had eight thousand German-Jewish and 12,000 displaced members. In the Soviet zone, where displaced Jews had not been permitted to settle, Jewish communities recorded four thousand members and were exclusively German in composition.

Between them, the two German states comprised eighty million inhabitants, seventeen million in the German Democratic Republic in the East, just over sixty million in the Federal Republic in the West. By any measure, Jews constituted a minuscule minority in post-Holocaust Germany, although the fact that some settled there at all and that remade communities emerged seemed out of kilter with the course of history. Looking back after fifty years, Moritz Neumann, then chairman of the Land Association of Jewish Communities in Hesse, asked:

How could it be that Jews were again living in Germany after everything that had happened? In Germany of all places? Did they have so little pride, such low self-esteem, that they put up next door to the perpetrators after they had been liberated from the death camps, that they brought children into this world and let them grow up in the former SS state that had only just been wrestled to the ground?[1]

For Robert Weltsch, there was no question to be answered. Until the rise of National Socialism in Germany he had been editor of the *Jüdische Rundschau*, a major Jewish cultural journal, and fled to Palestine in the 1930s. In 1946, he visited Germany to see for himself what had remained of Jews and their communities and famously wrote:

We cannot assume that there are Jews who feel attracted to Germany. It smells of corpses here, of gas chambers and of torture chambers. Yet, several thousand Jews are still living there. This remnant of Jewish settlement should be liquidated as soon as possible. Germany is no place for Jews.[2]

Social reality took a different turn. Jews did not or could not leave, communities were remade, and a Jewish presence in Germany continued. In each of the two German states, 'sojourners' constructed their own narrative and reasoning. In the East, membership of a community signalled distance from a Socialist order where religion was deemed out of line with political ideology and a collective future. Jews with an interest in shaping the emerging East German state, therefore, did not normally join Jewish communities but thought to rebuild their Germany after the Holocaust by embracing political activism.[3] Similarly, exiles who returned to East Germany positioned themselves not in its marginalised Jewish communities but in mainstream organizations of the Socialist state because it appeared committed to uprooting Nazism once and for all.[4] When the German Democratic Republic collapsed in 1989, Jewish communities had suffered years of Stasi surveillance and political harassment and their membership had dropped from around 4,000 in 1949 to just 402, most of them living in East Berlin.

No such meltdown occurred in the West. The political culture that developed in the Federal Republic lacked the 'prescribed anti-fascism' of its eastern counterpart which declared National Socialism and the Holocaust a legacy for West Germany and exculpated its own population and history of any wrongdoing.[5] Instead, West German political culture encompassed negative references to National Socialism and the Holocaust as its own unacceptable past that had to be condemned publicly and whose former victims had to be included publicly and demonstratively in order to legitimise post-war democracy. On the one hand, Jews who stayed in Germany regarded their presence there as provisional, sat on their proverbial packed suitcases and postponed a decision to leave until anti-Semitism would force them out or, more privately, until their children finished school, completed university studies, or had themselves decided whether to stay or go.[6] On the other hand, the very presence of Jews, regardless of their personal uncertainties whether to stay or go, enhanced the credibility of the Federal Republic. Some argued that it even served to whitewash a failure to address the Nazi legacies.[7] Others took the more charitable view that the presence of Jews had made German democracy more acceptable in the eyes of the world.[8]

No less significant is an aspect of democratic political culture that has largely been overlooked in the literature on Jews in Germany. It pertains to the rights of persecuted people to seek refuge and settle. In explicit reference to the Nazi years when Jews were trapped in Germany and deported to their death because no other country would accept them, and also as a signal that the democratic Germany they were creating wanted to distance itself from the past, the authors of the Basic Law, the written constitution for the Federal Republic, enshrined the right to political asylum as a constitutional right. This pledge benefited refugees from many oppressive regimes, notably from Communist and war-torn countries. It also benefited Jews who were forced to flee from regimes without religious tolerance. Commencing in the 1950s, several thousand Jewish refugees settled in Germany from Iran, Hungary, Poland, Romania and other countries where conditions had become untenable for them. Contrary to other asylum seekers, Jews received special assistance such as professional retraining, language instruction and welfare support from the West German state via its land governments while Jewish communities provided a cultural and social context to help with integration. When these newcomers arrived, the Zionist option did, of course, exist but not everyone had been persuaded to live by its rules. The Federal Republic could emerge as a preferred destination for Jews because it offered high living standards within a stable democratic framework. Some of the Jewish refugees had not personally suffered in the Holocaust and did not fear that Germany might be an SS state beneath a thin veneer of change. Others were glad to swap their threatened lives and livelihoods for a more secure and welcoming environment. Jewish newcomers also included – as migrants rather than refugees – several thousand Israeli citizens who, for whatever reason, ventured to live there. Unexpectedly West Germany became a preferred destination for Jews who searched, voluntarily or forcibly, for a new beginning.

Jewish communities assisted newcomers to find their place in an unfamiliar land and were themselves saved from attrition and fatal decline by the influx of newcomers. Without migration gains, the demographic imbalance of an ageing community with a high death rate and not enough births to generate natural growth would have taken its toll. As it was, Jewish community membership remained static at 30,000 for several decades because migration gains compensated for the losses incurred through deaths and emigration. Hidden beneath this apparent stability, howeyer, is a continuous process of revitalisation and change as new arrivals settled and shaped community life while others decided to leave. Jewish communities in West Germany were not destined for 'liquidation', neither did they flourish. For several decades, migration, emigration, births and deaths were finely balanced and kept overall membership numbers stable. A closer look reveals a significant process of centralisation. Small communities declined and disappeared because newcomers chose to live in big cities, near other Jews and viable Jewish cultural institutions. This dynamic stalemate of Jewish residency in Germany was blown apart in 1990 when large numbers of Jewish refugees began to arrive from the former Soviet Union. Nearly a decade later, Ignatz Bubis, who was then the chairman of the Central Council of Jews in Germany, reviewed how migration had underpinned and redefined the remade Jewish communities that emerged in 1945:

After the Shoah, there were hardly any German Jews left, while a quarter million displaced Jews lived in liberated Germany. They had been freed from concentration camps here or from forced labour compounds, or they came from eastern Europe to the western zones of occupation, especially to the American zone, in order to wait in a DP camp for a chance to emigrate. They came from Poland, Hungary, Romania. They came because they did not wish to remain in their home countries or could not go back there. On the one hand, anti-Semitism in Poland and other countries was intolerable, on the other hand, there were no opportunities to emigrate from there. Thus, they came here, lived in those camps. Of these 250,000 Jews, more than 230,000 emigrated. For the immediate post-war period, Weltsch was right. Until 1980, the number of Jews who lived in Germany remained stable at about 30,000, although there were always migration gains. There were also migration losses. These 30,000 also included two generations who were born in Germany. This means, in the first forty years after the Shoah, there was no significant Jewish migration into Germany. Between 1950 and 1990, the number of Jews fluctuated between 25,000 and 30,000. Jewish migrants, therefore, did not perceive Germany as an attractive country of residence. During the same period, many hundred thousands of Jews from all over the world moved to the United States or to Israel, but not to Germany. This changed only in 1990. This year saw the beginning of Jewish migration from the former Soviet Union. Up to the end of 1998, 45,000 Jews came to Germany, and with them came about 40,000 non-Jewish partners from mixed marriages. This is, perhaps, one of the reasons why they did not go to Israel. In the same period, however, 800,000 moved to Israel, another 400,000 to the United States and tens of thousands to other countries. Reservations about living in Germany have eased but they have not disappeared altogether.[9]

Migration and the Challenges of Integration

Jewish refugees who arrived prior to the onset of the recent 'Russian' migration preferred to attach themselves to one of the larger communities such as Berlin, Frankfurt, Munich, Cologne, Hamburg and Düsseldorf. They often settled in national groups and left their mark on the local culture. In Hamburg, four hundred Iranian Jews settled and enlivened local Jewish culture with their own rituals and with a lot more laughter than could be heard elsewhere.[10] In Düsseldorf, Romanians dominated regular community activities while Frankfurt am Main had attracted several thousand Israelis. They invigorated Jewish cultural life in the city although few took up formal community membership. Starting in the 1960s, German Jews have been outnumbered in all Jewish communities with the exception of Berlin.

The Jewish migration from the former Soviet Union accelerated and intensified this shift away from German-Jewish culture and towards diversity. Indeed, the migration redefined local cultures as newcomers everywhere outnumbered existing community members. The influx transcended all expectations. Within a decade, community membership more than trebled from 30,000 to 100,000 and continued to grow.[11] In the same period, the number of communities increased from 64 to 83 (see Appendix). Incoming Jews settled in towns where none had lived since the 1930s. Small communities that had been on the verge of extinction found themselves revitalised by the influx of newcomers, often growing larger than they had ever been in the past. In East Germany in particular, where state Socialist control had reduced Jewish life to tiny remnants in Berlin, Leipzig or Halle, Jews re-entered about a dozen towns to start communities from scratch.[12] Not unlike the communities of displaced Jews that had existed in the 1940s in Fürth, Darmstadt or – parallel to that for German Jews – in Hanover, these new communities were Russian-Jewish outposts, comprised and run by new migrants.

At the corporate level of land organizations and the Central Council, these developments constituted a significant, albeit manageable challenge.

Established structures absorbed the new as well as the expanded Jewish communities. While their clientele trebled, their purposes and policies remained the same. Above all, organized Judaism in Germany remained committed to the *Einheitsgemeinde*, the unified community where services followed quasi-orthodox religious rites and where specified Jewish traditions were upheld. Some such traditions, *kashrut* for instance, or how to observe the Sabbath, had willingly been adapted or abandoned in response to the non-Jewish environment and individual preferences. The approach to Halachic Law was different. It prescribes that only those persons can be regarded as Jewish and accepted as community members who were born to a Jewish mother.[13] Despite the high proportion of mixed marriages among Jews in Germany, community membership has remained narrowly defined and exclusive. However, many of the 'Russian' Jews who chose to migrate to Germany were married to non-Jewish partners and their children could not be considered Jewish. Thus, the rules of orthodoxy underlying German–Jewish organizations created additional difficulties for the very refugees who needed help after arrival. The emergence in Germany of 15 liberal communities with their untraditional approach to conversions, their practice of including non-Jewish partners and of treating women equally, suggests that the unitary model of the Central Council may begin to lose its shine.[14] This emergent diversity has been too recent and too marginal to benefit the new migrants.

The arrival of 'Russian' Jews exacerbated this diversity. In the Soviet Union and its successor countries, Jews had been defined – and discriminated against – by a stamp in the passport. Very few translated this ascribed nationality into a sense of identity or religious culture. Most abided by the state ideology and did not venture any kind of religious or cultural opposition. Their Jewish origins began to turn into a personal risk when anti-Semitism soared after Communist control collapsed. These state-defined Jews had no idea what might constitute a Jewish life in the home, in the community setting, or what to do in a synagogue. After arriving in Germany, they had to learn how to be Jewish although they soon outnumbered their potential teachers, and, in the case of new communities, were left to their own devices. Simultaneously, they also had to learn how to function in a western-style society, and how to build and rebuild their lives after migration.

On the face of it, Jewish migrants enjoyed a privileged status compared to individual refugees or asylum seekers. Classified as 'contingent refugees', they were admitted as members of a group without having to submit individual application papers or document their eligibility. This arrangement dates back to April 12, 1990 when the delegates of the first democratically elected East German parliament, the Volkskammer, voted unanimously to distance themselves from the treatment of Jews in their part of the country:

> We ask the Jews in the whole world for forgiveness. We ask the people of Israel for forgiveness for the dishonesty and hostility of official GDR policies towards the State of Israel and for the persecution and humiliation of Jewish citizens in our country even after 1945.[15]

Following this gesture of contrition, a 'contingent' of two thousand Jews from the collapsing Soviet Union were invited to settle in the GDR and help to rebuild Jewish life there. Of course, the GDR itself ended on October 3, 1990 when divided Germany was unified. Jewish migration from eastern Europe might have halted, had not the Central Council lobbied government ministers and political decision makers until the German parliament, the Bundestag, agreed in 1991 to admit 'Russian' Jews as 'contingent refugees', only this time without defining an upper numerical limit. In line with German policy pertaining to asylum seekers, the newcomers were to be dispersed, with regions and localities required to accept their share in line with population figures. Also like asylum seekers, they had to remain for at least seven years in the town to which they had been sent in order to qualify for material support. On behalf of the German public authorities and backed by the Central Council, Jewish communities and their welfare officers played a pivotal role in administering aid and developing programmes to assist integration, culturally as well as economically.[16] At the personal level, learning German or becoming acquainted with Jewish religious festivals, communities could help, although many perceived the sheer number of newcomers as a threat. At the macro-level of economic and social integration, the challenges could not be met as easily. Despite their privileged entry into the country, the newcomers remained foreigners by nationality and disadvantaged in their treatment:

> The Jews who arrived in the last couple of years, arrived at a time when general unemployment was already very high and even without language barriers it would have been very difficult for them to find work. As long as a German medical doctor is out of work or looking for a permanent surgery, no foreign doctor may be employed. We are encountering difficulties with obtaining German citizenship, but citizenship is very often the prerequisite for finding work, suitable accommodation and recognition. Let us stick with the example of the doctor: As long as this Russian Jew does not have a German passport, he is not allowed to practice medicine, and as long he cannot practice medicine, he is dependent on benefit and on material support from the Jewish

community. But, as long as he is dependent on benefit, he cannot obtain a German passport. It is a vicious circle, and the hope of this doctor to ever lead a normal life is diminishing.[17]

In November 2002, fifty years after Germany's post-war agreement to pay compensation to Holocaust survivors, the German government announced that the Central Council of Jews, like the Christian Churches, would henceforth receive state funding in accordance with their membership, estimated at two million Deutschmark per annum. The money recognised the strain imposed on Jewish communities who, after rebuilding 'ruptured and broken' institutions, were now challenged beyond their capacity by 'artificial growth'.[18] The apparent normalisation of community–state relations and the equal footing, in administrative terms, of Jews and Christians in Germany, has few of the hallmarks of stability, predictability and an assured future. Numbers, of course, do make a difference. With the Jewish population in Germany standing at 100,000 and growing, schools and other educational pathways for Jews have become viable in major communities such as Berlin or Frankfurt.

Could the emergence of an inner-Jewish diaspora with an exclusively 'Russian' membership obfuscate or even erase the divide between Jews and Germans? Do these newcomers share the Holocaust experience that has haunted the founder generations of the rebuilt communities? Does their detachment from even the rudiments of Jewish tradition and culture further erode religion that many had already seen as a worryingly feeble and fragile aspect of Jewish life in Germany? Will 'Russian' Jews become German-Jewish or remain Russians in orientation, preference and disposition? Are they the new *Paketjuden*, the packet Jews who, in the 1940s, joined communities only to secure material benefits? Or are they the new displaced Jews who might, over time, blend into or even invigorate Jewish community life in Germany? Ten years into the migration, Paul Spiegel, the successor of Ignatz Bubis as chairman of the Central Council of Jews in Germany, had no doubt that this would happen, albeit not immediately but within twenty years or so.[19]

Paradoxically, the Jewish population in Germany has been the only one in Europe to increase in numbers amidst a general decline which bypassed only the two major migration destinations for Jews: Israel and the United States of America.[20] Destination Germany can have different attractions. 'Russian' Jews may perceive it as an affluent country where their living conditions might improve. Or they may opt to go there because their non-Jewish partners might not find acceptance in Israel or because they could not obtain visas for the United States. Whatever the reasons, Germany has become a destination for Jewish migrants and its communities have tried to aid refugees after arrival and with their new start.

Jews in Germany: Assumptions and Identities

This remade Jewish setting seems a far cry from the 'liquidation' predicted for all Jewish life in Germany in the early post-war years. Yet, the critics have not fallen silent. Some claim that Jewish life in the country of the perpetrators can never be anything but a charade, a 'negative symbiosis' whereby Germans depend on the presence of Jews to make it appear as if their country and character had been reinvented while the presence of Germans cannot but remind Jews constantly of the Holocaust and its destructive impact.[21] Less complex and remarkably unaltered since liberation remains the Zionist perspective. Inside Germany, it made a shock appearance in 1996 during the first ever official visit to that country of an Israeli head of state, President Ezer Weizmann. He used his formal address to the German parliament to voice disbelief that Jews would want to live in Germany and accused those who did of whitewashing the German past and betraying Judaism itself. In earlier decades, Germany's Jews might have cringed, but remained silent. In the 1990s, they asserted their different and differing view. As chairman of the Central Council, Ignatz Bubis spoke for all Jews in the country when he stated: 'I have no cause to leave Germany.' A member of the council's executive, Moritz Neumann, rebuffed Weizmann's assumptions more forcefully:

> As far as religion and Jewish traditions are concerned, communities in Germany are more secure than many in other countries, including Israel. We Jews in Germany are, to be sure, no source of deep religiosity and we are, as far as I am concerned, nowhere near to securing a stable and traditional religious life. Compared with many Israelis, however, who stay in Germany either to visit or to live permanently, we can claim to be a stronghold of Jewish living and Jewish tradition.[22]

Not only establishment figures like Bubis or Neumann raised their voices to affirm their right to live in Germany as Jews. For the next generation, Daniel Cohn-Bendit, a member of the European Parliament for the Green Party and also a former protagonist of student protests in the 1960s who had grown up in France but settled in Germany, did not even think it necessary to provide elaborate reasons for his choice of place: 'I live in Germany today on the basis of my own free decision, and without any guilt feelings.'[23]

The founder generation of Jewish communities after the Holocaust had stayed in Germany because, for one reason or another, they could not leave it. Florence Singemann had lost 16 members of her family in the Holocaust. After being liberated in Bergen-Belsen she rejoined her non-Jewish husband in Erfurt and stayed because he stayed:

I did not want to stay there. I was terrified of the Germans. And I still cannot get over it. . . . The pain is like a tumour, it sits inside me and I cannot get rid of it.[24]

Moses Gercek was born in Poland. He and his brother were the only members of their family to survive. After liberation, they refused to wait in yet another camp and went to live in Munich. Attempts to emigrate to Canada failed because the brother suffered from a damaged lung. When his brother left for Israel in 1948, Moses Gercek did not join him but constructed his own narrative and quasi-collective mission in support of his decision:

If all Jews had left after the war, Germany would have been cleansed of all Jews and Hitler's dream, the Nazi dream, would have come true. We did not want to give the Germans this kind of satisfaction. But this is more in the line of demagogy. It is not the only reason why we stayed here. Another reason is, that we are *Zeitzeugen*, we have witnessed the events and can provide testimony. If there were no Jews in Germany, there would be no bad conscience. Germans and their government would think that they paid compensation and have nothing more to worry about or to regret. . . . We remained here in order to remind the Germans that they cannot pay off their guilt with money.[25]

At a more private level, Moses Gercek built a successful business while his brother in Israel barely made a living and needed material help. Of the two brothers, one stayed in Germany in order to enable the other, his wife, children and later grandchildren, to make ends meet in the land of the Jews.[26] Although 'no genius', Moses Gercek expanded his business 'bit by bit', got married, put down roots: 'I had to adjust and fit in.'[27]

Ignatz Bubis, who later rose to prominence as chairman of the Central Council for Jews in Germany, made a more deliberate choice. Liberated from a concentration camp aged eighteen, he made his way to Berlin in order to avoid being confined to a DP camp. Like most survivors, he had lost his family in the Holocaust, and repatriation to his home town of Breslau, now under Polish control, was not an option. Before deciding where to begin again, he actively explored what it might be like elsewhere:

This was the time when I thought I might want to go to Israel or to America. I was unsure of what to do, and did not decide until about 1949 or 1950. I even went to America and to Israel as a tourist to have a look, but then I decided to stay.[28]

Like Moses Gercek, he succeeded in business, first in Pforzheim in southwestern Germany and later in Frankfurt am Main where he settled because it provided a more viable Jewish community than the smaller town. After forty years in the city, he regarded Frankfurt as his *Heimatstadt*, his home town, and himself as 'a German citizen of the Jewish faith'.[29] This confident sense of belonging, however, conflicted with hidden assumptions, even among friends, that Jews belong elsewhere. At the reception in honour of Ezer Weizmann in January 1996, Bubis was asked – by a perfectly amiable and well meaning German guest – whether he had enjoyed the speech of 'his President'. The speaker, of course, meant the President of Israel, not of Germany.[30] Bubis refused to condone this kind of incident or excuse it as 'normal'. From his time as chairman of the Jewish community, he recalled:

> One of these days, the deputy chair of the local assembly and the Lady Mayoress of my hometown of Frankfurt am Main sent a friendly letter to the executive of the Jewish community. The city leaders wished, as they tend to do every year, happy holidays at Easter time and Passover to the Jewish community and the Christian churches. At the end, both expressed their hope that 'the peace process in your country' will continue. They meant well. After unification, social tensions have increased in Germany while racist and xenophobic violence soared suddenly. But, I, the astounded reader, had no idea that in my country, in Germany, a war had broken out. This was news to me. Of course, when the two senders wrote 'your country', they did not mean their own country. 'Your country' is, in the opinion of my Lady Mayoress and my deputy chair of my local assembly, Israel. Is Frankfurt, then, still my hometown? The Lady Mayoress and the deputy chair of the local assembly are, as I said, educated, friendly people who are well inclined towards me. They apologised for the wording, when they understood what they had said. But it had to be pointed out to them – by myself and others. And this makes one aware of the situation in which one lives as a Jew in Germany.[31]

Among the generation of founders and Holocaust survivors, many did not have the courage or the linguistic and cultural savvy to challenge the assumption that they did not belong. As we have seen, Jews were haunted by their own unanswered questions about Nazi persecution, about how and why so many Germans had contributed to implementing it, and whether some of them might be living next door to their former intended victims. Jews in Germany had always harboured a hope that Germans would revisit their past and learn to relate to Jews differently.[32] Until they could be sure, they would keep themselves to themselves. Even the children who were born and raised in Germany, grew up in Jewish enclaves. They met

Germans at school but did not invite them home to play.[33] At home, many families spoke Yiddish. Socially, they inhabited a world apart from their non-Jewish peers, all the more so since their parents associated marriage to a Jewish partner as a benchmark of their children's continued identity as Jews.[34]

The parent generation experienced and lived the distance to their German environment with unease and in silence. Their children and grandchildren have accepted that living in Germany might make them German by passport but will not do so by culture, orientation or identity. They live there as 'strangers' because they want to live as Jews.[35] In 1995, the Central Agency for Jewish Welfare and the weekly *Allgemeine Jüdische Wochenzeitung* invited youngsters between the ages of six and eighteen from all over Germany to explain what being Jewish meant to them in principle and in their daily lives. The organizers received 150 replies.[36]

The child respondents displayed an unfamiliar confidence in their 'difference'. In the playground, Hebrew served as a secret language, not something they should hide. Difference itself had become acceptable: 'It is stupid to look always for differences, because people are always different from one another.'[37] The acceptance of difference extended to issues of identity and to children who lived in Germany but whose parents had come from elsewhere. Difference lost its scariness, the 'otherness' of exclusion and fear. One 11-year-old boy explained: 'My father is Russian and my mother is Israeli. I am a Jew and I am not against foreigners because, to some extent, I am also a foreigner.'[38]

Some, of course, continued to subscribe to the Zionist vision of a country where everyone belonged. Alexander, aged eighteen, explained: 'I believe that a real Jew will always think of his country, where his ancestors were born and where we are always expected – Israel.'[39] A young Israeli shared the assumption that identification with Israel was straightforward, but also asserted that he could define his own relationship and distance to Germany and how to live there as a Jew:

> I as an Israeli do not have the problem of identity because I do have a homeland, and this is Israel. As an Israeli one does not know the problem of identity. One just has it. Therefore, it is possible to relate to Germans without prior assumptions, because one does not have to identify also with Germany. One does belong somewhere else and is only temporarily in Germany.[40]

Most young Jews in the survey, however, faced up to the conundrum of how to relate to the country where they were born and whose citizenship they may hold, but which destroyed their families and much of Jewish life in Germany and elsewhere in the past. These young Jews found themselves divided from the Germans among whom they had spent their lives and might spent their futures:

> I do have a problem of identity. Although I have lived in Germany since I was born, I do not feel myself to be German. I cannot see this country as my home because Germans have exterminated my family.[41]

Feeling uncomfortable, however, did not entail packing the suitcases to leave or hiding in silence, near invisible, in a Jewish enclave of family and friends. The young generation, and increasingly all Jewish generations from leaders to ordinary citizens, have begun to assert their right to be themselves. In the 1995 survey, a young boy aged eleven articulated the complex blend of confidence in his Jewish identity and unease in a German environment, where Jews and Germans remain divided by history and assumptions:

> I am, what I am, a Jew. Only, if someone comes along and asks me which race I belong to, I am a little bit afraid to answer. But I do answer!!![42]

APPENDIX

Jewish Migration and Community Development in Germany, 1945 to 2003

Year	Membership Total	Special Factors	Number of Communities
1945	15,000	Survivors inside the Third Reich in mixed marriages and in hiding	n/a
1946	21,454	Founding members, excluding DPs	87
1948	26,316	Members including German Jews and displaced Jews 'out of camp'	110
1949	20,496	Resettlement, largely completed February 1949	n/a
1950	24,431	Arrival of up to 2,000 'illegal' returners per annum	81
1955/6	15,684	1956, onset of *Soforthilfe* (emergency aid)	84
1959	21,563	6,316 'returners' joined communities since 1955	ca. 80
1960	21,755	No special developments	73
1964	25,132	Arrival of 1,300 Iranian Jews; also Israelis, but often not community members	73
1968	26,000	Estimated (Katcher) that majority now eastern European Jews	73
1970	26,799	Arrival of Soviet *olim* – Jews allowed to resettle; 3,000 to West Berlin	68

1980	28,173	Throughout decade, migration gains of 1,000 per annum, migration losses of 400	65
1990	28,488	2,000 'contingent refugees' accepted into East Germany in June; unification in October	64
1993	52,490	Influx of Jewish refugees from former Soviet Union; 15,000 became new community members	69
2003	ca. 100,000	Continued influx of new members from the former Soviet Union	83

Compiled from data provided by the *Zentralrat der Juden in Deutschland* in Berlin and the ZWST in Frankfurt am Main.

GLOSSARY

AJDC	American Joint Distribution Committee
Assembly Centre	Official term denoting DP camps
Bayrisches Hilfswerk	Bavarian Care Agency, based only in this region
Bezugschein	Coupon for Special Allocation
Bundestag	National parliament of the FRG
CID	Central Intelligence Department (US Army)
Committee of Liberated Jews	Organization(s) created and run by displaced Jews
D-Day	June 6, 1944, first day of the Normandy landing
DDT	(Dichlorodiphenyltrichloroethane) Disinfectant used for delousing
Death March	Forcible evacuation, normally on foot, of (mostly Jewish) prisoners from concentration camps and slave labour compounds in the closing months of the war
Death Trains	Forcible transport without food and water of Jews from concentration camps inside Germany in the closing weeks of the war
DM	*Deutsche Mark*, Deutschmark, i.e. German currency since 1948
DP	Displaced Person
DP Camp	Displaced Persons Camp
DP Centre	Displaced Persons Camp or special facility
ETO	European Theater of Operations, US Army term referring to Europe
Fremdarbeiter	Foreign workers forcibly conscripted or recruited on a voluntary basis to work inside Nazi Germany in industry and agriculture
FRG	Federal Republic of Germany
GDR	German Democratic Republic

Gestapo	*Geheime Staatspolizei*, Secret State Police in Nazi Germany
Ghetto	Designated and often hermetically sealed area where Nazis forced Jews to live
HIAS	Hebrew Immigration Aid Society
House of Commons	National Parliament of Great Britain
IRO	International Rehabilitation Organization
JAFP	Jewish Agency for Palestine
Jewish Community	Organization(s) created and run by German Jews
Jewish Relief	British-based Aid Organization for Jews (JRU)
Joint	American Joint Distribution Committee (AJDC)
JRSO	Jewish Restitution Successor Organization
JRU	Jewish Relief Unit
Jüdische Betreuungsstelle	Jewish Care Agency
Jüdische Gemeinde	Jewish Community
Komitee der befreiten Juden	Committee of Liberated Jews
KZ	*Konzentrationslager* (German for concentration camp)
Landesverband der Jüdischen Gemeinden	Regional Association of Jewish Communities
LSE	London School of Economics and Political Science
NAAFI	The Navy, Army and Air Force Institutes, i.e. the official trading organization of the British armed forces
Nazi	National Socialist
NSDAP	*Nationalsozialistische Deutsche Arbeiterpartei* (National Socialist German Workers Party)
Nuremberg Laws	Package of decrees announced at the Nazi party congression in 1935
OMGUS	Office of the Military Government in the US Zone
ORT	(Jewish) Organization for Rehabilitation and Training
SHAEF	Supreme Headquarters of the Allied Expeditionary Force
UNNRA	United Nations Relief and Rehabilitation Administration
VAAD HATZALA	New York-based Jewish charity to support Orthodox religious observance

LIST OF ARCHIVES

AJDC: American Joint Distribution Committee, Jerusalem (Archive), Israel
CZA: Central Zionist Archive, Jerusalem, Israel
IfZ: Institut für Zeitgeschichte, Munich (Archival Collection), Germany
IM: Imperial War Museum, London (Archival Collection), England
LBINY: Leo Baeck Institute, New York (Archival Collection), USA
LC: Library of Congress, Washington DC Manuscript Collection, USA
PRO: Public Record Office, London, England
StAF: Stadtarchiv Frankfurt am Main, Germany
USHMM: United States Holocaust Memorial Museum, Washington DC, USA
USNA: United States National Archive, Suitland, MD, USA
WLL: Wiener Library, London (Archival Collection), England
ZA: Zentralarchiv zur Erforschung der Geschichte der Juden in Deutschland, Heidelberg, Germany
ZfA: Zentrum für Antisemitismusforschung, Technical University Berlin (Archive), Germany

NOTES

Introduction

1. Martin Gilbert estimates that 330,000 Jewish survivors were liberated in Germany. See *Atlas of the Holocaust*. London: Dent, 1993, p.242.
2. The list of survivors compiled between June and December 1945 by Rabbi Abraham Klausner recorded a total of 30,000 Jewish survivors in Germany. For details, see chapter two of this volume.
3. Paul Celan, 'Todesfuge' (Death Fugue), 1945, reprinted in *Gate of Repentance. Services for the High Holidays*. London: Union of Liberal and Progressive Synagogues, 1973, p.483.
4. An exception to this rule were 700 German-Jewish survivors who had been liberated in Theresienstadt. Because they had relatives in the United States who provided affidavits, they were eligible to emigrate as soon as quota regulations permitted, and chose to wait in the DP Camp Deggendorf rather than re-enter German society for an interim period.

1. Experiences of the Holocaust and Strategies of Survival

1. For a detailed discussion see Michael Marrus, *The Holocaust in History*. New York: New American Library, 1987.
2. Martin Gilbert, *Holocaust: The Jewish Tragedy*. London: Harper Collins, 1986.
3. Wolfgang Benz, *Juden in Deutschland, 1933-1945*. Munich: Beck, 1989; Monika Richarz, ed., *Bürger auf Widerruf. Lebenszeugnisse deutscher Juden 1780-1945*. Munich: Beck, 1989.
4. In his *The Whitewashing of the Yellow Badge. Anti-Semitism and Philosemitism in Post-War Germany*, Oxford: Pergamon Press, 1992, Frank Stern documents how 'social annihilation' prepared and preceded 'physical annihilation'.
5. See for instance the survey of Jewish Holocaust experiences based on

conversations with survivors in Anton Gill, *The Journey Back From Hell.*
Conversations with Concentration Camp Survivors. London: Collins, 1988.

6. Yehuda Bauer, *The Holocaust in Historical Perspective.* Seattle: University
of Washington Press, 1978. See also the writings by Primo Levi on the
Holocaust and his experiences.

7. Eva Kolinsky, 'Experiences of Survival', *Leo Baeck Yearbook, XLIV*
(1999): 245–70.

8. Daniel Goldhagen, *Hitler's Willing Executioners. Ordinary Germans and
the Holocaust.* London: Little, Brown and Company, 1996. Although
Goldhagen's assumption that German anti-Semitism was specifically
'eliminationist' is not supported with research evidence, the book
provides an important account of anti-Jewish policy and actions in all
areas under Nazi control.

9. Lawrence Langer, *Holocaust Testimonies. The Ruins of Memory.* New
Haven and London: Yale University Press, 1991, p.16.

10. Ronald J. Berger, *Constructing a Collective Memoir of the Holocaust. A Life
History of Two Brothers' Survival.* Boulder: University of Colorado Press,
1995 uses the terms 'agency' and 'structure' to describe the parameters of
survival, 'The Berger brothers and other Jews who survived the
Holocaust did so in the face of a social structure that was systematically
organized by the Nazi regime to accomplish their death' (p.103).

11. Gerty Spiess, 'Hunger', *Süddeutsche Zeitung*, no. 75 (11 September
1948). LBINY, Papers of Hedwig Geng, AR 524/1587.

12. For a detailed discussion of research issues see Eva Kolinsky, 'Jewish
Survivors between Liberation and Resettlement' in Johannes Dieter
Steinert and Inge Weber-Newth, eds, *European Immigrants to Britain.*
Osnabrück: Secolo, 2001.

13. Lawrence Langer, *Holocaust Testimonies*, p.67.

14. David Bergman, Oral Testimony, recorded 18 July 1990. USHMM, RG
50.030 * 20, transcript p.36.

15. Ernest Weihs, Oral Testimony, recorded 30 May 1989. USHMM, RG
50.030 * 248, transcript p.27.

16. Hans Winterfeldt, whose story is recorded later in this chapter, admits to
eating the bread of Russian prisoners who had died next to him in the
hospital.

17. Hedwig Geng, 'Letter to Kurt', 28 January 1946, p.2. Quoted from a
collection of her documents and letters written after her liberation from
Theresienstadt. LBINY, AR 524/1587.

18. Hedwig Geng, Letter addressed to 'Meine Lieben', 26 January 1946, p.1.

19. Hana Bruml, Oral Testimony, recorded 27 February 1990. USHMM,
RG 50.030 * 0.43, transcript p.4.

20. Hana Bruml, Oral Testimony, p.37.

21. Reuven Danziger, 'No More Happy Days'. Unpublished memoir,
Natanya, Israel, 2002. Reuven Danziger survived various slave labour
camps and was liberated in Buchenwald in April 1945. He also lost his
father and younger brothers in the Holocaust.

22. Max Jacobson, *Mein Leben und Erinnerungen für Kinder und Enkel*

aufgezeichnet Leipzig im Jahre 1945/46, pp.1-52. LBINY, ME 330/1.
Max Jacobson wrote most of this account before his liberation in order to
have a record of his experiences for his children and grandchildren. All
details and quotations pertaining to Max Jacobson's survival are taken
from his account and translated into English by the current author.

23. Hans Winterfeldt, *Deutschland, ein Zeitbild 1926–1945. Leidensweg eines
deutschen Juden in den ersten 19 Jahren seines Lebens*. LBINY, MC 690,
p.48. All details and quotations pertaining to Hans Winterfeldt's survival
are taken from his account and translated into English by the current
author.

24. Bella Tovey neé Jacubowicz, Oral Testimony, recorded 15 February
1990. USHMM, RG 50.030 * 236. All details and quotations pertaining
to Bella Tovey's survival are taken from the transcripts of her recorded
testimony at USHMM.

25. Alice Lok-Cahane, Oral Testimony, recorded 4 December 1990.
USHMM, RG 50.030 * 051. All details and quotations pertaining to
Alice Cahane's survival are taken from the transcript of her recorded
testimony at USHMM.

26. Jewish women who had been deported from Hungary to Auschwitz were
made to wait in Block 25 before being taken to the gas chambers. See
Anton Gill, *The Journey Back From Hell*, p.26. In her memoir *Return to
Auschwitz. The Remarkable Life of a Girl who Survived Auschwitz*.
London: Sidgwick and Jackson, 1981, Kitty Hart describes Block 25.

27. Irma Grese was an SS guard who features in several narratives of
survival for her impressive appearance and for her cruelty. She was later
transferred to Bergen-Belsen and tried in September 1945 at the Belsen-
trial in Lüneburg and sentenced to death. See Eberhard Kolb, *Bergen
Belsen. Geschichte des 'Aufenthaltslagers' 1943–1945*. Hanover: Verlag für
Literatur und Zeitgeschehen, 1962, pp.177–85.

2. Unexpected Challenges: Liberating German Concentration Camps and Caring for their Survivors

1. Paul Johnson, *A History of the Jews*. New York: Harper and Row, 1987,
p.495; also Jacob Birnbaum with Jason A. Taylor, *'I Kept My Promise'.
The miraculous saga of a young man's survival through six labour camps
during the Second World War*. Lexington: Jason R. Taylor Associates,
1995, p.xi. The concentration camps were listed by the German
Government in *Bundesgesetzblatt*, 24 September 1977, pp.1787–852; the
figure for slave labour camps was provided by the Commandant of
Auschwitz, Rudolf Höss. The death camps were Auschwitz and Chelmo
in the Polish areas that were incorporated into the Reich, and Treblinka,
Sobibor, Majdanek and Belzec in the General Government area of
Poland.

2. The figures and the term 'populations' from A.H. Moffat, 'Report on
Concentration Camps', 29 June 1945, the first summary report on the

liberations prepared for the SHAEF. See USNA, RG 331/50/G-5/
5211/7/3 (Concentration Camps). A map of concentration camps inside
Nazi Germany depicting the situation as it had been in June 1944 lists
the names and locations of 140 camps. See Yaffa Eliah and Brauna
Gurewietsch, eds, *The Liberators. Eyewitness Accounts of the Liberation of
Concentration Camps.* Vol. I: Liberation Day. Oral History Testimonies
of American Liberators from the Archives of the Center for Holocaust
Studies. New York (Brooklyn): Center for Holocaust Studies, Documentation and Research, 1981.

3. SHAEF memorandum no. 39, dated 13 September 1944, revised and
   distributed November 1944. This Memorandum formed the basis of a
   'Guide to the Registration of Displaced Persons', dated 10 January 1945
   and distributed to field commanders. USNA, RG 260/121.
4. General J. Milner Roberts, interview conducted on 10 April 1992.
   USHMM, RG 50. 031 File 191, transcript p.19.
5. Eric Leiseroff, interviewed on 24 January 1979, in Yaffa Eliah and
   Brauna Gurewietsch, eds, *The Liberators, Eyewitness Accounts of the
   Liberation of Concentration Camps.* p.2.
6. Martin Gilbert, *Atlas of the Holocaust.* London: Dent, 1993, pp.223–4
7. Mayer Birnbaum with Yonason Rosenblum, *Lieutenant Birnbaum. A
   Soldier's Tale.* New York: Menorah Publications, 1993, pp.120–1.
8. *Stars and Stripes* (Paris), 30 April 1945. The issue also contains a report
   on a later visit, initiated by General Eisenhower, of 18 American
   newspaper editors and leading journalists, as well as a special delegation
   of the US Congress to Buchenwald.
9. *Stars and Stripes* (Western Europe edition), 10 April 1945, p.3.
10. David Malachowsky, interviews on 26 March 1975, in Yaffa Eliah and
    Brauna Gurewitsch, eds., *The Liberators*, p.12.
11. Report in *The New York Times*, 15 April 1945, p.9.
12. J. Milner Roberts, interview conducted on 10 April 1945. USHMM, RG
    50. 031 File 191, transcript p.15.
13. Egon W. Flesch and Edward A. Tenenbaum, 'Buchenwald. A Prelimi-
    nary Report', 24 April 1945, p.2. USNA, RG 331/50/G-5/2711/7.21.
14. 'Bericht über das Konzentrationslager Buchenwald bei Weimar' prepared
    by the Psychological Warfare Division of SHAEF in April 1945 and
    reprinted in full as *The Buchenwald Report.* Translated by David A.
    Hackett. Boulder: Westview Press, 1995.
15. Flesch and Tenenbaum, 'Buchenwald. A Preliminary Report', p.9.
16. *The Buchenwald Report*, p.236. Of the 9,000 prisoners who were marched
    to Buchenwald from Ohrdruf on 3 April, the Jews were also selected for
    the 'death trains'.
17. Details from *The Buchenwald Report*, p.271–9.
18. Flesch and Tenenbaum, 'Buchenwald. A Preliminary Report', p.14.
19. 'Buckenwald', report by Brig. Gen. Erich F. Wood, Lt. Col. Chas H. Ott
    and CWO S.M. Day, 16 April 1945, p.1. USNA, RG 331/50/G-5/
    2711/7.21.
20. Guy Stern, Oral Testimony, recorded 1 May 1990. USHMM, RG

50.030 * 223 (File 'Liberators'), transcript pp.1–12. Later in life, Guy Stern had a distinguished academic career as Professor of German at Columbia University, New York. In his testimony, he recalls how relatives in the United States provided affidavits that were unusable because they did not contain financial guarantees while an affidavit for him from a children's home in St. Louis was rejected because he had already passed his 14th birthday. In desperation, the family travelled to Hamburg to apply in person for visas at the US Consulate. Here, the Consul agreed to stamp the papers of the boy but not of the parents since, they were told, the United States accepted people only in certain employment categories, and Guy Stern's father did not fit them.

21. This and the following quotations from Guy Stern, Oral Testimony USHMM, RG 50.030 * 223.
22. Harry Herder Jr., 'The Liberation of Buchenwald'. Http://www.jewish. org.ForgottenCamps/Witnesses/HerderEng.html, p.6.
23. Details in Warren F. Draper, 'Report of Visit to Buchenwald Concentration Camp near Weimar Germany', 25 April 1945, dated 30 April 1945, pp.3–4. USNA, RG331/50/G-5/2711/7.21.
24. Report of a visit to Buchenwald on 27 April 1945 by a French Mission. USNA, RG331/50/G-5/2711/7.21.
25. Warren F. Draper, 'Report of Visit to Buchenwald', pp.3–4.
26. Lt. Col. Charles I. Schottland and Senior Commander M. Macdonald, 'Report on a Field Trip to Buchenwald', 12 June 1945, pp.1–3. USNA, RG331/50/G-5/2711/7.21.
27. Warren F. Draper, 'Report of Visit to Buchenwald', p.4.
28. Schottland and Macdonald, 'Report on a Field Trip to Buchenwald', p.2.
29. *The Buchenwald Report*, p.10, quoting a remark made by General Eisenhower on 13 April 1945.
30. Schottland and Macdonald, 'Report on a Field Trip to Buchenwald', p.3.
31. Cable from Twelfth Army Command to SHAEF, 9 May 1945. USNA, RG331/50/G-5/2711/7.21.
32. In June 1945, the East German regions of Saxony and Thuringia were handed over to the Russians in exchange for an American sector of occupied Berlin. Under Soviet control, Buchenwald became a *Spezialla-ger*; a detention camp for political detainees. Ursula Härtle and Walter Mönch, eds, *Buchenwald. Delikte, Denkmale, Erinnerungen*. Lauterbach: Euler Verlag, 1995. The volume does not mention that Jews were ever imprisoned in Buchenwald.
33. Mayer Birnbaum and Yonason Rosenblum, *Lieutenant Birnbaum. A Soldier's Tale.* p.139.
34. Schottland and Macdonald, 'Report on a Field Trip to Buchenwald', p.1.
35. For a detailed account, see Paul Kemp, 'The British Army and the Liberation of Bergen-Belsen, April 1945' in Jo Reilly, David Cesarani et al., eds, *Belsen in History and Memory*. London: Cass, 1997, pp.134–48. Also the collection 'Bergen-Belsen' at the archive of Imperial War Museum (IM) containing personal testimony from Belsen at the time of liberation.

36. General Sir Evelyn Barker, 'Report on the Liberation of Bergen-Belsen', Appendix B, dated 12 April 1945. IM, collection Bergen-Belsen, 84/59/1.

37. Memo 'Belsen Concentration Camp' 8C/484/G (O), dated 13 April 1945. Appendix A to General Sir Evelyn Barker, 'Report on the Liberation of Bergen-Belsen'.

38. Ibid., Appendix A, p.1.

39. In the first moments of confusion, however, one thousand Jewish survivors escaped to nearby towns such as Hanover and Celle where they later founded Jewish communities. See 'Survey undertaken at the request of UNRRA', 29 March 1946. PRO, FO 1052/294.

40. Jane E. Leverson, Report dated 6 May 1945 to the Jewish Committee for Relief Abroad, London, in Dr. A.R. Horwell, P78, IM, File 91/21/1, p.5.

41. Report by Lt. Col. R.I.G. Taylor in File 6, p.5, General Sir Evelyn Barker, IM 'Belsen', 1216.

42. Ibid., p.3.

43. Ibid., p.4.

44. Dr. A.P. Meiklejohn, 'London Medical Students' Work at Belsen' in *UNRRA Monthly Review*, July 1945, p.19. IfZ Archive, DW 102.001.

45. Col. S.G. Champion, 'The First Afternoon'. IM 'Belsen', File 93/11/1, p.3.

46. Meiklejohn, 'London Medical Students' Work at Belsen', p.19.

47. W.R. Williams, Letter to his son Tom, 18 April 1945, reprinted in Reilly, et al., eds, *Belsen in History and Memory*, London: Cass, 1997, pp.248–9.

48. 'Death Camp Victims Still Suffer', *Jewish Chronicle*, 1 July 1945, p.12.

49. These records are kept in the archive of the Imperial War Museum in London; some have been incorporated into its permanent Holocaust exhibition.

50. 'Memorandum for the Record' (Col. A.H. Moffat), 27 April 1945, USNA, RG331/50/G-5/2711/7, pp.1–2.

51. Ibid., p.2.

52. Dr. D. Bradford, Diary 18 April – 29 May 1945 (handwritten), IM 'Belsen' File 86/7/1, entry 28 April, p.1.

53. Dr. M. Coigley, Notebook, May 1945, IM 'Belsen' File 91/6/1, p.2.

54. Brigadier Glyn Hughes, the officer in charge of medical provisions at Belsen, quoted in Reilly et al., eds, *Belsen in History and Memory*, p.38.

55. Dr. P.J. Horsey, 'Typhus at Belsen', manuscript written in 1946, based on diary kept at Belsen 30 April to 14 May 1945. IM 'Belsen', 91/21/1 (R), pp.61–2.

56. Dr. T. Charters, letter to his wife, Belsen 15 May 1945, IM 'Belsen'. Con. Shelf, collection of letters p.131.

57. Statistical record for the camps and the hospitals at Belsen, itemised on a daily basis for the period 15 April 1945 to 26 May 1945, in papers relating to Dr. P.J. Horsey, IM 'Belsen'.

58. Dr. Meiklejohn, 'London Medical Students' Work at Belsen' in *UNRRA Monthly Review* July 1945, p.20. IfZ Archive, DW 102.001.
59. Zvi Asaria, *Wir sind Zeugen*. Hanover: Landeszentrale für politische Bildung, 1975. In the 1950s, Hermann Helfgott changed his name to Asaria and moved to Israel.
60. Ibid., pp.105–6.
61. *Jewish Chronicle*, 1 July 1945. See also Leslie Hardman's autobiographical account in Reilly, et al., eds, *Belsen in History and Memory*.
62. Isaac Levy, letter to T.T. Scott, DP-Section, UNRRA, London, dated 16 May 1945, p.2. IM File 91/21/1 (Collection Horwell).
63. Ibid.
64. Letter by Margaret Wyndham Ward to her mother Sarah Langlands Ward, dated 11 May 1945. British Red Cross Archives Library, London, T2/War.
65. Letter by Margaret Wyndham Ward to her mother, 19 May 1945.
66. Based on a report by one of the liberators, Josef Butterman, and cited in Abraham Hyman, *The Undefeated*. Jerusalem: Gefen Publishing, 1953, p.78.
67. Details from Jane Leverson, 'Report on Displaced Persons, Centre no. 267, Lingen, Germany', 6 June 1945. IM File 91/21/1 (R) (Collection Horwell).
68. Shalom Marcovitch, 'Report to the Jewish Relief Committee Abroad', 12 July 1945. IM File 71.21/1 (R) (Collection Horwell).
69. Details in Abraham Hyman, *The Undefeated*, pp.76–7.
70. Dr. A.J. Horwell, Letter to his family, dated 23 May 1945. IM File 91.21/1 (R). Horwell lobbied the Jewish chaplain Leslie Hardman on 16 May. He recorded his experiences in *The Story of Belsen*, which is kept in the 'Belsen' collection of the Imperial War Museum, London.
71. Quoted in *Jewish Chronicle*, 4 May 1945.
72. USNA, RG331/50/G-5/2711/7.4; a file note from SHAEF (G-5) of 27 April 1927 reported that Dachau surveillance had been carried out, and that a proposal to operate an airlift to surround the concentration camp in order to save the lives of survivors had been turned down.
73. William J. Cowling, 'Report on the Surrender of the German Concentration Camp at Dachau', 2 May 1945. http://remember.org/witness/cowling.html, p.1.
74. Letter by William J. Cowling to his family, started on 28 April and completed after the liberation of Dachau, ibid. p.2.
75. Cowling, 'Report on the Surrender', ibid. p.3.
76. Ibid. ibid. pp.3–4.
77. John Komski, Oral Testimony, recorded 7 June 1990. USHMM, RG 50.030 * 115, transcript pp.40–1.
78. Ibid. p.42.
79. Walter J. Fellenz, 'Impressions of the Dachau Concentration Camp Liberated 29 April 1945' in Yaffa Eliach and Brauna Gurewitsch (eds), *The Liberators*. Vol. I, p.37
80. Cowling, 'Report on the Surrender', p.5. Cowling also claims that

shooting at the SS began only after the electric fence had been disconnected.

81. Ibid., p. 2.
82. 75. Sixth Army Group Signed Devers to SHAEF, G-5, 4 May 1945; USNA, RG331/50/G-5/2711/7.3.
83. Cowling, Letter to his family, p.8.
84. 'Guide to the Care of Displaced Persons in Germany' dated 18 May 1945. USNA, RG 331/56/G-5, 2866 (Displaced Persons). This Guide brings together Memorandum no. 39, its revised version of 16 April 1945 and a guide to Assembly Centres (CA/d9) issued in September 1944. See also 'Concentration Camps', Draft Directive (no date) to COMDB/GOC-In-C-Army Groups, USNA, RG 331/56/G-5/2846.
85. P.H. Spivey, 'Report, Concentration Camps, Dachau', to Commanding General, 7th Army, 5 May 1945; pp.2–3. USNA, RG 331/50/G-5/2711/7.3.
86. Details in Otto Burianek, *From Liberator to Guardian. The US Army and Displaced Persons in Munich, 1945*. MA dissertation, Emory University, 1992, p.153.
87. Ibid., pp.159–60.
88. A Report by two senior SHAEF Displaced Persons Branch officials, Lt. Col. J.D. Faulkner and Lt. Col. V.R. Paravicini based on their visit on 6 May and published on 12 May 1945, states that it was unclear at the time whether the 'figure of the camp population' in Dachau (32,000) included those liberated at Allach. RG 331/50/G-5/2711/7.3, p.3. They also noted than 3,000 of the liberated survivors were Jews, and 2,000 held at Dachau were prisoners of war.
89. Interview by Paul Bradley, *The Voice of America*, with Col. Paul A. Roy, 22 July 1945. Records relating to the military career of Paul A. Roy (Dachau), USHMM, RG 19.032 * 01.
90. Interview with Paul A. Roy; also Cable on 'Dachau', 5th Army to SHAEF, dated 9 June 1945. USNA, RG 331/50/G-5/2711/7.3.
91. Paul A. Roy, 'Report on Dachau after Liberation', USHMM, RG19.032.
92. Cable from 6th Army Group to SHAEF, dated 6 May 1945. USNA, RG 331/277/G-5/277/7.3. The cable also mentions that 4,000 had been on death trains from Buchenwald of whom just 2,000 survived.
93. Roy, 'Report on Dachau after Liberation'.
94. Burianek, *From Liberator to Guardian*, pp.163–4.
95. M.J. Proudfoot, 'Report on Conditions in Dachau Concentration Camp, 2 July 1945', dated 9 July 1945. USNA331/50/G-5/2711/7.3. p.2.
96. J.D. Faulkner and V.R. Paravicini, 'Report on a Field Trip', 12 May 1945. USNA, RG 331/50/G-5/2711/7.3, p.3.
97. Ibid., p.2.
98. Proudfoot, 'Report on Conditions in Dachau', p.2.
99. International Prisoners' Committee, Press Activities, 19 July 1945. USHMM, RG 19.032 (Papers of Paul A. Roy).
100. Proudfoot, 'Report on Conditions in Dachau', pp.1–2.
101. 'Survey of the Inmates at Dachau Concentration Camp by Nationalities,

6 May 1945'. USNA, RG 331/50/G-5/2711/7.3. The data of this survey are also used in the 'Report on Concentration Camps' prepared by A.H. Moffit for the DP Branch at SHAEF on 29 June 1945. USNA, RG 331/50/G-5/2711/7.

102. Faulkner and Paravicini, 'Report on A Field Trip'.
103. Proudfoot, 'Report on Conditions in Dachau'.
104. By the end of July 1945, the Americans had repatriated seven million individuals from their zone of occupation while one million 'unrepatriables' remained.
105. 'International Prisoners Committee, Communique no. 34'. USHMM, RG 19.032 (Papers of Paul A. Roy).
106. Hyman, *The Undefeated*, p.38.
107. Details in Judah Nadich, *Eisenhower and the Jews*. New York: Twayne Publishers, 1953, pp.74–5.
108. Hyman, *The Undefeated*, pp.36–7.
109. Further to Abraham Klausner's work in Dachau and later in Feldafing, see also Alex Grobman, *Rekindling the Flames. American Jewish Chaplains and the Survivors of European Jewry, 1944–1948*. Detroit: Wayne State University Press, 1993, pp.65–70.

3. Beyond Survival: In Search of a Normal Life

1. Philip Auerbach, a survivor of Buchenwald, had been deported from Breslau in Silesia and later made a name for himself as the founder of the first German-Jewish newspaper, the *Jüdisches Gemeindeblatt*, based in Düsseldorf, and as State Commissioner for Restitution in Bavaria. Quoted from Auerbach's first report as State Commissioner in Joachim Schröder, *Politische und kulturelle Geschichte der jüdischen Displaced Persons anhand des von den USA verwalteten Lagers Föhrenwald in der amerikanischen Besatzungszone*. MA dissertation, University of Munich, April 1990, p.11.
2. Sama Wachs, cited from Jacqueline Giere and Rachel Salamander, *Ein Leben aufs neu. Das Robinson-Album. DP Lager. Juden auf deutschem Boden 1945–1948*. Schriftenreihe des Fritz Bauer Instituts, Frankfurt am Main, vol. 8. Vienna: Brandstädter Verlag, 1995, p.24.
3. Francesca M. Wilson, *Aftermath*. London: Penguin Books, 1947, p.69.
4. Paul Oppenheimer, *From Belsen to Buckingham Palace*. Wittness Collection. Newark: Beth Shalom, 1996, pp.147–50.
5. Charles Bruml, Oral Testimony, recorded 9 February 1990. USHMM, RG 50.030 * 042, transcript pp.29–30.
6. Benno Helmer, Oral Testimony, recorded 25 June 1990. USHMM, RG 50.030 * 093, transcript p.34.
7. Ibid., p.37.
8. Abraham Levent, Oral Testimony, recorded 20 October 1989. USHMM, RG 50.030 * 130, transcript, p.41.
9. Simon Schochet, *Feldafing*. Vancouver: November House, 1983, p.15.

10. Agnes Vogel, Oral Testimony, recorded 14 July 1989. USHMM, RG 50.030 * 239, transcript, p.11.
11. Ibid., p.12.
12. Ibid., p.13.
13. Abe Malnik, Oral Testimony, recorded 10 May 1990. USHMM, RG 50.030 * 145, transcript, p.36.
14. Ibid, p.38.
15. Solomon Krug, Oral Testimony, recorded 13 March 1990. USHMM, RG 50.030 * 107, transcript, p.11.
16. Ibid, p.24.
17. A similar medical and psychological approach is adopted by Kerry Bluglass, *Hidden Children*. London: Greenwood Press, 2004. Her study shows that most of the children became successful adults who had learned to cope with the experiences and memories of their past.
18. David Pablo Boder, *I Did Not Interview The Dead*. Urbana: The University of Illinois Press, 1949, p.xviii.
19. Ibid., pp.xviiii–xix.
20. Albert A. Hutler, Letter (to his wife), dated 3 April 1945. USHMM RG 19.028 * 26, p.1, Albert A. Hutler Papers, Displaced Persons Officer, Detachment Co2d, APO 758, Mannheim/Germany. File 'Letters'.
21. Albert A. Hutler, Letter (to his wife), dated 7 May 1945, p.1.
22. 'Report' (Mannheim), dated 4 April 1945. USHMM, RG 19.024*01. Albert A. Hutler Papers, File 'Articles and Military Records'. The same figure is also cited in a report prepared by the Mannheim office and dated 7 April 1945.
23. Albert A. Hutler, 'Weekly Functional Report', dated 5 May 1945. USHMM, RG 19.022 * 01. Albert Hutler Papers, File 'Reports – Seventh Army'.
24. Albert A. Hutler, 'Weekly Functional Report – Displaced Persons', dated 6 July 1945.
25. 'Weekly Functional Report', dated 28 June 1945.
26. Ibid.
27. Albert A. Hutler, Letter to his wife, 7 September 1945, typed draft p.2.
28. Albert A. Hutler, Letter to his wife, 7 May 1945. Women and children had to wait longer for their return home since Hutler felt it was necessary to secure passenger trains rather than cattle cars to ensure that they would travel in comfort.
29. Albert A. Hutler, Letter to his family, 15 May 1945.
30. Albert A. Hutler, Letter to his wife, 30 May 1945.
31. Ibid.
32. Albert A. Hutler, Letter to his wife, 23 June 1945.
33. Ibid.
34. Albert A. Hutler, Letter to his wife, 25 June 1945.
35. Albert A. Hutler, Letter to his wife, 17 August 1945.
36. Albert A. Hutler, Letter to his wife, 7 September 1945.
37. Albert A. Hutler, Letter to his wife, 16 September 1945.
38. Memoranda prepared by Seventh Army Headquarters on 'Responsibility

for Care and Control of Displaced Persons in Germany', 24 May 1945, and 'Organisation of UNRRA Administrative Establishment for Displaced Persons Operations in Germany', 5 September 1945. USHMM, RG 19.028 * 26, Albert A. Hutler, Papers. File: Articles and Military Records.

39. Albert A. Hutler, Letter to his wife, 26 September 1945.

40. Albert A. Hutler, Letter to his wife, 19 August 1945, pp.3–4.

41. For a concise overview see Wolfgang Jacobmeyer, 'The Displaced Persons Problem: Repatriation and Resettlement' in Johannes-Dieter Steinert and Inge Weber-Newth, eds. *European Immigrants in Britain 1933–1950*. Munich: Saur, 2003, pp.137–49.

42. SHAEF, 10 August 1944, 'Use of American and British Red Cross Personnel'. USNA, RG 260/138/152.

43. USNA, RG 260/176/16: 'Report on DP-Centres', 2 June – 14 July, 1945. The report also mentions that at the time, 810 UNRRA staff (from a projected 5,000) were deployed in the US zone, compared to 911 in May/June 1945.

44. 'Displaced Persons Operations'. Report of Central Headquarters (UNRRA) for Germany, April 1946, pp.63–4. IfZ Archive, DW 102.005, File no. 5774/77.

45. 'The Children of Kloster Indersdorf', UNRRA Review of the Month, October/November 1945. IfZ Archive, DW 102.001, File 56 17/76.

46. Details in Greta Fischer, 'Report: DP Children's Center Kloster Indersdorf', January 1946. USHMM, RG 19.034 * 06 (Greta Fischer Papers, Folder 2).

47. Martin Gilbert, *The Boys. Triumph over Adversity. The Story of 732 Young Concentration Camp Survivors*. London: Weidenfeld and Nicolson, 1996. See also the story of Kurt Klappholz later in this chapter.

48. Fischer, 'Report: DP Children's Center Kloster Indersdorf', p.25.

49. Ibid.', p.6.

50. Ibid., p.20.

51. Ibid., p.11.

52. Kloster Indersdorf, 'Disillusionment Following Liberation', Folder 2, p.1.

53. 'The Children of Kloster Indersdorf', UNRRA Review of the Month, Oct/Nov, 1945.

54. Giere and Salamander, *Ein Leben aufs neu, 1945–1948*. p.22. Includes quotes from early reports where carers describe displaced Jews as a 'hunted population' who was, at best, an object of welfare and caricature.

55. Wilson, *Aftermath*, p.117.

56. Henry B. Murphy, *Flight and Resettlement*. Unesco, Switzerland, 1955, pp.65–75.

57. Mary Heaton Vorse, 'This is the Story of Kurt Klappholz'. Typed manuscript, dated December 1945. USHMM, RG 19.034 * 09 (Greta Fischer Papers).

58. Gilbert, *The Boys*.

59. Lillian Roberts, 'Refugees – Who Cares? Address delivered at the Annual

Conference of the National Federation of Settlement', 12 September 1947. RG 19.043 * 04, p.5.

60. Kurt Klappholz, Testimony, transcribed tape, 1995, cited in Gilbert, *The Boys*, p.411.

61. Mary Heaton Vorse, 'This is the Story of Kurt Klappholz', p.9.

62. Ibid., p.10.

63. Fischer, 'Report: DP Children's Center, Kloster Indersdorf', section II.4.

64. 'This is the Story of Kurt Klappholz' Vorse, pp.6–7.

65. Roberts, 'Refugees – Who Cares?' p.9.

66. Fischer, 'Report: DP Children's Center, Kloster Indersdorf', p.20.

67. Roberts, 'Refugees – Who Cares?' p.1.

68. Fischer, 'Report: DP Children's Center, Kloster Indersdorf', p.6.

69. Ibid.

70. Ibid.

71. Anita Lasker-Wallfisch, '1925–1946. Told by Anita'. In Anita Lasker-Wallfisch Papers. LBINY, ME 305 (Safe), p.73. This chapter refers to Anita by her maiden name of Lasker, her name at the time of her liberation and new beginning. I should like to thank Anita Lasker-Wallfisch for her helpful comments on this section of the book.

72. Ibid., p.72.

73. Ibid., p.74.

74. Ibid.

75. Ibid., p.75.

76. Ibid., p.72.

77. Ibid., p.76.

78. Ibid.

79. Ibid., p.78.

80. A Memorandum issued by SHAEF to all Army Commands on 9 April 1945 stipulated that 2 Red Cross postcards should be issued to each liberated DP. A maximum of 25 words could be written in the small section reserved for personal communications. The postcards were to be sent by the military via Geneva to their mailing addresses. USNA, RG 260/173/35 (Folder: DP Communications).

81. Letter to her sister Marianne, 17 June 1945. In Anita Lasker-Wallfisch Papers. Part II, section III. LBINY, ME 305 (Safe).

82. '1925–1946. Told by Anita', p.80.

83. Letter dated 5 July 1945 by Renate Lasker to her sister Marianne. In Anita Lasker-Wallfisch Papers. Part II, Section IV. LBINY, ME 305 (Safe).

84. '1925–1946. Told by Anita', p.81.

85. Anita Lasker to Helli (the wife of her cousin Jack in Bristol), 30 July 1945. Anita Lasker-Wallfisch Papers, Part II, Section III. At the time, Anita Lasker was particularly impressed by the performance of the pianist. It was only later that she found out that it had been Benjamin Britten.

86. Anita Lasker to Helli, 30 July 1945.

87. Anita Lasker to Marianne, 8 June 1945.
88. Anita Lasker to Marianne, 15 June 1945.
89. Anita Lasker to Marianne, 8 June 1945.
90. Anita Lasker to Marianne, 19 June 1945.
91. Anita Lasker to Helli, 30 July 1945.
92. Ibid.
93. Lasker to Marianne, 25 June 1945.
94. Anita Lasker-Wallfisch, '1925–1946. Told by Anita', p.85. Emphases in the original.
95. Ibid., p.86.
96. Ibid., p.87.
97. Ibid.
98. Ibid., p.89.
99. For a more detailed account see Anita Lasker-Wallfisch, *Inherit the Truth, 1939–1945: the documented experiences of a survivor of Auschwitz and Belsen*. London: Giles de Mare, 1996.
100. '1925–1946. Told by Anita', p.97.
101. Renate Lasker to Marianne, 9 June 1945. Anita Lasker-Wallfisch Papers. Part II Section .IV. LBINY, ME 305 (Safe).
102. Renate Lasker to Marianne, 9 June 1943.
103. '1925–1946. Told by Anita', p.97.

4. Until the Gates Open: Waiting in Germany on the Road to Somewhere

1. One of the American soldiers who helped to bring supplies to St. Ottilien, and later issued a public appeal on behalf of its survivors in the United States, wrote a personal account of the events. Robert L. Hilliard, *Surviving the Americans. The Continued Struggle of the Jews After Liberation. A Memoir*. New York: Seven Stories Press, 1997.
2. A detailed account in Abraham Hyman, *The Undefeated*. Jerusalem: Gefen, 1993, p.79.
3. Hilliard, *Surviving the Americans*, pp.118–19.
4. Ibid., p.120.
5. Ibid., p.121.
6. *Frankfurter Rundschau*, 29 January 1946, p.1. The conference was held in Munich on 25 January and elected Zalman Grinberg as its president. In September 1945, liberated Jews in the British zone had organized their own conference, chaired by Josef Rosensaft, in Belsen. The unity of liberated Jews of St. Ottilien had given way to zonal divisions and rival organizations, although both shared the commitment to Zionism and the critical focus on provisions for displaced Jews in Germany.
7. 'Befreite Juden', quoting from Zalman Grinberg's closing address, *Frankfurter Rundschau*, 1 February 1946, p.2.
8. Details in *Frankfurter Rundschau*, 29 January 1946, p.1.
9. Quoted from Alex Grobman, *Rekindling the Flames. American Jewish*

Chaplains and the Survivors of European Jewry 1944–1948. Detroit: Wayne State University Press, 1993, pp.65–6.

10. A detailed account on Harrison's mission and the background to it can be found in ibid., chapter 3. Also Leonard Dinnerstein, *America and the Survivors of the Holocaust*. New York: Columbia University Press, 1982.

11. Sylvia Gilman, 'The American Jewish Conference – Spokesman for a United American Jewry', undated report (1946). Central Zionist Archive, Jerusalem, C7, 313/1, p.1.

12. Judah Nadich, *Eisenhower and the Jews*. New York: Twayne Publishers, 1953, p.38.

13. *New York Times*, 16 May 1945. The report of the first of these delegations was presented to both Houses of Congress, and received there in silence and shock.

14. Abraham Hyman, *The Undefeated*, p.45.

15. Details in Dinnerstein, *America and the Survivors of the Holocaust*, p.291.

16. Ibid., pp.39 ff.

17. In addition to Earl G. Harrison who was, at the time, US representative on the Intergovernmental Commission for Refugees (ICR), the team included Joseph J. Schwartz, the head of overseas relief and rescue services of the American Joint Distribution Committee, the main fund-raising body of American Jewry; Patrick M. Malin, the vice-director of the ICR, and Herbert Katzski, a staff member of the War Refugee Board.

18. Earl Harrison, 'Journal. May – July 1945'. Earl G. Harrison Papers, USHMM, RG 10.088, Folder 1. Handwritten notes, no pagination.

19. *The Department of State Bulletin* no. 13, 30 September 1945, pp.456–63. The full text of the Harrison Report is reprinted in Leonard Dinnerstein, *America and the Survivors of the Holocaust*, pp.291–305.

20. *New York Times*, 2 October 1945. The residents stressed that their conditions had been better than those portrayed in the report for a considerable time and not hastily improved since its publication. They did, of course, not know that the military had been given the opportunity to get improvements into place in early August 1945.

21. The Harrison Report, quoted from Leonard Dinnerstein, *America and the Survivors of the Holocaust*, p.292.

22. The Harrison Report, quoted as 'Report from Europe' in *The National Jewish Monthly* (November 1945), p.98.

23. Report on SHAEF policy towards displaced persons and persecuted persons in Germany, *New York Times*, 24 May 1945.

24. The Harrison Report, in Leonard Dinnerstein, *America and the Survivors of the Holocaust*, p.301.

25. Earl G. Harrison, 'The Last Hundred Thousand', typed draft, p.10. Earl G. Harrison Papers, USHMM RG 10.08812, Folder 2.

26. 'Report From Europe', *National Jewish Monthly* (November 1945), p.86.

27. The Harrison Report, in Leonard Dinnerstein, *America and the Survivors of the Holocaust*, p.298.

28. Earl Harrison, 'Journal, Visit to Belsen', 22 July 1945.

29. George Vida, *From Doom to Dawn. A Jewish Chaplain's Story of Displaced Persons*. New York: Jonathan David, 1967, pp.62–3.
30. Sylvia Gilman, The American Jewish Conference, p.3.
31. Earl Harrison, 'Journal'. According Harrison's notes, Weizmann estimated the number of Jewish survivors at 1.5 million and admitted that others in the Zionist movement did not agree with restricting entry. Harrison did not mention Weizmann's views in his report.
32. The Journal reveals that Harrison incorporated information given to him by Abraham Beckelman of the AJDC who ventured an estimate which, at the time, seemed inflated but was to prove too low from 1946 onwards when additional Jewish newcomers arrived from eastern European countries. Beckelman also indicated that only 3,000 further Palestine Certificates were to be granted and most of these had already been allocated to Jews in countries other than Germany, leaving the displaced persons there stranded.
33. Quoted from 'Report from Europe', *National Jewish Monthly* (November 1945), p.98.
34. On the diplomatic exchanges between the American President Harry S. Truman and the British Prime Minister Clement Attlee, and between the foreign ministers of the two countries, see Abraham Hyman, *The Undefeated*, pp.91ff.
35. Jewish Agency for Palestine, 'Report of Activities, 1946–1948'. Munich 1948 (signed by Dr. Chaim Hoffmer), pp.1–2. Institut für Zeitgeschichte (IfZ), Dw 379.001. Although JAFP arrived in June 1945, it took until December for personnel to organize an office and begin their work of assisting Jews with leaving for Palestine.
36. Abraham Hyman, *The Undefeated*, p.91.
37. Letter by General Dwight D. Eisenhower to President Harry S. Truman, 5 November 1945. Institut für Zeitgeschichte (IfZ), RG 84/POLAD, 736/25.
38. Ibid., p.1. Eisenhower also stressed that displaced persons already enjoyed more floor space in their living quarters than the 30 square foot per head to which American soldiers were entitled.
39. Ibid., p.2.
40. 'In accordance with the policy of this headquarters, such persons will be segregated as rapidly as possible into special assembly centers. Those who are Jews will be cared for in special Jewish centers.' Quoted in Judah Nadich, *Eisenhower and the Jews*, p.43.
41. 'Summary of DP Population', UNRRA, 24 August 1946. USNA, RG 19.034.06, Folder 'UNRRA'.
42. Letter. Eisenhower to Truman, 5 November 1945, p.2.
43. Military Government Office Greater Hesse, Historical Report for the period October 1945 – June 1946, p.448. IfZ, Fg 27, File 5827/78. See also Judah Nadich, *Eisenhower and the Jews*, p.126.
44. The 'Guide to Assembly Center Administration', dated 15 January 1947 reported that UNRRA had, from the outset, focussed on the care of displaced persons inside assembly centres although area directors could

decide whether individuals who were 'free living' should receive any support. From 22 November 1946 onwards, Administration Order no. 204 restricted care to persons living inside camps. IfZ, File DW 102.002.

45. The first AJDC representative, Ely Rock, arrived in Feldafing in June 1945 but objected to being allocated to the camp's UNRRA team. An AJDC office was finally opened in Munich in December 1945 to co-ordinate aid work in the US zone.

46. Irving Heymont, letter to his wife, 19 September 1945. USHMM, RG 19.038. Some of the letters are also published in Irving Heymont, *Among the Survivors of the Holocaust – 1945. The Landsberg DP Camp Letters of Major Irving Heymont, United States Army*. Cincinnati: American Jewish Archives, Hebrew Union College, 1982.

47. Irving Heymont, letter dated 19 September 1945.

48. Ibid.

49. Irving Heymont, letter dated 20 September 1945.

50. Ibid.

51. Ibid.

52. Ibid.

53. Irving Heymont, letter dated 1 October 1945.

54. Irving Heymont, letter dated 8 October 1945.

55. Ibid.

56. Irving Heymont, letter dated 4 October 1945, referring to an inspection tour led by General Mc Bride.

57. Irving Heymont, letter dated 2 October 1945.

58. Irving Heymont, letter dated 28 September 1945, describes Föhrenwald as 'ideal for a DP camp with fine housing for families. Being a compact, separate community, it is well suited for maintaining control and keeping the Germans at a distance. When the Jews and Germans are very close, there is tension and the possibility of clashes'. It took several weeks before Landsberg residents could be persuaded to move to Föhrenwald.

59. Letter dated 4 October 1945.

60. Irving Heymont, letter dated 8 October 1945.

61. Ibid.

62. Irving Heymont, letter dated 5 November 1945.

63. Irving Heymont, letter dated 13 October 1945.

64. Officially, Ben-Gurion was the chairman of the Histadrut, the Trade Union Organisations in the Yishuv, the Jewish settlement in Palestine. De facto, he was the future leader of a Jewish state. In 1948, he did indeed become the first Prime Minister of Israel. For details on the perception of Ben-Gurion by displaced Jews in 1945, see Judah Nadich *Eisenhower and the Jews*.

65. Irving Heymont, letter dated 22 October 1945.

66. Quoted in Abraham Hyman, *The Undefeated*, p.93.

67. J. Dijour, Director of HIAS, Program Germany and Austria to Ambassador Robert Murphy, US Political Advisor, Berlin. Memo headed 'The Jews in Germany. Situation and Immediate Solutions', 28 November 1945. The other six destinations were England (161),

Argentina (71), Brazil (73), Australia (34), Hungary (168) and Romania (63). The survey also includes information on the place of birth of residents and the extent of dislocation: Poland 3,740; Hungary 283; Romania 162; Lithuania 141; Germany 129; Czechoslovakia 106; Greece 58; Palestine 28 CZA, File 313/1.

68. Irving Heymont, letter dated 12 October 1945.
69. Irving Heymont, letter dated 29 October 1945.
70. Ibid.
71. While UNRRA administered displaced persons camps, food, medical and other supplies were procured by the army. The handover to UNRRA was delayed because teams remained understrength, and because UNRRA and the US army found it difficult to agree on how to share responsibility.
72. Irving Heymont, letter dated 6 December 1945.
73. Abraham Hyman, *The Undefeated*, p.110. Hyman reports that the Chief of Staff took Leo Scrole for a private conversation to the railway carriage that had been reserved for Hitler's personal use during the Nazi era. General Smith promised that additional camps would be opened and Scrole withdrew his resignation.
74. Irving Heymont, letter dated 6 December 1945.
75. See 'Survey of Conditions of Jews in the British Zone in March 1948', compiled at the request of UNRRA. PRO, FO 1052/294. For 1946, the recorded total was 14,178, including Jews living out of camp; for March 1948, 14,378.
76. Source for tables 4.1 and 4.2: Headquarters EUCOM Civil Affairs Division, report dated 8 April 1948. USNA, RG 260/120.
77. For a detailed discussion see Margaret Myers, 'Jewish Displaced Persons in the US Zone', *Leo Baeck Yearbook* XLIII (1997), pp.303–24.
78. Simon Schochet, *Feldafing*. Vancouver: November House, 1983, pp.159–62.
79. Headquarters of EUCOM, Civil Affairs Division, reported on 8 April 1948 that 29,051 Jews out of 3,082,339 displaced persons had been resettled from occupied Germany. USNA, RG 260/120.
80. Jewish Agency for Palestine, Report 1946–1948. IfZ, DW 379.001, pp.4–5.

5. Remaking Jewish Life in Post-war Germany

1. Monika Richarz, 'Einleitung' in Monika Richarz, ed., *Bürger auf Widerruf. Lebenszeugnisse deutscher Juden 1780–1945*. Munich: Beck, 1989, p. 54.
2. Boris Sapir, 'Germany', *American Jewish Yearbook*, vol. 49 (1947–48), p.363.
3. Displaced Persons Executive, 16 September 1945, cited in Reinhard Rürup, ed., *Jüdische Geschichte in Berlin. Bilder und Dokumente. Katalog zur Ausstellung 'Topographie des Terrors'*. Berlin: Hentrich Verlag, 1995,

p.330. Maor quotes different figures based on a list of Jews in Berlin after liberation: 2,183 = 28% 'privileged', 1,964 = 25% men married to non-Jewish women, 1,791 non-privileged 'star-wearers', 1,416 =18% 'illegals', i.e. survived in hiding, and 62 = 1% 'remigrants'. See Harry Maor, 'Über den Wiederaufbau der Jüdischen Gemeinden in Deutschland seit 1945.' Ph.D. diss., Mainz, 1961, p.2. For yet another version of Jewish residency in Berlin, see Erica Burgauer, *Zwischen Erinnerung und Verdrängung – Juden in Deutschland nach* 1945. Reinbek: Rowohlt, 1993, p.356.

4. Lutz Niethammer, 'Juden in Deutschland nach 1945', in *Living with/ without/against Jews after 1945 in Europe*. Proceedings of a conference held in Essen, published by the Evangelische Akademie, Essen, 1990, p.53.

5. Central Committee for Liberated Jews in Bavaria, September 1945, cited from Kurt Grosman, *The Jewish DP Problem*. New York: Institute of Jewish Affairs/World Jewish Congress, 1951, p.11.

6. The census collected information on Jewish residency in Germany by asking respondents to state their religion. It is impossible to say how partners in mixed marriages responded who had been defined by the Nazis as Jews although they were, by religious affiliation, Christians and had been baptised.

7. Details in Jael Geiss, *Übrig sein – Leben 'danach'. Juden deutscher Herkunft in der britischen und amerikanischen Zone Deutschlands 1945–1949*. Berlin: Philo, 2000, p.45.

8. Headquarters EUCOM Civil Affairs Division. Displaced Persons Statistics, 17 January 1947. USNA, RG 260/120.

9. Alexander Kohanski, 'Review of the Year 5705: Germany', *American Jewish Yearbook*, vol. 47 (1945/6), p.377. Kohanski's figure of 8,000 German Jews corresponds with observations by Harry Maor, 'Über den Wiederaufbau' that only about half the Jews in mixed marriages joined a Jewish community in 1945. Most of the Jewish women married to non-Jewish men appeared to have severed the links with Judaism that had been forced upon them.

10. Alon Tauber, 'Die Entstehung der jüdischen Nachkriegsgemeinde in Frankfurt am Main 1945–1949'. Unpublished manuscript, Heidelberg, 1998, p.2; also Fritz Stein, 'Ein neuer Abschnitt in der Geschichte der Jüdischen Gemeinde Frankfurt am Main', *Mitteilungsblatt der jüdischen Gemeinden und Betreuungsstellen*, no. 1, 7 December 1945, p.1.

11. Adolf Diamant, *Chronik der Juden in Leipzig. Aufstieg, Vernichtung und Neuanfang*. Chemnitz and Leipzig. Verlag Heimatland, Sachsen: 1993, pp.362–3.

12. Harry Maor, 'Über den Wiederaufbau', pp.1–2.

13. In the late 1950s, Maor conducted a survey among community founders and noted that 'although most were living in mixed marriages, they were characterised by the clear determination to continue the union on a voluntary basis into which they had been forced before. The years of

persecution had made many of them sorely aware of their Jewishness.'
Ibid., p.6.

14. See also the case study of Frankfurt in this volume which charts the
divides between German and displaced Jews at local level and the
eventual merger of 'community' and 'committee'.

15. Steffen Held, *Zwischen Tradition und Vermächtnis. Die Israelitische
Religionsgemeinde zu Leipzig nach 1945.* Hamburg: Dölling and Galitz
Verlag, 1995, p.13.

16. Renata Laqueur, *Schreiben im KZ. Tagebücher 1940–1945.* Bearbeitet von
Martina Dreisbach. Bremen: Donat Verlag, 1991, p.21.

17. Ibid., p.22.

18. 'Hier ist alles in Ordnung', ibid., p.22.

19. Ibid., pp.22–3. The term 'organize' was used by former concentration
camp prisoners and later by displaced persons to describe obtaining
goods by theft, stealth or another version of personal, illegal initiative.
This form of 'organizing' constituted an essential tenet of survival.

20. Renata Laqueur, *Schreiben im KZ*, p.25.

21. Entry for 17 March 1945 in Martha Glass, *Jeder Tag in Theresienstadt ist
ein Geschenk. Die Theresienstädter Tagebücher einer Hamburger Jüdin
1943–1945.* Hamburg: Ergebnisse Verlag, 1996, p.116.

22. Ibid., entry for 5 May 1945, p.118.

23 'Aufruf des Ältestenrates' cited in ibid., p.117.

24. H.A. Fierst, Report on SHAEF Displaced Persons Activities, 11 May
1945. USNA, RG 165/829/ SHAEF Reports. A cable from SHAEF to
21st Army confirmed on 23 May 1945 that 'distinguished nationals' had
been moved. USNA, RG 331/56 56/G-5/2852.

25. Martha Glass, *Jeder Tag in Theresienstadt*, entry for 28 June 1945, p.120.

26. Ibid., entry for 1 August 1945, p.122.

27. Gerty Spiess, *My Years in Theresienstadt. How One Woman Survived the
Holocaust.* New York: Prometheus Books, 1997, pp.186–7.

28. Ibid.

29. Ibid., p.190.

30. The house in the Kaulbachstrasse is not named by Gerty Spiess but can
be identified from other contemporary reports as the old folks home run
by the fledgling Jewish community in Munich that served as a reception
centre for Jews returning to Munich, and, as shown in Hedwig Geng's
narrative below, as a place of residency for those with nowhere else to go.

31. For the experiences of Hedwig Geng up to her liberation, see chapter
one.

32. Hedwig Geng, letter, 20 September 1945. Papers of Hedwig Geng,
LBINY, AR 524/1587.

33. Hedwig Geng, letter addressed to 'Meine Lieben' and dated 'Zweiter
Weihnachtsfeiertag 1945'.

34. The AJDC distributed some Red Cross parcels in October and
November 1945. Later, it shipped more suitable and diverse goods from
the United States for distribution in Germany.

35. Hedwig Geng, letter, 26 January 1945, p.1.

36. H. Ingster, 'Emigrieren oder Hierbleiben?' in *Jüdisches Gemeindeblatt*, vol. 1, no. 24 (19 March 1946).
37. Harry Maor, Über den Wiederaufbau', p.13.
38. Details in Vaad Hatzala, *Germany 1948. A Pictorial Review*. Ed. Nathan Baruch, 1948 (no place of publication).
39. The closure of displaced persons camps had commenced in 1947, and gathered speed in 1948 and 1949 as resettlement reduced residency numbers, requiring fewer camps. From 1948 onwards, housing units that had been confiscated from Germans for use as DP camps and former military barracks were also vacated and returned for German use. From 1949 onwards, the public authorities in the new West German state were put in charge of displaced persons administration, including running any remaining camps. Some Jews were reluctant to leave the sheltered environment of a camp. Just over one thousand chose to move to Föhrenwald in Bavaria and held out against closure until 1957.
40. Compiled and published by the Advisor for Jewish Affairs in March 1949; quoted from Harry Maor, 'Über den Wiederaufbau', p.19.
41. From the outset, observers from outside Germany condemned these communities for their patchy pursuit of religion and blamed the assimilated, essentially a-religious founders for these developments.
42. Letter by the executive of the Landesverband der jüdischen Gemeinden, Nordrhein to Herrn Ministerpräsident Dr. Amelunxen, 4 November 1946. ZA, File B1/2, Sheet 200 (Allgemeine Korrespondenz).
43. Karl Marx, 'Wir, die deutschen Juden', *Jüdisches Gemeindeblatt*, vol. 1, Sheet 16 (27 November 1946).
44. Kultusgemeinde Gross Dortmund, Korrespondenz mit Mitgliedern 1946–1948. ZA File B1/2, Sheet 11/E.
45. Siegfried Heimberg to Distribution P.G.C.C., c/o Mr. Caster, Essen (Villa Hügel), 11 November 1946. ZA File B1/2, Sheet 19 (Allgemeine Korrespondenz 1946–50).
46. Siegfried Heimberg, 'Bescheinigung', 30 March 1949. ZA File B1/2, Sheet 19 (Allgemeine Korrespondenz 1946–1950).
47. Letter by the Stadtdirektor Stadt Schwerte to Wirtschaftsabteilung, Landesverband der jüdischen Gemeinden Westfalen, 4 June 1947. ZA, File B1/2, Sheet 19/11.
48. In February 1947, the Council of Jewish Communities in the British Zone reported that 510 coupons were to be distributed, each entitling the recipient to half a Care Parcel. Based on community membership in the zone, the Council resolved that the allocation entitled every fortieth member to receive such a (half) parcel, leaving it to local communities to determine who were the most needy individuals. See 'Bericht über die am 25 und 26 Februar 1947 in Bremen stattgefundene Sitzung des Rates der jüdischen Gemeinden der britischen Zone', p.2. ZA, File B1/2, Sheet 200.
49. Letter by D.B. Wodlinger, Zonenrepresentative (*sic*) to Landesverband der jüdischen Gemeinden, Westfalen, dated 25 May 1946, confirming in writing that the AJDC was willing to pay 2,500 Reichsmark per month

but required 'regular and detailed accounts for this money at the end of every month'. The money was intended to help cover the organizational cost of Jewish communities in the region (ZA, B1/2, Sheet 200).

50. See the papers concerning 'Sozialarbeit Joint' in ZA, File B1/2, Sheet 368; no. 371 and no. 372.

51. 'Rundschreiben an alle jüdischen Gemeinden', dated 10 February, 1947 and signed by Dr. Hadassah Bimko. ZA, File B1/2 Sheet 25 (Z-K Belsen). A severe shortage of X-ray machines in Germany's ruined towns made it very difficult for needy German Jews to comply with this new rule.

52. Copy (*Abschrift*) of a letter by Ernst Huldschinsky, 2 July 1948 to Zentralkommittee der befreiten Juden in der Britischen Zone. ZA, File B1/2, Sheet 25.

53. Letter by Siegfried Heimberg, 19 July 1948 to Zentralkommittee, Belsen, p.1. ZA, File B1/2, Sheet 25.

54. Bavaria retained a separate care system, the 'Bayrisches Hilfswerk' that distributed aid to communities and through them to needy members. It was incorporated into the Central Jewish Welfare Agency in 1956.

55. For details and cases see ZA, File B1/2, Sheet 224 (Verband).

56. Circular (*Rundschreiben*) to all Jewish communities by the 'Bayrisches Hilfswerk', 1 June 1953. ZA, File B1/5, Sheet 190.

57. 'Bayrisches Hilfswerk', *Rundschreiben* no. 131, 5 October 1951. ZA, File B1/5, Sheet 190.

58. 'Bayrisches Hilfswerk', *Liste* 25, 4 November 1953, p.2. ZA, File B 1/5, Sheet 190.

59. Harry Maor, 'Über den Wiederaufbau', p.47; also Jael Geis, *Übrig sein – Leben 'danach'*, pp.47ff.

60. Cilly Kugelmann, 'Befreiung – und dann? Zur Situation der Juden in Frankfurt am Main im Jahr 1945' in Monica Kingreen, ed., *Nach der Kristallnacht. Jüdisches Leben und antijüdische Politik in Frankfurt am Main 1938–1945*. Frankfurt/Main: Campus, 1999, p.444.

61. Adolf Diamant, *Gestapo Frankfurt am Main. Zur Geschichte einer verbrecherischen Organisation in den Jahren 1933–1945*. Frankfurt/Main: Selbstverlag, 1988, pp.242–3.

62. In a letter to Max Cahn, the legal spokesman of the *Jüdische Gemeinde* in Frankfurt, and dated 30 October 1946, the State Commissioner for Jews, Dr. Kurt Epstein, explained that the sum of 35,000 had been a special allocation, not an entitlement. The *Betreuungsstelle* should be grateful to receive any sum at all rather than complain about the reduction. ZA, B1.13, A 65, Sheet 36.

63. Fritz Stein, File note, July 1945. ZA, B1/13, A 183, Sheet 31.

64. Diamant, *Gestapo Frankfurt am Main*, p.446.

65. Transport list with names, and letter to *Kultusgemeinde Frankfurt a.M.*, 17 August 1945. ZA, B1/13, A 178, Sheet 6.

66. According to a list compiled by the Welfare Department on 15 May 1945, there were 191 beds in ten emergency shelters, eight of them using hotels. In addition, the Jewish hostel for 25 residents was located in

Sandweg. Institut für Stadtgeschichte, Frankfurt am Main. Archive, Magistratsakten 8841.

67. Letter by the Frankfurter Versorgungshaus und Wiesenhüttenstift to Herrn Stein, 31 May 1945. ZA, B1/13, A 182, Sheet 11.

68. Letter by the Frankfurter Versorgungshaus und Wiesenhüttenstift to Herrn Stein, 12 June 1945. ZA, B1/13, A 182, Sheet 10.

69. August Adelsberger to Fahrbereitschaft Frankfurt/Main, file copy of letter, 19 May 1945. ZA, B 1/13, A 176, Sheet 16.

70. Letter by Fritz Stein to August Adelsberger, 23 May 1945. ZA, B1/13. A 176, Sheet 2.

71. List of residents addressed to the Office for Food, 14 September 1945. ZA, B1/13, A 176, p.35. Of the 31 residents for whom Stein obtained ration cards, 26 were women, five men. Half were aged 65 and over, just three under 25, the youngest was a girl of 14. See also Fritz Stein, 'Ein neuer Abschnitt in der Geschichte der Jüdischen Gemeinde Frankfurt am Main' *Mitteilungsblatt der jüdischen Gemeinden und Betreuungsstellen*, no 4 (7 December 1945), p.1.

72. ZA, B1/13, A 183, Sheet 26. From 28 February 1946 onwards, hotels were no longer available as temporary accommodation for German or displaced Jews in the city. Letter by Hauptverwaltungsamt Frankfurt to Besatzungsamt, 28 February 1946. Institut für Stadtgeschichte Frankfurt am Main, Archiv. Magistratsakten 8841.

73. Judah Nadich, *Eisenhower and the Jews*. New York: Twayne Publishers, 1953, pp.53–4.

74. E.g. the case of Frau Bär who was made to understand that she could move into the flat vacated by the wife of an imprisoned former Nazi only to find that the German landlord had given it to non-Jewish tenants, and the housing department declared itself powerless to intervene although, on paper, such ex-Nazis' flats were to be reserved for 'Jews and concentration camp inmates'. File note from Baumweg office, 21 June 1945, signed Helfrich. ZA, B1/13, A 183, Sheet 22. The head of the housing department was a member of the Jewish community and thought to be sympathetic to Jewish needs, but in reality proved unhelpful. See the letter of complaint by Erich Flörsheimer to the executive of the Jewish Community, reporting that Katz had been 'abrupt' while a Christian official finally helped. ZA, B1/13, A 519, Sheet 7.

75. Alon Tauber, 'Die Entstehung der jüdischen Nachkriegsgemeinde in Frankfurt am Main *1945–1949*'. Unpublished manuscript, Heidelberg, 2001, p.2.

76. Dr. Leopold Neuhaus, letter, 4 October 1945, for publication in the *Frankfurter Rundschau*. ZA, B1/13, A 183, Sheet 45.

77. Letter by Fritz Stein to Rotes Kreuz Krankenhaus, Frankfurt, 3 September 1945. ZA, B1/13, A 178, Sheet 5.

78. File note, handwritten, by Dr. Neuhaus. ZA, B1/13, A 181, Sheet 5.

79. Hauptverwaltungsamt. Referat für Sonderbetreuung, letter An die Jüdische Betreuungsstelle, z. Hd. Herrn Rabbiner Dr. L. Neuhaus, 23 August 1945. ZA, B1/13, A 180, Sheet 21.

80. Lore Geminder, 'Keine Wintermäntel', *Frankfurter Rundschau*, 29 August 1945, p.1.
81. Detailed description in Judah Nadich, *Eisenhower and the Jews*, p.103.
82. 'Wiederweihe des ersten jüdischen Gotteshauses in Frankfurt a.M.', *Frankfurter Rundschau*, 12 September 1945, p.1.
83. Leopold Neuhaus, 'In memoriam'. *Frankfurter Rundschau*, 9 November 1945, p.1.
84. Fritz Stein, 'Ein neuer Abschnitt in der Geschichte der Jüdischen Gemeinde Frankfurt am Main', *Mitteilungsblatt der jüdischen Gemeinden und Betreuungsstellen*, no. 4, (7 December 1945), p.2.
85. Details in 'Notiz an Stelle der am 4. 6. 1946 wegen Feiertag ausgefallenen Sitzung', compiled by Leopold Neuhaus. ZA, B1/13/A1, Sheet 35. *Reichsvereinigung der Juden* is the national association that had imposed by the Nazi state to centralize and control all matters pertaining to Jews.
86. Letter by Dr. Neuhaus to Jüdische Gemeinde, 'z. Hden. Herrn Stein', 22 November 1945. ZA, B1/13, A 181, Sheet 11.
87. 'Notiz für Herrn Dr. Neuhaus' by the head of the Wirtschaftsamt, Karry. ZA, B1/13, A 184, Sheet 18.
88. Neuhaus, undated memorandum (September/October 1945), ZA, B1/13 A 183, Sheet 43.
89. Minutes of the Jewish Community executive meeting, 29 October 1946. ZA, B1/13, A 1, Sheet 18. It took until December 1946 to institute the separate care centres, see the Minutes of the Jewish Community executive meeting, 14 December 1946. ZA, B1/13, A 354, Sheet 10.
90. Details on Zeilsheim in Judah Nadich, *Eisenhower and the Jews*, pp.57 ff. drawing on his personal experience as Jewish Advisor and Jewish chaplain in Frankfurt at the time.
91. For a recent study see Seev W. Mankowitz, *Life between Memory and Hope. The Survivors of the Holocaust in Occupied Germany*. Cambridge: CUP, 2002.
92. Letter by Dr. Leopold Neuhaus to Dr. Kurt Eppstein (*sic*), 4 June 1945 (*sic*), should read 1946. ZA, B1/13, A 65, Sheet 72.
93. File note by Fritz Stein, 3 July 1946. ZA, B1/13/A. Sheet 42.
94. Letter by Fritz Stein to 'Regierungsdirektor Dr. K. Epstein', 5 July 1946. ZA, B1/13/A 65, Sheets 62–63.
95. Cilly Neuhaus, 'Zum Geleite!' in *Mitteilungsblatt der jüdischen Gemeinden und Betreuungsstellen*, no. 1 (26 October 1945), p.1.
96. Monika Richarzz, 'Jews in Today's Germany', *Leo Baeck Yearbook*, ZXXX, (1985), pp.265–274 and Martin Jay, 'Resettlement of German Jews', ibid., pp.275–82.
97. The Jewish Agency had received 496 such certificates for the whole of 1946 and used them to send a group of unaccompanied children to Palestine. Report on Activities 1946–1948. IfZ, DW 379/001.
98. Sadie Sender, American Joint Distribution Committee Frankfurt/Main to Mr. Sharon L. Hatch, Chief P Welf&DP Division, OMGUS for Greater Hessen, 1 August 1946. ZA, B1/13, A 46, Sheet 51.

99. Details in Boris Pliskin, Leon Retter and Samuel Shlomowitz (Central Committee of Liberated Jews), 'An evaluation of the American Joint Distribution Committee program in the American occupied zone of Germany, from its inception to January 1947', pp.2ff. AJDC Archive Jerusalem, RG C7, File 1254.

100. Minutes of the Jewish Committee executive meeting, no. 1, March 1946. ZA, B1/13 A 44, Sheets 1 and 7.

101. On 28 March 1946, the chairman, David Werba, reported that local radio agreed to broadcast the notice for the first time and then twice daily on Friday, Saturday, Sunday and Tuesday. ZA, B1/13, A 44, Sheet 3. On 28 May 1946, the Committee also requested a list of all Jewish residents living in the vicinity of Frankfurt and received a list with 30 names. Letter by Der Landrat des Obertaunuskreises to Committee of Liberated Jews in Frankfurt/Main, 6 July 1946. ZA, B 1/13, A 521, Sheet 17.

102. Letter by Fritz Stein to the Jewish Committee, dated 1 April 1946. ZA, B1/13, A 44, Sheet 2.

103. 'Protokoll No. 2 der Sitzung beim Regionalkomitee', dated 2 February 1947, states: 'The existence of the Council of Five is, in our view, not necessary and should be disbanded.' ZA, B1/13, A 47, Sheet 65.

104. 'Revisions-Kommission beim Jüdischen Komitee Frankfurt'. Report, addressed to the Jüdisches Komitee Frankfurt, 10 May 1948. ZA, B1/13, A 48, Sheet 59.

105. Organizations Optejlung. Ajnwojnercol, dated 25 September 1947. ZA, B1/13, 973, Sheets 4–5.

106. E.g. Regional Komitet Frankfurt/M., 'Betrojung für Monat April 1948'. ZA, B1/13, A 64, Sheets 49–50.

107. Liste der Betreuten der Jüdischen Betreuungsstelle von Februar 1947. ZA, B1/13, A 64, Sheets 20ff.

108. Minutes of the Jewish Community executive meeting, dated 19 March 1947. ZA, B1/13, A 2, Sheet 41.

109. At the request of the Executive of the World Union of Progressive Judaism three of its leading rabbis including Leo Baeck met to advise Jewish communities in Germany on the issues arising from mixed marriages. The main recommendation consisted of consulting a Religious Court (Beth Din) to decide upon individual cases. See letter, 10 December 1947, in ZA, B1/13, A 2, Sheet 80.

110. Florian Ritter, 'Das "Displaced Persons" – Lager in Frankfurt am Main/Zeilsheim' in *Wer ein Haus baut, will bleiben. 50 Jahre Jüdische Gemeinde. Anfänge und Gegenwart* (Ausstellung des jüdischen Museums). Frankfurt/Main: Societätsverlag, 1998, pp.110–20.

111. ZA, B1/13, A 53, Sheet 17.

112. Regional Revisal (*sic*) Commission of Liberated Jews in Hesse, Protokoll No. 9, 9 July 1947, ZA, B1/13, A 47, Sheet 21.

113. Minutes of the Jewish Community executive meeting, 12 November 1947. ZA, B1/13, A 2, Sheet 76.

114. Minutes of the Jewish Community executive meeting, 20 August 1947. ZA, B1/13, A 2, Sheet 68. After discussion, the women were permitted

to distribute the donations they secured but refused a role in the community's 'official' welfare work.

115. See AJDC Inspector Samuel Kurta, Report to Abraham Cohen, District Direct or, 30 December 1948. The report covers the month of August 1948 and also includes forecasts of demand for September–November. ZA, B1/13, A 992, Sheet 9.

116. Report of the 'Revisionskommission', 15 May 1948. ZA, B1/13, A 48, Sheet 57.

117. ZA, B1/13, A 1343, Sheets 8–9.

118. Boris Pliskin, Leon Retter and Samuel Shlomowitz, 'An evaluation of the American Joint Distribution Committee Program', pp.7–8.

119. 'Memorial über die Besprechung und Vorkommnisse bei dem Städtischen Komitee von Frankfurt/Main', 24 November 1946. ZA B1/13, A 46, Sheet 8.

120. ZA, B1/13, A 1208, Sheet 15 contains a list of 432 extensions of residency permits obtained in May 1947 and valid until June 1948. See also ibid. Sheets 2 and 35 listing over one thousand applications for permits, each lasting more than one year.

121. Letter by Kurt Epstein to Regierungsrat Dr. Althans, 3 December 1946. ZA, B 1/13, A 46, Sheet 6.

122. Letter by Kurt Epstein to the Jewish Committee, Frankfurt, 3 December 1946. ZA B1/13, A 46, Sheet 7.

123. Letter by Emil Wulkan to Landeswirtschaftsamt Wiesbaden, Abt. Schuhwaren, 20 May 1946. ZA B1/13, A 526, Sheet 48.

124. ZA B1/13, A 527, Sheet 56.

125. Beprechung bei dem Ministeriun in Wiesbaden, file note, 8 September 1946. ZA, B1/13, A 46, Sheets 21–2.

126. Ernst Landau, 'Od lo awda tikwatenu' (Still no hope of work), *Jüdische Rundschau*, no. 12–13 (March 1947), p.13.

127. Jewish Committee executive meeting, minutes no. 17, 27 November 1946. ZA, B1/13, A 46, Sheet 16.

128. Jewish Committee executive meeting, minutes 23 April 1947. ZA, B1/13, A 2, Sheet 52.

129. Jewish Committee executive meeting, minutes no. 11, 26 June 1947. ZA, B1/13, A 47, Sheet 47. The Committee's own Rabbi, Thorn, managed to secure the funding from Vaad Hatzala.

130. In response to a request for information by OMGUS, Frankfurt operated 'feeding stations' for 5,430 individuals in November 1945, many of them former concentration camp prisoners. Those who could afford to pay were charged between 40 and 50 Pfennig for a meal, while 'the destitute do not pay'. USNA, RG260/1080/4 (Welfare Branch).

131. A letter to the Community, 17 April 1947, states that the Committee intends to open a kitchen together with the community, and requests use of the building in Theobald Christ Strasse, i.e. next to its supply store. ZA, B1/13, A 520, Sheet 5.

132. Jewish Committee executive meeting, minutes no. 17, 27 November 1946, ZA, B1/13, A 46, Sheet 16.

133. Biographical details in the letter by Emil Wulkan to Stadtrat Erich Hermann, a former friend of his brother in Breslau, 7 May 1947. ZA, B1/13, A 19, Sheet 24.
134. His list of Jews from Breslau contained 2,000 names. He reported that between 200 and 220 were 'saved' and returned to Breslau, and a further 96 were liberated in Theresienstadt. Most of this group opted for resettlement in the United States and had moved to the DP camp Deggendorf. 'I have in my possession a list of these Jews and of a large number of "mixed race" persons (*Mischlinge*).' ZA, B1/13, A 19, Sheet 49.
135. 'Memorial über die Besprechung und Vorkommnisse bei dem Stadtkomitee Frankfurt'. Copies sent to Joint, and the US Army Chaplains, Rabbi Miller and Rabbi Dalin. ZA, B1/13, A 521, Sheet 56.
136. *Frankfurter Rundschau*, 25 January 1947, p.3.
137. ZA, BA/1/13, A 46, Sheet 9.
138. Letter from the AJDC to Jewish community, 8 November 1946, asking for assistance with persuading the gas works to supply the Jewish kitchen. ZA, B1/13, A 521, Sheet 59.
139. Letter by David Werba and Emil Wulkan to Main Gaswerke, Frankfurt, 13 November 1946. ZA, B1/13, A 521, Sheet 60.
140. David Werba to Kriminal Polizei, 16 December 1946. ZA, B1/13/A 516, Sheet 13.
141. Letter by David Werba to Rabbi Dalin, Wiesbaden, 28 November 1946. The letter contains a list of 27 individuals held in four German prisons, including 8 in Preungesheim in Frankfurt. ZA, B1/13, A 520, Sheet 27.
142. Invitations to the inaugural meeting were sent out by State Commissioner Epstein who contacted the Committee but ignored the community. See Minutes of the Jewish community executive meeting, 23 December 1947. ZA, B1/13, A 2, Sheet 8.
143. Minutes of the Jewish Community executive meeting, 11 June 1947. ZA, B1/13, A 2, Sheet 61.
144. Letter by Regional Association of Jewish Communities to 'Committee of Liberated Jews', 26 August 1948. ZA, B1/13, A 1029, Sheets 20–1.
145. Federation of Hungarian-speaking Jews in Greater Hesse, minutes of meeting, 9 May 1948. ZA, B 1/13, B 48, Sheet 60; also the letter by Vaad Gius, Frankfurt to the Jewish Committee, dated 30 May 1948, ZA, B 1/13, B 48, Sheet 49.
146. Minutes of the Jewish Committee executive meeting, no. 26, 18 January 1949. ZA, B1/13, A 49, Sheet 28.
147. Minutes of the Jewish Community executive meeting, 20 August 1947. ZA, B1/13, A 2, Sheet 67.
148. Pro-forma of such a letter, 6 June 1950 in ZA, B1/13, A 1342, Sheet 1.
149. See ZA, B1, 13, A 1342, Sheets 10 and 22.
150. Minutes no. 8, Jewish Committee executive meeting, 6 June 1948. ZA, B1/13/A 48, Sheet 47; also ZA, B1/13, A 1025, Sheet 35: file note that, on 15 June 1948, the Central Committee of Liberated Jews had stopped payment of all salaries but sent a consignment of food instead.

151. Minutes no. 9, Jewish Committee executive meeting, 14 July 1948. ZA, B1/13, A 48, Sheets 40–3.

152. Minutes no 14, Jewish Committee executive meeting, 24 August 1948. ZA, B1/13, A 48, Sheet 29.

153. For a more detailed discussion, see Chapter 6 in this volume.

154. The cases are cited from a collection of letters in ZA, B1/13, A 1024, Sheets 21ff.

155. Letter, 28 June 1948, ZA, B1/13, A 1024, Sheet 18.

156. 'Sitzung der Sachbearbeiter der Betreuungsstelle', 25 August 1948 and 28 August 1948. ZA, B1/13, A 1299, Sheets 1–11. For each recipient, the list specifies the type of persecution or incarceration and the assistance applied for.

157. ZA, B1/13, A 1025, Sheet 45.

6. Jews and Germans: Distance, Distrust and New Beginnings

1. Simon H. Rifkind, a judge from New York, was the first of five Jewish Advisors to the US Chief of Staff. He was appointed in the wake of the Harrison Report in October 1945. He was succeeded in office by Philip H. Bernstein, a rabbi from Rochester, NY, Louis Levinthal, a judge from Philadelphia, Dr. William C. Haber, a professor of Law at the University of Michigan and Harry Greenstein, the director of the Jewish Charities and Welfare Fund in Baltimore. Major Abraham Hyman served the last four as deputy and took over as Jewish Advisor to wind up the office after the foundation of the Federal Republic of Germany. See USNA, RG 165/845/1, p.1.

2. Judge Simon Rifkind, 'Final Memorandum', 7 March 1946. Published in Congressional Record – Senate, April 1946, p.3392. USNA, RG 165/850/4.

3. Menache Mautner, 'DP Lager Deggendorf, 1945/6'. In Collection Ball-Kaduri. Yad Vashem. Quoted from copies in the archive of the IFZ, File 01/163.

4. Rifkind, 'Final Memorandum', p.3392.

5. For a recent account see Wolfgang Jacobmeyer, 'The Displaced Persons Problem: Repatriation and Resettlement' in Johannes-Dieter Steinert and Inge Weber-Newth, eds, *European Immigrants in Britain, 1933–1950*. Munich: Saur, 2003, pp.138ff.

6. Rifkind, 'Final Memorandum', p.3393.

7. Judge Simon Rifkind, Speech delivered at the Biltmore Hotel, April 2nd, 1946, p.2. USNA, RG 165/850/4.

8. Rabbi Philip S. Bernstein, 'Report to the Secretary of the Army', 26 October 1947, p.2. USNA, RG 165/845/1.

9. Ibid. p.11. Also *Stars and Stripes*, 14 August 1947, p.1 and 12, reported that General Lucius D. Clay, the US Military Governor whom Bernstein served as advisor, argued before the United Nations Sub-

Committee on Palestine that displaced Jews could not be absorbed into the German economy 'without revival of anti-Semitism'.

10. Adi Kreuz, 'Ausgehobene Hamsterlager', *Frankfurter Rundschau*, 26 September 1945, p.4.

11. Kurt Brode, 'Parasiten der Demokratie'. Letter to the editor in *Frankfurter Rundschau*, 26 September 1945, p.4.

12. Walter Kolb, 'Zum Neuen Jahr', *Frankfurter Rundschau*, 2 January 1947, p.1.

13. In 1946, for instance, Richard Merton, a director of the Metallgesellschaft, one of Frankfurt's leading businesses, was helped to return. See letter by the office of the Ministerpräsident für Grosshessen to Lord Mayor Dr. Blaum, 16 May 1946; also Blaum to Military Government in Frankfurt, 30 April 1946. Frankfurt also wooed the writer Franz von Unruh and the humanist Albert Schweizer. Institut für Stadtgeschichte, Frankfurt am Main. Archiv, Magistratsakten, MA 4.388.

14. Letter by Oberbürgermeister Dr. Blaum to Professor Dr. Ferdinand Blum, 3 October 1945. Institut für Stadtgeschichte, Frankfurt am Main. Archiv, Magistratsakten, MA 4.388.

15. Walter Kolb, letter, 14 April 1947.

16. Walter Kolb to Leopold Hanauer, 23 April 1947, Institut für Stadtgeschichte, Frankfurt am Main. Archiv, Magistratsakten, MA 4.388.

17. Maria Fulda, *Frankfurter Rundschau,* 11 January 1947.

18. Note from Fürsorgeamt to Stadtrat Dr. Prestal that Maria Fulda had received RM 1,128 Returner's Aid, and a further RM 100 special payment in January 1947. On 6 March 1947, Maria Fulda wrote to Walter Kolb, advising him that she was too ill to leave her house and attend the personal consultation he had offered. Institut für Stadtgeschichte, Frankfurt am Main. Archiv, Magistratsakten, MA 4.388.

19. Heinrich Meyer, letter to 'Dear Lord Mayor', *Frankfurter Rundschau*, 11 January 1947.

20. Fritz Uhlmann to Walter Kolb, 2 January 1947. Institut für Stadtgeschichte, Frankfurt am Main. Archiv, Magistratsakten, MA 4.388. On 8 January 1947, Kolb invited Uhlmann for a personal consultation with his Personal Assistant, although the file copy of the letter includes the handwritten remark that Uhlmann is a Communist Party member and activist.

21. Karl Enck, Hofheim/Taunus (Behelfsheim), letter to Walter Kolb, 1 January 1947. Institut für Stadtgeschichte, Frankfurt am Main. Archiv, Magistratsakten, MA 4.388.

22. Walter Kolb to Karl Enk (*sic*), letter, 7 January 1947. Institut für Stadtgeschichte, Frankfurt am Main. Archiv, Magistratsakten, MA 4.388.

23. Letter by 'Ältere Frankfurter Bürger' to Walter Kolb, 10 January 1947. Institut für Stadtgeschichte, Frankfurt am Main. Archiv, Magistratsakten, MA 4.388.

24. Carl Greiner, letter to Walter Kolb, 11 January 1947. Institut für Stadtgeschichte, Frankfurt am Main. Archiv, Magistratsakten, MA

4.388. Greiner refers to himself as an anti-fascist and also calls for the 'return of our eastern territories' (*Ostgebiete*).

25. Max Meyer, letter to Walter Kolb, 2 January 1947. In it, Meyer mentions that Jews in Shanghai had approached him on 24 September 1946 for help, but he had not replied since the Jewish community did not have the resources to help: 'The speech you gave yesterday gives me courage to recommend these people [exiles based in Shanghai] for return. On my own, I cannot promise them any guarantees.' Institut für Stadtgeschichte, Frankfurt am Main, Archiv, MA 4.388.

26. Fritz Stein, Jüdische Betreuungsstelle der Stadt Frankfurt, letter to Walter Kolb, 16 January 1947. Institut für Stadtgeschichte, Frankfurt am Main. Archiv, Magistratsakten, MA 4.388.

27. Anna and Richard Merritt, eds, *Public Opinion in Occupied Germany. The OMGUS Surveys 1945–1948*. Urbana: Illinois University Press, 1970.

28. For a good overview see Werner Bergmann, 'Sind die Deutschen antisemitisch? Meinungsumfragen von 1946–1987 in der Bundesrepublik Deutschland' in Werner Bergmann and Rainer Erb, eds, *Antisemitismus in der politischen Kultur nach 1945*. Opladen: Westdeutscher Verlag, 1990, pp.112–13.

29. *The Jewish Chronicle*, 12 September 1946. The Munich correspondent of *The Jewish Chronicle* reported similar problems in September 1947.

30. *Anti-Semitism. A memorandum*, prepared for the Foreign Affairs Committee of the Anglo-Jewish Association. November 1948, p.3. Wiener Library, London.

31. Adolph Diamant (*Geschändete Friedhöfe 1945–1980*, Frankfurt/Main: Selbstverlag, 1982), reports that in the late 1940s, about 12 cemeteries per year were desecrated. Between 1948 and 1957, 170 such desecrations took place, damaging at least 500 tombs. See also Joachim Prinz, *The German Dilemma. An Appraisal of Anti-Semitism, Ultra-Nationalism and Democracy in West Germany*. Report published by the Commission on International Affairs, American Jewish Congress, 1959, p.14. WLL (Press Cuttings 'Anti-Semitism').

32. *Anti-Semitism. A memorandum*, p.3.

33. Ibid., p.2. Philip Auerbach was later dismissed from his post, falsely accused of fraud and embezzlement in relation to his extensive restitution activities and wrongly convicted. When sentenced to imprisonment in 1952, he committed suicide. His innocence was subsequently confirmed on appeal.

34. *Ruhr Zeitung*, 29 June 1949. WLL (Press Cuttings 'Anti-Semitism').

35. Letter from the Foreign Office to A.G. Brotman, Board of Deputies, 16 March 1950. WLL (Press Cuttings 'Anti-Semitism'). Response to a report prepared by the Board of Deputies on 'Nationalism and anti-Semitism in Western Germany – September 1949 to February 1950'.

36. *Die antisemitischen und nazistischen Vorfälle. Weissbuch und Erklärung der Bundesregierung*. Bonn: Ministerium des Inneren, 1960. For a case study see Werner Bergmann, 'Die antisemitische Welle im Winter 1959/60' in Werner Bergmann and Rainer Erb, eds, *Antisemitismus in der politischen*

Kultur der Bundesrepublik nach 1945. Opladen: Westdeutscher Verlag, 1990, pp.253ff.

37. Philip S. Bernstein, 'Report', dated 26 October 1947, p.11. USNA, RG 165/845/1. Also *Stars and Stripes*, 14 August 1947, pp.1, 12.

38. Anti-Semitism in Germany. A memorandum prepared for the Foreign Affairs Committee of the Anglo-Jewish Association. November 1948. Wiener Library Archive. Collections Newspaper Cuttings and Reports.

39. OMGUS, 'Report on Survival of Anti-Semitism'. Berlin, 1 July 1947. USNA, RG 260/176/12.

40. Philip Bernstein, 'Program to Deal with Anti-Semitism', 16 July 1947. Central Zionist Archive (CZA), C 7/253.

41. OMGUS, 'Report on Survival of Anti-Semitism', p.1.

42. 'Denk ich an Deutschland in der Nacht', *Der Aufbau*, no. 12 (25 March 1949), p.105. The article continued to cite examples from the German press how overt anti-Semitic utterances are avoided but how Jewish individuals such as the Nuremberg prosecutor R.W. Kempner, Henry Morgenthau and also Lucius D. Clay, when he was perceived as being anti-German, were publicly identified as Jews (Clay wrongly as Morgenthau's son-in-law) and vilified.

43. OMGUS, 'Report on Survival of Anti-Semitism', p.2.

44. Ibid., p.3.

45. Quoted from a report about McNarney's comments 'on the problem of Jewish and displaced persons', *Frankfurter Rundschau*, 15 March 1947, p.5.

46. Ralph Giordano, 'Gedanken nach einer Fahrt durch Deutschland', in *Zwischen den Zeiten. Jüdisches Leben. Jüdisches Wissen.* vol. 1 no. 1 (October 1947), p.19.

47. Summary prepared by OMGUS of main recommendations of the report on anti-Semitism, USNA, RG 260/176/12.

48. OMGUS, 'Report on Survival of Anti-Semitism', p.5.

49. Ibid., p.6.

50. To this day, these fears continue to surface when Jews encounter uniformed German police. See the interviews in Lynn Rappaport, *Jews in Germany after the Holocaust. Memory, Identity and Jewish-German Relations.* Cambridge: Cambridge University Press, 1997.

51. *Congressional Record*, Monday April 1, 1946. 'Permission to address the House: German Police Kill and Plunder'. USNA, RG 165/819.

52. 'The DP center in Stuttgart is not in a real sense a camp. About 800 Jews are in a batch of apartment houses in one section of Stuttgart, another is in a former sanatorium. There has been almost no organization to speak of.' Cited from a letter by Harry Lerner, 19 October 1945, to his family. USHMM, R 19.029 * 01 (The Papers of Harry Lerner).

53. Uncorrected draft of a report by the chief of police in Stuttgart to the American Military Government of the city, dated 1 April 1946, quoted in Susanne Dietrich and Julia Schulze Wessel, *Zwischen Selbstorganisation und Stigmatisierung. Die Lebenswirklichkeit jüdischer Displaced persons und*

die neue Gestalt des Antisemitismus in der deutschen Nachkriegsgesellschaft. Stuttgart: Klett Cotta, 1998, p.192.

54. Ibid., p.194.
55. Letter by Harry Lerner to his wife, 23 January 1946.
56. Letter by Harry Lerner to his parents, 4 April 1946.
57. For a detailed account and local sources, see Susanne Dietrich and Julia Schulze Wessel, *Zwischen Selbstorganisation und Stigmatierung*, pp.198–201.
58. See Judge Simon Rifkind, Speech at the Biltmore Hotel, New York. USNA, RG 165/850/4.
59. Col. Wilson to OMGUS Württemberg-Baden; OMGUS Greater Hesse; OMGUS Bavaria, no date. USNA, RG 260/275/26.
60. Arthur T. Allan, Memorandum for Col. Wilson, 'Entrance of German Police into DP Camps'. No date. USNA, RG 260/275/26.
61. OMGUS Liaison and Security Office, report on 'DP Situation' to OMGUS Bavaria, 16 January 1948. USNA, RG 260/284/20.
62. Arno Rudert, 'Zeilsheim', *Frankfurter Rundschau*, 12 August 1947, p.2.
63. 'Rabbi Deplores DP Camp Conditions', *Stars and Stripes*, 2 February 1947, pp.1 and 12.
64. O.W. Wilson, Chief, Public Safety Branch to G-5, USFET, memo, 13 May 1946. USNA, RG 260/275/26.
65. Intra-Office Memorandum (OMGUS Public Safety) 'Policing DP Centers' from Theo E. Hall to Mr. McCraw and Mr. Urton, 25 November 1947. USNA, RG 260/275/26.
66. 'Entrance into DP Camps by German Police'. Memo from Public Safety Branch, OMGUS to the three OMGUS administrations in the US zone. No date, RG 260/275/26.
67. Report headed 'Riot' by Col. B.W. Gocke, Public Police and Safety Section, 29 April 1946. USNA 260/275/26.
68. Report headed 'Jewish DP Attacks upon American Soldiers at Windsheim' by Col. O.W. Wilson, Public Safety Branch, OMGUS Bavaria, 26 July 1946. USNA, RG 260/275/26.
69. Report headed 'Reported Riot Involving Jewish DPs', by Col. O.W. Wilson, 27 July 1946. USNA, RG 260/275/26. Wilson based his report on information he received from the Bavarian Rural Police.
70. *Zentralamt für Kriminal-Identifizierung*, Dr. Heindl, report to OMGUS Bavaria, Public Safety Branch, 19 January 1948. USNA, RG 260/284/20, pp.1–3.
71. Ibid., p.4.
72. Presidency of Rural Police, Bavaria. Report 'Perpetrators of Major Crimes', 16 January 1948. USNA, RG 260/284/20. The report showed that 1.2 per cent of displaced persons and 2.4 per cent of the German population had been convicted of black market offences.
73. Report prepared by OMGUS, Germany, January 1949, pp.1–4. USNA, RG 260/138/138.
74. Weekly report, 2 November 1945, by the chief of the German police to military government Counter Intelligence Corps (CIC) in Stuttgart,

quoted from Susanne Dietrich and Julia Schulze Wessel, *Zwischen Selbstorganisation und Stigmatisierung*, pp.154–5.

75. Memorandum (in English) headed 'Problems and Difficulties in Fighting DP Delinquency' by Präsidium der Landpolizei von Bayern to OMGUS Bavaria, 17 January 1948, p.1. USNA, RG 260/284/20.

76. William Haber to Edward Litchfield, Director of Civil Administration Division, OMGUS, 8 September 1948, and attached, a copy of Haber's Memorandum to the Commander in Chief, European Command, 31 August 1948. USNA, RG 260/284/20.

77. Edwin Hartwich, 'Roundup at a Railway Station', *New York Herald Tribune*. Copy in USNA, RG 260/350/10.

78. In Frankfurt, for instance, 10,000 people were rounded up in police raids between 1 January and 8 February 1947 of whom 408 persons were arrested, among them 14 DPs. USNA, RG 260/350/10.

79. A delegate of the Frankfurt local assembly, Schaub, at a meeting with the Lord Mayor of Frankfurt, following the creation of Zeilheim DP camp. Minutes dated 19 October 1946, in StAF (Stadtarchiv Frankfurt), Stadtkanzlei, File 1047/6, vol. 1.

80. The report purports to quote 'Jewish and German informers'. OMGUS Maintaunus, Major John C. Nelson to Director, OMG Hesse, 27 March 1948. USNA, RG 260/284/20.

81. Ibid.

82. Quote from a letter of protest by Chester B. Lewis to the Minister President of Württemberg-Baden, Reinhold Meier, quoted in a press release by the regional OMGUS office, 7 January 1949. USNA, RG 260/285/8.

83. 'Police Dictatorship in Württemberg?', *Neue Zeitung*, 13 January 1949. Translated copy of the article in USNA, RG 260/285/8.

84. James E. Hurley, 'Inviolability of the Home', Radio broadcast (script), Radio Stuttgart, 17 January 1949, p.4. OMG Württemberg-Baden. USNA, RG 260/285/8.

85. Letter by Chester B. Lewis to the Minister President of Württemberg-Baden, Reinhold Meier, quoted in a press release by the regional OMGUS office, 7 January 1949. USNA, RG 260/285/8.

86. Report by OMGUS Bavaria, Civil Administration Division Munich to the Civil Administration Division, Nürnberg, 15 February 1949. USNA, RG 260/285/8. In Munich for instance, 10,000 searches took place, 9,900 without warrant; in Landsberg, none of the 465 searches were backed by a warrant.

87. Ernest Leiser, 'Germans up to their old tricks'. OMG Berlin. USNA, RG 260/285/8.

88. Robert Solomon, Report 'After a Tour (Oct. 22–31, 1947) in the British Zone of Germany'. PRO, FO 1052/73, p.1.

89. Josef Rosensaft, *Jewish Chronicle*, 16 January 1948.

90. During his first visit to Germany from 30 January to 2 February 1947, Robert Solomon had met the Central Committee at Belsen, including chairman Josef Rosensaft and representatives of the Jewish Relief Unit,

The American Joint and the Jewish Agency. For the Jews at Belsen, the main topic for discussion was 'the question of emigration to Palestine. Colonel Solomon is one of the most influential people in this question'. The brief report on the visit prepared by secretary of the Central Committee, Dow Laufer, does not mention how Solomon responded to their concerns. Central Committee of Liberated Jews in the British Zone, Bergen-Belsen. *Rundschreiben* no. 4/19, 5 February 1947. ZA, B1/2, no. 25.

91. The American Forces journal *Stars and Stripes* carried regular reports and updates on the '*Exodus* 1947', the refugee ship laden with 4,500 Jews, including 800 children, that was stopped outside the port of Haifa by the British in July 1947, its passengers loaded onto three military vessels and forcibly returned, at first to France and, after refusing to disembark there, to Germany on 6 September 1947. The 'Exodus' incident sparked widespread protests among displaced Jews in Germany, and in the British zone an attempt to blow up a railway line.

92. 'Survey on conditions of Jews in the British zone of Germany'. March 1948. PRO, FO/1052/294.

93. Robert Solomon, 'Report', pp.1–2.

94. Ibid., p.2.

95. Details in Norman Bentwich, *They Found Refuge*. London: The Cresset Press, 1956, pp.144ff.

96. Robert Solomon, 'Report', p.4.

97. On leaving the United States for Germany, Harry Greenstein, the last of the regularly appointed Jewish Advisors, estimated that 2,700 'tubercular cases for whom Palestine would be the worst destination' would have to stay behind. 'Statement to the Press', USNA, RG 260/138/156.

98. Louis L. Kaplan and Theodor Schuchat, *Justice – Not Charity. A Biography of Harry Greenstein*. New York: Crown Publisher, 1967, p.112.

99. Harry Greenstein, 'The Future of Jews in Germany'. Minutes of the Conference held in Heidelberg, 31 July 1949. ZfA (Zentralinstitut für Antisemitismusforschung).

100. Only the Bavarian parliament voted against because it regarded the Basic Law as an instrument of centralisation that conflicted with its regional and separate interests.

101. A good account can be found in Michael Brenner, *After the Holocaust. Rebuilding Jewish Lives in Postwar Germany*. Princeton: Princeton University Press, 1997, pp.66ff.

102. See table 5.3.

103. For a detailed study of these early developments see Harry Maor, 'Über den Wiederaufbau der jüdischen Gemeinden in Deutschland seit 1945', Inaugural Dissertation, University of Mainz, 1961.

104. Abraham Hyman and Louis Barish, 'Report covering the period January 15, 1949 to February 15 1949', in LC, Papers of Emmanuel Celler, Box 17, p.7. Hyman and Barish were Acting Jewish Advisors at the time, prior to the arrival of Harry Greenstein in Germany.

105. In his final report dated 20 October 1948, William Haber estimated (p.3)

the 'hard core' of displaced Jews who were unable to leave at 1,000 TB cases, 2,170 invalids (one thousand of them with major problems), 100 'unaccompanied old people' and 75 cases of insanity, confined in institutions. In addition, he believed that 20,000 Jews were 'free-living . . . like the rest of the German population' and might not leave. AJDC, B6/2, C 45.096.4. In his Final Report, Abraham Hyman concluded all Jews 'with intention to remain in Germany' were of doubtful quality and character (p.11). AJDC, B6/2, C 45.096.4.

106. Joachim Prinz, 'The Future of Jews in Germany'. Conference, Heidelberg, 31 July 1949, p.46. ZfA.

107. Table 'Religious Character of Communities', in ibid., p.17.

108. Ibid., p.18.

109. Details of the survey were presented at the Heidelberg Conference. See ibid., p.14.

110. These problems have been studied especially with reference to Turks in Germany. See e.g. Aytac Eryilmaz and Mathilde Jamin, eds, *Fremde Heimat. Eine Geschichte der Einwanderung aus der Türkei*. Essen: Klartext Verlag, 1998; also Eva Kolinsky, *Deutsch und türkisch leben. Bild und Selbstbild der türkischen Minderheit in Deutschland*. Berne: Lang, 2000.

111. Prepared by the Joint on the eve of discontinuing all support for displaced Jews and their committees in October 1950. AJDC Archive, B5 C 45.016 (File 1947–1951).

112. Walter Friedrich, 'Wiedergutmachung für Juden', *Frankfurter Rundschau*, 14 January 1947, p.2.

113. Generalanwalt Dr. Philip Auerbach, 'Neues vom Stand der Haftentschädigung und Wiedergumachtung', in *Jüdische Gemeinde Fürth*, September 1949, pp.3–4.

114. Philip Auerbach, 'Der Stand der Wiedergutmachtung in Bayern' in *Jüdisches Gemeindeblat für die britische Zone. Sonderbelage in Wiedergutmachungsfragen*, 5 February 1947, pp.1–2.

115. 'Rückerstattung. Gesetz für die US- und die französische Zone. Und wann folgt die britische Zone?' *Jüdisches Gemeindeblat für die britische Zone*, 30 November 1947, pp.1–2.

116. A good overview in Andrei S. Markovits et al., 'Jews in German Society' in Eva Kolinsky and Wilfried van der Will, eds, *The Cambridge Companion to Modern German Culture*. Cambridge: CUP, 1998, pp.86–109.

117. 'Das Bekenntnis der Bundesregierung', quoted from *Allgemeine Jüdische Wochenzeitung*, 28 September 1951, p.1.

118. 'Chronik 1946–1996', *Allgemeine Jüdische Wochenzeitung*. 25 April 1996, p.9.

119. For an excellent account see Curt Garner, 'Remaking German Democracy in the 1950s: Was the Civil Service an Asset or a Liability?' *German Politics* 8, no. 3 (December 1997), p.39. Garner shows that between 1951 and 1954, the civil service grew by 20 per cent while the number of reappointed former Nazis increased by 40 per cent.

120. *Allgemeine Jüdische Wochenzeitung*, 28 July 1950.

121. Report on an Interview given by Hendrik van Dam to 'Revista Quencenal' (*Das Blatt*) in Bogota, in *Jüdische Sozialarbeit*, vol. 2 no. 3/4 (5 July 1957), p.26.

122. See e.g. Neima Barzel, 'The Attitude of Jews of German Origin in Israel to Germany and Germans after the Holocaust, 1945–1952', *Leo Baeck Yearbook*, vol XXXIX (1994), pp.271–301.

123. 'Israel und Wir' in *Allgemeine Jüdische Wochenzeitung*, 28 July 1950.

124. 'Jüdische Jugend lernt' in *Jüdische Illustrierte*, vol. 6, no. 4 (May 1956), p.14.

125. Hans Frey, 'Auswandern oder Hierbleiben?' *Jüdisches Gemeindeblatt* (9 November 1946).

126. Bericht des Generalsekretärs für die Periode Januar – August 1951. Düsseldorf: Zentralrat der Juden in Deutschland, 1951, p.1.

127. *Jüdisches Gemeindeblatt* (Frankfurt), vol. 1 no. 4 (July 1955), p.4.

128. A spokesman for the JRSO, Max Kreuzberger, explained the settlement to delegates at the Heidelberg Conference as follows: 'Just as the JRSO recognised that the Jewish communities exist and have a right to exist, and that they must accomplish their joint goals, just so the JRSO declared openly that the Jews who remained behind cannot claim to be heir and successor of property, which once belonged to big and prosperous Jewish communities. Whatever has been built up by and for 550,000 people in the course of many hundreds of years of history and designed for such a great number of people, cannot be claimed by 20,000 to 25,000 people. That, which is not needed by existing communities, should be used for the reconstruction work of Jews who have suffered greatly in all parts of the world, and who are attempting to make a new start'. In 'The Future of Jews in Germany', p.52.

129. Abraham Hyman, 'Final Report', 25 (AJDC, B6/2, C 42.096). The Stuttgart community, apparently, demanded 1.5 million Deutschmark for its 300 members, a sum the Joint branded as 'excessive'.

130. In 1952, the Federal Republic, under its chancellor Konrad Adenauer, signed the so-called Luxembourg Agreement. Brokered by the American Claims Conference, this landmark agreement committed West Germany to pay restitution money for the victims and survivors of the Holocaust to Jewish corporate bodies, including the State of Israel. East Germany (the GDR) refused to pay restitution of any kind. For a good summary see 'Entschädigung und Wiederaufbau. Gespräch mit Dr. Karl Brozik, Repräsentant der Claims Conference (CC) in Deutschland', *Tribüne. Zeitschrift zum Verständnis des Judentums*, 41 no. 164 (2002), p.98.

131. Peter Prager, *From Berlin to England and Back. Experiences of a Jewish Berliner*. London: Vallentine Mitchell, 2002, p.111.

132. 'Das kurze Gedächtnis der Deutschen', *Jüdisches Gemeindeblatt*, 10 December 1946.

133. Frank Stern, *The Whitewashing of the Yellow Badge*. London: Pergamon Press, 1992, p.253. He reanalysed a set of autobiographical narratives where Germans described their experiences during and after the war to determine what they mentioned and remembered about Jews.

134. Ibid., p.254.
135. See for instance 'Ein Land baut auf', *Jüdische Illustrierte*, vol. 6 no. 6–7, (June–July, 1956).
136. *Beilage (Allgemeine Jüdische Wochenzeitung)*, vol. 3 no. 7, (March 1953), pp. 1–2.
137. Heinz Galinski in *Der Weg. Zeitschrift für Fragen des Judentums*, vol. 8, no. 12 (20 March 1953), p.1.

Epilogue

1. Moritz Neumann, 'Gemeinschaft oder Gemeinde. Juden in Deutschland heute' in Otto R. Romberg and Susanne Urban-Fahr, eds, *Juden in Deutschland nach 1945*. Frankfurt/Main: Tribüne Verlag, 1999, p.167.
2. Quoted from Monika Richarz, 'Juden in der BRD und der DDR seit 1945' in Micha Brumlik, ed., *Jüdisches Leben in Deutschland seit 1945*. Frankfurt/Main: Athenäum, 1988, p.14.
3. Ulrike Offemnberg, *'Seid vorsichtig gegen die Machthaber'. Die jüdischen Gemeinden in der SBZ und der DDR 1945 bis 1990*. Berlin: Aufbau Verlag, 1998.
4. John Borneman and Jeffrey M. Peck, *Sojourners. The Return of German Jews and the Question of Identity*. Lincoln and London: University of Nebraska Press, 1995.
5. For a detailed discussion see Amos Elon, *Journey Through a Haunted Land. The New Germany*. London: Deutsch, 1967, p.109.
6. A personal account of these contradictions in Micha Brumlik, *Kein Weg als Deutscher und Jude. Eine bundesrepublikanische Erfahrung*. Munich: Luchterhand Literaturverlag, 1996.
7. Henryk M. Broder and Michel R. Lang, *Fremd im eigenen Land. Juden in der Bundesrepublik Deutschland*. Frankfurt/Main: Fischer Taschenbuchverlag, 1979; Micha Brumlik et. al. (eds.), *Jüdisches Leben in Deutschland seit 1945*. Frankfurt/Main: Athenäum 1988; Micha Brumlik, *Kein Weg als Deutscher und Jude. Eine bundesrepublikanische Erfahrung*. Munich: Luchterhand Literaturverlag, 1996; Michael Cohn, *The Jews in Germany 1945–1993. The Building of a Minority*. London and Westport: Praeger, 1994.
8. Moritz Neumann, 'Gemeinschaft oder Gemeinde', pp.167–8.
9. Ignatz Bubis, 'Erschütterungen sind zu überstehen' in Otto R. Romberg and Susanne Urban-Fahr, eds, *Juden in Deutschland nach 1945*. Bonn: p.11. In December 1998, the journal *Tribüne* interviewed Bubis for a special issue, published 1999. Bubis himself died in August 1999.
10. Details in Leo Katcher, *Post-Mortem. The Jews in Germany – Now*. London: Hamish Hamilton, 1969.
11. Zentralwohlfahrtsstelle der Juden in Deutschland e.V., 'Gesamtmitgliederzahlen von 1990–2002'. Frankfurt, 31 December 2002.
12. Susan Stern, *Juden im heutigen Deutschland*. Bonn: Internationes, 1997, p.10.

13. Orthodox conversion is possible but difficult to achieve, not least since rabbis themselves discourage it.
14. *The Jewish Chronicle*, 17 January 2003, p.17.
15. Quoted from Robert Guttmann, 'Ohne Anfang und ohne Ende. Stationen jüdischen Lebens in Deutschland', in Rombach and Urban-Fahr, eds, *Juden in Deutschland nach 1945*, pp.51–52.
16. The Central Welfare Agencies for Jews in Germany, (Zentralwohlfahrtsstelle der Juden in Deutschland e.V.) co-ordinated the assistance for Russian Jews and produced information materials for newcomers or their life and rights in Germany, e.g. *Leitfaden für jüdische Zuwanderer aus der ehemaligen Sowjetunion* (1996). Ignatz Bubis, then head of the Central Council, and Paul Spiegel, head of the Central Welfare Agency, co-signed the preface.
17. Ignatz Bubis, 'Erschütterungen sind zu überstehen', p.18.
18. 'German Jews get major state funding' in *Jewish Chronicle*, 22 November 2002, p.14.
19. Paul Spiegel, 'Jewish leader predicts new era for German community', *Jewish Chronicle*, 15 March 2002, p.10.
20. For a comprehensive account of these changes see Jonathan Webber, ed. *Jewish Identities in the New Europe*. London and Washington: Littman Library of Jewish Civilizations, 1994, esp. the chapters by Sergio DellaPergola and Julius Carlebach.
21. Dan Diner, 'Negative Symbiose', *Babylon*, vol 1 (1986), pp.9–20.
22. Moritz Neumann, 'Wir, die deutschen Juden', *Allgemeine Jüdische Wochenzeitung*, 25 January 1996.
23. Daniel Cohn-Bendit, 'Ein Widerwort an Israels Präsidenten Ezer Weizmann', *Die Zeit* no. 4 (1996), p.1.
24. Florence Singemann in *Im Haus des Henkers. Gespräche in Deutschland*, ed. Susan Heenen-Wolf, Frankfurt/Main: Alibaba, p.160.
25. Moses Gercek in ibid., p.14.
26. Ibid., pp.15–16.
27. Ibid., p.16.
28. Ignatz Bubis in ibid., p.173.
29. Ignatz Bubis in *Juden in Deutschland*, ed. Wilhelm von Sternburg. Berlin: Aufbau Verlag, 1996.
30. Ibid., pp.20–1.
31. Ibid., pp.19–20.
32. This notion of complementary monologues is developed by the first chairman of the Central Council for Jews in Germany, Hendrik van Dam, in *Die Juden und Wir*. Bonn: Council for Christians and Jews, 1957, p.57.
33. For examples see the interviews in Lynn Rapaport, *Jews in Germany after the Holocaust. Memory, identity and Jewish-German relations*. Cambridge: Cambridge University Press, 1997, p.83.
34. Lena Inowlocki, 'Normalität als Kunstgriff. Zur Traditionsvermittlung jüdischer DP-Familien in Deutschland' in Fritz Bauer Institut, ed.,

Überlebt und unterwegs. Jüdische Displaced Persons im Nachkriegsdeutschland. Frankfurt/Main: Campus, 1997, pp.267–89.

35. See e.g. Peter Sichrovsky, *Strangers in their Own Land. Young Jews in Germany and Austria*. London; Tauris, 1986; Henryk M. Broder and Michel R. Lang, *Fremd im eigenen Land. Juden in der Bundesrepublik*, and Micha Brumlik, *Kein Weg als Deutscher und Jude. Eine bundesrepublikanische Erfahrung*.

36. Quoted from Alexa Brum, '*Ich bin, was ich bin, ein Jude*'. *Jüdische Kinder in Deutschland erzählen*. Cologne: Kiepenheuer & Witsch, 1995, p.11.

37. Ibid.

38. Ibid., p.23.

39. Ibid., p.58.

40. Ibid., p.83.

41. Ibid., p.84.

42. Ibid., p.24.

INDEX